Guidebook to the LEED®
Certification Process

Guidebook to the LEED®
Certification Process

FOR LEED FOR NEW CONSTRUCTION, LEED FOR CORE & SHELL, AND LEED FOR COMMERCIAL INTERIORS

MICHELLE COTTRELL, LEED AP BD+C

WILEY

John Wiley & Sons, Inc.

100% Total Recycled Paper
100% Postconsumer Paper

This book is printed on acid-free paper. ∞

For general information on our other products and services, or technical support, please contact our Customer Care Department within the United States at 800–762–2974, outside the United States at 317–572–3993 or fax 317–572–4002.

Wiley also publishes its books in a variety of electronic formats. Some content that appears in print may not be available in electronic books.

For more information about Wiley products, visit our Web site at *www.wiley.com*.

Library of Congress Cataloging-in-Publication Data:

Cottrell, Michelle.
  Guidebook to the LEED Certification Process: For LEED for New Construction, LEED for Core & Shell, and LEED for Commercial Interiors/Michelle Cottrell.
       pages cm
  Includes index.
  ISBN 978-0-470-52418-3 (cloth); 978-111-801441-7 (ebk.); 978-111-8-01442-4 (ebk.); 978-111-8-01556-8 (ebk.); 978-111-8-01557-5 (ebk.); 978-111-8-01558-2 (ebk.)
  1. Sustainable buildings–Design and construction.   2. Leadership in Energy and Environmental Design Green Building Rating System. I. Title.
  TH880.C685 2011
  720'.47–dc22
                                                                            2010042352

Printed in the United States of America

10 9 8 7 6 5 4 3 2 1

Contents

Chapter 3

Building A Project Team _____ **37**

Foreword

We are in a new place and time.

Whether we call it a revolution, a paradigm shift, or a movement, the way we understand and imagine our built environment has radically changed in less than a generation. We are, together, on a journey to minimize our collective impact on Planet Earth so that she can continue to sustain life as we know it.

In terms of sustainable design and construction, we've only just begun developing tools that can help us create goals and metrics so that our defined paths are clear, attainable, and actionable. This book is one such tool.

As the leader of construction markets for BASF, the chemical company, I have worked with the author, Michelle Cottrell, on various sustainable construction initiatives. It may surprise people to know that innovations in chemistry are at the forefront of many sustainable building products and systems that reduce energy demand and increase durability, disaster resistance, indoor air quality, and speed of construction, to name a few benefits. Together, Michelle Cottrell and BASF, for example, have worked on projects that require consensus building and outreach to the trade, code officials, and the design community in order to effect tangible and measurable improvements in the way communities are built.

As this book goes to press, Michelle is working with BASF on the construction of our new U.S. corporate headquarters that we anticipate will achieve two LEED Platinum certifications; one under Core & Shell rating system (version 2.0) and another certification for the tenant space under the LEED for Commercial Interiors (version 3.0). The 300,000-square-foot, five-story complex, slated for occupancy by summer 2012, demonstrates BASF's commitment to sustainable development as a core business strategy.

And although we have all come far in a short period of time, we have far to go. As manufacturers, we need to continue developing, innovating, and improving our products and reducing environmental impacts. As designers, we need to explore high-performance building systems, like those that incorporate insulated concrete forms, structural insulated panels, polyurethane foam insulation, and pervious concrete formulation, to create integrated systems that capitalize on efficiencies. As builders and developers, we need to challenge and retrain the trades while increasing our own building science IQ. As appraisers and realtors, we need to acknowledge and market the value of better-performing buildings.

Regardless of where we fall on the value chain, we need to move the industry forward from the outside in or from the inside out. There is a reason for all of us to do so. For one thing, it is just good business.

At BASF, we know there is a demand for sustainable construction solutions. When, for example, we presented the BASF Near-Zero-Energy Home in Paterson, New Jersey, in 2005 (the first LEED Platinum home on the East Coast), thousands of visitors from every walk of life toured the home or visited our website eager to learn more about how they, too, could someday build, sell, design, or live in a near-zero-energy home.

Since that time, BASF has worked directly with several developers to systematize their green building practices using off-the-shelf technologies that optimize performance, increase profits, and reduce environmental impacts. The fact that these builders remained competitive during the economic downturn and have emerged as postrecession market leaders is empirical proof that the marketplace is more than ready for the wide-scale adoption of sustainable, high-performance communities.

Obtaining LEED certification is one trusted and verifiable way of achieving that end. I encourage you to embrace this manual. Share it with your colleagues so that, together, we can catapult LEED certification efforts as a core strategy for mainstreaming sustainable construction.

Jack R. Armstrong
Leader, Construction Markets
BASF, the Chemical Company

Acknowledgments

Persistence is *key*! Ste, I could not have done this without your love and encouragement. Thank you so much for motivating me, and distracting me with meteorology, inertial navigation systems, the 60 acronyms for instruments, and gyroscopes! Two people on a mission in life, ready to accomplish so many things together.

Thank you to each of my contributors! Thank you for offering your LEED project experiences and images. Your perspectives helped to diversify the guidebook and bring exponential insight to the process. A very special thank you to Jack Armstrong for an inspiring foreword and always offering intriguing opportunities. Your perspective on the market brings an insightful and positive outlook supported by your international exposure, experience, and knowledge.

I would also like to thank all of my clients, GreenEdu staff, and colleagues for your support as I was accomplishing this endeavor. Zach, my GreenEdu partner, I know it was a challenge (to say the least), so for that I thank you!

I would also like to thank my family for granting me the time and space allowing me to focus on another book. Gina Fischetti, thank you for always being there to celebrate with me as I accomplished each chapter (even if it was over video chat)! Dad and Di—you have always been so supportive, eager to see the final product, and ready to party! Thanks for all your help with Izzy!

Thank you to all my friends and colleagues for your interest in my progress and encouragement along the way. A special thanks to Kristina Holloway, I continue to be inspired by your perseverance and persistence! Never give up! And Dirk DeSouza, you rocked my laptop with your forwarded tracks; just when I needed that kick of energy, you were there! And when I needed an escape, you were right there, ready and willing! "Thanks for being there, thanks for being my friend, thanks for being around, thanks for everything, thanks for being you!" (Christian Sol).

I would not have all of these opportunities if it were not for my editor at Wiley, John Czarnecki, Assoc. AIA! Thank you for presenting me with this endeavor and for your continued collaboration. The experience has been extremely rewarding, as everyone at Wiley has been nothing but amazing to work with.

And Mom, I will never be able to thank you enough for all your cheer and help! You have always been there to listen to me ramble on about everything and anything and for that I will always be grateful! BBQ pool day rewards are *the best!*

Introduction

Figure I.1 This LEED Gold certification plaque at the Waterfront Technology Center in Camden, New Jersey, denotes the achievements of the design and construction team and signifies the intended performance of a project. Image courtesy of Stephen Martorana, LEED AP BD+C of the New Jersey Economic Development Authority.

As the green building movement continues to transform the design and construction industry, owners and developers are becoming more and more cognizant of the competition to develop energy-efficient buildings. They are becoming even more aware of the need to design and construct spaces that will operate in a beneficial manner for the occupants and users, the environment, and themselves, as the owner (see Figure Intro.1). Owners are beginning to scrutinize their site selections for environmental impacts, and then they are requesting architects and engineers to assess the environmental impacts of their choices in materials and equipment. These types of decision-making changes are resulting in the need for contractors to become more aware of the impacts from the demolition and construction processes. Together, the design and construction factors are transforming building operation and maintenance.

Professionals may find themselves asking, "How is it possible to manage all of these factors that affect energy use?" or "How do we assess the environmental impacts of our decisions as architects, engineers, and contractors?" Over the past 10 years, measurement tools, such as ENERGY STAR®, Green Globes®, and U.S. Green Building Council's (USGBC®) Leadership in Energy and Environmental Design (LEED®) rating systems, have been introduced to the industry as a means to implement a process, suggest strategies, dictate requirements, and provide reference standards in which to measure and track a building's performance. In more recent years, USGBC's LEED rating systems have become the more prominent tools in which to measure a building's performance during design and construction, as well as operations and maintenance.

Project teams on a sustainable mission often look to specialists to navigate through the different LEED rating systems and the applicable certification requirements and standards. Therefore, a managing choreographer knowledgeable in these factors is necessary, in order to help to make the process more streamlined and efficient. With the introduction of this manager, or LEED coordinator, the design and construction teams are able to focus on and then follow through with their responsibilities as part of the process, where the LEED coordinator focuses on the certification requirements and is not distracted by the details of design or construction. This three-part guidebook details those requirements of the integrative design and construction approach of high-performance buildings necessary during the LEED certification process, to assist coordinators lacking LEED project administration experience.

The LEED for New Construction and Major Renovations™ (NC), LEED for Core & Shell™ (CS) and LEED for Commercial Interiors™ (CI) rating systems will be discussed throughout this guidebook for their similarities and differences to each other, as related to the process of certification. Incorporating aspects of the LEED certification process, including LEED-Online, throughout this guidebook is intended to provide a level of expectation and understanding for a LEED coordinator new to the process, especially when he or she may not be a LEED Accredited Professional (AP) or LEED Green Associate.

As most of the readers of this guidebook will already be aware of the need for and benefits of sustainability and high-performance buildings, as well as the environmental impacts of the current building stock in the United States, this type of information will be omitted. Instead, the key concepts of sustainability, high-performance buildings, and the integrative design process will be discussed throughout this guidebook, ensuring the understanding of the critical terms and concepts that continue to alter the traditional design and construction methods and processes. Case studies of projects awarded LEED certification are presented throughout this guidebook, as a means to highlight successful strategies to learn from. Perspectives from many of the different primary team members, such as owners, architects, engineers, contractors, manufacturers, and commissioning authorities, are also presented throughout the book, as the certification process is meant to be integrative and a successful LEED coordinator needs to be knowledgeable of the roles and responsibilities of each of the team members they might be managing.

Part I of this guidebook will provide an introduction to each of the three LEED rating systems geared toward commercial projects and the integrative design process, along with a description of how the two correlate. The integrative design process helps to evaluate the benefits of green buildings and to provide the value proposition for each of the building project types, including new construction, base building projects, and tenant improvements. Every project has triple-bottom-line goals and, therefore, environmental, economical, and social benefits. The

LEED coordinator is an integral component to help outline each of these benefits for each type of project along with the different project team members.

Part II of *Guidebook to the LEED® Certification Process* will introduce the concepts of the process during the design phases, beginning with the eco-charette. The eco-charette is an opportunity to gather the entire team at the very beginning of a project and establish the critical elements of the project, such as the owner's program requirements and the project goals. As the project advances through each of the design phases, it is imperative and critical to encompass the principals of the National Institute of Building Sciences' (NIBS) *Whole Building Design Guide* to focus on the triple-bottom-line goals of the project. This guidebook will highlight those vital principals in a concurrent manner with the certification requirements.

When approaching the design of a high-performance building, a team should focus on the site design, the building's orientation, daylighting opportunities, lighting and power needs, the building envelope, and the mechanical systems. This guidebook will not necessarily focus on these types of detailed aspects for architects and engineers, but will instead outline and illustrate the important milestones for the design team to achieve in order to prepare for the Design Review submission to Green Building Certification Institute (GBCI) after the construction documents are completed.

Part III of *Guidebook* will focus on the LEED certification process during the construction phase of a project. Carrying the integrated and process-related concepts from design through the construction phases of the project will assist the team with the process of managing a LEED project during construction through certification award. A detailed approach of responsibilities and tasks of the general contractor, subcontractors, and the owner will be illustrated, while also providing an overview of the responsibilities of the commissioning agent (CxA) during the construction phase of a project, as related to the LEED certification process. The requirements and process of the final submission to GBCI for documentation review, after substantial completion or possibly occupancy, will be reviewed in this guidebook, as well as an approach to operations, as related to the certification process for the NC, CS, and CI rating systems.

Guidebook to the LEED® Certification Process is intended to provide LEED AP owners, developers, project managers, and design professionals with an overview of how to steer through the LEED certification process under the 3.0 rating systems. LEED APs have the education of understanding the LEED rating systems, but may be missing the experience of managing the documentation from the team during the certification process, or even having just participated on a project seeking LEED certification. This guidebook will provide these professionals with a tool to refer to, in conjunction with the LEED reference guides applicable to their project types.

PART 1 KEY CONCEPTS

chapter 1

Measuring Green

The LEED Rating Systems

As the first Leadership in Energy and Environmental Design (LEED®) rating system was implemented on projects, U.S. Green Building Council (USGBC®) recognized the need to develop multiple rating systems to speak to different project types, scopes, and typologies. LEED needed to address not only new construction projects, but also tenant improvements and fit-outs, retail, healthcare facilities, homes, schools, major renovations, existing buildings, and core-and-shell projects. A rating system was also needed to focus on the neighborhood, connecting pedestrians to their home and the activities they rely on for entertainment, work, and education and community resources.

In 2004, USGBC launched the LEED for Commercial Interiors™ (CI) rating system to focus on tenant improvement projects in the commercial market sector primarily aimed at corporate, retail, and institutional project types. "Tenants who lease their space or do not occupy the entire building are eligible."[1]

In 2006, the LEED for Core & Shell™ (CS) rating system was launched with intentions geared toward developing speculative commercial buildings focusing on the building envelope, structure, and singular building-level systems, as opposed to campus-level efficiencies. This rating system offers a precertification aspect that is not offered in the other ratings systems. Precertification provides the base building owner/developer to market to potential tenants and financiers the unique and valuable green features of a proposed building.[2] The LEED for Retail™ and LEED for Healthcare™ rating systems are currently in pilot phase, while LEED for Neighborhood Development™ was recently released after two and a half years. LEED for Existing Buildings is currently in its third version as LEED for Existing Buildings: Operations and Maintenance™ (EBOM). LEED for Schools™ is also available under its third version under the LEED 2009 suite of rating systems.

As an outcome of its success, LEED has become an internationally utilized benchmarking tool, providing third-party verification that a project has implemented sustainable and efficient practices during the design and construction phases, as well as the postoccupancy methods of operations and maintenance. This voluntary certification has become the mainstream tool in analyzing the performance of buildings for owners, developers, architects, engineers, real estate professionals, construction managers, lenders, government officials, scientists, and citizens across the world. As a result of the adoption of green building strategies on an international level, in 2002, eight nations joined together to form the World Green Building Council (WorldGBC) to help to increase the market transformation on a global scale. Since then, other countries, such as Canada, India, and Italy, have created their own green building councils and some have revised and adopted their own rating systems.

On April 27, 2009, USGBC launched LEED 2009 providing more consistent and streamlined, yet flexible, parameters for measuring the performance of buildings and projects. USGBC now presents the LEED for New Construction and Major Renovations™ (NC), LEED for Core & Shell, LEED for Schools, LEED for Healthcare, and LEED for Retail rating systems into one comprehensive book, the *Green Building Design & Construction (BD+C) Reference Guide.* USGBC now presents the LEED for Commercial Interiors and LEED for Retail Interiors rating systems into another book, the *Green Interior Design & Construction (ID+C) Reference Guide.* The LEED for Existing Buildings: Operations and Maintenance and LEED for Existing Schools rating systems have been compiled into a third book, the *Green Building Operations & Maintenance (GBOM) Reference Guide.*

Although LEED NC is primarily aimed at new commercial office buildings, the rating system can be applied to many other uses, including institutional buildings (Figure 1.1), hotels, and residential buildings of four or more habitable stories. The rating system also addresses major renovations of existing buildings. According to the BD+C reference

Figure 1.1　The Duke Law Star Commons project in Durham, North Carolina, by Shepley Bulfinch, obtained its certification under the LEED for New Construction and Major Renovations rating system. Photo courtesy of Kat Nania, Shepley Bulfinch.

guide, "a major renovation involves major heating, ventilating, and air-conditioning (HVAC) renovation, significant envelope modifications, and major interior rehabilitation."[3] It is the responsibility of the project team to determine if LEED NC is applicable based on the scope of work, where maybe LEED EBOM or LEED CS may be the more appropriate rating system to use.

The LEED rating systems are characterized by the percentage of space the owner/developer occupies versus the tenant. For LEED NC, the owner or tenant must occupy more than 50 percent of the building's leasable square footage. "Projects in which 50% or less of the building's leasable square footage is occupied by an owner, the team should pursue LEED CS certification."[4] The LEED CS rating system is also ideal for a developer with control over the design and construction of the entire base building systems but not the spaces to be leased by future tenants. These base building systems may include the mechanical, electrical, plumbing

(MEP), and fire-protection systems. LEED CS is a good fit for "commercial office buildings, medical office buildings, retail centers, warehouses, and lab facilities."[5]

The LEED CI and LEED CS rating systems were developed to work in conjunction with one another. As mentioned earlier, LEED CS was developed to certify the core (composed of spaces that support the base building including mechanical and equipment rooms; elevators and stairwells, restrooms, lobby areas, and other owner-occupied or -operated spaces) and the shell (including the perimeter walls; roof, and ground floor of the building) of a building and therefore creating the environment for a tenant seeking LEED CI certification. This does not mean a tenant would not be able to certify their space in a non-LEED-certified core and shell project, but it would make the process a bit easier. This will be explained in more detail in Chapter 4.

The Key Concepts of LEED

The Categories

Each of the LEED NC, LEED CS, and LEED CI rating systems are broken down into five environmental categories: Sustainable Sites (SS), Water Efficiency (WE), Energy and Atmosphere (EA), Materials and Resources (MR), and Indoor Environmental Quality (EQ). There are two additional categories, Innovation in Design (ID) and Regional Priority (RP) that are offer bonus point opportunities.

The ID category offers points for exemplary performance and addresses factors that are not described in the other categories focusing on methodologies and practices implemented during the design and construction phases, as well as during the operation of the facility or space. Therefore, project teams have two ways to be awarded points within the ID category:

1. Substantially exceed the defined benchmarks in the other categories by the means of exemplary performance.

2. Develop and implement an innovative strategy not detailed in the other categories of the rating system, accomplishing an unprecedented achievement.

The other bonus category, Regional Priority, provides the opportunity for projects to earn points for complying with credits from the five main categories that would be an extraordinary achievement given the limitations within their zip code, as determined by USGBC. For example, a project that earns two points under MR Credit 5: Regional Materials in South Florida, where obtaining locally extracted, processed, and manufactured construction materials and products is quite challenging, USGBC recognizes this achievement by awarded the project an additional bonus point under the RP category. More information for this category will be detailed later in the chapter.

Sustainable Sites

The Sustainable Sites (SS) category "addresses environmental concerns related to building landscape, hardscape, and exterior building issues"[6] impacted by site selection and development. The category "discourages development on previously undeveloped land; minimizes a building's impact on ecosystems and waterways; encourages regionally appropriate landscaping; rewards smart transportation choices;

controls stormwater runoff; and reduces erosion, light pollution, heat island effect and construction-related pollution."[7]

The BD+C reference guide depicts the requirements for both the LEED NC and LEED CS rating systems, including the following SS category concepts:

- Selecting and developing the site wisely
- Reducing emissions associated with transportation
- Planting sustainable landscapes
- Protecting surrounding habitats
- Managing stormwater runoff
- Reducing the heat island effect
- Eliminating light pollution

Since a tenant would most likely look at existing buildings in which to lease their space, the LEED CI rating system addresses base building design elements outside of the tenant improvement scope for point opportunities. In the ID+C reference guide, the SS category addresses the following concepts to address when seeking LEED CI certification:

- Selecting a building that has developed its site wisely
- Selecting a building with sustainable landscapes
- Selecting a building that protects surrounding habitats
- Selecting a building that manages stormwater runoff
- Selecting a building that reduces heat island effects

- Selecting a building that reduces light pollution
- Selecting a building with water-efficient landscaping
- Selecting a building that uses on-site renewable energy
- Selecting a building that reduces potable water consumption
- Selecting a building within close proximity to public transportation or implements other strategies to reduce emissions associated with transportation

Water Efficiency

The Water Efficiency (WE) category addresses possible strategies and technologies that help to reduce the amount of potable water used and disposed of. LEED CI addresses water efficiencies in both the SS category, as well as the WE category depending on whether the approach is an owner/base building-related strategy, a reduction by the tenant's usage, or sometimes a combination of both. The category in the LEED NC and LEED CS rating systems addresses water use reduction strategies in the interior and exterior of the building with the following concepts:

- Monitoring water consumption performance
- Reducing potable water consumption
- Reducing water consumption to save energy and improve environmental well-being

Energy and Atmosphere

Whether designing an interior fit-out or a new, ground-up building, the design team needs to not only be aware of what materials and components are being utilized for construction, but the method in which the building/space is/are constructed and how efficiently the components will work together. The Energy and Atmosphere (EA) category "encourages a wide variety of energy strategies: commissioning; energy use monitoring; efficient design and construction; efficient appliances, systems and lighting; the use of renewable and clean sources of energy that are generated on or off-site; and other innovative strategies."[8] Commissioning (Cx) is defined as "a quality-oriented process for achieving, verifying, and documenting that the performance of facilities, systems, and assemblies meets defined objectives and criteria"[9] by the ASHRAE (American Society of Heating, Refrigerating and Air-Conditioning Engineers) Guideline 0, The Commissioning Process. The Cx process will be discussed in more detail in the next chapter.

While LEED NC and LEED CS analyze the overall energy use and efficiency of building systems and how they work together, LEED CI breaks out the components of lighting power, lighting controls, HVAC, and equipment and appliances and assesses the individual performance of each component (see EA Credit 1: Optimized Energy Performance in the reference guide). This approach is due to the limitations a tenant faces as they typically do not have the ability to impact whole building systems. It is common to find more similarities within the NC and CS ratings systems, as compared to CI.

The EA category promotes three kinds of activities:

- Tracking building energy performance—design, commissioning, monitoring

- Managing refrigerants to eliminate chlorofluorocarbons (CFCs)

- Using renewable energy (for NC and CS as CI addresses renewable energy in the SS category)

Materials and Resources

During both the construction and operational phases of a building, a large amount of waste is generated and an abundant amount of materials and resources are consumed. Therefore, the Material and Resources (MR) category promotes strategies to reduce waste, reuse of materials, and recycling practices for project teams to implement to reduce the burden of the built environment. The category addresses the preservation and availability of resources for future generations by encouraging "the selection of sustainably grown, harvested, produced and transported products and materials."[10] Within each of the rating systems, the category focuses on the following three concepts:

- Selecting sustainable materials

- Practicing waste reduction

- Reusing and recycling

Indoor Environmental Quality

Differing from energy efficiency, water use, and sustainable development practices, the quality of the indoor environment has an important role in green building practices, as the indoor environment significantly impacts the health and well-being, productivity levels, and quality of life of people. Building related illnesses may have driven the awareness for improvement from a liability aspect, but productivity has also helped to change the approach to designing the built environment. The Indoor Environmental Quality (EQ) category focuses on the following strategies to address these challenges:

- Increasing ventilation

- Managing air contaminants

- Specifying less harmful materials
- Allowing occupants to control desired settings
- Providing daylighting and views

Prerequisites versus Credits

Each of the rating systems details and defines prerequisites and credits throughout each of the five main categories mentioned above. A prerequisite is a mandatory component of the rating systems, necessary to achieve certification. Meeting the requirements of a prerequisite ensures each project that achieves certification will perform to a minimum level of performance. Each of the eight prerequisites in the LEED NC and LEED CS rating systems, and the seven in LEED CI, are absolutely required to earn certification. Within the LEED NC and LEED CS rating systems, there is at least one prerequisite in each of the main categories, while LEED CI does not have a prerequisite defined in the SS category. Even though credits to do not have to be attempted in every category, each of the prerequisites must be met. For example, if a project team is not attempting to earn any credits within the WE category, the project must still meet the requirements of Prerequisite 1: Water Use Reduction. Notice, too, neither the ID category nor the RP category include any prerequisites, as pursuit in either category is not required because they are considered bonus categories that offer extra point opportunities. Refer to the rating system scorecards in Appendix A to see the value of prerequisites and credits within each category.

Each of the rating systems is based on a 100-point scale, with 10 additional bonus points possible for innovation in design, exemplary performance, and regional prioritization. Because the rating systems are based on a point program, there are different

levels of certification possible, based on the number of points the project earns: Certified, Silver, Gold, and Platinum. Table 1.1 describes the point range of each level of certification.

Table 1.1 LEED Certification Levels

Certification Level	Point Range
Certified	40–49
Silver	50–59
Gold	60–79
Platinum	80+

Therefore, a minimum of 40 points, in addition to meeting the requirements for each of the prerequisites, is required to earn LEED certification for any project, regardless of the rating system as they are all based on the same point scale.

Credit Weightings

There is another significant change in 2009: The LEED rating systems now account for "the potential environmental impact and human benefits of each credit with respect to a set of impact categories."[11] After assessing the environmental or human effect (i.e., climate change or resource depletion), based on the timing of the impact (i.e., construction, operations), each impact or benefit is quantified by a combination of approaches (i.e., life-cycle assessment, transportation analysis). LEED 2009 uses the U.S. Environmental Protection Agency's (EPA's) Tool for the Reduction and Assessment of Chemical and Other Environmental Impacts (TRACI) environmental impact categories and the weightings developed by the National Institute of Standards and Technology (NIST) to determine the weight for each credit. From these assessments, the following parameters have been established and incorporated into the LEED 2009 rating systems:

- All LEED credits are worth a minimum of 1 point.

- All LEED credits are positive, whole numbers; there are no fractions or negative values.

- All LEED credits receive a single, static weight in each rating system; there are no individualized scorecards based on project location.

- All LEED rating systems have 100 base points; ID and RP credits provide opportunities for up to 10 bonus points.

Exemplary Performance

Throughout each of the rating systems, there are opportunities to earn points for exemplary performance, indicating that a project has exceeded the requirements of the credits detailed in each of the other categories. The extra point is earned by meeting the next percentage increment in the threshold progression. For example, in the MR category, Credit 2: Construction Waste Management, a project would earn 2 points for diverting at least 75 percent of the construction waste from a landfill. There is an opportunity to earn one exemplary performance point should the project team divert at least 95 percent of the construction waste from a landfill or incineration facility. All exemplary performance points are tallied in the ID category. Each rating system allows for a total of three exemplary performance points to be awarded, although there are many opportunities provided throughout the rating systems. For example, LEED CI offers 20 exemplary performance opportunities, while LEED NC offers 21 and LEED CS offers 22 opportunities dispersed throughout the rating systems.

It is helpful to read through the exemplary performance point details for SS Credit 3 in LEED CI and SS Credit 4 in LEED NC and LEED CS, as there are multiple opportunities available within the Alternative Transportation credit, but a project can earn only one exemplary performance point within the Alternative Transportation credit. The same applies for SS Credit 6 for LEED NC and LEED CS and EQ Credit 4 in LEED CS; although each offers an opportunity to earn an exemplary performance point, only one can be earned within the Stormwater Design and the Low-Emitting Materials credit suites.

LEED CI differs from LEED NC and LEED CS when tallying up exemplary performance points. In CI, Sustainable Sites Credit 1: Site Selection, Option 2, offers four opportunities to earn exemplary performance points:

- Path 4: Heat Island Effect—Nonroof

- Path 5: Heat Island Effect—Roof

- Path 10: Water Use Reduction

- Path 11: On-Site Renewable Energy

The point for SSc1, Option 2, is logged under Path 12, but note that only one point may be earned under this path. Therefore, the project team should seek only one of these paths for exemplary performance. Refer to the ID+C reference guide for the requirements for exemplary performance for each of these credits to determine which path is most appropriate for your specific LEED CI project.

Regional Priority

Another new addition to the LEED 2009 rating systems, the RP category, awards points for recognizing and addressing geographically specific environmental technologies and strategies. Each of the rating systems offers up to four points to be achieved under this category. Although the rating systems define six credit opportunities qualified by the project's zip code, it is up to the project team to determine which four credits they wish to attempt. Project teams will need to refer to the USGBC website to search a database with Regional Priority credit opportunities specific to the applicable zip code and download the spreadsheet for the state in which the project is located. The spreadsheet will list six credit opportunities specific to the project's zip code. For example, for a project located in Tampa, Florida, with a zip code of 33607, it would be possible to earn an RP point for meeting any of the following:

Regional Priority Credit Opportunities for 33607 Zip Code

SSc2
SSc4.1
WEc2
EAc1(28%)
EAc2(13%)
MRc5(20%)

Therefore, if a project in the Tampa area is able to meet the requirements for WE Credit 2: Innovative Wastewater Technologies, the project would earn two points under the Water Efficiency category, as well as an additional bonus point under the RP category. Once a project is registered with LEED-Online, the RP opportunities will be noted on the project's scorecard.

Minimum Program Requirements

As part of the update of LEED 2009, USGBC has further developed the minimum program requirements (MPRs) for a project pursuing LEED certification. Similar to a prerequisite, a project must meet and adhere to each of the MPRs in order to achieve LEED certification, regardless of the rating

system being pursued or the certification level sought.

Project teams should refer to the USGBC website at www.usgbc.org/DisplayPage.aspx?CMSPageID=2102 for more detailed information about each of the following MPRs and for the most current requirements. At the time of printing, every project that registers under a LEED 2009 rating system must adhere to the following MPRs[12]:

- Must comply with environmental laws

- Must be a complete, permanent building or space

- Must use a reasonable site boundary

- Must comply with minimum floor area requirements:
  - LEED NC and LEED CS: minimum of 1,000 square feet
  - LEED CI: minimum of 250 square feet

- Must comply with minimum occupancy rates:
  - Project must have at least one full-time equivalent (FTE) occupant. FTE determination is discussed in Chapter 6.
  - Should the project have less than one FTE, the project cannot seek any of the available credits within the IEQ category, although the prerequisite *must* be met.

- Must commit to sharing whole-building energy and water usage data for five years. If CI projects are unable to comply due to the lack of submetering of their space, the project is exempt for complying with this MPR.

- Must comply with a minimum building area-to-site area ratio: Gross floor area cannot be less than 2 percent of the gross land area (with LEED project

OWNER'S PERSPECTIVE
Going for Gold

By M. Christie Smith, CAWA
Executive Director for the Potter League for Animals

Figures 1.2 and 1.3 The Potter League for Animals project in Newport, Rhode Island, by ARQ Architects, implemented a green roof, focused on materials with recycled content and reduced the facility's water consumption, making it the first animal shelter in the United States to earn LEED Gold certification. Images courtesy of Lucinda A Schlaffer of ARQ Architects.

The Potter League for Animals found the LEED process to be exciting and definitely worth pursuing (Figures 1.2 and 1.3). Six years ago, when the board of directors committed to LEED practices, it was a risk for our small nonprofit humane society. By the time our fund raising and construction started, there was so much more general information about sustainable design and buildings that our supporters were impressed we were so forward thinking. The LEED component helped our fund raising and donor support and, most significantly, was firmly compatible with our mission.

The best practices for a modern, efficient facility for animals naturally align with the best practices for green buildings, and for this reason the Potter League never considered the LEED process to be an additional expense. We engaged ARQ Architects as they fully understood both the challenges of LEED certification and the unique complexities of animal shelter design. At the time, few general contractors in the area had LEED experience, so we selected an excellent firm eager to learn. The result of this united commitment from owner, architect and contractor is a highly functioning building that is the first to receive LEED Gold in Rhode Island and the first animal shelter in the country to achieve Gold certification. As a leadership building, the staff, volunteers, and board of directors have made a commitment to share our lessons and progress with others.

Best of all, the impact on our two- and four-legged clients is astounding. The animals have quiet, stress-free, light-filled living spaces, and visitors are not assaulted with depressing chain-link, noise, and odors so typical in animal shelters. LEED was an important goal, but the joys of living, visiting, or working in this building are the real benefits.

boundary). CI projects that do not include site work within the scope of work and LEED boundary are exempt from complying with this MPR.

Please note: "If it becomes known that a LEED project is or was in violation of an MPR, certification may be revoked, or the certification process may be halted. These situations will be handled on a case by case basis according to GBCI's challenge policy."[13]

Checklists/Scorecards

Appendix A in this guidebook includes the checklists (also referred to as scorecards) for the three rating systems addressed in this book: LEED NC, LEED CS, and LEED CI. The other ratings systems can be found at the USGBC website, www.usgbc.org.

The LEED Certification Process

Green Building Certification Institute

In 2009, USGBC engaged Green Building Certification Institute (GBCI) to coordinate the LEED certification process. GBCI was once responsible only for administering the accreditation/credentialing process for professionals, but is now responsible for managing the certification process as well. Project teams will interact with GBCI to register and certify a project, while USGBC will still be responsible for updating and maintaining the LEED rating systems and education programs. Figure 1.4 summaries the roles of the two parties.

Registration

Typically, a LEED coordinator completes the registration process the project for the team, as this person

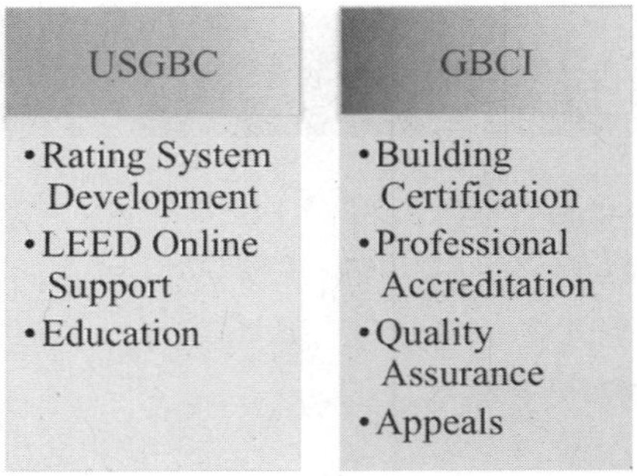

USGBC	GBCI
• Rating System Development • LEED Online Support • Education	• Building Certification • Professional Accreditation • Quality Assurance • Appeals

Figure 1.4 The Roles of USGBC and GBCI

will assume responsibility of the documentation process, including inviting other team members to the site, assigning prerequisites and credits to each team member, and communicating with GBCI for documentation review. LEED-Online refers to this role as the project administrator. Because this guidebook is written for purposes of the LEED coordinator, the two terms will be used interchangeably. Note, any team member, including the owner, can act as the project administrator.

The coordinator will need to visit the LEED-Online website (www.leedonline.com) in order to start the process. The coordinator will need to establish an account with GBCI and sign in, to begin the project registration process as a member or nonmember of USGBC. GBCI accounts are free but USGBC membership is not. Members of USGBC are national and are therefore limited to corporations or companies and not individual people. Individual professionals can become members of USGBC only at the local chapter level. Membership status impacts the fees for project registration and certification review. Visit the USGBC website for more information on becoming a national and/or local member.

Once the coordinator is signed in to LEED-Online, there is a "Register New Project" tab. Clicking on this tab will begin the online registration process with GBCI. The coordinator will need to acknowledge the eligibility of the project by reading through the LEED Certification Terms and Conditions for Project Registration. This is considered Step 1, as seen in Figure 1.5, and requires a review of the following terms and conditions:

- Definitions

- Scope of Binding Agreement

- Overview of the LEED Certification Process

- Payment and Adjustment of Fees

- Documentation and Application Review Policies

- LEED Project Registration Cancellation Policy

- Registration of a Project subject to an Award, Final Denial, or Revocation of LEED Certification

- Certification Audit and Revocation

- Certification Expiration Policy

- Information Sharing

- Project Monitoring

- Minimum Program Requirements

- Intellectual Property

- Release and Limitation of Liability

- Waiver of Consequential Damages

- Indemnification

- Notice of Claim

- Mediation

- Governing Law

- Venue

- No Third-Party Beneficiaries

- Miscellaneous

After agreeing to the terms and conditions, the coordinator is presented with his or her own contact information, including national membership status, to confirm accuracy. Step 2 of the registration process begins with three questions in reference to the type of registration (i.e., single project, multiple projects) and provides an option if more assistance is required to determine the most appropriate rating system. The next screen will provide the list of rating systems from which to choose, as well as two other options: precertification for LEED CS projects (as discussed earlier in the chapter) and recertification for existing buildings. Step 2 concludes with acknowledgment of the MPRs.

Step 3 consists of the display of a sample scorecard for the rating system selected, while Step 4 requires the following project information (editing allowed after project is registered):

Project Title:
Address:
City:
State/Province:

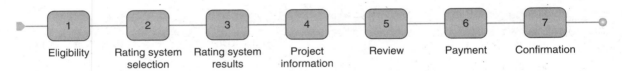

| 1 | 2 | 3 | 4 | 5 | 6 | 7 |
| Eligibility | Rating system selection | Rating system results | Project information | Review | Payment | Confirmation |

Figure 1.5 The Steps of Project Registration

Country:

Zip Code/Postal:

Anticipated Construction Start Date:

Anticipated Construction End Date:

Gross Project Square Footage:

Confidential Project: Yes or No

Would you like to notify your local chapter of this project registration?

Anticipated Project Type (i.e., health care, office, lodging, public assembly, etc.):

Anticipated Certification Level:

The coordinator will have an opportunity to review the project information prior to proceeding to Step 6 and inputting in the payment information. Depending on the membership status, the fee to register will be either $900 (members) or $1,200 (nonmembers) regardless of project type, rating system, location, or size (except for LEED CS precertification). See Certification Fees section in this chapter for more information, but always refer to the GBCI website for the most up-to-date pricing information.

LEED-Online

Once a project is registered, the project administrator will receive an email confirming the project registration and will be issued a project access ID. The project administrator will be able to log on to LEED-Online and see a display of all of their registered projects. Once a specific project is selected, the administrator will then have the ability to invite other team members to have access to the specific project. The invited team members will receive an email invitation to join the LEED-Online site from GBCI by means of providing them with the same project access ID specific to the project. Once the team members have joined, the team administrator will be able to assign the team members a role (i.e., architect, engineer, owner, contractor, etc.).

The team administrator will also have the access to indicate which credits will be attempted for the specific project, per the scorecard of the rating system being utilized. The team administrator will then assign each credit and prerequisite a team member role to indicate who will be responsible for which. A team member can be assigned to multiple prerequisites and credits, but each prerequisite and credit can be assigned to only one team member. This does not indicate that only the team member can view the prerequisite or credit; it just implies that the team member will be responsible for uploading the documentation applicable to the prerequisites and credits in which they are assigned. For example, the civil engineer's role may be assigned to the SS prerequisite and four of the SS credits, but the landscape architect and all of the other invited team members can view that prerequisite and the credits.

LEED-Online serves as a portal for team members to share documentation with each other and eventually with GBCI. GBCI will use LEED-Online to review the documentation to verify compliance and ultimately award certification and, if so, what level of certification based on the number of points earned. LEED-Online serves as a centralized location for communication with GBCI, as questions may arise, clarification may be needed, or additional documentation may be requested proving compliance. Remember, LEED is a self-evaluating process, but it is third-party verified. Therefore, a member of GBCI will not visit the project site, but merely use the documentation posted to LEED-Online as an indication of compliance.

Credit Interpretation Requests and Rulings

Just as in the design and construction process, questions arise during the documentation review of the LEED certification process. In the construction industry, we refer to those questions as RFCs (requests for clarification) or RFIs (requests for information). With LEED, we refer to those questions as CIRs (credit interpretation requests).

At the time of printing, an online CIR database exists for projects registered pre-LEED 2009 in which teams can query to find answers to their questions not detailed in the reference guides or on the USGBC and GBCI websites. Although the database is accessible, neither USGBC nor GBCI will post any new CIR question and responses (known as credit interpretation rulings) as of June 2009.

Within the LEED 2009 rating systems, a CIR database does not exist because CIRs issued for LEED 2009 projects will be project specific. Project administrators should note the existing CIR database is not to be referred to for any project registered under any of the LEED 2009 rating systems. Therefore, a project team will need to submit a CIR through LEED-Online should they need administrative and technical support pertaining to MPRs, prerequisites, and credits for any of the rating systems. At the time of printing, the CIR process is undergoing changes, so it is best to consult the GBCI website for the most current procedures for submitting a CIR.

The project administrator can submit a CIR at any point after the project is registered. The CIR should be specific to *one* LEED prerequisite, credit, or MPR requirement. The USGBC website details the following key CIR submission requirements and concepts:

- "The ruling will only apply to the project for which the CIR was submitted, and there will be no corresponding entry in the CIR database. Accordingly, the CIR ruling will not be precedent setting and will not carry forth and apply to other projects submitted by the same Project Team nor be available as a ruling for other projects registered by other project teams."[14]

- "Project teams should note that neither the credit language nor the minimum achievement thresholds can be changed through the CIR process. Furthermore, CIR rulings do not in any way guarantee that a LEED MPR, prerequisite or credit will be satisfied or achieved. The project Applicant must still demonstrate and document satisfaction of all LEED requirements during the LEED certification process. In addition, project teams must adhere to the CIR rulings received for their projects."[15]

- "CIRs shall contain only the specific inquiry and the essential background information necessary for a ruling. CIRs shall not contain in excess of 600 words or alternatively 4000 characters including spaces. Furthermore, Project teams shall not submit attachments, cut-sheets, plans or drawings with any CIR."[16]

Review and Certification

Project teams have the option to submit for either a split review process (one after the completion of the construction documents and the other after substantial completion) *or* just one certification review at the end of construction. The end of construction or substantial project completion is defined as "the date on which the building receives a Certificate of Occupancy or similar official indication that it is ready for use."[17]

Project teams that submit for the split review (two reviews) will have more success with earning certification, as opposed to those project teams that wait until the end of construction to submit for review. The main reason for this success is due to a preliminary design review, as it allows the project team to get a snapshot of the project's performance and progress in terms of certification level, compliance, and potential earning of points. This allows the project team the opportunity to attempt additional points, if needed, during construction, in order to aim for a preferred certification level.

Should the project team decide to pursue a split review, they would submit a complete application for a preliminary design review through LEED-Online, including payment. It is suggested that you submit for this review after the construction documents are completed, with as many design prerequisites and credits as possible to gauge the project's potential, although only one design credit or prerequisite is required for submission for review. LEED-Online denotes prerequisites and credits with a pencil for those eligible for design review and a hammer for those qualified for a construction review.

Once submitted, GBCI will then review and submit preliminary comments back to the project team (if needed), through LEED-Online, for all credits and prerequisites submitted with the design review application. As noted in Figure 1.6, within 25 business days after the application is submitted, the team will see whether those credits and prerequisites are "anticipated" or "pending." Should more information be requested from GBCI with a "pending" indication, the project team then has 25 business days to respond through LEED-Online. Once the team resubmits for review, a final design review should be received within 15 business days with an "anticipated" or "denied" indication for each prerequisite and credit submitting for review.

The same process will begin again at the project's substantial completion for a preliminary construction review, response to preliminary construction review, and final construction review. The construction review application is submitted via LEED-Online, following the completion of the design review phase and within two years of substantial project completion. The construction review application may include design *credits* not previously reviewed but *must* include any design *prerequisites* not previously reviewed. The construction review application must include enough credits (including the "anticipated" credits from the design review) to earn the minimum certification level.

Review Phase	Time Frame
Project Team submits for Preliminary Design Review	25 Business Days for reply from GBCI
Project Team to respond to comments from GBCI	25 Business Days
Final Design Review by GBCI	15 Business Days
Project Team submits for Preliminary Construction Review	25 Business Days for reply from GBCI
Project Team to respond to comments from GBCI	25 Business Days
Final Construction Review by GBCI	15 Business Days

Figure 1.6 The Certification Review Time Frame

Project teams wishing to expedite the review process by GBCI can opt to pay an additional fee of $5,000 at either or both application review submittals. The expedited fees paid are intended to decrease the review time by GBCI in half. As with any fee, project teams are encouraged to visit the GBCI website for the most current pricing.

Appeals

The appeals process applies to the CIR ruling process, as well as the certification review process pertaining to a particular MPR, prerequisite, or credit. A project team may issue an appeal to GBCI should they wish to challenge a decision.

The appeals process works similar to the certification review process. There is a first-level appeal that is issued to GBCI through LEED-Online within 25 business days from the coordinating determination (i.e., CIR ruling, certification review). The GBCI website indicates that the appeal must be issued with payment and the following information:

- Supplemental documentation applicable to the MPR, prerequisite, and/or credit in question.

- An explanation of the denied situation. "If the appeal pertains to a response to a Credit Interpretation Request, the Project Team must include an explanation addressing the contested guidance provided with the Credit Interpretation Request response."[18]

Once a project team issues an appeal, GBCI will indicate an acknowledgment of the submittal within five business days. GBCI will then locate individuals not previously involved with the project to review the information submitted. The review team will respond to the

project team within 20 business days of the appeal submission date with a decision. The response from GBCI shall include technical information detailing their decision.

Should the project team be dissatisfied with the first-level decision of the appeal, the team may issue a final appeal within 25 business days from the decision rendered from the first-level appeal. All second-tiered appeals must be submitted in writing to GBCI (not through LEED Online).

When a final appeal is submitted, an appeals board is created to be composed of three GBCI president-appointed (in consultation with GBCI chair) persons. The project team has 10 business days to review the names of the three appointed individuals and respond to GBCI with any conflicts that would affect the review of the appeal. GBCI will determine if a conflict exists in order to disqualify the individual from serving on the appeals board. This board shall meet within 60 calendar days and render the final decision (by means of a majority vote) on the matter at hand within 10 business days after the board meeting.

See the section on certification fees in this chapter for costs involved in issuing an appeal to GBCI. The GBCI website offers the most current and up-to-date information, as fees may change. The fee listed pertains to each appeal submitted for each credit, prerequisite, or MPR challenge at each level of appeal.

Certification Fees

Consult the GBCI website for detailed and current information pertaining to the fees associated with both project registration and certification. Just as with registering a project, there are different fees for members and nonmembers of USGBC for certification review. For certification review, notice that the fees are also dependent on the size of the project seeking certification. Fixed rates and available if the project size is less than 50,000 square feet or more than 500,000 square feet. If a project falls between 50,000 square feet and 500,000 square feet, there are rates to multiply by the square footage specific to the project to find out what the certification review fee is specific to the project at hand.

Notice the different fees for design review, construction review, and the combined design and construction review, as the options were discussed previously (i.e., split review). As you can see, it does cost more to go for a split review, as compared to one combined review after construction, but it is well worth it! Other key fee components to recognize are the precertification option for LEED CS projects, as well as the fees for appeals, expediting review times, and CIRs.

Resources and Tools

There are multiple resources and tools to refer to while working on a LEED project. Teams are encouraged to review the CIR database, refer to the USGBC and GBCI websites, and consult the appropriate reference guide to gather more information. It is suggested to contact GBCI prior to submitting a CIR to avoid unnecessary fees. When contacting GBCI, it is recommended to submit questions via the website, as compared to calling, as the responses are typically more appropriate and detailed.

The USGBC website also contains a "Resources and Tools" section where any project team member can download addenda for each of the rating systems and additional support specific to each of the rating systems, such as multiple building certification, daylight diagrams, and vertically attached buildings. The

GBCI website also has a "Resources" section for credit interpretation request information, fees, and the *GBCI LEED Certification Manual.*

There are other websites offering guidance to strategies and documentation examples, such as *www. Harvard.edu* and *www.leeduser.com* (membership required). LEEDuser's website is most helpful as a forum in which to post questions to the community and read answers from others (as the CIR database used to function). The prerequisite and credit information is mostly rewritten from the reference guide and therefore not as helpful although at the time of printing, they were adding more documentation examples. Also, be sure to visit the e-learning page on USGBC's site and download the free project profiles to learn how other teams implemented strategies to help their projects earn LEED certification.

Using the Reference Guides

The reference guides are intended to serve as a tool to describe the intentions behind the rating systems, including the prerequisites and credits. Within each reference guide, each prerequisite and credit is introduced with the intent and requirements described. You will the find following sections on the subsequent pages:

• Benefits and Issues to Consider

• Related Credits

• Summary of Referenced Standards

• Implementation

• Timeline and Team

• Calculations

• Documentation Guidance

• Examples

- Exemplary Performance

- Regional Variations

- Operations and Maintenance Considerations

- Resources

- Definitions

Project teams are encouraged to consult the appropriate reference guide to ensure the intentions of each prerequisite and credit are achieved. Every primary team member should obtain their own copy of the reference guide to ensure constant and frequent access opportunities. LEED coordinators should be mindful of the credit relationships, as noted in the related credits section for each of the prerequisites and credits in the reference guides, to ensure efficiencies of scale to help assess triple bottom line benefits. Referenced standards will provide additional information to help achieve the requirements detailed. The implementation section will help the team to determine the strategies and technologies to achieve compliance. LEED coordinators should always keep track of the timeline to ensure that the team is focused on the proper requirements at the right time. Knowing how to perform the individual calculations and the documentation requirements, will allow the LEED coordinator to assist the individual team members to complete the credit submittal templates. The Examples section will highlight some submittal templates and other documentation requirements instances. If any exemplary performance opportunities are available for the credit, the next incremental threshold will be listed or any other details concerning the requirements to comply to earn the bonus point. The Regional Variations section provides some insight to the applicability of the credit from a geographic standpoint. For those project teams thinking ahead and interested in pursuing the EBOM certification, note the Operations and Maintenance Considerations section for details on synergies of prerequisites and credits currently being pursued and those pertaining to the EBOM rating system. For additional information, the Definitions and Resources sections describe the terms applicable to the prerequisite or credit and provide links to more information specific to the topic.

The Next Steps of Coordinating a LEED Project

Now that there is an understanding of the components of each of the LEED Green Building Rating Systems™ and key concepts, and the project is registered, the second step of the LEED coordination strategy, the process, and importance of building a project team will be presented in the next chapter. The following describes the approach and strategy the LEED coordinator will manage until the certification is awarded (and where it is defined and discussed in the book):

The Integrative Project Delivery Process (Chapter 2)
Building a Project Team (Chapter 3)
Site Selection (Chapter 4)
The Eco-Charette (Chapter 5)
Part II: The Design Phases
Schematic Design and Design Development Phases (Chapter 6)
Construction Document Phase (Chapter 7)
Part III: The Construction Phase
Coordination with the Construction Team (Chapter 8)
Monthly Reports (Chapter 9)
Construction Completion (Chapter 10)

OWNER'S PERSPECTIVE
Two Questions Every Owner Must Answer for Their LEED Project

By Chet M. Roach
Project Manager of Brailsford & Dunlavey

Two individuals are interested in buying a new car. Buyer A drives to the local car dealership, walks up to the nearest sales associate and tells them that he has no idea what kind of car he wants, that he doesn't care about any particular features a new car might offer him, and that he doesn't care how much the new car costs. Buyer B takes 10 minutes before heading to the dealership to write down her criteria for buying a new car—she wants a four-door SUV with four-wheel drive, that received at least a three-star crash test rating, and that gets more than 20 miles per gallon in the city. She also wants to spend no more than $20,000. Which buyer will likely be more satisfied with their purchase? Why?

Clearly, Buyer B, with a proactive approach that establishes the criteria through which to judge individual vehicles, will not only be more likely to purchase the right car, but will also more efficiently find the car that is right for her. Buyer A is more likely to follow the sales associate around the lot for hours, frustrated and confused by the overwhelming number of options available, and purchasing a car that might exceed his budget.

While many people approach simple, everyday tasks in this way (grocery shopping with a list, establishing personal monthly budgets, etc.), in my experience, many owners dive into LEED projects without any overt criteria by which the success of their pursuit of LEED certification can be measured. Without clear definition of what you want to buy, why you want to buy it, and how much you can spend on it, an owner will likely become overwhelmed with the LEED process and invest in a LEED project that is potentially not the best fit for them.

In order to ensure that an owner's approach to a LEED project puts them in the position to not only "buy the right car," but also to accurately understand their success or failure, following are the two questions that every owner must answer, even before the design process begins:

Question 1: Why are we pursuing a particular LEED status on our project?

Each institution must understand the *strategic goal* that the construction of a LEED facility is trying to achieve. Generally, owners' answers fall into one or more of the following categories:

- To minimize the environmental impact of the project
- To reduce the long-term costs of operating the facility
- To create a highly visible marketing or publicity tool
- To meet a mandate or requirement put in place by a governing body

Each of these answers necessitates a starkly different approach to sustainable design. For example, the decisions that an owner makes on a LEED Silver building should vary when dealing with a project intended to meet an established mandate rather than one that focuses on reducing operating costs. There is no single solution or magic combination of LEED credits that is right for every owner—or even for the same owner pursuing different types of projects.

Question 2: How much money are we willing to invest to achieve LEED status on our project?

There is currently much discussion among industry professionals that constructing a LEED-certified project does not carry a financial premium when compared to constructing a non-LEED facility, due to the evolution of best practices and so on. Whether or not this statement is true, I will leave that debate for others. What is certain is that it is a major mistake for an owner to ignore LEED in budgeting for the cost of implementing a LEED project. Not doing so will leave the design team with no option but to pursue credits exclusively based on their cost, which will not necessarily serve an owner's strategic goals, as defined in an institution's answer to Question 1. Rather, establishing a clear budget for LEED premiums allows the owner to manage the pursuit of credits within a defined framework and lets an owner make informed decisions in selecting credits that are consistent with their goals. That being said, failing to clearly allocate funds for these LEED premiums on the front end of the project will result in one of two outcomes:

- A facility that does not meet the institutional goals of the project
- A project that is over budget as a result of meeting its institutional goals

As Buyer B's approach to car shopping mitigates the risks of wasting time with options that do not fit her established criteria, an owner honestly answering the two questions above will create a more efficient approach to managing a project team through the LEED process. Without clear answers to these questions, the owner risks spending money on credits that do not fit within their strategic purpose, as well as encounters budget concerns on their project.

chapter 2

The Integrative Project Delivery Process

A new construction project is typically the most expensive entity a person or company will acquire. Although the individual items used to construct the project are continually and repeatedly produced, the building is a unique conglomerate traditionally designed and constructed by two separate entities. Better yet, the traditional approach to contracts for the different teams does not allow them to work in collaboration, but instead against one another. Would it not make more sense for an owner to approach this undertaking in an integrative fashion to allow for the most efficiencies?

The *integrative* process of a green building project is critical in the success of achieving Leadership in Energy and Environmental (LEED®) certification (Figure 2.1). As stated in *The Integrative Design to Green Building*, "it is not the collaboration of many minds that is the problem—it is the process by which they collaborate."[1] In

Figure 2.1   The integrative project delivery process requires team coordination. Photo courtesy of Steelcase.

CONSTRUCTION MANAGER'S PERSPECTIVE
From Design to Reality

By Bassam Tarazi , LEED AP
Project Manager of Omnibuild LLC

As a construction manager, it is your job to make sure that all the pieces fit into the puzzle as they were intended. It should be no surprise that the puzzle pieces that show up on-site do not always fit the way they do on the box. Visions, models and design intent are a necessity on any large-scale project, but in the end, it's the constructability of the design that will have the final say.

In my experience at Omnibuild, from the LEED consulting side to the LEED construction side, I have been able to fight for the integrity of a design one day and the realities of site conditions the next. But it seems that the realities of site conditions tend to be the trump card in this deck. I was recently working on a project that had wanted to implement a rainwater retention tank in the space, which would then filter the water and have it reused on-site. A wonderful idea from the get-go, theoretically designed correctly on paper, but when it came time for the actual build-out, the realities of site conditions jeopardized the ability of us being able to install the unit at all. The hurdles that had not been thought of were:

- Where would the stormwater overflow drain be pumped? The drawings had it going directly to the floor below, tying into another drain. However, on-site, there was a low ceiling stairwell directly below the tank's location.
- The four-inch storm drain had to travel from the back of the space to the front of the space (where the tank was), maintain its pitch, dodge air-conditioning units and ducts, and stay above a soffit ceiling.

A rainwater retention tank was something that not every architect/engineer has the utmost experience with, so while what they put on paper was a 100 percent sound design, our reality as construction managers on-site was a completely different world. From the outset, we knew that the pitched four-inch water line could not travel "as the crow flies" from the stormwater drain to the tank inlet. Our job was to prepare for a construction game of "Operation." We had to ensure that this pipe did not affect air-conditioning unit locations or duct runs even before the heating, ventilating, and air-conditioning (HVAC) units were on-site.

On a LEED job, communication is key. If you have an ego, it's best to leave it at the door because in order to accomplish LEED Platinum or LEED Gold, it is impossible for any one professional service company or trade to carry the entire slack for the job. The painting contractor is as important as the architect, and everyone needs to understand that.

But as a construction manager with LEED experience, you cannot just focus on the "construction" points. If you see something that affects the entire credit breakdown, then you have to say something. On a different project, when inputting some information into LEED online, I had noticed that the head LEED consultant had been counting on the installation of new low-flow fixtures and toilets in the bathroom, but due to the project deciding to go after the resource reuse credit, we were going to leave the fixtures as is. It wasn't that he forgot, it's just that there are so many things to keep track of on LEED projects that some things slip through the cracks. That is why each and every trade/professional service has to have its head on a swivel watching the backs of everyone else. Only then can a symbiotic professional relationship really blossom.

conjunction, the achievement of obtaining LEED certification will depend on not only the commitment of the owner, but also the motivation of the rest of the project team. The role of a LEED coordinator will play a crucial role in continuing the motivation of the project team beyond the commitment of the owner (as important as it may seem), as well as the integrative effort of the entire team. Therefore, understanding the differences between the two different approaches will help to inform a LEED coordinator how to work more efficiently and succinctly with the integrative process.

The Differences of a Traditional Project versus an Integrative Project Delivery

The integrative project delivery (IPD) process differs from the conventional process in a multitude of ways, including communication, risk, rewards, contracts, technology, and compensation. A team working in an integrated fashion will appreciate:

- A clear understanding of the project goals

- Increased communication, reducing errors, omissions, and assumptions

- A clear determination of roles and responsibilities to eliminate overlaps and gaps

- A clear and present value of meeting time

- A definitive and measurable game plan for processes during design and construction, including milestones

- Optimized decision making by the use of modeling, simulations, and other design tools, such as life-cycle assessments

- The ability to design high-performance buildings that will be easy to maintain and operate

These initiatives will encourage communication and collaboration in exciting and unconventional means. The idea is to think outside the box and encourage team members to leave their comfort zones. Although a mechanical engineer may have never collaborated with an electrical engineer in regards to the actual lighting power density impacting the requirements for conditioning air, the HVAC system will perform more effectively once this conversation is entertained.

The collaborative approach encourages a team effort, therefore sharing not only the risks, but the rewards as well. Due to the interactive nature of the IPD process, every team member is engaged throughout the entire process, therefore encouraging a greater buy-in. For example, an architect selecting paint colors to reduce the number of required lighting fixtures is going to become more engaged in the design of the HVAC system because of the efficiencies their selections bring to the table.

The Project Team Members

Understanding the processes of design and construction, from a traditional or conventional standpoint versus that of sustainable projects, begins with an understanding of the players involved in the process. A more detailed description of the roles and responsibilities of the following team members will be presented in the next chapter.

Architect. Responsible for the design of green building strategies, including overall site planning and interior spaces

MEP engineer. Responsible for the design of the energy and water systems of a building, more specifically, the mechanical, electrical, and plumbing components, including thermal impacts

GENERAL CONTRACTOR'S PERSPECTIVE
The Importance of Integration for the Success of LEED Projects

By Travis Hall , LEED AP
Project Engineer at Howard Shockey & Sons, Inc.

A jail may seem an unusual facility to seek LEED certification, but in reality the daily functions of a jail hold tremendous opportunity for increased efficiency and more environmentally friendly strategies available through the LEED program. These types of strategies were implemented in the construction of the Western Virginia Regional Jail located in Salem, Virginia—the first regional jail in Virginia to seek LEED certification (Figure 2.2). I served as the project engineer for the general contractor, Howard Shockey & Sons, Inc., and these are a few lessons learned from the contractor's perspective.

Figure 2.2 The Western Virginia Regional Jail in Salem, Virginia, constructed by Howard Shockey & Sons, Inc. Photo by Travis Hall, LEED AP of Howard Shockey & Sons, Inc.

A jail, by virtue of its constant operation, uses a tremendous number of resources. Water is one resource that can be used more efficiently through advanced plumbing techniques. To reduce the amount of water used in flushing toilets, a vacuum-assisted waste system was installed. Construction of this system took meticulous planning by the design team, coupled with training for our plumbing contractor, in the unorthodox rules of vacuum waste piping. For instance, typical plumbing plans are schematic in nature and allow for flexibility in the exact locations of fittings and so on. In the case of a vacuum system, calculations by the design team determine locations of pipes and fittings, and the system must be constructed within close tolerance to the plans. In an effort to be sure that we were on the same page as the designers, we constructed a mock-up cell mechanical chase in a warehouse, where we installed vacuum waste piping as we intended to install it in the hundreds of chases on the job. Several reviews of the mock-up by the design team allowed us to resolve conflicts, as well as precut piping, which ultimately reduced installation time and wasted materials.

In a vacuum system, all toilet waste pipes are run above ceiling and converge at a central location, where collection tanks hold the waste until it is pulled into a municipal sewage system. In order to plan for the massive number of pipes entering this central mechanical room, our plumbing contractor created three-dimensional computer-aided design (CAD) renderings, which were followed closely during construction. These up-front planning procedures paid dividends during the installation of the system in the form of saved time on the construction schedule and avoidance of costly mistakes.

One of the LEED credits that we had hoped to earn, but did not, required a level of recycling of our construction waste. Disposal companies in the rural area we were building did not offer commingled recycling dumpsters, and it is our experience that in order to obtain this LEED credit commingling is a must. A commingled dumpster accepts all types of waste—recyclables in the waste are separated off-site. Instead of this method, we were forced to have multiple dumpsters to accommodate recycling of metal, cardboard, and so on. Frequently, foreign materials thrown into a dumpster caused the load to be rejected by the recycling facility and thrown into a landfill. The waste company we used during construction of the jail now offers commingled dumpsters and promises at least 80 percent recycling, whereas on the jail project, we obtained only 23 percent recycling using separate dumpsters.

Another recycling effort in the LEED program is the use of building materials that have high levels of recycled content. For example, installing a rubber floor made of recycled tires would contribute to earning this LEED credit. Calculations for this credit are based on the cost of the material. In the case of the jail project, a majority of the structure was precast concrete with a small section of traditional steel beams and metal stud walls. Concrete accounted for 65 percent of material cost for Construction Specification Institute (CSI) divisions 2 through 10, but contributed only 12 percent of the recycled content of the building. This is due to the fact that the only recycled product in concrete is fly ash, typically composing 1 to 2 percent of the mix. Conversely, the steel we used on the building accounted for 22 percent of material cost for CSI divisions 2 through 10, but contributed 70 percent of the recycled content of the building. The concrete masonry unit (CMU) and brick we installed did not contain any recycled content. Be aware that this credit may not be feasible if your dominant building materials are not carefully selected to conform to this credit's requirements.

There were several LEED Innovation in Design credits in this project, focusing on alleviating waste during the long-term use of the building. For instance, a siphonic roof drain system was installed to harvest rainwater off of the five-acre roof. The

continued

rainwater was collected in underground cistern tanks and then pulled back into the building for laundry use (Figure 2.3). The laundry was also designed to reuse rinse water from the previous load as wash water for the next load. These water-saving strategies will, according to design estimates, save 2 to 4 million gallons of domestic water and sewer discharge each year. From a construction standpoint, these systems took special planning to build. The siphonic piping was actually less complicated than a conventional system to install because it could be run flat, while the laundry rinse water reuse system was a challenge given the complicated plumbing that had to be coordinated between the laundry contractor and the plumbing contractor. The design team should clearly delineate where the building plumbing system stops and the laundry plumbing system starts.

The paperwork involved with documenting all of these LEED credits seemed as large a task as the actual construction. As the contractor's LEED administrator, I educated myself by attending several LEED seminars and eventually passed the LEED

Figure 2.3 The cistern tanks for siphonic roof drain system at the Western Virginia Regional Jail in Salem, Virginia. Photo by Travis Hall, LEED AP of Howard Shockey & Sons, Inc.

accreditation exam. While becoming a LEED Accredited Professional (AP) was not required, it does give an owner more confidence in the knowledge and willingness of the general contractor to complete their required credits. LEED projects typically require collection of submittals, paperwork, and photos during construction—tasks that cannot be done as an afterthought when the project is finished. For this reason, the general contractor must be given adequate instruction from the design team before construction begins, clearly outlining what is expected from them in terms of LEED compliance and documentation.

The jail was a traditional design-bid-build project, where the general contractor was given a list of LEED requirements to accomplish, which in some cases were not feasible, as in the case of waste management. This can be problematic for the general contractor if these LEED credits are made contractual obligations. I am currently working on a design-build project where we were made integral during the design process and especially in the selection of LEED credits. This has proven to be very beneficial for the project. An early engagement of the general contractor allows for buy-in and ownership of the credits that the contractor will be responsible for. It also allows the contractor to add their experience and knowledge.

While not an easy process for the general contractor, it is evident that construction of certain LEED credits has long-term benefits for the owner through increased efficiency in the use of resources and materials. As this type of building becomes more popular among owners, it is in the interest of the general contractors to educate themselves and create processes within their company to execute a successful LEED project.

Landscape architect. Responsible for the selection of trees and plants, the impacts of shading, and water efficiency for irrigation; also responsible for vegetated roof design

Civil engineer. Responsible for site design, including stormwater management, open space requirements, and site protection

Contractor. Typically referred to as the GC, short for general contractor; responsible for the demolition (if required) and construction of a facility, including site work

Facility manager. Also referred to as a building engineer; responsible for maintaining a building and its site during operations

Commissioning authority (CxA).– Responsible for the commissioning process, including drawing review during design and equipment installation and performance review during construction

Owner. Defines the triple bottom line goals and selects the team members for a project; can be a developer and does not have to be the end user

End users/occupants. The inhabitants of a building and therefore should be the main priority when designing for comfort and productivity

The Traditional Approach

There are substantial differences between conventional and sustainably driven projects, specifically with the phases of the design and construction processes:

Phases of the Traditional Project Delivery

- Predesign/Programming

- Schematic Design phase

- Design Development phase

- Construction Documents phase

- Agency Permit/Bidding

- Construction

- Substantial Completion

- Final Completion

- Certificate of Occupancy

Phases of Integrative Project Delivery

- Conceptualization

- Criteria Design

- Detailed Design

- Implementation Documents

- Agency Coordination/Final Buyout

- Construction

- Substantial Completion

- Final Completion

- Certificate of Occupancy

Although they have different names, the key difference of the phases depends on who is involved and when, when comparing a traditionally designed and constructed building versus one that is designed with sustainable initiatives. For example, with a traditionally designed project, an owner may hire a civil engineering firm or environmental team once they select a piece of property. Once the environmental reports are completed and they have an idea of how their building can fit on the site, the site plan is handed off to an architect. The architect then works with the owner to detail the program requirements (known as the Programming phase) and then begins to design the building (known as the Schematic Design phase). The architect then works with an engineering team (typically composed of a mechanical, electrical, and plumbing engineers and a structural engineer, if needed, depending on the project type). These professionals typically work independently of each other to complete their tasks (known as the Design Development phase). Remember, with a traditional design project, the architect has already designed the building and is now handing off the plans to the engineers to fit the building systems into the building that was designed without their input. Once the basic design elements are established, each professional works to complete a set of construction documents (CDs). Notice that the responsibilities are segmented just as the communication is fragmented.

What happens next with the CDs varies with different project types. Typically, these documents are first issued for permit review by the local municipality. It is quite common for most project types to send the CDs out for bid to a number of contractors about the same time as the drawings are issued for permit review (known as a design-bid-build project type), while other project types have the contractor engaged as one entity with the architect from the beginning (known as a design-build project type).

At this point in a design-bid-build project type, the contractor is given a short period of time in which to evaluate the drawings and provide the owner with a fee to provide demolition services (if required) and to construct the building, including site development work. They are given an opportunity to submit requests for information (RFIs) about the requirements or design elements during this bidding process, but then they are held to the quote they provide. Remember, the contractor was not engaged during the design phases, so they are not familiar with the hundred of hours that were put in to develop the information detailed in the CDs for the project and are required to dive in quickly, sometimes making assumptions about the construction requirements. *Most of the time*, projects are awarded based on the lowest bid, but think about the implications by doing so. If the lowest bidder wins the job, where are they cutting corners? Is quality being compromised? How were the subcontractors selected? Are they aware of the LEED goals and requirements? Was a critical element omitted? No one likes to lose money, as that is just bad business, but is this really the best way to select a contractor? Do we want to award the project to a contractor that knows the least about the project?

Once the permit is received, the contractor is selected and the construction cost is agreed upon, the phases of the design process are over and the construction process begins. Just as the design process has four phases, the construction process does as well. Construction commences the process, traditionally with little involvement from the design team. The next phase, Substantial Completion, includes the final inspection process and when the owner issues a "punch list." The owner compiles a punch list while walking the space with the contractor and notes any problems requiring the contractor's attention. Final Completion is next, followed by the Certification of Occupancy. Once the Certificate of Occupancy is received, the building is then permitted to be occupied.

The Integrative Approach

When compared to the traditional project delivery method, the integrative design process for sustain-able design projects involves different phases of design and construction as shown in the previous list, and remember that the main differentiator is determined by the team members, particularly how and when they are involved. For a project seeking LEED certification, the owner may engage a number of consultants early in the process to assist in selecting the property or tenant space. They may retain an architect to evaluate the site for building orientation options to capitalize on natural ventilation or day-lighting opportunities. They may hire a civil engineer to research the stormwater codes and to determine access to public transportation. A LEED consultant may be engaged to assist with evaluating the triple-bottom-line goals particular to a project site or tenant space. Think about the benefits of bringing the landscape architect and the civil engineer on board simultaneously so they could work together to reveal the opportunities to use stormwater collection for irrigation needs. If the site were already determined, the owner would bring all of the consultants (including the general contractor) together to review the economic, social, and environmental goals collaboratively. This goal-setting meeting, or eco-charette, is a key component of the first step of a sustain-able project and is therefore part of the first design phase of Programming or Predesign, as the integrative process should be started as early as possible. The eco-charette will be discussed in greater detail in Chapter 5.

After the eco-charette and during design, the project would benefit from the collaboration of multiple team members. For example, the integration of a lighting designer, an architect, and an HVAC or mechanical engineer could help to reduce first costs for lighting, HVAC supply and distribution systems, operating costs, and environmental impacts connected with manufacturing and operations by simply addressing paint color! By increasing the light reflectance value (LRV) of the paint color selections, the number of lighting fixtures required can be reduced. Therefore, it is essential for the LEED coordinator to encourage this type of interaction and communication for the success of the project.

Design Tools

Another key difference with a green building project is the use of energy modeling and Building Information Modeling (BIM). These tools allow the design team to find efficiencies and conflicts within their design intentions. They can model the proposed building systems to evaluate and predict the performance of the components specific to the project's location and site. These technologies allow the design team to specify systems and equipment sized appropriately for the particular building. Because the tools allow for the project to be evaluated from a three-dimensional perspective, design teams also have the opportunity to find conflicts with building components and systems. For example, there could be a contradiction with the structural beams and mechanical ductwork at certain locations with the specified finished ceiling height. Think about the project Bassam Tarazi described earlier in the chapter. Perhaps the project team might have been able to implement a stormwater retention tank if the team utilized a 3D design approach to recognize the conflicts that prohibited the strategy.

The design teams can also use these tools to determine the estimated energy and water savings as compared to implementing traditional building systems. These tools are used throughout the design phases to bring more efficiency to the project for all team members to capitalize on for awareness. For example, a conversation between an architect and an HVAC engineer was mentioned earlier to depict a different approach to designing mechanical systems. Traditionally, a mechanical engineer might design the HVAC system based on charts and tables laid out by industry standards such as the American Society of Heating, Refrigerating, and Air-Conditioning Engineers (ASHRAE), whereas a project seeking LEED would encourage communication between disciplines, as well as the integration of design tools, such as energy modeling, to design the building systems.

Time and Money Savings for IPDs

Projects utilizing an integrative design approach bring the entire team together early in the design process, thus allowing for the opportunity for everyone to work more collectively, which can actually save time and money. One of the biggest misconceptions of LEED and green building methodologies is that they cost more than conventionally designed and constructed buildings. Building sustainably does not mean adding green features, thus adding to the project's economic bottom line. Building sustainably means building in an integrative fashion, taking advantage of efficiencies of design solutions. For example, incorporating a green roof is not an addition or an applied green feature, although one of the most visible attributes of a green project. Including a green roof allows the project to take advantage of a thermal barrier between the indoor environment and the outdoors, therefore reducing the impact of the urban heat island effect and the burden on the mechanical systems. A green roof also helps to address stormwater management issues, which brings another advantage to the project. Therefore, if a green roof were to be "value engineered" out of a project, the decision would impact

GENERAL CONTRACTOR'S PERSPECTIVE
Involving a Construction Manager during Design

By Michael J. Parnell, LEED AP
Sr. Project Manager at Hunter Roberts

Being involved with the project in the Preconstruction/Design Development stage plays a critical role in understanding how and why certain LEED points are being attempted, and allows for a new perspective to be given to the design team from the construction manager's point of view. The construction manager can provide feedback to the architect and engineers as to how certain elements of the design can work within the project budget, or if there are other means and methods to accomplish the design intent at reduced cost or with greater efficiency. And if you are able to have the individual that will be actually managing the Construction phase of the project as your preconstruction lead, you will enjoy even greater success as that individual will have the advantage of being involved with each of those design decisions and will be more keenly tuned into the project's LEED goals.

---

more than the roof system specification, but instead how the building performs as a whole.

Time savings can be addressed during design and construction. Although the integrative approach may appear as though it will require more time during design as more components (such as daylighting, life-cycle assessments, and indoor air quality) are addressed over a conventionally designed structure, that is not the case. The key is to engage the right team members at the right time. For example, a lighting designer does not need to be at a project meeting to discuss stormwater management strategies.

A project's schedule can be reduced because the project's goals are reinforced throughout every step of the process, as shown through the avoidance of the "value engineering" process that can happen on a conventionally designed project. Value engineering (VE) can take place when the bidding contractors respond with a construction cost much higher than

anticipated by the owner and design professionals. In response to this high price, the design team begins to remove design elements from the original scope of work to try to get the construction cost better aligned with the project budget. IPD projects avoid this time inefficiency because the team established the goals at the beginning and incorporated an integrated budgeting approach. For example, if the goals include designing a high-performance envelope that may cost more than a conventionally designed envelope, the mechanical systems may be reduced, therefore balancing the budget and aligning with the project goals. This approach includes optimizing on a whole-building approach concentrating on the linkages of components, thus adding efficiencies. An IPD project can also avoid the process of VE because the team, including the contractor, is evaluating the elements and drawings continuously throughout each of the design phases to ensure compliance with the budget. Eliminating the VE process not only saves time but also money; as every revision requires at least one consultant's

ENGINEER'S PERSPECTIVE
Integrated Design and Collaboration

By Robert Diemer, PE, LEED AP
Partner at In Posse LLC

Much has been said in the green building movement about the importance of integrated design. I truly believe this to be the path to achieving the highest levels of performance for the lowest first cost and environmental impact, and I take it to be one of the fundamental tenets of sustainable design. It can come about only when a project team is dedicated to the idea of integration and functions in a collaborative way. However, more often than not, I see team members embrace integrated design as a concept, but the reality of how to achieve it is often left to chance. In my mind, it is the collaborative spirit that is most lacking in the building industry, and I believe it is the key to achieving the highest levels of success.

I was first attracted to sustainable design because I wanted to design buildings—not the mechanical systems in buildings, not a piece or part or system, but the entire building. I also felt that within the framework of sustainable design, my contribution to the building process would be leveraged and enhanced through the collaborative, integrated process and result in a project that was greater than the sum of its parts.

Collaboration is very difficult to achieve on a building project. The industry is not integrated. and most projects are made up of many individuals working for different companies with diverse goals. I am not surprised that some projects end up with finger-pointing, blame shifting, or even litigation, as in this environment, collaboration is the last thing on people's minds.

True collaboration evolves from mutual understanding, respect, and ownership for the entire outcome. If all team members try to understand and appreciate what fellow team members are trying to accomplish, respect the value of what each contributes, and reflect on how their own actions affect the others, a spirit of collaboration can develop. Collaborative team members understand that their individual success is linked to the success of all other team members, and therefore, they take ownership for helping everyone succeed. The stance of "it's not my problem" is altered to "it's our challenge and how do we fix it?"

The obvious parallel to this are successful sports teams. It is rare for a team to rise to championship levels without team members developing a sense that their individual success depends on the success of the team. Time after time, teams with superior talent but a lack of teamwork have fallen short. The following are some ideas on how the building industry can become more collaborative:

1. Hire people who are curious and have the ability to look at the big picture. This is a particular challenge for engineers who are often quite good at seeing the "trees" but often overlook the "forest."

2. Reflect on process as much as solutions. Spend time thinking about how to improve the process of design and construction.

3. Be willing to educate others. Explain to fellow team members what you are trying to accomplish and why.

4. Take ownership for the entire outcome. We can't be collaborative if we care only about good performance on the systems we design without regard to all the other project outcomes.

5. Be collaborative within your company. If we can't collaborate among ourselves, how can we hope to collaborate with others?

---

time to implement the changes to the drawings and specifications.

In summary, traditionally designed projects differ from IPDs in terms of teams, process, risk, communications, agreement types, and phases. Remember, conventional project teams are fragmented, whereas green building teams work more collectively. An IPD project's process is more holistically approached, while a traditional project is more linear. The risk is separated with a fragmented, traditional project as compared to an IPD. In terms of communicating ideas and concepts, traditional projects are presented in a two-dimensional format, while sustainable projects work with BIM technologies to allow for the opportunity to find conflicts. Agreement types can vary, but with an IPD there is more collaboration to encourage a multilateral approach as compared to a unilateral approach of a conventional project. Finally, the phases change names from a traditional approach versus an IPD.

LEED and IPD

The achievement of LEED certification relies heavily on the implementation of the IPD process. It is the role of the LEED coordinator to bring the project team together to encourage a collaborative environment. A LEED coordinator needs to develop a process to support the questioning of assumptions and inspire the team to think differently. As a result of this interaction, the LEED coordinator also needs to acknowledge the different aspects of insight and to understand how to find the common merit, process, and intent. It is encouraged that you create a thought process for each of the disciplines to participate in to understand the opportunities for efficiencies of building components, systems, and technologies and to capitalize on those interrelationships. It is critical for project decisions not to be based on the traditional approach, experience, or implementation, but instead because it makes sense for the project and aligns with the goals for the project. The next chapters will focus on research and analysis after each milestone, which may result in more time dedicated initially, as opposed to the final stages as found with the traditional approach, but will ensure a cohesive, holistic, high-performance project. This is not meant to imply the "on-time, on-budget" mentally needs to change, but just the process in which it occurs.

chapter 3 **Building a Project Team**

Selecting the right team members for a specific project could mean the difference between achieving certification or not. As discussed in the previous chapter, bringing all of the team members together as early as possible will help add to the success of the project. This chapter will help you assess the different parameters involved with each role to assist with the decision process and focus on the critical measures.

To aid with the understanding of the possible Leadership in Energy and Environmental Design (LEED®) credentials of prospective team members, the following section details of the credentialing system, as the new system involves three tiers:

1. LEED Green Associate

2. LEED Accredited Professional (AP) with Specialty

3. LEED Fellow

The Tiers of the Credentialing Process

The LEED Green Associate tier is applicable for professionals with a basic understanding of green building systems and technologies. LEED Green Associate professionals have been tested on the key components of the LEED rating systems and the certification process. This level of credentialing is the first step to becoming a LEED Accredited Professional (AP).

The next tier, LEED AP with Specialty, is divided into five types (of specialties). This credential denotes professionals with LEED project experience and who have passed one of the following types of exams. It should also be noted the previous credentialing system only had one tier composed of the LEED AP credential. Therefore, any professional with LEED AP and not one of the specialties, was credentialed under the previous system.

1. *LEED AP Building Design + Construction* (BD+C). This credential tests concepts related to new construction and major renovations, core and shell projects, and schools. This specialty will also cover retail and health care applications in the future.

2. *LEED AP Interior Design + Construction* (ID+C). This credential tests information related to tenant improvement and fit-out project knowledge for commercial interior and retail professionals.

OWNER'S PERSPECTIVE
Building a LEED Team

By Bill Stoller of Stoller Vineyards

Figure 3.1   The Stoller Winery in Dayton, Oregon, is located atop a scenic knoll that provides the slope required for gravity flow wine production, thus improving the quality of the wine and conserving energy by avoiding the need for pumps. Photo courtesy of Mike Haverkate, Stoller Vineyards.

We used a consulting firm to oversee the LEED certification process of Stoller Winery (Figure 3.1). They were vital to our success. Everyone on the project was educated on what their role was in making sure we were doing all we could to follow the proper process, including recycling of materials, where to purchase material, tracking the content of the materials, the surrounding environment, transportation impacts of construction, and so on. It had to be a total team effort among the architect, contractor, and the subcontractors. When organized, it is not difficult to attain. Our only problem was the inexperience of the team (except the consulting firm, of course), as no one had worked on a LEED building prior to our construction. As a result of dedicated teamwork, in the end, we were delivered a high-performance, sustainable building constructed with recycled content and salvaged and regional materials. Energy efficiency was our biggest success, as the building ended up being 70 percent better than what code requires. The solar technology is actually producing at a higher efficiency than first expected (Figure 3.2). We have been able to deliver between 53,000 and 58,000 kWs each year back to the grid, translating into over a 50 percent credit to our electric bill for normal usage (excluding harvest processing). This energy-efficient achievement was made possible not only by the high-performance envelope and renewable energy features at Stoller, but also because our barrel room is 100 percent cooled by the natural capacities of the earth. We are also quite proud to report another sustainable achievement: our contractor was able to divert over 95 percent of the waste generated during construction from landfills. Overall, we are very pleased to have the LEED designation and are proud of what we have accomplished.

Figure 3.2 Stoller Vineyards in Dayton, Oregon, generates electricity on site by the means of photovoltaic panels mounted on the roof. Photo courtesy of Mike Haverkate, Stoller Vineyards.

3. *LEED AP Operations + Maintenance* (O+M). This credential covers existing building project knowledge specific to operations and maintenance issues for existing buildings.

4. *LEED AP Homes.* This credential applies to professionals experienced in the residential market.

5. *LEED AP Neighborhood Development* (ND). This credential tests whole or partial neighborhood development project knowledge.

Finally, the third tier of the credentialing system, LEED Fellow, is the highest level of credentialing and is meant to signify a demonstration of accomplishments, experience, and proficiency within the sustainable design and construction community. The requirements of this credential were released in November of 2010, synonymous with the acceptance of applications for individuals with over eight years of LEED credentials and project experience nominated by individuals with over 10 years of experience.

What Is a LEED Coordinator?

Understanding the role of a LEED coordinator can help to find the perfect candidate to manage the process for certification. Many inexperienced owners and other team members might have the misconception that a LEED coordinator completes all of the documentation to be submitted for certification review. Experienced LEED project team members understand the role of the coordinator a bit more and understand that this is not the case. Remembering the context of Chapter 1 and the process of registration and certification, the project administrator is responsible for managing the coordination of key stakeholders and guiding the team through the process, including the assessment and evaluation of the team's documentation for certification review. A project administrator or LEED coordinator is well versed in the aspects of sustainable design and the requirements of LEED, but is not expected to be an expert in all of the details to achieve the strategies and technologies. If this were the case, we would not have architects, engineers, contractors, and other professionals, we would just have one expert knowledgeable in all the different realms of design and construction—quite a difficult undertaking for any one person. Therefore, a LEED coordinator should be thought of in terms of a LEED project manager, one that guides a project team but not one that completes the individual tasks to be accomplished.

What Are the Responsibilities of a LEED Coordinator?

During the preliminary stages of a project, a LEED coordinator can help an owner or developer select the rest of the project team. They can also help with assessing the probability of compliance for LEED certification during site selection. This could include working with a broker to define the goals of certification to ensure, at the very least, that the prerequisites can be met. This is incredibly important for a tenant looking to earn LEED for Commercial Interiors™ (CI) certification, as the base building could attribute to earning up to five points. Base buildings can also hinder certification altogether. For example, in order to comply with Energy and Atmosphere (EA) Prerequisite 3: Fundamental Refrigerant Management, if any part of the heating, ventilating, and air-conditioning (HVAC) system within the proposed leased space is to be modified to meet the needs of the build-out, no chlorofluorocarbon (CFC) refrigerants are allowed. This may or may not be feasible due to the base building systems in place. In other situations where certification might not be hindered by existing base building components, but there is the opportunity for it to become a big challenge, a LEED coordinator could add value to the owner by helping them to understand the level of commitment required. For example, in order to comply with EA Prerequisite 2: Minimum Energy Performance, a tenant space needs to meet the energy performance criteria of

ENGINEER'S PERSPECTIVE
The LEED Challenge and the Role of Project Coordinator

By Wayne Howell, PE
Principal at Clive Samuels & Associates

LEED building certification has become the norm for building projects across the country, and many states and municipalities have mandated meeting LEED requirements in their building and energy codes. Clients and owners have embraced the green movement and want their buildings to be environmentally responsible. Meetings that previously discussed how the space can best meet the needs of the clients, space allocations for people, product, and energy-efficient equipment, and budget, now take the discussions to the next level. How can these optimal engineering and architectural designs meet LEED requirements?

Having an independent LEED project coordinator, whose job is to manage the LEED aspects of the project, can facilitate the process. The project coordinator's focus is only LEED, and while the engineer or architect can successfully be the LEED leader, they are also tasked with their own design duties for the building systems or structures.

Each company that is a member of the design team usually has LEED-accredited professionals and people familiar with LEED project requirements on staff, and they bring their expertise to the design discussions. Initial project meetings are now design charrettes, where each team member suggests design ideas or features that can be added to the project, and additional energy-related and environmental features are examined. Discussions ensue about the project implications, benefit to the environment, initial cost of the proposed feature, return on investment, and so on.

Additional items are then discussed and examined for inclusion in the project. The LEED project coordinator then produces the LEED project checklist where each credit is assigned to a team member, coordinates initial setup of the project with U.S. Green Building Council (USGBC®), and then follows the team's progress. They may review the online templates and provide suggestions to a team member who may not have worked with this template previously. They will also review uploaded support documentation for compliance with requirements—with just the right amount of information.

When necessary, the LEED coordinator may be required to submit a credit interpretation request (CIR) to LEED on behalf of a project with special considerations. One Clive Samuels & Associates project in particular required a CIR by LEED on how to handle submission requirements for a complex, multiphase, multiowner, multibuilding, commercial mixed-use redevelopment project in Austin, Texas, where multiple mixed-use buildings have multiple occupancy and usages within the same building footprint. The project coordinator was instrumental in securing the correct approach for the project.

The LEED project coordinator as team member can complement the other team members' LEED work so the project meets the requirements and more easily make it through the project review process and, in some cases, secure the proper starting point for complex projects.

American Society of Heating, Refrigerating, and Air-Conditioning Engineers (ASHRAE) 90.1-2007. If space in an older building is an option, this typically means additional insulation will need to be included in the scope of work for the tenant improvement in order to comply with this prerequisite. Is this a cost the owner is willing to pay for in order to get the tenant in the building? Or is this a cost the tenant will pay for because of their commitment to achieve certification? Who will be responsible for the utility costs during operations? The answer might help to negotiate a solution, as an increase in energy performance most likely will result in a utility savings down the road. Integrated budgeting will be discussed in Chapter 5, as there are ways to offset this additional up-front cost, but these cost considerations are mentioned for the purposes of understanding the role and importance of a LEED coordinator prior to site selection.

For a LEED for New Construction and Major Renovations™ (NC) or LEED for Core & Shell™ (CS) project, although not a matter of complying with the requirements of a prerequisite, employing a LEED coordinator prior to site selection could add value to the process. For example, certain Sustainable Sites (SS) credits should be addressed prior to selecting the site, such as access to public transportation or the remediation of a brownfield site. However, in most cases with NC and CS projects, the owner or developer typically approaches the LEED coordinator after site selection.

After the team is compiled and the site is selected, a LEED coordinator's role includes coordinating and conducting the eco-charette and design integration meetings during the design phases and of course, registering the project with Green Building Certification Institute (GBCI). The key is to keep the project team focused and on schedule to submit for certification review after construction documents. This requires a lot of support and encouragement, as well as patience and persistence. During construction, a LEED coordinator typically will be responsible for training the contractor and their subcontractors, material tracking through submittal reviews, indoor air quality (IAQ) inspections, and managing the construction waste.

Looking for a LEED Coordinator?

For those readers who are looking for a LEED coordinator to assist with their project, there are many aspects to consider. How do you know what to look for in a LEED coordinator if you have never worked on a LEED project? Readers, beware—the fact that a professional has earned their LEED Accredited Professional (AP) status does not mean they are qualified to be the team administrator for your project seeking LEED certification. This actually falls true for any LEED AP and their role on a project seeking certification. Therefore, it is critical to ask the LEED AP candidate a few questions when looking for a LEED coordinator:

- Is your firm involved with USGBC?

- How many LEED credentialed professionals does your firm employ? What specialty are the project contact's AP credentials in (i.e., Building Design and Construction [BD+C], Operations and Maintenance [O+M], Interior Design and Construction [ID+C], etc.)?

- How many projects have you registered with GBCI?

- How many projects have you worked on that earned LEED certification?

- Have any of your projects earned the same level of certification the current project is seeking?

- Have you worked with the rating system the current project is looking at?

- Have any of your projects used the same technologies or strategies the current project team is planning on incorporating into the project (i.e., green roof, chilled beams, etc.)?

- How do you determine your fees?

Fees for LEED Coordination

For those readers who are looking for insight on consultancy fees for LEED certification process coordination and documentation management services, be aware that prices vary for these consultants just like most consultants. You will find that some fees are based on a percentage of benefit of incentives or per task, service, or even worse—by credit. As LEED itself is based on a holistic approach, so should LEED consulting services. How else would you reap the benefits of a dedicated person to the success of earning certification? Therefore, LEED coordinators should base their fees on design- and construction-side services. It obviously makes the most sense for the same consultant to manage the documentation process during both design and construction, but it can work if split into two—just not as efficiently and effectively. For example, the architectural team might have a dedicated LEED AP managing the effort during the design phases, but not have the contract to support the contractor during construction. The contractor may have in-house support to help produce the required documentation, or they may subcontract out these services. In either case:

- Who is responsible for reviewing the information prior to submitting to GBCI for review to ensure consistency and accuracy?

- If the architectural team is the main contact (project administrator) on LEED-Online, are they responsible for the final submission for certification review? Who is responsible for following up with GBCI and the certification body after each review submission?

It is important to point out none of the version 3.0 LEED rating systems require a LEED AP to be part of the project team. Therfore, it is merely encouraged to ensure the LEED consultant is also a LEED AP with certified project experience.

Experience has shown that once construction begins, the documentation efforts for LEED have a tendency to fall by the wayside. Traditionally speaking, general contractors have been responsible for scheduling and coordinating the construction of buildings, not tracking materials for recycled content, regional manufacturing and extracting points, or volatile organic compound (VOC) content. This may be one of the reasons why there are so many projects registered, but not certified. Therefore, it is important to address the roles and responsibilities of each of the team members as soon as possible.

For a project seeking LEED certification, its success relies on consistency and dedication. Not only do the owner and the project team need to be committed to the environmental goals determined at the onset of the project, but having a LEED coordinator managing the documentation during both the Design and Construction phases aids the project's success. Accordingly, it is best to ensure that one person is in charge and responsible for reviewing all of the documentation prior to submitting for certification review.

Selecting the Rest of the Team Members

A LEED coordinator is sometimes hired before the rest of the design team and, in that event, an owner or developer may look to the LEED coordinator for help

PROFESSIONAL PERSPECTIVE
The Value of Certification

By Mark Hanson, PhD, LEED AP
Director of Sustainable Services at Hoffman LLC

Hoffman's experience is that a green or sustainable project at a Silver, or even a Gold, level can be provided at equal to or less than conventional cost (Figure 3.3). However, in the early stages of a project, one comes to the point in the discussion with the owner where some of that first cost savings will need to be given up if one is going to do formal certification under USGBC's LEED program. And if one is in a situation where a green project is above conventional cost for whatever reason—including the pursuit of a high Platinum certification level perhaps—then the owner is facing additional first cost. Some owners will give up some of the first cost savings, while others don't see the value. In round numbers, we have found this cost to be roughly $100,000 for a medium-sized project, around 50,000 to 100,000 square feet. That cost does not include the commissioning cost. We recommend commissioning regardless of whether formal certification is being done.

The clearest statement of the value of certification that we have heard came from one of our project owners, which was a public school district. The school district administrator's comment was that certification led her team to think differently,

Figure 3.3 The River Crest Elementary School in Hudson, Wisconsin, by Hoffman, LLC, was the first elementary school in the state and second public school in the nation to earn LEED Gold certification. Photo courtesy of Fotographix and Hoffman, LLC.

which led them to act differently. The acting differently included both the close collaboration on various green decisions during the design and construction process, as well as ongoing actions in operating the new school and in managing other properties in the district. During the discussion of miscellaneous electrical loads in the school, the owner initially said that they wanted to leave computers on after hours for various reasons, including system updates. A few months later in the project, the district decided it would be better to change their operations, saving energy costs and resulting in an adjustment in the energy model used in the certification. Later, the school district informed us that they saw so much value in the change that they had implemented the policy district-wide. This is but one example of the attention and partnership that emerged in achieving a LEED for Schools Gold certification.

Our experience with owners who decide not to pursue certification is that there is a tendency to be less focused and committed to sustainable achievements as might otherwise be done. We find owners less attentive to sustainability, and they sometimes let decisions languish. And if the owner is less committed, the project team will also tend to reduce its focus. This can result in some erosion of some LEED points, as the project may slip from the equivalent of Gold into a Silver level, for example. The attitude seems to be that if a green project is not going to be formally certified, maybe we don't need to do this or that, and we can reduce the first cost even further. This is not a wrong decision. It is a different decision that can, and in our practice does, result in buildings that are still green—but not to the same degree—and, of course, do not have the third-party review that LEED provides.

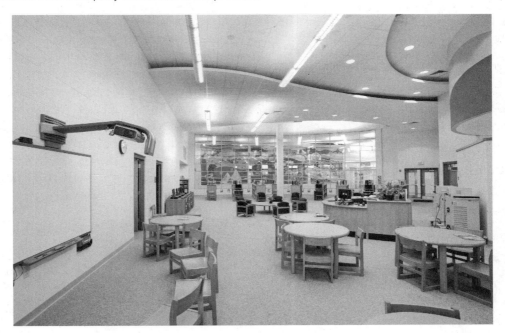

Figure 3.4 The media center at the River Crest Elementary School includes local materials, Forest Stewardship Council (FSC)-certified wood products, and strategies to ensure a quality indoor environment for the students and teachers. Photo courtesy of Fotographix and Hoffman, LLC.

compiling the rest of the project team. A LEED coordinator typically has a database of networks available for resources with LEED certification experience. It is important to refer or suggest team members with credentials beneficial to the project that will add experience and efficiencies. Some questions a LEED coordinator might ponder when thinking of possible team members might include the following:

- Which architects, engineers, and contractors have earned their LEED AP credentials?

- Are they familiar with the process for integrative projects?

- Have they worked on LEED registered projects, and are they familiar with LEED-Online?

- Which architects, engineers, and contractors are familiar and experienced with LEED and the certification process?

- Have their projects achieved certification? If not, why?

- Have they worked with the specific rating system the project will be working with?

- Do they have the regional experience specific to the project to understand the local requirements?

- Do they evaluate decisions based on life-cycle costing?

- How many staff members are LEED credentialed? Will they be assigned to the project?

- What is their involvement with USGBC?

These are general, yet critical, questions to ask yourself as you are compiling a team of professionals for the project you are working on. More questions are detailed below, specific to each discipline. Overall, when looking to professionals who have worked on projects earning LEED certification, you will find they understand:

- The benefits of green building

- The integrative project delivery (IPD) process

- The LEED rating systems and the strategy synergies

- Their documentation responsibilities for a LEED project

- The different strategies and technologies for compliance, including products and materials

- The process for submission to LEED-Online

Building off of a professional's prior experience will not only save a client money, but add efficiencies to a project. There is nothing that costs a project, and therefore a client, more than a team member's learning curve (although, ironically enough, it could be the owner's own learning curve adding to the project's cost). Even though there is an increasing number of LEED-certified projects across the country, there is still a large number of professionals (LEED APs included) yet to work on one. Although the new credentialing system has addressed this issue, the problem still exists. The inexperienced are unsure how to estimate the time commitments required, and therefore might overcharge for their services. What are they basing their fees on?

Due to the nature of the integrative design process, selecting team members with a positive attitude can make all the difference. Each member will be expected to work as a team and not as independently as they would on a conventional project. Experienced team members with positive attitudes have the right combination for a successful, certified project. Depending on the specifics of each project, the technologies and systems will determine the types of professionals required, but here is a breakdown of typical members (including some from the list in the previous chapter):

- Owner/Developer
- Real estate attorney/Broker
- Architect
- Interior designer
- Lighting designer
- Civil engineer
- Landscape architect
- Mechanical/electrical/plumbing (MEP) engineer
- Structural engineer
- Commissioning agent (CxA)
- General contractor and their subs
- Construction manager

The Owner/Developer

This is the most crucial member of the team, and that is not intended due to the economic deliverables the owner and/or developer bring to the team. The owner/developer has the capacity to motivate or demotivate the entire team. It is much easier to inspire an entire team from the top down, as compared to the hired consultants trying to enthuse an owner about green building benefits and values. For NC and CS projects, an owner will not only help to set the goals for a project, but will also play a crucial part creating and implementing policies, such as recycling, smoking, and tenant guidelines. The owner as tenant will serve as a critical role for CI projects as well, for the purposes of lease agreements and negotiations with the building owner or developer. A tenant has

the opportunity to impact the site and building as a whole, therefore influencing more than their leased space, thus having a greater environmental impact.

The Real Estate Attorney/Broker

For each project type, a real estate attorney and/or broker will play a role in the process. Although they are not typically responsible for submitting documentation for certification review, their role can help make the up-front process more efficient, especially for CI projects.

A LEED-credentialed broker understands the requirements for certification and how a site's location can play a major role when tallying up points. They may already have surveyed different building owners and/or management companies to prequalify the buildings for possible selections. After a site has been selected, these professionals will assist with lease negotiations, as they are familiar with green lease provisions to ensure that the tenants' environmental goals are not compromised.

The Architect

An architect's role on a project seeking certification is important from beginning to end. They are typically responsible for building the design team, as they are involved with each of the team members helping to evaluate sustainable solutions appropriate to the project type setting the pace for construction and operations. For example, they need to collaborate with the engineering team and the CxA to develop envelope solutions, including glazing and insulation, to ensure that the mechanical equipment is sized appropriately. For NC and CS projects, the architect's qualifications pertaining to building orientation design, will affect the success of passive design strategies for daylighting

ATTORNEY'S PERSPECTIVE
The Risks of Green Building

By Stephen T. Del Percio
Attorney at Arent Fox LLP

As green building practices continue to proliferate, the legal community is just beginning to consider the ramifications that sustainability will have for traditional concepts of construction and real estate law. With only a handful of insurance claims and reported lawsuits arising out of green building projects that have been reported to date, much of the discussion among industry stakeholders and their attorneys about green building risk has been theoretical. Nevertheless, there are some key concepts through which stakeholders should review their contracts and other documents in connection with green building projects until those legal issues have been more fully flushed out. Green building risks can generally be considered under three broad umbrellas: regulatory and policy risks, financial risks, and performance risks. Each of these general types of risks have different implications for different industry stakeholders, but each must be addressed in any contract or lease where the underlying project or building contemplates green features.

Regulatory and policy risks refer to the rapidly changing legislative landscape that may apply to a given green building project. For example, since 2002, there has been a 200 percent increase in state- and local-level green building programs across the country. For developers and their project teams, determining which regulations apply to their project may be a challenge, particularly given the lack of uniformity associated with most regulatory activity. One of the few reported lawsuits arising out of a green building project to date—*Shaw Development v. Southern Builders*—stemmed from the parties' failure to acknowledge specific technical requirements of the applicable state-level green building tax credit program. Understanding regulatory requirements and translating associated responsibilities into contract documents will continue to be of primary importance for project teams, particularly as pending federal legislation casts a long legal shadow over state and local programs that have already been enacted.

The financial risks of green building are myriad and still being assessed by developers, insurers, sureties, and underwriters. The types of risks that these parties are considering include what many still believe to be increased green construction costs, the costs associated with third-party certification under programs such as LEED, and a project team's failure to earn tax credits or other financial incentives that may be anticipated by the owner. In this context, scopes of work, third-party certification responsibilities, and limitations on liability provisions in contracts are critical for parties to consider. For example, a consultant's failure to submit certain documentation in support of a specific LEED credit, which causes the project to miss the anticipated level of certification and associated tax credits, could expose the consultant to a disproportionately large amount of liability compared to its total contract amount. While this type of scenario ties back into regulatory and policy risks, it demonstrates the unique nature of green building projects and necessity for an active risk management strategy throughout the design, construction, and certification processes.

Finally, the actual performance of green buildings once occupied remains a question mark. While data suggests that some green buildings do perform quite well, that same data has identified many green buildings that do not. The developer or landlord who touts its project's green features to entice potential tenants may be exposing itself to claims for fraud or misrepresentation if those features do not perform as advertised. Design professionals may specify new or emerging building systems or technologies without performing sufficient due diligence, or otherwise engage in more "aggressive" design on behalf of a client seeking to push the green design envelope. More practically, designers or consultants who provide third-party certification services must be careful to keep their professional liability insurance in place by avoiding language or other representations in their contracts that could be construed by their insurer as the equivalent of a warranty or a guarantee that the project will ultimately achieve a specific level of certification.

As green building practices continue to proliferate, the legal community is just beginning to consider the ramifications that sustainability will have for traditional concepts of construction and real estate law.

---

and ventilation. For CI projects, they would need to develop a strategy to address indoor air quality and water conservation. For any project type, they need to have experience with specification development and writing for sustainable products and materials, waste management, and recycling.

The Interior Designer

The role of an interior designer is important on any project type, as they are responsible for selecting finishes and furniture options, as well as furniture layout. Therefore, they need to be familiar with environmentally preferred products and materials, including paints and coatings, adhesives and sealants, flooring finishes, ceiling finishes, and furniture. They also need to be aware of furniture layout to improve occupant satisfaction and productivity by the means of visual access to the outdoor environment and acoustical performance. The interior designer is also typically involved with light fixture selections and placement. Therefore, they will need to be aware of energy-efficient options and able to converse with an engineer to ensure optimized use. The architect typically assumes these responsibilities if an interior designer is not hired for a specific job.

The Lighting Designer

A lighting designer is typically hired to specifically address the lighting requirements on highly complex project types, such as museums, retail spaces, and hospitality projects. Since lighting is one of the largest uses of energy, it is recommended that you engage a lighting designer to find efficiencies and optimize usage. Therefore, they need to be extremely familiar with energy-efficient options to suggest to the team and implement into the drawings and specifications. For a project seeking LEED certification, a lighting designer would typically manage the light pollution, as well as daylighting strategies. The documentation requirements of the Indoor Environmental Quality (EQ) credits for daylighting and views typically requires a lighting designer to be responsible for the simulation modeling to show compliance with the credit requirements. Therefore, before hiring a lighting designer and daylighting specialist, you are encouraged to inquire about their experience with modeling software and whether they have ever submitted for credit review for LEED.

The Civil Engineer

An important team member for NC and CS projects, the civil engineer is deeply involved with addressing the prerequisite and the majority of the SS category credits. They need to be aware of local codes and ordinances pertaining to stormwater management, parking, and other zoning requirements. They should have experience with low-impact site design and natural methods to address stormwater management systems, such as pervious pavement and bioretention systems. Should your NC or CS project wish to pursue Water Efficiency (WE) Credit 2: Innovative Wastewater Technologies, you should select a civil engineer with experience in the design of alternative wastewater treatment systems.

The Landscape Architect

A landscape architect is typically hired to design the site and address plant and vegetation types and locations. For a project seeking LEED certification, a landscape architect will need to address how these decisions will affect wildlife habitats, biodiversity, irrigation reduction or elimination needs, natural fertilizers, and integrated pest management strategies. For NC or CS projects, if a green roof is desired, a landscape architect would play an important role to determine the appropriate vegetation and the design for maintenance access, in conjunction with the architect and contractor.

The MEP Engineer

Although typical thought of as one role, a mechanical/electrical/plumbing (MEP) engineer has many different responsibilities as related to building systems and energy efficiency. Each of the systems needs to be addressed individually and cohesively to achieve a high-performance result.

The Mechanical Engineer

The role of the mechanical engineer is essential in a LEED project, as not only do they help to create a thermal barrier between the indoor and outdoor environments, but they need to be able to evaluate and assess the building's performance as a whole, typically through the means of energy modeling or whole-building simulation. They need to be familiar with the Montreal Protocol in order to address refrigerants and comply with the requirements of LEED. Depending on your project goals, you may want to inquire about their experience working with mixed-mode ventilation strategies, ground-source heat pump systems, radiant flooring, or energy recovery units. In any case, ensuring that the mechanical engineer is familiar with energy modeling software and that they have submitted for prerequisite and credit review is critical.

The Electrical Engineer

The electrical engineer addresses the energy demands of the building systems, including sensors and controls. Therefore, they must be familiar with strategies and technologies to increase the efficiency of electric power and distribution to reduce demand requirements. They are also responsible for designing any on-site renewable energy systems, including photovoltaic panels and wind turbines, with the possible help of a subconsultant or specialist. They will need to interact with the civil engineer for site lighting and curfew regulations for sequencing.

The Plumbing Engineer

The plumbing engineer is responsible for water reduction strategies regardless of the project type. They need to be familiar with the Energy Policy Acts (EPAct) of 1992 and 2005 to understand the documentation requirements of LEED. Achieving a 40 percent water savings is not atypical for most NC and CS projects, so you are encouraged to inquire how the plumbing engineer plans on optimizing the

ENGINEER'S PERSPECTIVE
Offsetting the Costs of Energy Modeling and Commissioning

By Paul Meyer, PE
Horizon Engineering

When owners are considering LEED certification for their projects, they are often reluctant to pay for commissioning and energy modeling engineering services. In some areas of the country, utility companies offer cost sharing or direct funding of these services such as the New York State Energy Research and Development Authority (NYSERDA). If you are not lucky enough to be in an area served by one of these utilities, there is still hope. The Energy Policy Act of 2005 created the Energy Efficient Commercial Buildings Tax Deduction. This tax deduction could reach up to $1.80 per square foot, but requires an energy model and building commissioning to achieve the maximum dollar amount. Since LEED also requires an energy model and building commissioning, the tax deduction could offset these soft costs. Obviously, the size of the project is directly related to this benefit.

If we assume an office building project seeking LEED certification, the cost of energy modeling and commissioning should pay back with a building around 20,000 square feet in size. Above this size, the tax deduction should exceed the increased commissioning fees and the owner will therefore be "making money." If we increase the size of the project to 50,000 square feet, the tax deduction should be approximately $24,000 more than the cost of the energy model and commissioning combined.

To qualify for EPAct 2005, the IRS Notice 2006–52 states that the project must be certified to reduce total annual energy and power costs to at least 50 percent less than a baseline reference meeting the requirements of ASHRAE/IESNA 90.1–2001 solely through changes to the building envelope, lighting, and HVAC. Since the LEED NC and CS versions 3 are based on exceeding the ASHRAE/IESNA 90.1–2007 requirements, you should be able to meet this percentage.

water use for flush and flow fixtures. Plumbing engineers with experience with waterless urinals typically can offer some advice on the different types and the associated life-cycle cost assessments. Should the team wish to implement solar hot water systems or capture stormwater for reuse, a plumbing engineer should be familiar with these strategies to bring efficiencies and value to the team. Depending on the system, the plumbing engineer will most likely work in close collaboration with the civil and the CxA to discuss the collection system and its capacity and capabilities for indoor use.

The Structural Engineer

A structural engineer's insight, specifically related to a project seeking LEED certification, is most valuable as it pertains to reuse. Working with a structural engineer on a major renovation project, can possibly help to salvage, maintain, or reuse structural components and avoid waste and disposal, as well as the need for virgin materials to rebuild. Structural engineers can also be responsible for developing the concrete mix designs and for a LEED project this could include the recycled content of fly ash, therefore affecting

Materials and Resources (MR) and possibly Innovation in Design (ID) credits.

The Commissioning Agent

The Whole Building Design Guide (WBDG) website states, "commissioning assists in the delivery of a project that provides a safe and healthful facility; optimizes energy use; reduces operating costs; ensures adequate O&M staff orientation and training; and improves installed building systems documentation."[1] The role of a CxA ensures the long-term performance of a project by coordinating with the project team during design and construction to make sure building systems are designed properly and then installed, calibrated, and perform the way they were intended. Therefore, their role benefits the owner from a cost perspective and the occupants from a safety and comfort standpoint. Unfortunately, the role of CxA is typically misunderstood and the return on investment (ROI) they bring, and therefore the consultant is seen as an additional cost. It is typically the responsibility of the LEED coordinator to enlighten the owner on the value and benefits of a CxA, as their involvement is critical to certification and a justifiable expenditure. Why wouldn't an owner want an experienced, third party verifying the accuracy and performance of one of the most expensive business decisions they will make?

The Cost-Effectiveness of Commissioning New and Existing Commercial Buildings: Lessons from 224 Buildings (http://cx.lbl.gov/2009-assessment.html), updated in 2009, and Lawrence Berkeley National Laboratory's 2004 *Cost-Effectiveness of Commercial-Building Commissioning: Meta-Analysis of Energy and Non-Energy Impacts in Existing Buildings and New Construction* (http://eetd.lbl.gov/emills/PUBS/PDF/NCBC_Mills_6Apr05.pdf) are two studies project teams can refer to in order to educate themselves on the benefits and cost-effectiveness of commissioning. When comparing the two for new construction, the average cost of commissioning has gone up $0.16 from $1 per square foot, yet the ROI has been reduced from 4.8 years to 4.2 on average (based on energy savings).

The LEED coordinator might also have to help the team decide whether enhanced commissioning will be pursued. Although the benefits far outweigh the up-front cost, this may be a challenge to overcome. It is suggested that CxAs provide proposals to separate their fees for fundamental and enhanced services to give the owner some insight on the cost differentials from a soft-cost perspective. Typically, CxAs charge about 20 to 30 percent more for enhanced commissioning services, depending on the amount and complexity of the systems included, although this cost is not in line with the double scope of work required.

LEED Requirements of a CxA

As with any prerequisite, EA Prerequisite 1: Fundamental Commissioning requires a LEED project to perform to a minimum performance level. Therefore, the LEED rating systems not only require a minimum number of building systems to be commissioned, but also define the minimum qualifications of the selected CxA. Note that the term *commissioning agent* is also used interchangeably with the term *commissioning authority*.

Although they do not need to be LEED projects, a CxA is required to have documentation proving their experience of commissioning at least two building projects prior to the commencement of the LEED project. The owner typically hires the CxA, as the authority must be independent of the design and construction teams,

COMMISSIONING AGENT'S PERSPECTIVE
Selecting a Commissioning Authority

By Bill Lodato, PE, LEED AP
CxA of Innovative Facility Solutions, Inc.

Commissioning is a quality process that is designed to ensure that the owner's requirements are achieved, that the owner is provided a project that functions as intended, and that they have the documentation and knowledge to not only operate and maintain but also enhance their facility. To achieve this type of success on your project, it is important to understand that both the scope and rigor of commissioning services can vary widely. The scope can range from complying with the minimum LEED requirements to whole building commissioning while the rigor can vary from the LEED prerequisite to that required to satisfy oversight of regulated industries. Aligning the scope and rigor of commissioning with your project involves understanding the commissioning process, the complexity of the project, the various risk factors, and the responsibilities of all project stakeholders.

In terms of scope, at a minimum, LEED requires that the heating, ventilating, air-conditioning, and refrigeration (HVAC&R) system and controls, lighting and daylighting controls, domestic hot water systems, and on-site renewable energy systems be included in the commissioning scope. Owners and developers who recognize the benefits of the commissioning process often extend the scope to additional building systems and building components, such as water reuse systems, building envelope, and fire-suppression systems. Although not specifically required for LEED certification, these types of building systems require a high degree of reliability and are therefore worth consideration for inclusion in the commissioning scope, as doing so can help the team pursue an Innovation in Design credit.

Although it may be good practice for commissioning authorities to visit the job site to review systems as they are being installed, facilitate regular commissioning meetings, and be diligent in discovering issues before they impact the project, these tasks are not necessarily required for LEED compliance. Scope of services can range from a simple review of paperwork developed and submitted by design/construction professionals to full site presence, regular field inspections and observations, regular meetings, execution/witness of all testing, conducting training, creating as-built drawings, and so on.

Commissioning checklists, the most recognized work product of the commissioning process, can also vary substantially. They can be simple spreadsheet checklists that generally describe the tests steps, while others are full test protocols that contain the purpose, process, and acceptance criteria for each test; document all deviations on standard forms, identify and include all supporting documents as attachments, and follow a chain of command for approval/acceptance.

The approach to commissioning on any project is as unique as the project itself. Some factors to consider in determining the scope and scale of the commissioning process include:

- What cost, schedule, and quality aspects of the project are most important?
- How complex is the project and the building systems?

continued

- How confident are you in the project team's coordination, competence, and integrity?
- What level of documentation and owner/occupant training is anticipated?
- How involved will the owner be in the quality aspects of the project?

Professional project consultants, such as the commissioning authority, are typically hired through a process of selection based on qualifications, followed by the negotiation of actual desired work scope and fees. A proper request for qualifications for commissioning services will describe the project, its perceived complexities, the schedule milestones, and the commissioning objectives. Selecting the commissioning authority for your project based on a thorough work scope, definition of deliverables, and negotiated price with the firm most qualified for the project's needs has unique advantages. This approach provides a process to jointly develop the scope and complexity of the commissioning activities with the firm most suited for your project; it develops realistic budgets and time frames; and it embraces a collaborative, team approach to project quality.

---

although it is permitted to utilize a qualified employee or contractor of the owner. For projects smaller than 50,000 square feet, it is permitted to have one of the team members with the qualified experience perform the commissioning (Cx) responsibilities. In either case, the CxA cannot be the engineer of record for the project and must report their findings directly to owner.

The Role of a CxA during Design

By the end of Chapter 6, you will understand the importance of involving a CxA as early in the design process as possible, but for now it is important to understand the role they will play and why that role is so critical to the success of the project as a whole. The information below is presented as if the CxA is hired to comply with both the prerequisite and the credit for fundamental and enhanced commissioning.

After the CxA is selected and after the eco-charette (discussed in more detail in Chapter 5) is conducted to establish the goals of the project as a team, the commissioning agent works with the owner to establish the owner's project requirements (OPR). The OPR includes the overall goals of the project

and is issued to the design team to develop a basis of design (BOD) for the energy-related building systems, such as lighting, domestic hot water, HVAC&R equipment and controls, and any renewable energy generated on-site. The Cx process continues with the development of a commissioning plan and then with a review of the design drawings and specifications, prior to the development of construction documents, to avoid design flaws and ensure that the environmental goals are included, such as water and energy use reductions. Therefore, intense collaboration between the engineers and the CxA is critical.

The Role of a CxA during Construction

The CxA works diligently during construction to ensure the building system equipment is installed, calibrated, and performs appropriately and efficiently to avoid construction defects and equipment malfunctions. Simultaneous with the architect's and engineer's review, it is also required for the CxA to review the contractor's submittals pertaining to the building systems being commissioned to ensure alignment with the OPR and BOD. The CxA must also create a systems manual for the operations and maintenance staff

Table 3.1 The Differences between Fundamental and Enhanced Commissioning

Phase	Step	Task	Fundamental	Enhanced
Pre-design and Design	1.	Designate CxA	Owner or project team	Owner or project team
	2.	Document OPR; Develop BOD	Owner or CxA; Design team	Owner or CxA; Design team
	3.	Review OPR & BOD	CxA	CxA
	4.	Develop & implement a Cx Plan	Project team or CxA	Project team or CxA
	5.	Incorporate Cx requirements into construction documents	Project team or CxA	Project team or CxA
	6.	Conduct Cx design review prior to mid-construction documents	N/A	CxA
Construction	7.	Review contractor submittals applicable to systems being commissioned	N/A	CxA
	8.	Verify installation and performance of commissioned systems	CxA	CxA
	9.	Develop systems manual for commissioned systems	N/A	Project team or CxA
	10.	Verify that requirements for training are completed	N/A	Project team or CxA
	11.	Complete a summary commissioning report	CxA	CxA
Occupancy	12.	Review building operation within 8 to 10 months after substantial completion*	N/A	CxA

* Review building operation within 8 to 10 months after substantial completion for LEED CI projects and within 10 months for LEED NC and CS projects.

to understand how the space is intended to operate and function. Before the building is occupied, the CxA helps to educate the facility management teams on the operation and maintenance strategies specific to the building. After construction, the CxA is responsible for creating the final commissioning plan to include with the rest of the required documentation for final certification review. Within 8 to10 months after substantial completion (depending on the rating system), the CxA returns to the site to ensure the building systems are working accordingly and address any needed adjustments with the operations and maintenance staff. Table 3.1 summarizes the tasks, responsibilities, and differences between the prerequisite and the credit.

The Contractor

Selecting the right general contractor (GC) for a LEED project is essential to a project's success. The GC is responsible for implementing every concept developed during design. Therefore, their involvement during design can only contribute to the success of the project, as they are aware of the goals and strategies prior to receiving a set of CDs to competitively bid on. They can assist the team with budgeting and layout strategies learned from past experiences. How many times does a contractor indicate they could add efficiencies to a project but are constrained by the requirements detailed during design or contract language? The goal is to capitalize on their insight as most owners or design professionals do not have experience procuring materials or the lessons learned in the field actually assembling the systems they design.

During construction, the GC integrates with the CxA and is typically responsible for following the information detailed in the project specifications. The specifi-

cations would include the environmental goals specific to LEED, including the procurement of materials: with recycled content, with low-to-no volatile organic compound (VOC) content, with local/regional extraction, processing, and manufacturing locations, with rapidly renewable composition, and classified as certified wood. As compliance is measured through a valuation of material cost of the project (typically Construction Specification Institute [CSI] MasterFormat^{TM} Divisions 3–10), the GC should review these procurement goals and the documentation requirements with each of their subcontractors to ensure a common understanding.

The contractor will need to be aware of indoor air quality (IAQ) management strategies, including the Sheet Metal and Air Conditioning National Contractors Association (SMACNA) Guidelines for Occupied Buildings under Construction. The contractor also needs to understand the cost and time ramifications of flush-out and air quality testing requirements. Remember, cost is not necessarily associated with the actual flush-out, but instead the time could imply costs, as the space is not occupied but turnover has taken place considering substantial completion may have been awarded by this time. This is critical for NC and CI projects only, since CS projects are not eligible to pursue EQ Credit 3.2: Construction IAQ Management Plan—Before Occupancy.

The GC will also need to determine how they will address construction waste if the team would like to attempt the point opportunities of MR Credit 2: Construction Waste Management. The contractor will be responsible for developing and implementing a construction waste management plan detailing how they intend on reaching and satisfying the waste diversion goals of the project. The IAQ and waste management strategies are coordinated with the mechanical subcontractor and waste hauler.

The Mechanical Subcontractor

The GC should verify that each of the subcontractors, especially the mechanical subcontractor, have read the Division 1 specifications to ensure that all the requirements are addressed for LEED compliance. The Division 1 specifications typically include the IAQ goals for the project, during construction and prior to occupancy, and the mechanical subcontractor plays an important role to achieving these objectives. They need to ensure that they include the proper Minimum Efficiency Reporting Value (MERV) filter products in their quotes and understand the housekeeping and protection strategies of the SMACNA Guidelines. Selecting a mechanical subcontractor with LEED project experience will add to the efficiencies of the process during construction.

The Waste Hauler

The waste hauler plays a critical role in earning the construction waste management credit to divert from landfill disposal. An experienced hauler will know to check the Division 1 specifications for the construction waste goals and requirements for each material. Both the GC and the waste hauler have to determine the appropriate compliance path relevant to the project. For example, in an urban setting with little site space, a commingled approach may be better, and the GC may feel more confident to achieve high levels of waste diversion if the containers are sorted off-site. Providing multiple containers intended for on-site separation of waste is another option. In either case, a waste coordinator needs to be established, typically required to be a LEED AP, to develop a construction waste management plan. The LEED coordinator should explain the documentation requirements to the intended waste hauler to achieve a higher level of understanding and compliance and, therefore, success.

Contracts

Successful projects are tied to a common understanding of goals, intentions, and commitment of the entire project team. Contracts that address these parameters ensure an identification of roles and responsibilities, and therefore eliminate confusion for the duration of the project, although sometimes it is difficult for the team to achieve this level of understanding before the goals of the project are defined.

Traditionally, team members are given basic requirements on which to base fees, such as LEED certification goals. If an owner asks for a minimum of LEED Silver certification, what does that mean? How does the team achieve it and what cost implications does it have on the design team *and* the owner? Would it not be advantageous to avoid change orders in the future by declaring the expectations prior to concocting and signing a contract?

Therefore, it is advised to approach the contract agreements in a different manner for project teams pursuing LEED certification. The following process will require a bit of creativity for an owner seeking a project team based on a design competition, but essentially, the competition could act as a preliminary goal-setting exercise for the owner to verify the qualifications of the competing teams.

For a qualification-based team selection process, it is suggested to gather a project team of the essential

WASTE HAULER'S PERSPECTIVE
How LEED Has Changed the Waste Industry

By David Cardella of Cardella Waste

Last year in the United States, we produced 143.5 million tons of construction waste, and only 28 percent was recycled. This may not seem like we have recovered very much, but it actually comes out to 40.2 million tons of waste diverted from landfills. This is also a vast improvement over years past. The LEED standards inspire us to divert 50 to 95 percent of the waste stream, depending of the number of points desired and certification level sought. LEED is changing not only the way companies handle their building waste; it is also changing the standards for which we build and operate them.

LEED has changed the way contractors, building managers, and owners have thought about and handled their waste over the past decade. They are turning to their waste experts to assist them in developing waste management plans for their facilities. Waste management plans have improved the recyclable recovery from the waste stream and lowered the overall cost of disposal. LEED has given the industry the framework and desire to manage waste streams in an environmentally responsible manner.

The development of the waste management plan is crucial for reducing and managing the entire project's waste stream. This plan should be considered in the Preconstruction phase of the project and should involve the waste vendor. Depending on the waste recycler's experience, they can assist or write the waste management plan for the project. Cardella Waste has worked on well over a hundred LEED projects, and we are continually updating and improving our waste management plans.

The site space for LEED projects in the New York Metro area has been a challenging issue and makes on-site recycling impractical. The contractor would then engage a company, such as Cardella Waste, who would be able to collect the waste and deliver it to a material recovery facility for off-site separation and documentation. Since my company also operates the facility, it makes tracking and documenting the recyclable recovery rates easier for contractors and consultants. We have used this type of recycling for thousands of construction projects, whether they were seeking LEED certification or not.

---

consultants together to evaluate, discuss, and determine the appropriate triple-bottom-line goals first, then to approach the contract agreements afterwards. Although there may be some hesitation from the team members for a lack of commitment for the bigger picture immediately, agreeing to conduct the research to prepare for the eco-charette and attending the goal-setting meeting to establish not only the goals, but the roles and responsibilities, will benefit the project and the team members in the long run. Once the team is aware of the intentions and the level of commitment required, then it is the appropriate time to establish the applicable contracts and fees to outline and define these factors. The contracts should reinforce the integrative nature of the project and avoid the code-minimum performance directives.

LEED COORDINATOR'S PERSPECTIVE
The LEED Coordinator: No One Understands Me!

By Steve Leone, AIA, LEED AP

"Let me introduce you to our LEED coordinator, who will make certain we get this project certified." If I had a nickel …

One of the most common misunderstandings in the world of LEED certification is the role of the LEED coordinator. Having acted in this capacity on nearly a dozen projects, I have had to spend an inordinate amount of time explaining and reminding teams exactly what this role comprises. Even after crafting what I thought was iron-clad contractual language, in the not-so-small print that is highlighted up front in the scope of services section of the contract, I've had to enumerate my tasks and activities to owners, contractors, and design consultants. I've even had this issue with some of my own internal design teams on which I am acting as LEED coordinator (my day job is being a licensed architect).

On nearly every LEED project that I've been involved with, someone on the team at some point in the process has confronted me with the comment, "What are you responsible for then?" or "Isn't that your job?" On more than one occasion, it has been less than friendly fire. The confusion stems primarily from the lack of understanding of the still relatively new process. Let me offer some examples of the questions and issues I've faced with lesser or greater degrees of contention and frustration:

"Why is my project manager spending time gathering all these documents? We don't have the fee for that"—from a design firm principal. Well, I admit, this point of confusion has begun to fade as teams realize that this is a team-centric process and, most importantly, the LEED coordinator is not the lead (not LEED) project manager. In fact, no professional team should relinquish authority for their respective disciplines as they carry the liability. In some cases, the LEED coordinator may not have any formal training in a building industry discipline.

"Your input on specifications is too broad; I need you to tell my subs exactly what to purchase"—from a developer/builder client. This was clear evidence of not understanding that a LEED project is no different than one not seeking LEED and that flexibility is required in the "buy-out" of the trades. Why would one restrict the purchase of any given component when pricing and availability are so fluid? Naming a specific product or system without allowing alternatives will restrict competitive bidding, and that will certainly lead to the claim that "LEED costs more." The developer/builder understood that explanation very clearly.

"Here are my sub's material purchase orders. Will you approve them for recycled content?"—from a general contractor. A real source of confusion is when the project transitions into the Construction phase. This is especially true if the contractor has not been brought in early in the design process or in a public-bid scenario. Again, when the team hears that there is a LEED coordinator on the project, they feel they are relieved of LEED-related duties.

continued

Thankfully, as more teams go through the process and become better educated, this trend is changing. Those same teams that have challenged the scope of my services recognize after completing a LEED project that, at most, the LEED coordinator is one cog in the wheel and that there is no way one individual can guarantee a successful project outcome.

So what about that contract language? I've reviewed a number of documents intended to clearly delineate the LEED coordinator's scope, including some templates, such as the one published by the American Institute of Architects, AIA B214. The U.S. Green Building Council's web links and reference guides are certainly good resources. While there is no way to cover every issue or situation, these are good places to start.

My contracts have included the following sentences and phrases intended to provide clarity. As stated in the actual contracts, there is no implied guarantee of certification in the language shown below:

- The LEED coordinator shall be responsible for working in tandem with the owner and owner's consultants to review and track the LEED requirements for the specific project listed below as it proceeds through the certification process.
- The LEED coordinator is not responsible or liable for judgments, decisions, or selections of building systems, products, aesthetics, or building performance of any kind. The owner and its professional team must submit requested and required documentation as necessary to meet LEED criteria and/or achieve LEED certification.
- The LEED coordinator shall organize and manage the LEED design documentation as submitted by the owner's professionals and certification process and shall not be responsible for design of building systems or their installation requirements.

One of the things I've done more recently is to change the title from LEED coordinator to LEED administrator if for no other reason but to better align it with the USGBC's term. The term *administrator* might imply to some that the role carries less responsibility than that of a *coordinator,* though both are defined by the same adjectives.

I hope this brings us closer to being on the same page.

After the eco-charette, the owner can distribute a request for qualifications (RFQ) based on the requirements of the project to find the best-suited consultants. This can include the roles of the attendees of the eco-charette, or it can be used to find the missing disciplines required, such as a lighting designer or landscape architect. Regardless, the final contracts should address the following, in addition to the typical contract language covering scope of work for each particular discipline:

- The project's definition, including the triple-bottom-line goals specific to the project
- The roles and responsibilities of each team member, including documentation requirements for LEED certification review
- The meeting time commitments for research and analysis and design integration meetings
- Accountability and milestones
- Preliminary LEED scorecard

chapter 4

Site Selection

Figure 4.1 Villa Montgomery Apartments, a remediation project in Redwood City, California, by Fisher-Friedman Associates, earned LEED Gold certification under the LEED NC rating system, for compliance with multiple Sustainable Sites strategies, including brownfield site selection and remediation. Photo courtesy of FFA.

This chapter focuses on the components of site selection to assist the team in understanding the impacts for achieving Leadership in Energy and Environmental Design (LEED®) certification. A LEED coordinator can play a critical role for LEED for New Construction and Major Renovations™ (NC), LEED for Core & Shell™ (CS), and LEED for Commercial Interiors™ (CI) projects by assisting the owner to select a site with maximum capability for earning

points toward certification (Figure 4.1). This can be especially important for projects seeking Gold and Platinum certification levels, where obtaining as many points as possible is critical to the success of earning a high-level certification.

Education Is Key

A LEED coordinator should be ultimately familiar with the incentives and assistance available within the region in which a project is intended. Potential assistance can include technical resources, design assistance, financial grants, or reduced financing rates for construction costs. Having availability and insight to all-encompassing resources covering these opportunities will help to minimize effort for research for the coordinator, owner, and the rest of the project team. Compliance with the requirements of these opportunities could determine the possibility of a project moving forward and ultimately its success.

Resources

For a high-performance green building project seeking LEED certification, especially one designated as a brownfield or one with on-site renewable energy,

TAX CONSULTANT'S PERSPECTIVE
An Introduction to Understanding Section 179D

By Dennis J. Stilger, Jr.
Managing Member at Concord Energy Strategies, LLC

The general public and federal government are becoming increasingly aware of the key role that the built environment plays in positioning the United States on a more sustainable path. As this relates to the use of natural resources a variety of federal, state, and local incentive programs have been launched to push the private sector to adopt more energy efficient and environmentally friendly methods of doing business. One of the most prominent incentive programs launched by the federal government is the Energy Efficient Commercial Buildings Deduction, also known as Internal Revenue Code Section 179D.

Originally passed as part of the Energy Policy Act of 2005, and expanded upon in IRS Notices 2006–52 and 2008–40, Section 179D of the Internal Revenue Code allows for a one-time tax deduction, worth up to $1.80 per square foot for any new construction or retrofit placed in service since 12/31/05 and before 1/1/14. The commercial project must meet specific energy efficiency benchmarks. Qualifying for the deduction is based on the energy efficiency of the new construction or retrofit as compared to American Society of Heating, Refrigerating, and Air-Conditioning Engineers (ASHRAE) 90.1–2001. For any new construction or retrofit that meets a 50 percent energy power cost reduction as compared to the ASHRAE 90.1–2001 standard, a deduction worth $1.80 per square foot is available. For those buildings that do not meet the 50 percent reduction, there are partial deductions available. These partial deductions are worth up to $0.60 per square foot and are created as a result of a $16^2/_3$ percent energy power cost reduction (for construction put in service or retrofitted in 2006 and 2007) in any of the three following subsystems: heating, ventilating, and air conditioning (HVAC), interior lighting, and building envelope. The total energy power cost reduction for subsystem deductions was updated in IRS Notice 2208–40 and, as of 2009, now require a 20 percent reduction for lighting and HVAC systems and a 10 percent reduction for the building envelope in order to qualify. One of the more unique provisions of this tax incentive program is the fact that for newly constructed or renovated public buildings, a tax deduction is allowed for the lead designer of the energy-efficient property—meaning that architects, engineers, energy service companies (ESCOs), and other design professionals are in the position to reap considerable tax benefits for their public design work.

While qualification for the deduction is based on the energy efficiency of the retrofit or new construction, the IRS has mandated that in order to claim the Energy-Efficient Commercial Buildings Deduction (179D), the building owner must have an independent third-party verify the energy savings required to generate the deduction and certify the savings, as well as complete a site visit to verify that the building has been built to the specifications used to create the energy model. Furthermore, in order for designers of public buildings to claim the 179D deduction for their design work on municipal projects, the owner's representative for the municipal building must sign a form allocating the deduction to them. The designer(s) must still contract to have an independent third-party energy study, certification, and site visit completed under the guidelines prescribed in Section 179D of the Internal Revenue Code.

In order to take advantage of this substantial tax savings programs, designers of energy-efficient public buildings or private building owners are required to consult with an independent firm that deals with certifying EPAct/179D deductions. The criteria for qualifying for the deduction is not difficult to meet if LEED certification is already being sought, but does require specialized modeling (using one of 13 software packages approved by the Department of Energy [DOE]), a professional engineer to certify the new energy-efficient design, and the study along with the certification must be completed by an independent third-party provider. In addition, a professional engineer or licensed contractor unrelated to the taxpayer claiming the deduction and licensed in the jurisdiction where the building is placed in service must complete a site visit, as outlined by the National Renewable Energy Laboratory's *Energy Savings Modeling and Inspection Guidelines for Commercial Building Federal Tax Deductions.*

As the number of federal, state, and local programs mandating energy efficiency and LEED certification in the built environment expands, so do the opportunities for the designers of buildings, as well as owners of buildings, to reap significant tax savings through the Section 179D program. In a number of municipalities, LEED certification for public and private buildings is now mandated, and the number of programs requiring increased energy efficiency is constantly growing. In Kentucky, for instance, all state construction projects placed in service since July 1, 2009, where the Commonwealth of Kentucky pays 50 percent or more of the total capital cost, must be designed to meet high-performance building standards, as mandated by Kentucky House Bill 2. Programs like those in Kentucky are beginning to be found throughout the United States. This provides the opportunity not only for the built environment in the public sector to be more energy efficient and environmentally responsible, but also for the designers of these projects to take advantage of considerable tax savings through the 179D deduction.

---

the LEED coordinator is encouraged to visit the DSIRE website (www.dsireusa.org) to inquire about the local, state, and federal opportunities available. These incentives and policies could also include those posted by utility companies. The site includes opportunities available for projects incorporating renewable energy and/or energy efficiency measures. For each state, the site provides the following information:

- Financial incentives, including tax credits and incentives and rebate, grant, and loan programs

- Rules, regulations, and policies, including energy codes, solar contractor licensing, equipment certification, net metering information, and laws pertaining to renewable energy systems

- Related programs and initiatives

Owners and tenants wishing to take advantage of these incentives, including the 179D tax deduction (as Dennis Stilger mentioned earlier) or accelerated depreciation, should seek the advice of a consulting firm specializing in green building projects.

USGBC and GBCI as a Resources

In addition to assistance and incentives, a LEED coordinator should also be aware of legislation and ordinances pertaining to LEED, as quite a number of local, state, and federal agencies have adopted some form of the benchmarking tool. At the time of publishing, the U.S. Green Building Council (USGBC®) website stated, "various LEED initiatives including legislation, executive orders, resolutions, ordinances, policies, and incentives are found in 45 states, including

442 localities (384 cities and 58 counties), 35 state governments, 14 federal agencies or departments, and numerous public school jurisdictions and institutions of higher education across the United States."[1]

The Questionnaire

A questionnaire should be distributed to the owner for the team to fully understand their expectations at the onset of the project, to help the team evaluate the alignment of site selection criteria. This questionnaire should present the possible triple-bottom-line goals of the project, including:

Economic

What are your economic goals for this project?
What kind of benchmarks will you use to measure the success of achieving the economic goals?
Will others use different benchmarks to evaluate this project?

Social

What kind of social benefit do you want this project to provide for the community?
Are you required to provide any types of social amenities?
What kinds of benchmarks would you use to measure the social benefits of this project?

Environmental

What environmental principles do you think are important to this project?
What environmental principles are important to you as a developer/tenant?
Are there company-established environmental guidelines or regulations to conform to?

How will you evaluate the environmental goals?
Is there an expected level of LEED certification to be achieved?
Is there an expected or anticipated payback period for environmental features or amenities?
Do you believe incorporating environmental features will add value to this project? If so, how?
What is motivating you to incorporate environmental features?

The owner's representative should consult the CEO and other executive members of the developer or tenant's team, for input and insight as necessary to ensure alliance from the company as a whole. The results of the questionnaire will help the LEED coordinator, and the rest of the project team, to position the opportunities of the site with the overall goals for the project.

Initial Assessment

A thorough evaluation and assessment of the opportunities specific to the site during the predesign process will not only result in a conclusive report involving zoning and development codes, but will also inspire the design team to focus on the building orientation, shading, and ventilation opportunities moving forward. This report will be much more in-depth for an NC or CS project, as compared to a project seeking LEED CI certification.

Evaluating a site for an NC or CS project differs from the criteria for a CI project, for existing conditions reasoning. The design team for an NC or CS project will have the ability to decide on building orientation, how to develop a site, and select the building systems, whereas a CI project will have to evaluate what exists to verify compliancy. For example, Sustainable Sites

BROKER'S PERSPECTIVE
LEED-Certified Development Properties vs. Traditional Development Properties

By Marie Taylor, LEED AP
Senior Vice President of NAI Capital

Figure 4.2 The proposed Citrus Avenue Business Park in Fontana, California, designed by Steve Martinez, Martinez Design Group, Inc., Irvine, CA; and developed by Oxford Land Development, LLC, Pasadena, CA; will provide high performance buildings for commercial tenants. Rendering courtesy of J Bullock and Associates, Pasadena, CA.

I have worked as a real estate broker in southern California for the last 7.5 years and became a LEED Accredited Professional 1.2 years ago. There are several ways that working as a broker on a LEED-certified development project can prove to be very different from the experience of working on a traditional development project. I faced challenges in the areas of valuing, cost analysis, marketing, and acquiring construction funding for a LEED project during one of the worst real estate downturns in history.

While working on my first LEED project, my initial approach was to give this development a premium for the LEED accomplishments. However, that approach caused a myriad of challenges, such as valuing the property for lease and for sale. This project was a high-tech light industrial business park, and valuations were looked at in traditional manners, such as income-producing analysis and the comparables approach for the sales valuation. Typically, the sales comparables approach is based on similar properties in a given territory. The challenge was that for this particular project there were no similar LEED-certified projects in the territory, or any surrounding territories, for that matter. Therefore, the valuation was done on the highest-end business parks in the territory. This was also the same approach for the lease analysis side.

The second challenge in valuation was proving the cost savings. Currently, cost savings for LEED-certified buildings are not readily available. Typically, a broker wants to know exactly how many dollars will be saved per year by any energy-efficient

continued

designs so that the calculations will be reflected in the value analysis. But those numbers are impossible to calculate until the broker knows which components of the particular LEED rating system are going to be used and has a set of completed drawings that can undergo a cost-savings analysis. In this particular instance, my client was nowhere close to this stage. The closest thing I could use to generate these calculations were some general numbers on cost savings for "green" buildings.

The third challenge was marketing my client's project. Only one out of the four listing services has a search value for LEED buildings. It is against USGBC's policy to advertise a proposed LEED project as a LEED-certified building prior to obtaining the certification. The certification is not granted until the building has been constructed and met all the requirements of the process. This regulation proved to be an obstacle in letting brokers know that this proposed LEED project existed when it could not be stated as such in the development stage. USGBC has since introduced a precertification opportunity for spec buildings pursuing the LEED CS rating system, granting this marketing opportunity and therefore raising more awareness.

Funding was the fourth challenge. While trying to secure a construction loan in mid-2008, real estate in the Inland Empire of California had taken a major hit, and getting a loan was difficult. We thought that since the development was a LEED proposed project, it might make it easier to find funding. To value the property for lenders, we looked at every LEED-certified project in San Bernardino and Riverside counties and found that they were 100 percent leased. We also found that they were leased for at least a 20 percent premium over other properties. We also found approximately 100 companies or corporations in the United States, many of them Fortune 500 companies that integrate some type of "green" into their commercial buildings. The state of California and many other entities lease space only in LEED-certified buildings. But, still, lenders wanted to see some preleasing activity and, in this case, we were in a market where that was virtually impossible.

Even with all of the challenges mentioned, our society is becoming more "green." As the sustainable momentum continues, the commercial real estate industry stabilizes, and as marketing tools adapt to creating search-friendly LEED fields, the challenges of marketing LEED-certified buildings will decrease. It would benefit the industry if all listing sites had a field designated for LEED registered properties for those properties about to undergo construction or rehabilitation, as well as for LEED-certified properties.

(SS) Credit 1: Site Selection requires a CI project team to select a base building that was awarded LEED certification, or the team will need to look into the many different path options to verify applicability and conformity. These paths include green building strategies such as stormwater design, heat island effect, and light pollution reduction. Typically, these components exist, and therefore it is critical for a CI project team to evaluate a site's potential contribution toward LEED points prior to signing a lease, whereas an NC or CS project team has the ability to impact the approach during design. Whichever LEED rating system is being pursued, the opportunity to evaluate the site prior to final selection will help to optimize point potential.

LEED for New Construction and LEED for Core & Shell

LEED NC and CS project teams will need to research the requirements and impacts of compliancy for the parameters covered by the different rating systems, especially prerequisites. For example, most jurisdictions require erosion and sedimentation plans as detailed in SS Prerequisite 1: Construction Activity Pollution Prevention, but this should be confirmed by a civil engineer familiar with the region.

The project teams will then need to evaluate the site location components for applicability and to determine which credits to pursue to earn points within the SS category. The LEED coordinator shall remind each team member to consult the latest version of the appropriate reference guide (including errata posted online) containing the applicable rating system intended to be pursued for more detailed requirements for conformity. The following credits are encouraged for evaluation for the likeliness to achieve when evaluating sites, and therefore should be pursued. Remember, for the purposes of LEED, urban infill projects are best. as they offer the most point earning potential.

SS Credit 1: Site Selection

- Both the NC and CS rating systems indicate that the project should avoid inappropriate sites for development. These six types of sites include: prime farmland; previously undeveloped land whose elevation is lower than 5 feet above the elevation of the 100-year flood; land used as a habitat for endangered species; land within 100 feet (or distance defined by superseding jurisdiction) of any wetlands; previously undeveloped land that is within 50 feet of a body of water that currently supports or could support fish, recreation, or industrial use; or previously established public parkland. The civil engineer typically is responsible for this research for compliancy. For information and verification of the zone for the 100-year floodplain, the civil engineer should consult the Federal Emergency Management Agency (FEMA) website or the local municipality. The U.S. Fish and Wildlife website will provide information about endangered species, as well as an inventory map for wetland areas. The team may need to seek the guidance of a qualified professional to survey the site and assess the environmental characteristics of the site.

SS Credit 2: Development Density and Community Connectivity

- In order to comply with this credit, the project team has two options. The first option is to select a previously developed site with the minimum potential density of 60,000 square feet per acre net. The project team will typically need to rely on a public agency's geographic information system (GIS) database in order to determine compliance with this option. The second option, which is usually easier to document, is to select a previously developed site that is within a half-mile of a residential area and that has pedestrian access to at least 10 basic services. If it is a mixed-use proposed development, one of the basic services can be counted from within the project boundary. Remember, up to two restaurants can be included in the calculations, and up to two basic services may be anticipated, therefore at least eight must be operational.

SS Credit 3: Brownfield Sites

- Developers that select sites needing remediation and/or that are classified as a brownfield site by a local, state, or federal government agency are eligible to earn a point for this credit. Sites containing asbestos may also qualify for this credit. Project teams shall verify compliance with testing for contaminants by engaging environmental consultants, if certification documentation is not available. It is a good idea to contact the local Environmental Protection Agency (EPA) Office of Solid Waste and Emergency Response for support, as well as local regulators for compliance rules and to inquire about any financial assistance available.

SS Credit 4: Alternative Transportation

- These credits aim to reduce the use of the automobile for commuting to the project site. Therefore, teams are encouraged to select a site with access to public transportation in terms of rail station or bus stop proximity. Remember, campus and private bus lines are valid solutions as well. Project teams should note sites with convenient bike pathway access and should also look into the availability for discounted parking opportunities and car-sharing programs as well. Should a site be selected that does not comply, project teams are encouraged to work with the transit authorities to inquire if future plans include additional stops for bus routes or coordinate a shuttle service with the owner.

SS Credit 5.1: Site Development—Protect or Restore Habitat

- To assess the environmental characteristics of a site, consult with an ecologist, government official, or other qualified professionals. These characteristics would include wetlands, sloped areas, special habitat areas, and forested areas to be protected.

Energy and Atmosphere (EA) Credit 2: On-Site Renewable Energy

- Project teams should evaluate the possibility of including on-site renewable energy systems, should the owner wish to incorporate the strategy into the environmental goals. Teams should evaluate the potential for creating the energy demand sought and may wish to engage a consultant to help them determine the appropriate system, feasibility, and available and applicable incentives.

LEED for Commercial Interiors

Tenants wishing to pursue the LEED CI rating system are encouraged to disclose this goal as early as possible to the broker or leasing agent they are working with. Prior to beginning the search for a site, it is helpful to establish some preliminary environmental goals and to survey the future occupants to inquire about commuting location points. Where is the majority of the staff traveling from to get to work? What kind of amenities do they need nearby to utilize during their lunch breaks or before and after work? Perhaps site selection may be prioritized by proximity to public transportation to help reduce the impact of automobile transportation and need for an abundant amount of parking and/or ride share programs.

When approaching different building owners, it is important to remember that it is not only the building and site, but also the landlord that will help the tenant to receive certification. The tenant has the option to lease within a previously LEED-certified or noncertified, new or existing space. Any team member could consult the USGBC website for a list of all certified projects to which they could look for a leasing opportunity. In a noncertified existing building, the developer or owner may need to be educated

ENERGY PROVIDER'S PERSPECTIVE
Power Purchase Agreements

By RJ Donnelly, LEED AP
Vice President at Donnelly Energy Solutions

Today, many businesses, schools, municipalities, and nonprofits would like to benefit from clean, abundant, renewable power. However, there are many reasons that some may be unable to finance, own, or operate a renewable energy system on their property. For these entities, an investment vehicle has been created to help achieve those ends.

A power purchase agreement (PPA) is a legal contract between a producer of energy (provider), and a consumer of energy (host). Under such an arrangement, the provider finances, designs, builds, owns, maintains, and monitors an energy-producing asset (such as a solar array or wind turbine) on the host's property and sells the power back to the host at a negotiated rate with escalators for a predetermined amount of time. A PPA typically falls outside the realm of regulated utility companies since the seller of energy is an independent power producer (IPP).

The PPA is the central document that establishes the terms and conditions of the energy transaction. Most PPAs have standard terms for the purposes of insurance, taxes, legal issues, ownership, and so on between the provider and the host. A PPA is typically 5 to 30 years in duration, with clauses to renew the contract, purchase the energy-producing equipment from the provider, or remove the equipment from the property at the end of the term.

The first PPA was created in 2006, spurred on by recently enacted state and federal incentives for renewable energy systems. The revenue streams of most PPA installations are so favorable that they may allow the provider to supply energy to the host at below-market rates. Cash flows for PPA investments are derived from a combination of federal tax credits, tax deductions from accelerated depreciation of the system, federal grants, state incentives (rebates and/or sale of RECs or renewable energy certificates), low-interest loans, and the sale of power.

There are many reasons for a host to enter into a PPA, but the most popular reasons are as follows: (1) the host does not have adequate access to capital in order to fund the installation of a power-producing asset; (2) the host does not have the desire or the resources to maintain a power-producing asset; (3) the host does not have the expertise to design, engineer, and install a power-producing asset; (4) the host may not be a taxpayer (municipalities, places of worship, nonprofits, etc.) and cannot fully take advantage of the tax benefits.

A PPA is a highly effective arrangement for all parties involved because the provider typically earns a high return on investment and the host benefits from inexpensive, clean, renewable power.

on the benefits of green building and the strategies involved, but a motivated and determined tenant has the opportunity to negotiate a few leveraging points as related to the lease agreement. Finding out about how much of the building is occupied could help the tenant to negotiate, as the owner may be motivated to make improvements to in turn lease the space and make the rest of the available space more marketable. Inquiring about the type of lease preferred could be another negotiating point for a project team. In terms of a net lease, the tenant is typically responsible for paying for their utility usage, whereas with a gross lease, the owner incurs the utility expenses. A gross lease type would encourage an owner to make improvements, whereas a net lease type would encourage the tenant to be as efficient as possible. Remember from the previous chapter that working with the right brokerage team may help to simplify the search with a list of prequalified properties from which to choose.

Prior to signing a lease, a tenant is encouraged to inquire into the possibility and compliancy with the following key credits that may impact the point-earning potential for the project:

SS Credit 1: Site Selection

- Projects have the opportunity to earn up to five points for this credit, and therefore tenants should evaluate the opportunities to comply as early as possible, as the location of the base building is critical to earning this credit. The easiest way to comply is to select a space to lease within a previously certified LEED building. Otherwise, a team would need to refer to the 12 following paths in which to combine to earn up to five points. Remember, these strategies may already be in place, or the tenant can encourage the building

owner to improve the facility (except for Path 1: Brownfield Redevelopment, of course). Appendix B has a checklist for project teams to use specific to this credit. Teams should refer to the ID+C reference guide for the detailed parameters to comply, as the list below provides an overview of the concepts:

Path 1. The base building was built on a remediated brownfield site.

Path 2. The existing base building site has implemented a stormwater quantity plan to reduce the amount of runoff equal to the amount prior to development should the imperviousness prior to development equal 50 percent or less; or if the imperviousness equals more than 50 percent, the plan should reduce the predevelopment rate by 25 percent. If the existing site does not comply, the owner and the facility manager will need to consult with a civil engineer and/or a landscape architect to determine site modification strategies, should the team wish to pursue this point.

Path 3. This compliance option is available for base building sites that have stormwater treatment systems in place created to remove total suspended solids and total phosphorus.

Path 4. Applicable for project sites that provide shade for impervious surfaces, such as parking areas, walkways, and fire lanes. If these impervious areas are composed of light-colored materials and have a high solar reflectance index (SRI), this strategy could also comply with the requirements. Open-grid paving solutions to increase the impervious area and reduce the heat island effect could also meet the requirements for this path.

Path 5. Base buildings that reduce the impact of the heat island effect with a high SRI roofing material or by a roof covered with vegetation would meet

ARCHITECT'S PERSPECTIVE
Seeking LEED CI Certification for a Hotel: The Challenges and Benefits

By Michael F. Maurer, AIA
Gettys

As with any building type, there are challenges and opportunities in designing a building to achieve LEED certification. While designing Hotel Felix (www.hotelfelixchicago.com), Gettys, acting as Design Architect, Interior Designer, Procurement Agent, and Development Partner, found ways to simplify the challenges and capitalize upon the opportunities.

Many people still perceive that there is an increased cost to design a building for LEED certification. While this may be somewhat true, any additional costs are quickly disappearing as manufacturers and vendors of building materials respond to the demand for cost-effective products that contribute to LEED certification. The amount and variety of green products and systems from which designers can now specify, coupled with contractors' growing familiarity and experience with LEED requirements, is eliminating any cost differential. In the design of Hotel Felix, as with all of the LEED designs that Gettys creates, we were able to present a menu of LEED qualifying items to our client with a cost associated with each point. It is a bit more difficult to quantify the benefit or payback period of each item, but our client could very easily choose which LEED points they wanted in order to achieve the desired LEED rating while fully understanding any cost impact.

Fortunately for the design of Hotel Felix, many LEED-contributing aspects were "built in" to the program (Figure 4.3). SS Credit 2: Development Density/Community Connectivity point, as well as SS Credit 3.1: Public Transportation were a given based upon the site's location in downtown Chicago. The bicycle storage we installed not only benefits the employees, but is an amenity to the guests as well, many of whom bring their bikes to take advantage of the wealth of bike routes and trails throughout the city. The hotel's management has advanced the green aspect of SS Credit 3.3: Alternative Transportation, Parking Availability by offering free parking for hybrid vehicles!

Hotel Felix is an independent boutique hotel. During the early stages of development, though, we considered aligning with one of the major hotel brands. There is an operational benefit in doing so in that brand loyalty and reward points help to attract guests, but it also requires that the design conform to brand standards that aren't always perfectly aligned with the property's goals. For example, not all of the major brands would allow the low-flow showerheads we intended to use. Fortunately, most brands have now realized the benefit and desirability to the guest of LEED design and are modifying their standards to eliminate any conflicts. Building codes, as well, are incorporating many of the same good design practices that contribute to LEED certification. Chicago's mechanical code is very progressive, reducing the difference between basic code-conforming design and LEED-contributing design in HVAC Energy Performance.

We still find ourselves reminding clients that green design does not need to look like hemp and granola. We like to say that you needn't sacrifice any luxury to be LEED-certified. That said, there are certain design elements that guests in an upscale hotel expect. We used quite a bit of imported stone in the public areas (a lobby of Joliet or

continued

Figure 4.3 Hotel Felix in Chicago, designed by Gettys, successfully earned LEED CI Silver certification; its urban location helped earn SS Credits 2 and 3. Image courtesy of Gettys.

Indiana limestone would not have made the same impact!). Quite often, the real difference in LEED is what the guest does not notice–the lack of off-gassing smells, for example. We used low-emitting materials throughout the property.

Controllability of systems is a critical aspect in hotel design. Whether traveling for business or leisure, guests are often more focused on their plans for the day than they are on turning off the lights as they leave the room or are burdened with luggage and boarding passes as they check out. The use of heat and motion sensors in the room controls ensures that the energy is not wasted (in a hotel, motion sensors are not enough–you can't turn down the thermostat if someone sleeps very soundly!).

The success of Hotel Felix demonstrates the value of LEED certification for hotels. There are many large corporations and governmental agencies that require their employees to stay in a LEED certified hotel if one exists in their destination city. There are even more guests who stay at Hotel Felix because its green aspects conform to their own lifestyle preferences. They appreciate not only the LEED design but also the management's commitment to respecting the environment in every aspect of the hotel operations. From the use of bleach-free cleaning supplies to partnering with Tesla, the makers of premium electric cars, Hotel Felix truly follows through on its commitment to being green!

Figure 4.4 Hotel Felix incorporates many sustainable design strategies such as incorporating low-emitting materials and products with recycled content. Image courtesy of Gettys.

the intentions of this compliance path. Should the roof have a combination of the two heat-retention mitigating solutions, the tenant would have the opportunity to pursue this path as well.

Path 6. Base buildings that reduce their light pollution also have an opportunity to help the tenant earn a point towards this credit. Base buildings would need to address the nonemergency interior luminaires with a direct line of sight to any building openings in terms of input power during after hours or their shielding to avoid polluting the exterior environment with an excessive amount of light, in order to pursue a point.

Path 7. CI projects can earn up to two points by leasing in a base building that reduces the amount of potable water needed for irrigation by the means of a high-efficiency irrigation system, by reusing collected rainwater, or by using recycled site water.

Path 8. Tenants seeking CI certification can earn an additional two points for occupying within a base building that eliminates the need for potable water for irrigation.

Path 9. Base buildings that reduce the need for potable water for sewage conveyance or that treats its wastewater on-site can lend a point earning opportunity to its tenants pursuing LEED CI certification.

Path 10. Signing a lease for space within a base building that reduces water consumption by at least 30 percent (excluding water used for irrigation) and requires tenants to comply within their space could provide a tenant with the opportunity to earn a point for this compliance path option. Remember, this point earning opportunity is only eligible for projects that intend to occupy 50 percent or less of the building's total square footage, to avoid "double dipping" on points with the WE category.

Path 11. A base building with an on-site renewable energy system that provides a portion of the energy for the building allots a tenant the opportunity to pursue this compliance path. Remember to consult the reference guide for eligible systems. The tenant may want to look at buildings that can provide enough energy with the ability for net metering back to the utility grid at times when the supply exceeds the demand.

Path 12. If the project team can determine other quantifiable green building strategies that increases performance employed by the base building or site, the team could earn another point. Teams are encouraged to consult other LEED rating systems and Innovation in Design (ID) credits previously awarded to other projects to inquire about opportunities in which to comply. This path could also be utilized as an opportunity in which to tally Exemplary Performance in one of the previous compliance paths for SS Credit 1: Option 2.

SS Credit 2: Development Density and Community Connectivity

- Just as with NC and CS projects, in order to comply with this credit, the project team has two options in which to abide by. The first option is to select a previously developed site with the minimum potential density of 60,000 square feet per acre net. The second option is to select a previously developed site that is within a half-mile of a residential area and that has pedestrian access to at least 10 basic services. If the base building is a mixed-use development, one of the basic services can be counted from within the project boundary. Remember just as with NC and CS projects, up to two restaurants can be included in the calculations and up to two basic services may be anticipated.

SS Credit 3: Alternative Transportation

- Just as listed previously for NC and CS projects, these credits aim to reduce the use of the automobile for commuting to the project site. Therefore, teams are encouraged to select a site with access to public transportation in terms of a rail station or bus stop proximity. Remember, ferry service and campus and private bus lines are valid solutions as well.

- Tenants will need to discuss the options to include bicycle racks for their employees and visitors, should there not be any or enough in place.

- Building owners will need to provide preferred parking for the building occupants participating in carpool or vanpool programs in order for the project to be eligible to earn two points under the third opportunity within this credit.

- Tenants should also look into the availability for discounted parking opportunities and car-sharing programs as well.

WE Prerequisite 1: Water Use Reduction

- Project teams will need to evaluate the building for compliance with this mandatory prerequisite, based on occupancy. Base building potable water consumption will need to be calculated for fixtures and fixture fittings in common areas, as well as those to be included in the tenant's scope of work. Should the base building not comply, the tenant will need to address fixture replacement or improvements, such as flow restrictors and aerators, as part of the lease negotiation.

EA Prerequisite 2: Minimum Energy Performance

- Project teams will need to inquire about the capability of the existing building systems to optimize energy performance for the tenant space in accordance with ASHRAE 90.1–2007. If the building owner exclusively controls these systems, and will not be part of the tenant's scope, then these systems will be exempt from compliancy. If the systems are to be included in the scope, the project engineer is encouraged to start the dialog early about strategies to comply, such as adding controls and outdoor air intakes.

- Depending on the performance based or prescriptive approach the team wishes to pursue, energy modeling may be needed to determine compliancy and understand the necessary actions for the tenant. The team may wish to inquire what the building's ENERGY STAR® rating is with the facility manager and to ask for the rating statement. If the building is not rated, a conversation with the facility manager is suggested to understand the maximizing efficiency opportunities for the tenant space. If the base building received LEED certification, an energy model may already exist and can be modified and used for the CI project as a design tool and for documentation purposes.

EA Prerequisite 3: Fundamental Refrigerant Management

- Should the tenant improvement work include revisions to the HVAC system, the team will need to ensure there is zero use of chloroflurocarbon (CFC)-based refrigerants. Engaging in a discussion with the facility manager will be necessary if the tenant's HVAC system ties into the base building systems. If CFC-based refrigerants are utilized in the existing system, a phase-out plan will be required in order to still comply with this prerequisite.

EA Credit 3: Measurement and Verification

- Should the team wish to pursue this credit, it is encouraged to discuss with the building owner prior to signing a lease for a tenant space that occupies less than 75 percent of the total building area. In order to comply, the team will need to install submetering equipment for the tenant's space and/or include a lease provision referencing the tenant's obligation to pay for their energy usage and for these costs to be excluded from the base rent.

MR Prerequisite 1: Storage and Collection of Recyclables

- Tenants should discuss current recycling policies and procedures with the building owner or management company to determine the opportunity to provide storage and collection areas for the tenant's waste to be reduced. If a policy exists, what types of materials are collected for recycling? Does the policy meet the requirements of the prerequisite? The team should inquire if a waste stream audit has been completed for the building.

MR Credit 1: Tenant Space—Long-Term Commitment

- A longer lease term will prove beneficial for the owner, and the tenant will then be able to pursue this credit toward certification.

EQ Prerequisite 1: Minimum Indoor Air Quality Performance

- Project teams will need to ensure that the base building HVAC system can supply sufficient ventilation to meet the provisions of ASHRAE 62.1–2007. The outside air quality may be impacted by heavy traffic, proximity to adjacent industrial sites, or nearby waste management sites.

EQ Prerequisite 2: Environmental Tobacco Smoke (ETS) Control

- Tenants should look to buildings that prohibit smoking in order to comply with this prerequisite. Should the building permit smoking, the project team will need to ensure that the tenant space can be isolated from these smoking areas and may need to design for separate ventilation systems. Exterior designated smoking areas need to be located away from the building entrances, any operable windows, and outdoor air intakes if smoking is allowed on site.

Narrowing Down the Search

As soon the available properties have been reduced down to two or three, it is recommended to coordinate a meeting with the owner, the facility manager, a mechanical/electrical/plumbing (MEP) engineer, a construction manager or contractor and/or the property management company to review the environmental opportunities specific to each site. This collaboration will allow the opportunity to clarify the strategies or intentions for the building that was not addressed by requirements or options within the LEED CI rating system, such as a green cleaning policy or operational practices for pest management.

A tenant looking to lease space within a LEED-certified CS building should engage the LEED coordinator to help them to understand the requirements described in the tenant guidelines (if applicable) as relating to sustainable design to understand the impacts of their build-out and operations. Do the guidelines or any other building standards list any strategies to comply with?

For some base buildings, the finish standards available may mitigate the opportunity to comply with LEED requirements, such as paints, carpets, and light fixture options. Although these standards may be in place for consistency and the ease of maintenance, the choices should be improved for performance, to maximize efficiency, and to reduce the burden on the environment and occupants by addressing such factors as VOCs, place of manufacture, and recycled content.

Understanding that every tenant's goals may differ and no two projects are exactly alike, project teams are encouraged to use this guidebook as a tool for beginning the certification process and to learn the basic integrative approach. If a tenant has more leveraging points, should they occupy a major portion of a building, or bigger goals, such as including the installation of on-site renewable energy systems into their project scope, the LEED coordinator and the rest of the project team must engage to understand these goals for the site and project overall to properly address the feasibility.

Addressing Sustainability in the Lease

Although the same person with the role of the broker does not typically play the role of the LEED project administrator, a coordinator may assist an inexperienced broker during the lease compilation. Continuing with the integrative strategies for the design and construction process, the lease should be developed in a similar approach by including environmental standards. To protect both parties, the three most important things to address are consistency, transparency, and accountability to ensure the implementation and continuation of green strategies by the owner and for the cooperation and participation of the tenant. It is also important to decide how to green the lease: either by integrating the changes within the body of the agreement or by adding a rider to detail the environmental goals and objectives. The responsibility and allocation of expenses should also be addressed in the lease, including initial improvement and ongoing operational costs. This financial inclusion should also address the rights and assignment of any incentives, grants, or rebates as a result of the sustainable strategies. The lease should also include the LEED checklist specific to the tenant's space and detail the requirements for improvements and strategies in order to achieve certification. Just as with the LEED certification process itself, the roles and responsibilities for each strategy should be defined as well. Project teams wishing to obtain more information can refer to the *Green Office Guide* published by USGBC, the *BOMA Green Lease Guide*, or the *Energy Efficiency Lease Guidance*.

Addressing the lease does not only apply to projects seeking CI certification. LEED CS projects can look to earning exemplary performance points for mandating future tenants to comply with certain LEED CI prerequisites and credits, such as fundamental and enhanced commissioning and indoor air quality management during build-outs. Project teams are encouraged to refer to the BD+C reference guide, Appendix 4, for more details about lease inclusions and tenant requirements for exemplary performance.

BROKER'S PERSPECTIVE
Sustainable Design Leads to Good PR and Improved Bottom Line … If Tenants Can Find a Way to Care

By Scott Steuber, LEED AP
Cushman & Wakefield Inc.

During a July 2010 conversation with a local CEO facing a December 2012 lease expiration, I asked whether LEED certification will be a criterion for the company's office search. Mind you, at the time this company was located in the only LEED-certified building in downtown Los Angeles. He responded emphatically: "Unless it has a direct impact on my bottom line, I could care less."

Although awareness of LEED and sustainable design has certainly spread (partially due to the shrinking premium associated with sustainable improvements), tenants are still skeptical. The desire to be a good corporate citizen can take a company only so far. As found with the disinterested CEO above, and most of my other middle-market clients, the consideration that ultimately drives the decision is **financial impact on the bottom line**.

Despite my constant efforts to educate tenant clients on the benefits of sustainable design and LEED CI certification, **the current tenant mind-set of short lease terms and limited to no capital expenditure presents a roadblock**. The Great Recession has impacted tenants' real estate strategies in two key ways that has made it difficult for tenants to pursue LEED CI certification. Due to cost-saving pressures and tenants' inability to forecast future business viability, tenants are (1) renewing or seeking out second-generation space and (2) targeting shorter leases terms. For renewals or second-generation space alternatives, tenants are requesting that landlords convert concessions to rent discounts or abatement. For the shorter-term leases, landlords are not interested in offering significant tenant improvement allowances. These factors lead to minimal capital going into the premises, thus limiting opportunities to make sustainable design improvements and making it impossible to achieve LEED CI certification.

To combat the above sentiment, I recommend implementation of the following strategies that I have found helpful in assisting corporate office tenants to score well with public relations while still performing well financially.

Structure leases to financially incentivize tenants to pursue LEED CI. In most leases, any operating expense save resulting from LEED CI–related improvements is typically shared on a pro-rata basis among neighboring tenants. A solution to this issue is to submeter the tenant premises so that you can work with your client's and the landlord's attorneys to draft a lease document that (1) replaces pro-rata allocation of energy use with actual tenant usage and (2) defines baseline energy use for tenant. Modified gross or full-service gross lease structures are the best way to accomplish this.

Focus on opportunities to improve employee productivity. Evidence supports that green buildings and interiors (1) reduce employee sick days (due to factors such as low VOC materials and better overall air quality), and (2) lead to a more comfortable work environment (due to factors such as natural lighting and reliable temperature controls). However, although employees may be spending more time at the office, are they collaborating on work-related projects or gossiping in the hallways? Working side-by-side with an architecture firm, real estate brokers can assist corporate tenants in evaluating worker performance by comparing the results of their employees to industry benchmarks. These findings are then used to inform new workplace strategies that incorporate sustainable design and allow for pursuit of LEED CI certification. While the direct connection between improved employee productivity and financial performance is challenging to pinpoint, metrics that illustrate sustainable design elements improving worker performance help build a strong case for pursuit of LEED CI.

Although a tenant's initial reaction to LEED certification is to "care less," when embraced, sustainable design can impact the bottom line through a rethinking of standard lease terms and by creating a more inspiring and comfortable work environment.

Continuing the Effort to Prepare for the Goal-Setting Meeting

Once the team has evaluated the above factors for LEED compliancy, they should expand their analysis to include additional parameters to meet the intentions of the owner's goals. The project team should engage in preliminary programming exercises, blocking and massing studies, daylighting and energy analyses, and developing a preliminary assignment of costs in order to determine the benefits and impacts of LEED certification. These preliminary studies for NC and CS projects should address the site's potential for building orientation to capitalize on passive design solutions for shading, ventilation, and daylighting opportunities. The team should evaluate what the air quality conditions are for natural ventilation prospects for NC and CS projects, as well as occupant comfort in terms of the existing indoor environment for CI tenants.

Once the site has been selected for its ability to align with the project's triple-bottom-line goals and to optimize the opportunity to earn the maximum amount of points, the team should prepare for the eco-charette by summarizing the efforts thus far and for the continued alignment with LEED requirements. The next chapter discusses the goals for the eco-charette and who should attend.

chapter 5

The Eco-Charette

Remember from the introduction, the eco-charette is an opportunity to gather the entire team at the beginning of a project to establish critical elements of the project, such as the owner's program requirements (OPR) and the project's triple-bottom-line goals. A Leadership in Energy and Environmental Design (LEED®) scorecard should be completed during the eco-charette to be utilized as a reference and summary of the goals of the project for the entire project team. This is also the appropriate time to delegate and assign the roles and responsibilities of each of the team members, to create a checklist of tasks to be completed during each of the design phases, and establish the budget and schedule for the project. The team should also become familiar with LEED-Online, as it becomes the centralized location for project information and, ultimately, the tool for certification review. If they are not familiar with the web-based tool, the eco-charette is a great opportunity to demonstrate how the navigate the site. Constant education of the requirements of LEED and the integrated design process ensures a team-oriented environment to pursue and meet the project goals.

Since each project is unique in a multitude of ways, it would be impossible to concoct one to-do list to address every project. Therefore, the following information is to be used as a guideline to be adjusted as needed. For example, a LEED coordinator may be presented with a project with site preparations taking place at the same time as design development, thus requiring the design team to adjust to the preliminary decisions of the developer. In another case, the owner may have hired a limited team to assist with a municipality's design review board for rezoning or approval for development, and therefore may have some challenges to address as it relates to LEED compliance. In any case, this book outlines the tasks to take place and it is up to the team to find the right solution to meet their needs.

ARCHITECT'S PERSPECTIVE
Collaborative Design

By Gary Moshier, AIA, LEED AP
Moshier Studio

Figure 5.1 A charette for the Pennsylvania Department of Conservation and Natural Resources' Elk Viewing Station project at Moshier Studio. Photo courtesy of Moshier Studio.

The design and construction of a high-performance green building is, by necessity, a collaborative and iterative process. In order to uncover and explore a full range of options, a process must be employed that explores the expectations of the participants and builds a basis for communication and collaboration. We use an initial charette process, or collaborative workshop, to start the project and build rapport between the stakeholders and the project team (Figure 5.1). The stakeholders can include the owner organization's management, employees, representative users, neighbors (including students form local high schools and colleges), city officials, and utility companies. The project team typically includes the owner's representative, architects, designers, engineers, landscape architects, and commissioning agents.

The charette is half- to full-day meeting that moves between general sessions to gain background and insight into certain topics, breakout sessions to explore different aspects in greater depth, and report-out and discussion sessions to arrive at the conclusions. Various members of the design team facilitate the sessions, and all members of the project team are asked to participate. The result of the charette is the establishment of the design parameters, goals, and objectives of the project at all levels, functional within the context of the community and within the environment at large. This is often referred to as the "triple bottom line" of economics, environment, and social equity or well-being. The charette group is reassembled at several key review points during the design process so the design team can report back on achievement of the goals and to garner further input and support.

The goals established in the charette are documented in the owner's project requirements (OPR) and becomes the cornerstone of the commissioning process, as well as the touchstone for all project team meetings and reviews. In smaller projects, with shorter design cycles and fewer people involved, the project goals are "front of mind" for the team members. On larger projects, it is incumbent on the project architect and project leaders from the various design disciplines and contractors to check the work product against the goals at the project milestones. Challenges to this arise daily as budget, schedule, and aesthetics are balanced, but if the goals are clear and concise, we have found that the group can collectively work through the issues to a successful conclusion. The result of applying a collaborative approach and integrated design process is a building design that is a direct response to the needs and desires of the owner.

Prior to the Meeting

In order to have a successful goal setting meeting, a number of key consultants should attend to offer their expertise and insight. Therefore, the list of attendees should, at a minimum, include the LEED coordinator, design team including the architect and interior designer, mechanical/electrical/plumbing (MEP) engineering team, the civil engineer, the commissioning agent (CxA), and the owner, including the different representatives that can speak about the economic, social, and environmental goals and impacts for the project. The lighting designer should also attend, if possible. If it is a new construction project, it is a good idea to also have the structural engineer at the meeting as well. For a LEED for Commercial Interiors™ (CI) project, the landlord or building owner should also attend. In any case, the meeting will benefit from having a general contractor or construction manager, as well as a cost consultant with green building experience.

The LEED coordinator needs to prepare the attendees for the integrative approach of the meeting and to ensure commitment and insight from each participant. To put the design team on the right path, the team members should be required to conduct some initial research prior to the meeting to determine the

CIVIL ENGINEER'S PERSPECTIVE
The Importance of Deciding to Pursue LEED Early in the Design Process

By Geoffrey B. Nara, PE, LA
Civil & Environmental Consultants, Inc.

It cannot be emphasized enough to make the decision very early in a project's process to pursue LEED certification, and ideally before the design team is assembled. Important key decisions are made when the design phase commences that are difficult, and typically expensive, to adjust or correct later in the process. Not planning appropriately, including not choosing experienced LEED designers and contractors, will certainly result in added costs, and may completely preclude the ability to attain the LEED certification.

Our design team was contracted to provide initial site evaluations and master planning services for the development of an 80-acre property located in an existing office park that had strict, environmentally oriented development regulations. The project was for a corporate headquarters consisting of a proposed 1 million-square-foot campus, with adequate parking to meet the client's higher-than-average needs. The goal was to design the site with the buildings centrally located, with parking within reasonable pedestrian access. The challenge was to make nearly 4,000 parking spaces blend into the natural landscape, with topography of the property playing a key factor in the design due to the presence of steep slopes and streams. The final site plan concept had an equal distribution of parking spaces surrounding the buildings, utilizing terraced parking lots to make the proposed grading conform to the existing terrain and to allow natural treed buffers to remain, while preserving natural open space.

While the design team encouraged the owner to consider pursuing LEED at the beginning, it was resisted due to a perception of adding to the project's cost. With the extremely aggressive schedule and a need to obtain environmental permitting and approvals in almost unrealistic time frames, the design team convinced the owner that incorporating sustainable design practices into the site work would enable the reviewing environmental agencies to more readily accept the project's impact and gain approvals more quickly.

As construction plans were prepared, the designers incorporated stormwater quality best management practices (BMPs) by creating planting strips between each bay of parking, with each acting as an individual bio-swale to improve water quality while managing stormwater runoff. The site was also oriented to minimize tree removal, leaving a 200-foot natural treed buffer surrounding the site, and impacting only about 60 acres of the 80-acre site. Rain gardens and a series of "wet" stormwater management ponds, which were designed to encourage wildlife habitats to remain, were incorporated into the design to also address runoff. A stream running through the site was buffered from the development by existing trees as well, and even a bridge crossing the stream was very sensitively incorporated into the design.

The reviewing environmental agencies were extremely pleased to see the incorporation of so many sustainable and responsible features, and the team was successful in obtaining construction permits on the very fast-tracked schedule.

Construction was ready to commence. It was then that the owner decided that pursuing LEED would be good for their corporate image and position in the community, and challenged the design team to obtain certification. While the project architect and the MEP and structural engineers' teams scrambled to accommodate design modifications, the civil/site engineer was well positioned to meet LEED criteria. By convincing the owner the sustainable design elements would accelerate the review process for permitting, it also enabled them to already meet almost all of the design elements for LEED. The design modifications to fulfill a few additional LEED points were minor and fairly readily obtained.

This scenario easily would have been different had there not been a very strong, LEED-experienced team of architects, engineers, and contractors involved in the design, and had these sustainable design elements not been incorporated by the civil/site engineer. Had the project started with a more typical and traditional design approach, the design for the site would have had drastic modifications when deciding to later pursue LEED. Almost certainly, more of the surrounding tree buffer would have been impacted. Design time and fees to modify what likely would have been one stormwater pond, as a typical dry basin, to be a series of wet basins would have added considerably to the project. Adding the bio-swales and rain gardens may not have been feasible, which would have likely meant sacrificing LEED points for stormwater quality issues. Without question, it would have meant delaying the start of construction for weeks, and possibly months, for design changes and what would have been a much greater struggle to obtain the environmental permitting.

---

prospective goals, strategies, and achievements specific to the project, assuming the site has been selected at this point. As discussed in the previous chapter, initial assessment prior to the site selection will help to add efficiency at this stage. If the site was selected prior to evaluating the environmental capabilities, the owner should receive the questionnaire, as depicted in the previous chapter, and the design team should engage in site evaluation, preliminary programming exercises, blocking and massing studies, daylighting and energy analyses, and developing a preliminary assignment of costs.

Agenda

Although this book is meant to provide tools to a LEED coordinator during the design and construction processes, it is not meant to cover all of the general aspects of meeting preparation, such as selecting a meeting venue, projection equipment, and refreshments and food. With that being said, it is important for the LEED coordinator to distribute an agenda to all the participants to provide them with the goals of the meeting. The agenda should address the following:

- Introduce the project

- Introduce the project team

- Define, discuss, and determine the project's triple-bottom-line goals

- Assign the roles and responsibilities for each of the team members

- LEED-Online training

- Moving forward: Project registration, task lists, and schedule for the next design integration meeting

The Goal-Setting Meeting

The LEED coordinator is typically responsible for gathering the appropriate team members for this critical milestone. Accordingly, the coordinator should be familiar with the attendees and the project in order to make introductions, create the integrative environment, and set the pace for the meeting. Remember, the next step is to create the OPR; therefore, the meeting should produce the information required to assist the owner and CxA.

Determining the Triple-Bottom-Line Goals

In lieu of a *point-chasing approach*, a project team should evaluate what solutions and strategies align with the triple-bottom-line goals for the project. With that being said and knowing the project's goals include earning LEED certification, grab the applicable reference guide, the corresponding scorecard, and dive in!

Remember, LEED is meant to be a tool with which to measure performance for a building or space. Therefore, the most important deliverable from the goal-setting exercise is the LEED scorecard, as it will be utilized for the duration of the project as a summary of the goals of the project for the entire project team to achieve collectively, but never meant to supersede any local, state, or federal regulation.

The team should start by evaluating the minimum project requirements (MPRs) as mentioned in Chapter 1. The owner should be ultimately clear on the intentions and risks if the project falls out of compliance. Each of the prerequisites should then be detailed and evaluated by the coordinator and discussed with the attendees to ensure compliance. Remember, all prerequisites are required and include:

- **Sustainable Sites (SS) Prerequisite 1: Construction Activity Pollution Prevention** (not required for LEED CI projects). Most municipalities require

such action, and this should not be a challenge to comply with. It basically requires the civil engineer to develop an erosion and sedimentation control plan.

- **Water Efficiency (WE) Prerequisite 1: Water Use Reduction, 20 Percent.** With the right fixture selections, a team can typically achieve at least a 35 percent water reduction. Remember, the approach is slightly different for a CI project, depending on the amount of building square footage the tenant will occupy.

- **Energy and Atmosphere (EA) Prerequisite 1: Fundamental Commissioning of Building Energy Systems.** This requires engaging a CxA to perform a minimum of 7 of the 12 tasks listed in Chapter 3. The CxA should be in attendance to confirm tasks and responsibilities with all of the other team members and clarify any misconceptions or challenges.

- **EA Prerequisite 2: Minimum Energy Performance.** A team needs to determine if a prescriptive or a performance-based approach is better suited for the project. LEED for New Construction and Major Renovations™ (NC) and LEED for Core & Shell™ (CS) projects will look to American Society of Heating, Refrigerating, and Air-Conditioning Engineers (ASHRAE) 90.1-2007 to achieve at least a 10 percent energy reduction as compared to the standard. CI projects will need to comply with the mandatory provisions of the same reference standard, reduce the lighting power density by 10 percent below the standard, and they will also need to provide ENERGY STAR® appliances and equipment (equivalent to at least 50 percent of rated power).

- **EA Prerequisite 3: Fundamental Refrigerant Management.** This is much easier for a LEED NC or

CS project to comply with, as most new equipment is not chlorofluorocarbon (CFC) refrigerant–based due to the Montreal Protocol. LEED CI project teams should have had a conversation with the building manager to ensure compliance or a strategy to comply (i.e., a phase-out of CFCs or install separate heating, ventilating, and air conditioning [HVAC] from the base building).

- **Materials and Resources (MR) Prerequisite 1: Storage & Collection of Recyclables.** Again, a much easier prerequisite for LEED NC and CS projects as long as the space has been dedicated to storage and collection of recyclables. A LEED CI project team should have discussed with the building owner or manager to ensure there is a policy in place and will then need to dedicate the space within their leased space for the collection of the five minimum materials to comply.

- **Indoor Environmental Quality (EQ) Prerequisite 1: Minimum Indoor Air Quality Performance.** NC and CS project teams will need to plan for the HVAC system to comply with ASHRAE 62.1, and CI project teams will need to ensure the base building system can meet the requirements for ventilation.

- **EQ Prerequisite 2: Environmental Tobacco Smoke Control.** Compliance depends on the smoking policy for the building. LEED CI projects should verify the location(s) for designated smoking areas to ensure compliance.

It is then advised that the attendees start evaluating the opportunities and impacts of each credit, category by category (Figure 5.2). Each credit should be assigned "likely," "possible," or "unlikely," depending on the applicability and conformity with the triple-bottom-line goals of the project. It is best to avoid definitive "yes" achievements as a conservative approach might avoid conflicts of expectations later down the road. The level of confidence to meet the requirements could be the determining factor between "likely" and "possible." For example, if the project is located in an urban area with access to a rail and/or bus line(s) meeting the requirements of the alternative transportation credit, a team could mark the credit as "likely," as they are convinced they can earn the points. If there is only one bus line and another is proposed, the team should mark the credit as "possible" as compliance is yet to be definitive and confirmed. In this case, compliance will be determined once the project is submitted for final certification review. By completing this exercise, the project team would have collectively determined how the project would pursue LEED certification specific to the project.

For an NC or CS project, it is a good idea to inquire about the goal for continued certification when pursuing points, more specifically certifying under the LEED for Existing Buildings: Operations and Maintenance™ (EBOM) rating system at a later date. This will help to understand the future impacts, opportunities, and goals for pursuing credits now and to seek out as many alignments and consistencies as possible for future certification with the EBOM rating system. For example, selecting native and noninvasive plantings requires little to no water and fertilizers, therefore easing the burden on the Operations and Maintenance staff to pursue EBOM SS Credit 3: Integrated Pest Management, Erosion Control and Landscape Management Plan, and WE Credit 3: Water Efficient Landscaping. Up-front determination of sustainable goals will not only impact the ability to pursue LEED points during design and construction for an NC or CS project team, but will also ensure that the certified project is on the right path to operate in a sustainable

Figure 5.2 The engineering team at Schlenger/Pitz & Associates, Inc. in Maryland identifies applicable LEED credits to pursue for a project prior to the actual eco-charette. Photo courtesy of Schlenger/Pitz & Associates, Inc.

fashion and will be able to approach EBOM certification in a straightforward and efficient manner.

For any project type, the following strategies should be considered at the eco-charette specific to the goals of the project:

- **Indoor Air Quality (IAQ).** Strategies to improve IAQ should be addressed, as it has an impact on the health of the occupants, not only during occupancy but during construction as well. Increasing ventilation, carbon dioxide monitoring, and mitigating the presence of chemical and pollutants within the building will help to improve the well-being and productivity of the occupants, concurrently reducing the liability of the owner. During construction, the use of low-emitting building products and materials will reduce the negative impacts of off-gassing for the construction workers.

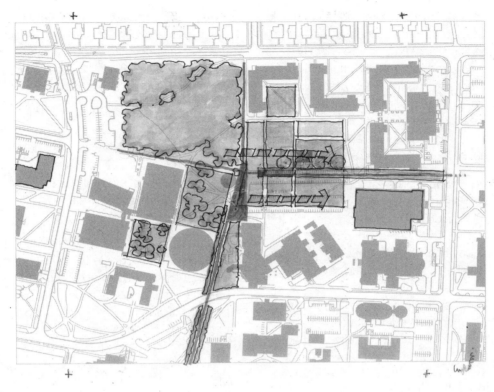

Figure 5.3 A diagram to study site implications at Pennsylvania State University's School of Architecture and Landscape Architecture in University Park, Pennsylvania by LaQuatra Bonci Associates. Photo courtesy of LaQuatra Bonci Associates

- **Site Selection and Development.** The site and the building should be considered as a continuous whole within the community setting. The project should address ways for the building to coexist within a natural ecosystem while reducing its impacts on the environment and infrastructure (Figure 5.3). Be sure to discuss site lighting and open space concepts and strategies. These two issues can conflict with the owner's perceptions of use. For example, hotels, restaurants, and retail settings might expect higher levels of lighting than permitted for the purposes of LEED. Some other owners might object to leaving land undeveloped and preserving open space as they wish to develop as much as possible.

- **Daylighting.** A green building should include ways to reduce energy demands, including the need for artificial lighting. Early decisions addressing building orientation, envelope selections, and floor plate layout and design can help the team to optimize daylighting strategies, to not only reduce energy consumption, but also to provide the occupants with access to the exterior environment.

- **Water Efficiency.** Increased life-cycle and maintenance costs are associated with large amounts of water consumption. Therefore, the team should address strategies to reduce indoor water consumption for flush and flow fixtures, as well as the amount of water required for irrigation. If the project does not plan on including any vegetated areas, remember planters or garden space can contribute to earning this credit if they are included within the LEED boundary line and cover more than 5 percent of the building site area.

- **Energy Performance.** The amount of energy required for building operations is directly related to its design. Project teams should focus on the building's massing and orientation, material selection and composition, the construction methods used, the envelope selection, and the energy-related building systems as a means to reduce the demand. It is not essential to determine the exact strategy and percentage reductions over the reference standard, but instead to focus on the applicable options and the associated feasibility.

- **Building Materials.** The project should evaluate the life cycle of its building products and materials to minimize the environmental impacts associated with transportation, off-gassing, and the need for virgin materials in order to construct and maintain the building. Be sure to discuss material life expectancy and any specific needs. LEED NC and CS project teams can typically earn MR Credit 4 with concrete, steel, gypsum wallboard, and acoustical ceiling tiles.CI projects typically have an easier effort with MR Credit 5 as local materials only have to be manufactured within 500 miles of the project site in order to earn one point (whereas NC and CI projects need to comply with material extraction and processing requirements as well).

- **Occupant Comfort.** The building should maximize thermal, lighting, and acoustical performance to increase productivity by the means of occupant comfort. If teams are concerned with thermal comfort and credit compliance, they may want to consider implementing a raised access floor, as it offers the most cost effective flexibility and individual controllability.

- **Construction.** Construction activities should be addressed to continue the effort for the project that will be established during design. Contractors should be aware of construction waste and IAQ management strategies, procurement requirements, the interaction required with a CxA, and development restrictions.

- **Operations.** Ultimately, the team should address strategies to encourage the design and construction of a high-performance building that is easy to operate and maintain. To develop these strategies, the insight of facility managers should be included to gain up-front knowledge to help during design. For example, tracking and monitoring strategies should also be addressed, such as EA Credit 5: Measurement and Verification to ensure the team is aware of the data and how they will use it. Otherwise, the investment is not well spent. In return, the project team should plan to educate the Operations and Maintenance staff about the intentions of the new structure's performance and train them to understand how the building systems operate and the associated maintenance that is required.

The team should also take advantage of the goal-setting exercise to address potential challenges with the team. Have the fiscal year-end activities been taken into consideration? What happens if there is a merger or acquisition? Are finances finalized? What is the backup plan if there are bank credit limitations? Are there any material shortages to be concerned about? Are there any internal or external hurdles that could present themselves?

CONTRACTOR'S PERSPECTIVE
LEED Certification: Hurdles to Success

By Holly Hawkins, LEED AP, ASHE
Director of Sustainable Services of Tri-North Builders

We have been involved in all aspects of the LEED process—from the owner saying they want a green building, all the way through hanging the plaque on the wall and celebrating our successes; from Commercial Interiors, New Construction, and Core & Shell, to the pilot program LEED for Retail. We have encountered differences and similarities in each of these rating systems, as well as when LEED was decided within a project and what the contractual relationships are. The LEED process itself is most collaboratively successful when the contractor, architect, and engineer are hired in conjunction with each other in a design-build format. This allows the greatest success with the LEED charette, allowing the team to incorporate green principles while seeing real-time costs associated. In gathering people for the LEED charette, one person needs to be selected as the leader. This person should review the owner's scope and the LEED checklist to identify potential points suitable for this project. Dispersing this list to the project team for their review will facilitate the discussion during the LEED charette. The actual meeting could take as little as an hour, or as long as several days, depending on the scale of work, which certification level you are seeking, and the overall budget of the project.

We have not been blessed to work on a project where we have a limitless budget—usually, it's quite the opposite. With many of the projects we have worked on, the budget has been approved long before the notion of LEED was even considered. When this occurs, careful consideration needs to be made on every aspect of the project and all of the "low-hanging fruit" are reviewed in detail. We've had projects, for example, where solar was removed from the project, even though the simple payback was less than eight years, because it was determined that increasing the R-value of the insulation and improving the exterior glass created more value to the project and freed up some much needed money for the nonprofit owner's educational programs.

Documentation is a beast within itself as related to review time and inconsistencies across review teams. Although U.S. Green Building Council (USGBC®) and Green Building Certification Institute (GBCI) are trying to streamline the process to better assist all of us in faster-reviewed project turnovers, the last review we submitted still took a little less than six months. As a contractor, this is very difficult to address with owners. When we turn over the building, they would like the plaque on the wall or for that plaque to appear very shortly after, for they are excited about the building and would like to promote it to colleagues and customers. The other drawback is that once a project is completed, most people don't feel the paperwork is as big a priority to complete, because the building is done and the owner moved in, so there is no hurry.

Another hurdle is that every review team looks at your submittal paperwork differently. We recently had a project where the review team told us they felt our building couldn't be as efficient as what the energy model and the construction drawings showed. As a company, we struggled with how to address a reviewer's feelings rather than facts, as the

continued

reference guide would lead you to believe. Another example is when the review team questioned a number of items on a project due to the project's being attached to another building that opened in phases—when in actuality the project was a stand-alone building and the entire building opened on the same day. This made us wonder if all the drawings, pictures, and descriptions we uploaded were even reviewed.

These types of hurdles can be frustrating at times, but we feel it is important to remember it only helps to keep us on our toes and helps to solidify the integrity of our submittals.

Integrative Budgeting

The strategies and technologies to consider to ensure compliancy for LEED offer many different synergies and trade-offs. With the overall goal of integrating building systems to function in a cohesive fashion for a high-performance building, the process of developing a budget should be approached in a similar manner. Prior to the goal-setting exercise, the project team should have assembled a preliminary assignment of cost. Typically, most project teams are confronted with three additional costs that are not considered in traditional projects: LEED coordination fees, CxA fees, and LEED registration and certification review fees. With the inclusion of these fees, the savings in another line item must offset them in order to balance the budget. It is the interaction of the team, working and thinking as a whole, that will allow this budget balancing as all the different aspects of the building are considered. In some cases, it is the pursuit of earning LEED certification that will allow for the team to pursue incentives (as Dennis Stilger suggested in the previous chapter with the pursuit of the EPAct/179D tax reduction) and grants, therefore offsetting up-front costs while still granting the end user the continued operational savings. It might also be necessary to bridge the gap between up-front costs and operational savings that would occur because of sustainable strategies, such as commissioning. It is for these reasons that the proper team members attend the charette to understand these opportunities and coordinate the two budgets. For example, hiring a lighting designer might add to the up-front costs, as will smaller, more efficient exterior light fixtures, but the operational savings and rebates for ENERGY STAR® lamps could offset these initial costs and result in a more uniform and consistent lighting design as compared to using fewer high-output, inefficient fixtures.

Roles and Responsibilities

At the eco-charette, the coordinator assists the team with assigning and establishing the roles and responsibilities of the design and construction teams as related to LEED documentation. As each prerequisite and credit is discussed, the team shall assign the member that will be responsible for the documentation requirements, recognizing that there may be multiple contributing parties. For example, EQ Credits 4 are all construction-side credits and would therefore fall to the general contractor to upload the documentation for proving compliance. Although, in order to know how to comply, the design team must detail the requirements for selecting the materials that meet the credit requirements, as typically defined in the specifications for the contractor to adhere to. Therefore, those particular credits require contributing details from the design team, although the contractor will be responsible for uploading information to LEED-Online for certification review by GBCI.

Appendix C includes a roles and responsibilities matrix for each of the three rating systems, including the design and construction phases for each prerequisite and credit for each contributing and responsible party for documentation. Notice that some credits can be assigned to a number of individuals. For example, EA Credit 5: Measurement and Verification for LEED NC and CS projects, (EA Credit 3: Energy Use, Measurement and Payment Accountability for LEED CI projects) can be assigned to the CxA, mechanical engineer, the facility manager, or even the energy modeler. It is up to the team to determine who is best suited for each prerequisite and credit based on his or her contracted scope of work. The idea is not to create documentation for the purposes of proving compliance with LEED requirements that was already created by another team member for construction documentation. This is the key reason why a LEED coordinator is not responsible for most prerequisite and credit documentation. For example for an NC or CS project, if a landscape architect is developing plans specifying native plantings, why would another team member be responsible for SS Credit 5.1 or WE Credit 1?

Checklist of Tasks/Develop a Road-Map

In order not to lose focus on the initiatives established at the meeting, and to avoid going back into a traditional silo approach to design, the LEED coordinator must stay on top of the team to ensure continued collaboration and integration. It is essential to determine a schedule for future integration meetings and who will be required to attend whether they are in-person or via telephone/video conference. The number of these meetings, their intent, and the time in between shall be based on the scope of the specific project and the project schedule.

It is important to clarify the requirements for documentation and the time necessary to complete the proof of compliance. If addressed from the beginning, the effort will be streamlined and fall naturally into alignment with the documentation needed for permit review and construction. If the team falls back into the traditional approach to design, the project's success may be compromised and they might feel overwhelmed, scrambling at the end to go back and compile the necessary information. Therefore, it is essential for the coordinator to push the design team to complete their documentation to be uploaded to LEED-Online quickly after the construction documents are issued for permit review/construction.

It is suggested for the LEED coordinator to encourage the team to submit for a Design Review with GBCI after the completion of the construction documents. Therefore, Figure 5.4 lists which prerequisites and credits are eligible to be submitted at that time for an initial review. The team will need to address all prerequisites and credits in some capacity during design; therefore, Figure 5.4 should be referenced only for a list to be completed prior to construction. Although Figure 5.4 aligns with LEED NC project teams, LEED CS and CI project teams can coordinate the effort with the following list, but bear in mind the numbering might be different. For more detailed information, Appendix D provides a chart to depict which prerequisites and credits are characterized as design or construction credits to indicate when they can be submitted for certification review specific to the rating system the team is pursuing.

Introduction to LEED-Online

LEED-Online is intended to function as an online resource and forum for a project team. It is the project administrator's responsibility to setup the site

Prerequisites and Credits Eligible for Design Review for LEED NC

Sustainable Sites

- ☐ SS Credit 1: Site Selection
- ☐ SS Credit 2: Development Density & Community Connectivity
- ☐ SS Credit 3: Brownfield Redevelopment
- ☐ SS Credit 4: Alternative Transportation
  - Public Transportation Access
  - Bicycle Storage & Changing Rooms
  - Low-Emitting & Fuel-Efficient Vehicles
  - Parking Capacity
- ☐ SS Credit 5: Site Development
  - Maximize Open Space
- ☐ SS Credit 6: Stormwater Design
  - Quantity Control
  - Quality Control
- ☐ SS Credit 7: Heat Island Effect
  - Roof
- ☐ SS Credit 8: Light Pollution Reduction

Water Efficiency

- ☐ WE Prerequisite 1: Water Use Reduction
- ☐ WE Credit 1: Water Efficient Landscaping
- ☐ WE Credit 2: Innovative Wastewater Technologies
- ☐ WE Credit 3: Water Use Reduction

Energy & Atmosphere

- ☐ EA Prerequisite 2: Minimum Energy Performance
- ☐ EA Prerequisite 3: Fundamental Refrigerant Management
- ☐ EA Credit 1: Optimize Energy Performance
- ☐ EA Credit 2: On-Site Renewable Energy
- ☐ EA Credit 4: Enhanced Refrigerant Management

Materials & Resources

- ☐ MR Prerequisite 1: Storage & Collection of Recyclables

Indoor Environmental Quality

☐ EQ Prerequisite 1: Minimum Indoor Air Quality Performance

☐ EQ Prerequisite 2: Environmental Tobacco Smoke (ETS) Control

☐ EQ Credit 1: Outdoor Air Delivery Monitoring

☐ EQ Credit 2: Increased Ventilation

☐ EQ Credit 5: Indoor Chemical & Pollutant Source Control

☐ EQ Credit 6: Controllability of Systems
- Lighting
- Thermal Comfort

☐ EQ Credit 7: Thermal Comfort
- Design
- Verification

☐ EQ Credit 8: Daylight & Views
- Daylight
- Views

Innovation & Design Process

☐ ID Credit 1: Innovation or Exemplary Performance

Figure 5.4. Prerequisites and Credits Eligible for Design Review for LEED NC

after registration, to invite the other the team members, indicate the credits to be attempted and assign each of the prerequisites and credits. During design and construction, the idea is for team members to post information to share with the other team members.

While at the goal-setting exercise, it is advised to show the team members the site and how to navigate around. The coordinator should show the team members how to log on and with what information, how to get to the specific project, and where to find the information they might be looking for. It would also be helpful to review what a credit

submittal template is and how to use it. The LEED-Online website contains a short video that might be useful to have everyone watch. While everyone is engaged, it is also recommended to show the team where to find additional help during the next phases of the project, such as where to purchase a reference guide and where the CIR database is located. It might also be helpful to review what a licensed profession exemption (LPE) form is at this time, as it helps to simplify the documentation efforts. This form "can be used by a project team's registered professional engineer (PE), registered architect (RA), or registered landscape architect (RLA) as a streamlined path to certain credits,

OWNER'S PERSPECTIVE
The Execution of a Certified LEED NC Project

By Mike Barbera, LEED AP
Senior Project Manager at Project Management Advisors, Inc.

Figure 5.5 The project team relied on their experience to work in an integrated collaboration, helping to earn LEED Gold certification for the Sanford-Burnham Medical Research Institute at Lake Nona, Florida. Photo courtesy of New York Focus.

Overall, this project was very successful and rewarding, having achieved LEED Gold certification when the initial goal was Silver (Figure 5.5). The LEED certification process ran efficiently most of the time due in large part to working with a very experienced and highly accomplished architect, Perkins+Will. They managed the LEED efforts and allowed the design to evolve efficiently. Equally important was contracting technically skilled professionals with LEED process experience, including civil, mechanical, and electrical engineers and the general contractor. These professionals addressed, implemented, and/or found complementary alternatives for design feedback and ideas coming out of the charette. Surrounding yourself with qualified experts will give you the confidence to step back and allow them to develop and properly implement your strategies.

LEED requires energy-driven systems to be commissioned, and due to the complexities of the building's MEP systems and integration of subsystems, there were numerous commissioning items to resolve. Again, by relying on professionals with relevant experience—in this case the MEP engineer with in-house energy modeling capabilities and experience using the software—we were able to manage the impact of these items and verify that the design-specified requirements were met.

Finally, but not of least importance, we found it critical to make sure the commissioning scope was clearly defined. Our approach was to ensure that every team member knew his/her role, so there was no confusion, and nothing would get missed. We asked the commissioning agent to be fully engaged and to lead the effort. We found that, with this approach, the owner learned more about the facility during the commissioning process than at any other time, therefore requiring heavy owner participation. Through the process, we also learned not be afraid to expand the commissioning scope to include process-related systems. Although these systems are not required to be commissioned for the certification process, they are energy consumers, and it only benefits the owner to confirm that these process systems are operating at their greatest efficiency within design parameters.

Figure 5.6   The cafeteria at Sanford-Burnham Medical Research Institute incorporates natural daylighting strategies, helping to reduce the need for artificial lighting and connects the staff members with the outdoor environment. Photo courtesy of New York Focus.

Table 5.1 LPE Eligible Credits

	RATING SYSTEM		
	NC	CS	CI
SS Credit 1 Site Selection	-	-	PE and RA
EA Prerequisite 2: Minimum Energy Performance	PE and RA	PE and RA	-
EQ Credit 1: Outdoor Air Delivery Monitoring	-	-	PE
EQ Credit 5: Indoor Chemical & Pollutant Source Control	PE (mechanical)	PE (mechanical)	PE (mechanical)
EQ Credit 6.2: Controllability of Systems: Thermal Comfort	-	-	PE

bypassing otherwise-required submittals."[1] LEED-Online indicates registered interior designers (RID) are eligible to use this form as well. Table 5.1 indicates the credits with LPE capabilities.

Momentum after the Eco-Charette

It is intended for the coordinator to follow-up with each of the attendees with a summary of the goal-setting meeting, including a completed roles and responsibilities matrix, as well as a completed score-card. A schedule for the design integration meetings and milestones should also be distributed, along with a project team contact list of all the key team members from each discipline. Most attendees typically leave the meeting with a list of items to research or clarify, as these outstanding items should be documented in a task list by the coordinator and also issued to the team. Each team member should follow up with the coordinator with a status of the information, at which time the coordinator should update the task list and redistribute to the team. These continual means of communication will help keep the momentum of the team, which was ignited at the kickoff meeting.

Whether the project is registered or not, the completed scorecard will help the LEED coordinator set up LEED-Online as the rating system is selected and the credits the teams plans on pursuing have been determined. This completed scorecard will also help the owner and CxA compile the OPR, as discussed in the next chapter.

PART 2 THE DESIGN PHASES

chapter 6 Schematic Design and Design Development Phases

By Chet M. Roach
Project Manager of Brailsford & Dunlavey

Buyer B, using her clearly defined selection criteria, has now narrowed her search down to a particular model of car—the DEEL. The DEEL is available in two options—the DEEL X, which provides the buyer with a base-level vehicle that meets all of the functionality requirements (answer to Question 1) and DEEL Y, which exceeds the performance of DEEL X with multiple environmentally friendly upgrades. DEEL X is under the established budget, and DEEL Y exceeds it (answer to Question 2). Each of the upgrades found on DEEL Y is available individually and can be added to DEEL X at the buyer's discretion. Now, how does the buyer determine which options are right for her? First, the buyer must revisit her purpose for the use of the vehicle. In this case, our buyer is concerned with minimizing the environmental effects of her car, as well as showcasing her environmental consciousness.

Now, with the purpose/goal and budget for the vehicle in mind, the buyer must evaluate each upgrade individually. The buyer must decide whether to decline each specific upgrade or to increase her budget to incorporate it. However, this decision cannot be made in a vacuum, as the potential upgrades all produce varied benefits and costs that must be considered before finalizing her optimal upgrade package.

While this approach seems reasonable for buying a car, many owners do not treat the development of Leadership in Energy and Environmental Design (LEED®) projects in this way. In order to avoid missing the intended purpose of the facility and exceeding your budget, below are the steps that an owner should take during the project to ensure that they retain maximum control throughout the LEED process:

- **Hold an Initial LEED Discussion with Project Team.** The owner must discuss their answers to Questions 1 and 2 with the project team (project manager, architect, engineers, builder, LEED consultant, etc.) early in the process to

continued

provide clarity on why the owner wants to pursue a LEED project, as well as how much of the project budget the owner is willing to invest to achieve the purpose/goal of the facility. This conversation should happen at the beginning of schematic design (SD).

- **Preliminary Filtering Workshop by Project Team.** At 50 percent SD, the owner should have the project team review the exhaustive list of all LEED credits available through U.S. Green Building Council (USGBC®), and determine which of the credits are not possibly achievable. For example, there is a credit available for redeveloping a Brownfield site, but most sites would not fall under this category, making this credit impossible to achieve. Once all of the possible credits are identified, the Builder should provide an initial range of costs for implementing each particular credit. These costs should be viewed as premiums when compared to the most cost-effective design solutions that would be used to deliver a non-LEED building. For clarity, instruct the builder to provide the premium when compared to "developer quality" construction of the same facility type.

- **Initial Presentation of All Options to Owner.** The owner should then direct the project team to present each possible credit with its associated cost premiums, as well as the most likely methods of implementing each credit. This will then establish the total number of potential credits that the project can achieve, as well as the total cost to implement all of the credits. At this point, the owner can provide helpful feedback about each credit using their criteria established during the initial LEED discussion.

- **Presentation of Potential Approaches to LEED for the Project.** Additionally, the project team should present three scenarios to achieve the targeted level of LEED certification in different ways:

  - **The Most Cost-Effective Method.** This approach details achieving the targeted level of LEED certification with cost as the only factor. The owner's purpose/goals are not a factor when developing this approach to LEED credits. This provides the owner with the most cost-effective approach to a LEED project.

  - **Completely Purpose-/Goal-Driven Method.** This approach provides the owner with maximizing the project's outcome to match the previously identified purpose/goals for the facility. Cost is not a consideration in this approach.

  - **The Hybrid Approach.** This approach challenges the project team to use their judgment to create a recommended list of credits that can be pursued to attain the specified level of LEED certification. The team is encouraged to maintain the purpose/goals of the project, while also selecting credits that may be more cost-effective.

  The owner can then review the three approaches for LEED in order to begin narrowing down the exhaustive list of credits to those that they definitely want to pursue, most likely want to pursue, may want to pursue, and do not want to pursue.

- **Understanding the *Payback* Calculation for Engineering Disciplines.** At approximately 90 percent SD, the mechanical/electrical/plumbing (MEP) engineers will have reached a critical point in the conceptual design of the building's components (mechanical, plumbing, building envelope, etc.) that affords them more information about the actual implementation costs and operating benefits of the options for these systems. In general, the more energy efficient a building component is to operate (thus more likely to achieve more LEED credits), the more expensive the initial investment is for the system. However, the engineering team should be able to provide the different *payback* calculations for each option being considered. For example, thicker insulation used in the walls of the building will incur a larger initial cost increase when compared to thinner insulation, but the thicker alternative has a *payback* of less than five years. This means that the premium to purchase the thicker insulation is paid back in less than five years due to the reduction in energy usage. Using this *payback* information to better understand the holistic costs and benefits associated with each design solution, the owner is better equipped to determine if a particular LEED credit merits its initial investment.

- **Presentation of "Final" LEED Credit Information and Selection of Credits to Pursue.** At 100 percent SD, the design team should now have enough information to provide the builder with more refined details pertaining to the preferred method of implementing a particular credit, which will increase the usefulness of the cost estimate for each LEED credit. At this point, the owner should have the following information to make a final decision about which credits to pursue:

  - The functionality of each credit—what am I getting if I pursue this credit?

  - The implementation method for each credit—how am I going to achieve this credit?

  - The initial investment cost for each credit when compared to the design alternative—how much am I going to spend to pursue this credit?

  - The *payback* calculation for credits, when necessary—how long will I have to use the building before I recover the cost of my investment?

  With this information, the owner can review the available LEED credits and select those that they determine to be the most appropriate for the project with respect to both the purpose/goals of the project, as well as within the finalized budget for LEED premiums.

- **Revisiting LEED Credits through the Design Process.** The project team should review the targeted LEED credits as the design progresses at 100 percent design development and 50 percent construction documents to inform the owner of any changes in the cost or program associated with achieving a particular credit (i.e., achieving credit X will require that the mechanical room be 50 square feet larger than was expected, which costs Y dollars more to complete). If the owner determines that the cost or programmatic changes warrant abandoning a particular credit rather than continuing its pursuit, the owner can direct the design team to do so.

- **Design Phase vs. Construction Phase Submissions.** LEED credits are broken into two categories—Design phase and Construction phase. The Design phase credits can be submitted for review by the governing body (USGBC reviewers) prior to the beginning of construction. I always recommend submitting the design credits for review during the Construction Documents phase. This will allow time for the design team to address any issues that arise from the reviewer's comments that could pose problems in achieving a particular credit and mitigates the risk of investing money in credits that will not produce official recognition from USGBC.

As Buyer B approaches purchasing a car with respect to her initial goals and budget in mind, so, too, must an owner approach their LEED project. Buyer B will use the resources available (sales staff, local mechanic, internet research, etc.) to gather the information that she needs in order to make the best possible decisions with respect to her goals and budget. An owner should challenge the project team to provide them with all of the important information that they need to take control of the process. At the very least, do not make a decision about the pursuit of a particular credit without fully understanding its functionality, method of implementation, initial investment cost, and payback calculation. When the owner implements this process, the outcome will be a better knowledge of the investments that it is making, as well as a heightened sense of ownership and satisfaction with the final product.

By this time, the project team has been compiled, the site has been selected, and the eco-charette has occurred. It is now time for the project team to dive in and develop the program and concepts for the project, including the shape, size, and envelope. Tenant improvement projects typically are shorter in duration, but should still go through the same steps as a ground-up, new construction or major renovation project.

In order to achieve the goal of submitting for a design-side review at the end of the Construction Documents phase, all of the design-side prerequisites and credits should start to be addressed, during these next two phases. Remember, the goal is to submit as many for review in order to gain the most benefit of the split-review. Although not all of the prerequisites and credits listed below are submitted for a design-side certification review, they need to be addressed in order to comply with the requirements during construction. Appendix D includes a checklist of design side prerequisites and credits to be addressed during the design phases, for the LEED coordinator to copy and distribute to each of the team members as a reminder of the goals for a design-side certification review.

Full Time Equivalent Occupants

Once the program is established, project teams will need to account for the occupant usage to calculate compliance with Sustainable Sites (SS) alternative transportation credits and Water Efficiency (WE) prerequisite and credit for indoor water consumption. The full-time equivalent (FTE) occupancy is an estimation of actual building occupation in terms of hours occupied per day and is used to determine the number of occupants for the building that will use the fixtures. FTE is calculated by dividing the total number of occupant hours spent in the building per day (each full-time employee is assumed to be in the building for 8 hours) divided by eight. Therefore, full-time employees have a value of one. Part-time employees must also be considered in the calculations, if they work four hours a day, they have a value of 0.5. If a building has 100 occupants, 50 of whom work full time and 50 of whom work part time, the FTE for the project is 75. It is also important to remember to include transient occupants in FTE calculations. For example, if a project team were designing a library, they would need to account for the visitors to the library, as well as the staff and employees. These visitors are thought of as transient occupants for the purposes of LEED. The credit submittal templates will separate full-time occupants, part-time occupants, and transients in order to perform the calculations necessary. Project teams will need to calculate the numbers and the responsible party will need to post on LEED-Online Project Information Form 3: Occupant and Usage Data. As with the other LEED-Online project forms, project teams will enter information one time to maintain consistency across all credits. The other required project forms as related to LEED-Online will be discussed in the next chapter.

Design Integration Sessions

The LEED coordinator will be responsible for determining the schedule and frequency for the design integration meetings with the design team. It is typical after the charette to allow the team to digest the information and pursue the goals, but do not allow too much time to pass before checking in with the team again. The schedule will need to follow the deliverables during design, but bear in mind the greater goal for a design review submission. Therefore, from a LEED perspective, the main purpose of the design integration meetings is to keep the team focused and on pace to complete the documentation required for certification review. The primary goal overall, however, is to help encourage communication and coordination as early as possible to develop strategies for performance. **The earlier decisions are made and triple-bottom-line conformity is confirmed, the fewer the number of changes later that would require additional time and money.**

The design integration meetings can be conducted in person or via teleconference or videoconference, depending on the agenda and complexity of the discussion points. Experience has shown more success with a combination of communication methods. Use the conference calls as follow-up to outstanding tasks or to have a smaller group discussion with specific team members. For example, the entire project team does not need to be on a call to discuss the recycling strategy for collection and storage. Use the in-person meetings to bring the entire team together for bigger-picture discussions, such as the building envelope or site design.

It is typical to use a spreadsheet to organize the strategy for each prerequisite and credit and the outstanding tasks for each as well. Each of the design integration meetings can then use this spreadsheet to organize the meeting, starting from the SS category and working through each prerequisite and credit for all of the subsequent categories, including Innovation in Design (ID) and Regional Priority (RP). The spreadsheet should be updated after each meeting and distributed to each team member to keep every-

one up to date on the outstanding issues and tasks to be completed. Therefore, the spreadsheet should define a due date and a responsible team member to ensure that each team member understands the expectations and holds everyone accountable.

The goal is to complete each design-side prerequisite and credit simultaneous with the completion of the construction documents, so the spreadsheet should be organized and updated to reflect this goal. For example, at the first design integration meeting, a spreadsheet should be distributed to the project team with all of the tasks to be completed for the design review. As each task is completed, it should be removed or crossed out, therefore reducing the tasks as the project moves forward. This can act as a motivator for the team to check everything off the list and for them to see identifiable progress.

Incorporating a Green Roof

If the project team is incorporating a green roof, be sure to address the average rainfall, appropriate soil types, and regional plant species (Figure 6.1). The

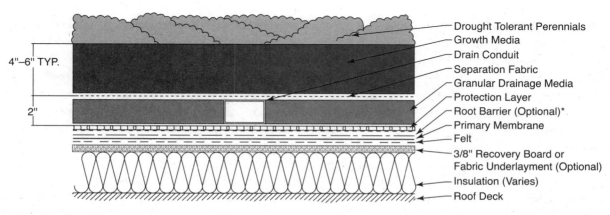

Figure 6–1 Assessing the different components of a green roof serves as a reminder of all of the different team members required to develop an appropriate solution. Image courtesy of Roofscapes, Inc.

GREEN ROOF TECHNICAL EXPERT'S PERSPECTIVE
An Overview of Green Roof Assemblies and Benefits

By Melissa Muroff Esq.
Principal of Roofscapes, Inc.

If you visited the green roofs of the world, you would soon find that you could classify the vast majority of earth's green roofs into four general categories:

- Single media over a moisture management mat
- Single media over a sheet drain
- Dual media
- Dual media over a reservoir sheet

Media, in this case, refers to the specially engineered "soil" used on green roofs.

A roof is a roof, right? Maybe, but all *green* roofs are not created equal (Figure 6.2). Dissect any green roof and you'll find a somewhat consistent anatomy: the plants are established in a mineral-based, engineered media, which is separated from a drainage/water retention layer by a root-permeable filter fabric. The drainage/water retention layer is installed over a root barrier (if necessary) and protection layer (to protect the integrity of the waterproofing membrane). Irrigation, slope stabilization, and other variations can be incorporated as well. Although the single media assemblies tend to be thinner than the dual media assembles, the real distinction among all of these types is the drainage/retention layer. This layer greatly impacts how water is managed and leveraged on the roof, and appropriate water management will dictate whether a green roof lives and thrives or dies.

Necessity is the mother of invention. One could argue that these four general types of green roofs evolved to address five broad variables: (1) local climate, (2) cost, (3) load constraints, (4) preferred plant palette, and (5) performance (including basic thrive requirements, stormwater management, thermodynamics, and biodiversity). Every green roof designer and provider is expected to deliver, on budget, a green roof using the specified plants that satisfies both load and basic thrive requirements in the local climate. Strangely, however, most green roofs are not required to achieve any environmental performance objectives, such as particular stormwater management, thermodynamic, and biodiversity requirements. Even compliance green roofs (green roofs built to satisfy local government regulations—typically, stormwater, green space, or urban heat island–based regulations) usually are not required to demonstrate specific performance capabilities. Generally, compliance green roofs must only meet or exceed a stipulated thickness. A four-inch green roof composed of nursery media and peat moss might weigh and cost less than a similarly thick green roof composed of industry-standard mineral media, but the long-term performance of the green roof with the nursery mix and peat will be disastrous, and the plants over time will fail. Therefore, it is important to determine the right assembly based on the specific project conditions, using materials that comport with industry- standard guidelines and testing methodologies (see Quality Assurance of a Green Roof below).

Figure 6.2 The green roof at PECO in Philadelphia, Pennsylvania, has a 3-inch unirrigated sedum assembly with a moisture management mat at the drainage layer. Image courtesy of Roofscapes, Inc.

Stormwater Management

From a civil engineering perspective, green roofs function as rooftop detention basins, and they can be modeled as such. During design, civil engineers are typically engaged to calculate the stormwater management performance capabilities of on-ground detention basins, so why aren't green roofs (and, for that matter, other low-impact development measures) held to the same standards? Considering the square footage of roofs in heavily built-up cities, the potential impact of green roofs on combined sewer overflows (CSOs) and nuisance flooding for many temperate-climate cities is dramatic. Green roofs can substantially reduce stormwater runoff volume and rates in urban areas, if addressed properly.

continued

Energy

In temperate climates, green roofs have been able to show energy benefits in both summer and winter; however, annual reductions in energy consumption rarely exceed 5 percent. The largest energy cost-reduction benefits occur in climates with long warm seasons. Methods for measuring the unique thermodynamics of green roofs can be incorporated into building envelope models to assess how well green roofs reduce cooling costs. When contemplating how a green roof cools a building and the ambient air above it, think forests, not insulation. Insulation works well when dry, and a green roof is almost never dry. In fact, the water in the green roof is the magic ingredient that dictates how well the green roof cools. The (a) evapotranspiration of moisture from the green roof plants and (b) the heat sink created by the media, moisture, and plants both effect cooling much more than a green roof's insulative properties.

Examples

In many southwestern climates, at least six inches of media and irrigation are required to assure that the green roof will thrive. Irrigation in arid climates poses its own challenges, and more LEED credits can be earned by avoiding irrigation; however, irrigation maximizes the green roof's energy performance—potentially reducing annual cooling costs by 30 percent! This kind of energy savings may be able to justify the additional reinforcements required to support the green roof's 40 psf deadload (at least) and a process for reclaiming the building's greywater for the green roof's irrigation, rightly conserving valuable potable water resources.

Alternatively, many northern cities struggle to comply with the U.S. Clean Water Act and control their combined sewer overflows. The relatively short warm season in these climates generally precludes the kind of energy benefit that green roofs can impart in the southwest; however, green roofs can be optimized to reduce maximum annual runoff volumes and rates. Green roofs in urban environments can be a powerful technology in the stormwater management toolkit.

Biodiversity

Striking a balance between plant and animal biodiversity goals, budget, irrigation limitations, and load constraints can be challenging—but doable. The green roof industry is just beginning to develop an integrated body of knowledge regarding the behavior of plants on green roofs (particularly nonirrigated roofs), the appropriate use of native vegetation on green roofs, successful planting in different microclimates, understanding normal green roof plant succession, strategies for attracting desired wildlife, and the long-term management of evolving roof meadows.

Other Green Roof Design Drivers

In addition to the five major variables that influence the selection of the appropriate green roof assembly, a laundry list of other drivers and factors also impact the ultimate green roof design, including the purpose of the green roof (amenity, demonstration, educational, compliance, values-based, marketing); relevant municipal regulations, subsidies, incentives, and taxes; rooftop microclimates; locally available materials; irrigation (if used) strategies, and maintenance resources. Although these factors and drivers must be considered in concert, all designs should at least (1) accommodate the varied green roof microclimates, (2) minimize irrigation requirements, and (3) leverage the natural succession and behavior of the plantings.

Modular (Tray) Green Roof Systems

Sedums, for example, normally migrate within the green roof, settling in the most suitable microclimate. This particular plant behavior favors contiguous, built-in-place green roofs. Modular or tray green roof systems interrupt that natural dynamic, thereby undermining long-term plant durability. Moreover, tray systems are vulnerable to "edge effects," in which temperature variations are exaggerated at tray perimeters, resulting in poorer plant growth. When drainage perforations become clogged, water accumulates in trays, and plants drown. Built-in-place or contiguous green roofs take advantage of the horizontal connectivity of the media and root systems to better manage water and to facilitate the plants' natural succession behavior. Compared to tray systems, built-in-place green roofs tend to be (1) more drought-tolerant, (2) less dependent on irrigation, (3) better stormwater management tools, (4) aesthetically more pleasing, and (5) more viable overall. Interestingly, tray systems also tend to be more expensive than contiguous green roof systems. Finally, leak detection, repair, and restoration—if ever required—is actually complicated by tray systems and easier to facilitate on contiguous green roof assemblies.

---

team should also account for waterproofing and draining issues for the different types of systems available. Engage the structural engineer to assist with the load requirements to support the additional weight. The mechanical engineer should also be included in the discussions for the design of the roof, as it impacts the thermal separation between the interior and the exterior environments; the civil engineer will also need to determine how the roof will impact the stormwater flows on site. The contractor and their subcontractor responsible for installing the system should be a part of the design process for a vegetated roof to thoroughly understand the system and its integration with other building systems. There are many credit synergies for implementing a green roof, as there are many benefits for the environment, and project teams are encouraged to utilize the reference guides for more information and to contact a technical expert well versed in green roof technologies appropriate for the project type and region. This

consultant may be crucial, depending on the local ordinances and requirements specific to vegetated roofs, as variances may be needed. He or she may also be knowledgeable about the different rebates that may be available for installing a green roof, depending on the location and municipality or state.

There are different kinds of green roofs (see Green Roof Technical Expert's Perspective by Melissa Muroff, Esq.) and therefore different components contained within. Project teams are encouraged to select native and adaptive plantings that require little to no maintenance and will not produce airborne seeds. Coordination is encouraged between the landscape architect, civil engineer, and green roof technical expert to evaluate the soil type, average rainfall, and local plant species to ensure biodiversity. If irrigation is needed, teams are encouraged to reuse stormwater and reduce the demand for potable water to be delivered from the municipality.

Collecting Stormwater

There are multiple benefits of capturing stormwater, and therefore it is important to understand how a project team would design to collect and reuse the water. Project teams need to evaluate different options to determine the appropriate collection systems for their specific project. Systems can range from small barrels to large cisterns (Figure 6.3) to permeable surfaces. If the water is collected from the roof, the teams need to be cognizant of the roofing materials not to contaminate the water, such as asphalt. Therefore, implementing metal, clay, or a concrete material–based roofing product might be a better option for these types of projects. Regardless of the system desired, project teams are encouraged to evaluate the following:

- **Water Budget.** How much precipitation is expected versus how much water is needed for the purpose the water is intended?

- **Drawdown.** How much water is needed in between rainfalls?

- **Drainage Area.** How will the water be collected to store? Will it be a permeable surface? If so, what is the size of the surface to determine how much water can be collected?

- **Conveyance System.** Different pipes will be needed as stormwater and greywater pipes are not allowed to be connected to potable water lines.

- **Pretreatment.** Screen and/or filters will be needed to remove debris from runoff.

Figure 6.3 Stormwater is collected on-site and stored in cisterns at the Utah Botanical Center's Wetland Discovery Point building and used to flush toilets, as well as irrigate the site, therefore reducing the need for potable water. Photo courtesy of Gary Neuenswander, Utah Agricultural Experiment Station.

- **Pressurization.** A pump maybe required depending on the system.

Addressing the Prerequisites and Credits

As described earlier, at the first design integration meeting after the charette, a task-oriented spreadsheet is to be distributed to the project team. It is suggested that this spreadsheet be organized by category with the prerequisites and the project's specific credits contained within. One of the goals is to determine if the credits are still achievable as the project moves forward. Another goal is to keep the team focused and on schedule to complete the design-side credit documentation so a certification review and a permit review can be conducted simultaneously. Project details tend to change throughout the design phases and therefore it is critical to keep the impacts to credit achievement in mind at times of revisions. This might indicate a change in compliance path and pursuit of a credit all together, as long as it does not include noncompliance with a minimum program requirement (MPR) or prerequisite. The last goal to address during the Schematic Design and Design Development phases includes addressing the construction credits in the drawings and specifications in order to set the pace for the construction team to follow.

Sustainable Sites

Regardless of the rating system or project type, the SS prerequisites and credits that are typically addressed during these two phases of design include:

SS Prerequisite 1: Construction Activity Pollution Prevention (for NC and CS projects)

- The civil engineer or landscape architect is typically responsible for this construction prerequisite. They will need to evaluate the site for erosion-prone areas to address the applicable soil stabilization strategy. They should also verify the soil conditions to help with determining the strategies for other SS credits, such as stormwater management and the drainage options. They need to document these strategies in an erosion and sedimentation control (ESC) plan as a means to give instruction to the contractor, particularly for rainstorms or other erosion-causing occurrences. Typically, this is required for most jurisdictions and should not be an additional effort to comply with LEED. Since a narrative is also required for certification review, it is beneficial for the responsible party to write the narrative when the comparison with the local jurisdiction's requirements is completed, as the information will be fresh.

- Additionally, the civil engineer or landscape architect should determine if a stormwater pollution prevention plan (SWPPP) is required, and therefore an ESC plan might already exist and meet the intentions and requirements of the prerequisite.

- Note that this prerequisite has a synergy with SS Credit 5.1, as setbacks are stipulated to preserve existing vegetation.

SS Credit 1: Site Selection

Although this credit is typically evaluated by this phase of a project, the process for documentation needs to commence.

- *For LEED for New Construction and Major Renovations™ (NC) and LEED for Core & Shell (CS) Projects:* The project team should start

ARCHITECT'S PERSPECTIVE
Managing Passive Loads

By Gary Moshier, AIA, LEED AP
Moshier Studio

Figure 6.4. The McGinnis Education and Conference Center in Sharpsburg, Pennsylvania, by Moshier Studio earned its LEED Silver certification by designing for the building as a whole and integrating the building systems to work cohesively. Photo courtesy of Moshier Studio.

One of the basic tenets of sustainable or green design that is most often overlooked, if not by the designers, at least by those who are writing about and learning from green buildings, is the management of passive loads. Effectively managing these loads is at the core of what is often called "whole building" or "whole systems" design (Figure 6.4), which is the attitude and practice of maximizing the efficiency of every component of the building to the point of having each one fulfill several roles and to contribute to the minimization of some other, more expensive component, on either a first or ongoing cost basis. It is both the right and the responsibility of the architect to take on this task. No other member of the team has the skills necessary to collect the various inputs of climate, orientation, site, structure, context (cultural and physical), materiality, program, and aesthetics and synthesize the building envelope to work in concert with the various systems.

Figure 6.5 Moshier Studio incorporated daylighting strategies for the McGinnis project near Pittsburgh. Photo courtesy of Moshier Studio.

continued

There are many fine examples of buildings that not only balance the management of passive loads with the aesthetics, but also are, in fact, beautiful because they do it so well. Most indigenous architecture uses the forms and materials that have been proven over time to be efficient of energy and resources. That is not to say that modern technology, especially regarding materials and assemblies, cannot improve on these solutions, but it is important to make these improvements within the context of history and the local climactic conditions and to stretch beyond the limitations imposed by suboptimal site conditions and context.

As we give form to our buildings, we should always question our moves and assumptions. Can I extend the comfort zone through effective ventilation? Can that ventilation occur naturally? Does shading the glass keep the summer heat and glare out while allowing heat and light to enter in winter? Am I optimizing for daylight (Figure 6.5)? What about views to the outside? Am I using the most appropriate glass technology for the application, climate, and orientation? What about insulation? Is it the right amount in the right place relative to heat and moisture flow? Where is the vapor barrier? Is the air barrier in the right place? Is it vapor permeable? How does the moisture that either enters or is generated inside the building get out? If I make the envelope better, can I reduce or eliminate an energy-using system like heating, air conditioning, fans, or lighting?

Fortunately, these questions are easier to answer with certainty than ever before. We now have powerful software to model our buildings at all stages of the design process. Material manufacturers and basic researchers have a wealth of empirical data available to help us make these decisions. As the tools and information get better, we need to use them effectively to make our buildings more comfortable, durable, efficient, and relevant.

---

developing a list of strategies in order to preserve the site's ecological features while also complementing them. The developer may wish to engage the community for comments during the preliminary design phases to avoid frustration at a later time.

- *For LEED for Commercial Interiors™ (CI) Projects:* If a LEED-certified base building is selected, the project team should utilize this time to obtain the certification review comments for the base building and/or the final scorecard for the base building to help determine other strategies pertaining to the CI space. If a previously certified space was not selected, and the project team is pursuing one of the other compliancy paths, the team should start collecting the documentation proving compliance if the project site has already implemented the strategies. If the owner has agreed to the site improvements for the project to comply, the teams are encouraged to work together to ensure that the improvements will meet LEED requirements as detailed for this credit. Tenants might consider adding the requirements of the improvements to the lease agreement to ensure that there is an immediate understanding between the parties. In either case, it is also a good idea to review local codes to compare the strategies and regulation compliancy in particular to stormwater management and rainwater collection and reuse strategies. For Path 6: Light Pollution Reduction, teams are encouraged to also begin to look at the tenant space to ensure compliancy. Refer to SS Credit 8 below for more information. For Path 11: On-Site Renewable Energy, besides the verification of the eligibility of the installed system(s), the project teams will need to determine how much energy the system(s) provide in comparison to the amount of energy the building requires in terms of cost. See Energy and Atmosphere (EA) Credit 2 below for more information.

SS Credit 2: Development Density and Community Connectivity

- To comply with the Development Density option, the responsible party determined at the eco-charette (typically the architect or civil engineer) will need to calculate the total area of the site and then the total square footage of the building to determine the density of the site. The density radius will then need to be calculated using the equations in the reference guides. The team would then use the density radius to determine the density boundary in order to generate a spreadsheet of the properties contained within. This spreadsheet will include the building square footage and the site area of the inclusive properties, except for undeveloped public areas, public roads, and right-of-way areas. The responsible party might find it useful to seek geographic information system (GIS) database information from a public agency to streamline this effort, as it could require a long amount of time to document otherwise.

- To comply with the Community Connectivity option, the responsible party will need to develop a site map with a half-mile radius shown from the main building entrance. All residential developments and commercial buildings that are located within this radius should be noted, as well as a minimum of 10 basic services (as defined in the reference

guides). It might be helpful to think of basic services as those one might visit to run errands during their lunch break or before or after work (i.e., library, grocery store, pharmacy, etc.). The responsible party for this design credit will need to prepare a spreadsheet for at least 10 basic services, including the business name and the service type. Google Earth is typically very helpful with the documentation requirements of the option.

SS Credit 3: Brownfield Redevelopment

- *For NC and CS Projects:* Typically by this time, as the site is already secured or leased, the applicability and credit compliance is determined. If this is not concluded and contamination is suspected, the owner should engage an environmental engineering firm to pursue a Phase II environmental investigation to determine compliance. This test will sample for contaminants in the soil, air, and water and may require further testing. If contamination exists, remediation experts are suggested to coordinate a schedule and determine the proper clean-up technologies and strategies to not destroy the natural features of the site. The owner should evaluate options for incentives should contamination be found.

- *For NC Major Renovation Projects:* There may be some evidence of asbestos-containing materials within a building built prior to the mid-1970s. An environmental professional should be engaged to evaluate the site and conduct an inventory. They will also be able to determine the extent required to be removed and the type of remediation necessary.

- *For CI Projects:* In order to comply with this credit, the base building would have needed to be constructed on a remediated site. The brokers or leasing agent for the building should be contacted to obtain the appropriate documentation.

- The documentation for this credit can typically be completed prior to the completion of the construction documents. Once the site has been remediated or documentation proving compliance has been received, the responsible party should upload it to LEED-Online and complete the submittal template, including a narrative summarizing remediation strategies implemented.

SS Credit 4.1 (LEED CI SS Credit 3.1): Alternative Transportation—Public Transportation Access

- To earn this credit, site location is paramount. The responsible team member should determine which of the two compliance paths to pursue: existing rail station or bus stop proximity. The local transit authority should be contacted for maps and schedules to upload to LEED-Online. They will also need to create a site vicinity plan to depict compliance from the building's main entrance.

- Teams should also consider creating a comprehensive transportation management plan for a bonus point under the Innovation in Design (ID) category, to assess the value and applicability of strategies to reduce the use of the automobile for commuting.

- This credit should be completed on LEED-Online as soon as documentation is obtained for public transportation compliant with the credit requirements. This will alleviate the coordinator's time at the end of the Construction Document phase to review other credits.

SS Credit 4.2 (LEED CI SS Credit 3.2): Alternative Transportation—Bicycle Storage and Changing Rooms

- *For NC and CS Projects:* Depending on the use (and size for CS projects) of the endeavor, the team will need to supply both bicycle storage/racks and shower and changing rooms or just bicycle storage/racks. Teams should start the evaluation of the different options for bicycle storage to ensure alignment with the budget and to determine the proper placement on the site. Coordination among the architect, landscape architect, and the civil engineer is encouraged for the racks and coordinating pathways; for the showers, the plumbing engineer and architect need to synchronize their intentions to ensure compliancy for distance, quantities, and access. CS project teams can use the alternative compliance path that dictates future tenants will comply with the credit requirements.

- *For CI Projects:* The project team will need to supply both bicycle storage/racks and shower and changing rooms in order to comply. Teams should start evaluating the different options for bicycle storage with the building owner to ensure alignment with the budget and to determine the proper placement on the site. Coordination among the base building architect, owner, tenant, architect, and, if needed, the landscape architect and/or the civil engineer is encouraged. Remember, the shower and changing facilities does not need to be located within the tenant space, but cannot be compromised by other occupants, and the facilities have to be free for tenants. Base building and tenant design team coordination is suggested for site design for the racks and plumbing revisions or accommodations for shower facilities. If a tenant will have access to a nearby gym or other facility with showers, the responsible team member will need to generate a map indicating a complying distance from the building entrance.

- Project teams will need to determine the full-time equivalent (FTE) number of occupants and the number of peak-time visitors for the entire building to then determine how many bike racks and showers to provide. LEED CI projects will need to conduct these calculations for just the tenant occupants, not to include all of the building occupants. LEED CS projects may need to consult Appendix 1 in the BD+C reference guide for default occupancy counts. LEED-Online will help to ensure that these calculations are consistent for related credits. Whichever rating system is being pursued, all calculations shall be rounded up to determine required showers and bike racks. For example, if the FTE calculation results in 4.2 showers required, the project team will need to provide 5 showers.

- The responsible team member for this credit will need to gather the cut-sheets for the racks or bicycle storage solution and will need to demonstrate that the racks/storage are solely for building occupants' use (public-access bike racks do not qualify). They will also need to create a plan showing the location of the bicycle racks/storage and shower locations. Remember, the showers do not need to be within the building, but within 200 yards of the building entrance. This implies facilities, such as an adjacent gym, that the FTEs will have access to will comply with this credit granted there are enough showers to meet the requirements.

SS Credit 4.3: Alternative Transportation— Low-Emitting and Fuel-Efficient Vehicles

- NC project teams have four options from which to choose to comply with this credit, while CS project teams have just three compliance options. Engaging in a conversation with the owner at the goal-setting meeting should have determined the path to pursue that is proper for the specific project.

- If refueling stations are to be implemented, the fuel type should be surveyed. Project teams should also research the local codes and requirements for alternative fuel types. Remember to keep the budget in mind for up-front costs, installation, and maintenance requirements. Besides a plan showing the locations of the refueling stations, the responsible team member will also need to collect data on the fuel type, manufacturer, model number, and the capacity of the implemented strategy.

- If cars are to be purchased, the owner's procurement representatives should be informed of requirements for compliancy as early as possible. If the FTE was not calculated to pursue the previous credit, the project team will need to complete this calculation to determine the number of cars needed to comply with this credit. The responsible team member will need to gather documentation detailing the manufacturer, model, and fuel type for the vehicles purchased.

- Coordination among the owner, the architect, and the civil engineer is encouraged to determine the preferred parking strategy for location of the reserved parking stalls. Remember, discounted parking options are available as well. A site plan will be required depicting the designated parking spaces, or documentation indicating the discounted parking program depending on the strategy the team is pursuing.

- If a vehicle-sharing program is to be implemented, the responsible team member will need to gather the contractual agreement to upload to LEED-Online.

SS Credit 4.4 (LEED CI SS Credit 3.3): Alternative Transportation—Parking Capacity

- Project teams should start by researching the local zoning code to determine parking provisions as early as possible, as this could impact site design. Project teams are also encouraged to research local and state incentives for carpooling programs. If a comprehensive transportation management plan is developed and depicts a lower demand for spaces than the minimum spaces required by local code, the team is encouraged to pursue a variance to provide less parking.

- *For NC and CS Projects:* Project teams will need to determine which option is applicable based on the type of project. If the FTE was not calculated to pursue the previous credits, the project team will need to complete this calculation to determine the number of cars needed to comply with this credit. LEED CS projects should consult Appendix 1 in the BD+C reference guide to determine the default occupancy counts to use for the calculations. In either case, the responsible team member will need to provide a site plan indicating the amount of parking, including designated parking spaces. Local zoning code documentation will also need to be uploaded to LEED-Online. Whichever compliance path option is pursued, project teams that are also pursuing SS Credit 4.3 need to be cognizant to add the preferred parking requirements for this credit to the requirements from the previous credit.

- *For CI Projects:* Depending on how much of the building the tenant occupies, the project team will need to determine which case is applicable to the project and then which option to pursue. Because compliancy with this credit can be impacted by the lease negotiations, it is best to address prior to finalizing an agreement. FTE calculations are based on the tenant occupants (not the whole building) and must be consistent with related credits. The responsible party will need to prepare a site plan showing the parking availability, including the designated spaces for carpools and/or vanpools.

SS Credit 5.1: Site Development—Protect or Restore Habitat

- Although this is credit is not eligible for a design side review, it is important to address the requirements in the plans and specifications for the contractor to implement during construction.

- Whether or not the site was previously developed will determine which case to pursue. Civil engineers and landscape architects will need to coordinate for any site revisions specific to existing hardscape areas to be replaced with vegetation, water bodies, soils, or other ecosystems. Remember, implementing turf grass is not a compliant strategy for this credit. Landscape architects should be engaged to determine native, adaptive, and noninvasive planting selections appropriate for the region and can help to streamline the documentation effort using the licensed-professional exemption (LPE) form. The architect, civil engineer, and landscape architect should coordinate to ensure compliancy for building footprint to open space proportions and to verify if the limited site area can accommodate construction activities. The contractor should be given clear direction for disturbance boundaries to protect and preserve existing natural areas that aligns with SS Prerequisite 1.

- Remember, if the project team is also pursuing SS Credit 2 and incorporating a green roof with native and adaptive vegetation, previously developed projects can take advantage of the credit synergy and alignment.

SS Credit 5.2: Site Development—Maximize Open Space

- The credit submittal template will require the owner to sign off declaring the open space relevant to the project seeking certification will remain open

LANDSCAPE ARCHITECT'S PERSPECTIVE
A Landscape Architecture Perspective on the LEED Certification Process

By Aiman Duckworth, ASLA, LEED AP
Landscape Designer and Associate at AECOM

With current LEED rating system requirements, a site alone cannot receive a LEED certification. A LEED certification requires a building. Yet, site considerations and innovative contributions from landscape architects on a multidisciplinary team create a solid foundation and framework for successful LEED-certified projects. A landscape architect brings particular expertise in site, habitat, and water to a team. The following recommendations provide a snapshot of simple, yet important site and landscape considerations as applied in the LEED certification process.

1. **Bicycle parking is more than a site furnishing.**

   Bicycle parking and circulation should be designed in tandem with other modes of transportation, not added late in the project when specifying site furnishings. If a project is at a point where automobile parking or circulation is being discussed, bicycle parking should be as well. Calculate spaces required for the site program and for LEED credit achievement early, and design for appropriate locations for safety and convenience to encourage use. Put yourself in the position of the cyclist and consider the particular requirements that they may have as employees, residents, and visitors. The *Bicycle Parking Guidelines,* published by the Association of Pedestrian and Bicycle Professionals, provides one useful reference for layout and locations of bicycle parking.

2. **Translate LEED credit requirements to work with your design process.** Don't use them as a separate set of calculations after your design is complete.

   For example, in the *Green Building Design and Construction (BD+C) Reference Guide*, under the SS credit for Site Development—Protect or Restore Habitat, for greenfield sites, the project cannot disturb beyond 10 feet from surface parking and walkways. With a maximum of a 3:1 slope to return from proposed to existing grade, that translates to a maximum difference between proposed grade and existing grade elevation of 3.3 feet. Steeper slopes and walls could also be considered in some locations to tighten up the limit of disturbance. Translate requirements for other features in a similar manner. This allows consideration of this credit in early site design exercises before the limit of disturbance is even graded out. With a handful of simple references and responsible site design, you can determine early in your process if this or other credits can be achieved with the site program.

3. **Don't be limited to concrete paving to reduce the heat island effect.**

   For many projects, concrete paving is a relatively inexpensive and durable material that has an easily referenced solar reflectance index (SRI). If a design proposes all concrete paving materials, the SS Heat Island Effect, Nonroof credit is often easily achieved. Design inertia, cost, and lack of SRI reference data can create a design comprised entirely of plain gray concrete. Do not let achieving this credit limit creativity or create visual glare issues. Luckily, many paving manufacturers, including asphalt, are now catching up to the market demand for SRI information. If a paving product lacks information, negotiate to have it tested. Contact paving product representatives, and create a product resource library of photos and samples of materials that have documented SRI measurements. The variety of paving tones, colors, and materials that can reduce the heat island effect comprise far more than bright white paving.

continued

4. **Do not ignore materials and resources in the landscape.**

    For Materials and Resources (MR) credits, such as Recycled Content, Regional Materials, Rapidly Renewable Materials, and Certified Wood, credit achievement is calculated by material cost. Projects pursuing LEED certification often have a much higher total unit cost for building materials as compared to site materials. Landscape materials and furnishings can therefore be easily overlooked, and the entire Materials and Resources category sometimes ignored with respect to the site. However, every product and material choice can add up to a substantial impact on a project as a whole. Gather references and push the site materials forward for inclusion in materials calculations, for the good of the project. Also, consider where regionally produced and sourced planting can contribute to materials credits.

5. **Look for opportunities to move beyond the credits.**

    LEED credits can be generators and supporters of varied and interesting design ideas. Consider credits for restoring habitat. Designed landscape habitats, properly demonstrated to have linkages to larger habitat resources, can contribute measurably to urban habitat diversity and health. A native plant palette may be an easy solution to creating habitat, but is only one component of an ecosystem. What connections to larger habitat patches and corridors can the project make? Does the project have unconsidered opportunities for a bird garden with properly designed nesting and feeding areas? A butterfly garden? Beehives? A more complete ecosystem and food cycle design? What are the local animal species in the project area? What do your local species require beyond just a native plant list?

---

space for the life of the building. Project teams are encouraged to ensure that the owner will comply with this requirement before spending any time researching or calculating compliance requirements.

- Project teams will need to research the local zoning codes to determine which compliance path is most applicable for the project and then to understand how much vegetated open space to provide in order to comply. Remember, wetlands or naturally designed ponds with low slopes can count as open space as well.

- The civil engineer shall be responsible for a compact parking and roadway strategy and to work with the architect and owner for a minimal footprint design in order to design connections with adjacent ecosystems. The civil engineer will also need to prepare a site plan indicating the amount of open space to be provided in comparison to the building footprint.

- Remember, if the project team is also pursuing SS Credit 2 and incorporating a green roof, previously developed projects can take advantage of the synergy and alignment with this credit as well. If the team is pursuing SS Credit 5.2 but not incorporating a green roof, pedestrian pathways and hardscape areas can contribute to earning this credit as well. For projects that implement flow-thru planters, these areas can count toward open space allotments.

Coordination of the entire project team is encouraged to evaluate the site design on a holistic level, as the layout might impact as many as five other credits. Site visits will most likely be required in order to understand the natural hydrology, topography, and soil infiltration rates for the site to determine the most appropriate strategies. Generally speaking, strategies should include a reduced building footprint and increased pervious areas. Designing for bioretention areas and infiltration swales will keep the budget in line, but depending on the site, other more expensive strategies may be required in order to achieve these next two credits.

SS Credit 6.1: Stormwater Design—Quantity Control

- Engaging a civil engineer to help to determine the stormwater runoff rates and volumes with help to decipher which compliancy case is best suited for the project and then to determine which option to pursue. Most use the Rational Method to determine the peak discharge rates as it applies to sites less than 200 acres. Teams looking for more information about this calculation are encouraged to visit http://onlinemanuals.txdot.gov/txdotmanuals/hyd/the_rational_method.htm#i1026532.

  Sites with existing imperviousness of 50 percent or less will have two options to choose from. Both require a stormwater management plan to be developed that addresses either the postdevelopment peak discharge rate or the erosion of receiving stream channels. Teams pursuing the latter option will also need to compile a narrative describing the strategies that protect the waterways from erosion and maintain the runoff below maximum levels.

  Project teams working with sites that have an existing imperviousness greater than 50 percent will also need to implement a stormwater management plan where the runoff volume is decreased by at least 25 percent from the two-year, 24-hour design storm.

  The engineer will need to complete a stormwater assessment plan, including the pre- and post-development conditions, and the stormwater management strategies, including water quality treatment and rainfall estimates. Once the strategies are determined, the LEED calculations should be completed to ensure compliance, as the strategies may need to be revisited. Be sure the strategies address not only the rate of runoff, but also the volume.

  The civil engineer and the landscape architect can then work together to address the impervious and pervious areas of the site to incorporate permeable paving and stormwater harvesting solutions. State and local codes should be researched to determine any restrictions for stormwater harvesting and its reuse. Some jurisdictions regulate how long water can be held for and if any treatment is required for reuse.

  Project teams are encouraged to analyze the costs associated with the proposed stormwater management strategies to ensure alignment with the budget.

  For LEED CI Projects: As detailed in Chapter 4, compliancy with this credit (under SS Credit 1: Option 2, Path 2) should be evaluated prior to signing a lease. Should modifications be needed to comply with this credit, the lease should include these provisions. If this determination was not addressed prior to signing the lease, the team should engage in a conversation with the building owner, base building civil engineer, or facility manager to evaluate applicability and compliance and to determine if the site design needs to be modified.

SS Credit 6.2: Stormwater Design—Quality Control

- The civil engineer and landscape architect should evaluate the nonstructural and structural measures in which to comply. Nonstructural measures, such as vegetated swales or rain gardens, are typically pursued as the up-front and long-term cost implications are lower and they can help to recharge the groundwater. If structural controls are implemented,

CIVIL ENGINEER'S PERSPECTIVE
Innovative Sustainable Civil and Site Design for a Nature Center Renovation and Expansion

By Geoffrey B. Nara, PE, LA
Principal of Civil & Environmental Consultants, Inc.

While this project was focused on using sustainable design to solve challenging project issues, each challenge became an opportunity to be used as an educational feature for visitors at this expansion of a nature center. Many of these elements can be easily adapted to most site designs. This work included civil engineering, survey services, ecological services, and an innovative on-site septic system design for a new building and site expansion as part of a multidisciplinary team of architects, engineers, and scientists. The project team employed green design principals to complete the project with a goal of LEED Silver certification.

In the earliest stages of design, site challenges for the project team included:

- A pristine, natural area with a small available disturbance footprint for a new building and expanded parking facilities
- The need to preserve existing nature center functionality during construction so visitors could continue to enjoy the experiences it provides
- A high-quality fishing stream adjacent to the facility, which limited stormwater and wastewater design options
- A wide variability in visitor attendance, creating considerable ranges of water use and wastewater production
- No public water or sanitary sewer services, steep slopes, and poor soils for on-lot septic systems
- A need to maximize stormwater infiltration from the project in poorly draining soils
- Poor groundwater quality from the well, necessitating groundwater treatment for iron removal
- High LEED performance standards
- The seemingly ever-present "limited project budget"

The team, necessitating creative solutions to these factors, embraced these challenges. Accordingly, the civil/site team incorporated the following sustainable design solutions:

- A stormwater collection and infiltration system design using a series of underground open-grated lightweight structures (like plastic milk crates) to promote groundwater infiltration due to a larger surface area exposure on all sides of the structure
- Ensuring all facilities for stormwater were above the stream's floodplain elevation to further promote infiltration, even during high rainfall and stream-flooding events;
- An evaluation to ensure no impacts to threatened and endangered species, wetlands, and cultural resources
- An evaluation of soils for on-lot septic management and landscaping purposes to ascertain the best location for infiltration fields (in this instance, the "best" location was 2,500 feet away and up a 600-foot slope!)

- Evaluation of the site soils for the design of a grass-paved parking lot to further minimize stormwater runoff

- Evaluation and design of pervious paving around the building for its walks and plazas (the only "impervious" concrete paved areas were for the handicapped parking spaces)

- Design for the modernization and treatment of the potable water supply well

- Design of a unique drip irrigation wastewater treatment system on steep, poorly drained soils with high seasonal water table (up that hillside)

- Design for the treatment of wastewater by a greenhouse-based "Marsh Machine" wetland treatment system

The owners were very pleased to have so many different sustainable design elements, and incorporated almost all of them as education exhibits. Signage and plaques denote the unique use of the sustainable design features, how they work, and how they improve or help the environment. Perhaps the most unique is an exhibit using water from the waste-water treatment system to house fish and other aquatic life. Signage explains how water from the bathrooms is treated and cleaned so that wildlife can use the same water.

A prominent local university had designed a solar, sustainable design house as part of a national competition. The nature reserve facility was so successful that the university's house was relocated from the university campus to an area next to the nature center's grass parking lot as a permanent additional exhibit.

---

the responsible team member will need to list and describe the pollutant removal capabilities for each strategy. Annual rainfall treatment calculations will determine the success of the proposed solutions.

- Project teams are encouraged to analyze the costs associated with the proposed stormwater management strategies to ensure alignment with the budget.

- The responsible party will also need to develop a stormwater management plan including the best management practices to be followed on-site and how they capture and treat stormwater runoff.

- *For LEED CI Projects:* As detailed in Chapter 4, compliancy with this credit (under SS Credit 1: Option 2, Path 3) should be evaluated prior to signing a lease. Should modifications be needed to comply, the lease should include these provisions. If this determination was not addressed prior to signing the lease, the team should engage in a conversation with the building owner, base building civil engineer, or facility manager to evaluate applicability and compliance and to determine if the site design needs to be modified.

SS Credit 7.1: Heat Island Effect—Nonroof

- Although this credit is not eligible for a design-side review, the project team will need to determine the combination of strategies if at least 50 percent of the parking is not placed under cover during the design phase. Coordination between the civil engineer, landscape architect, and architect will help to ensure compliance with credit and minimize the hardscape areas on-site. Remember, this credit can align with SS Credit 6.1 to recharge the groundwater supplies, if open-grid paving is incorporated into the solution. It is easiest to comply if hardscape areas are limited.

LANDSCAPE ARCHITECT'S PERSPECTIVE
Use 3D Modeling Tools for a Quick and Accurate Measurement of Tree Shading

By Aiman Duckworth, ASLA, LEED AP
Landscape Designer and Associate at AECOM

Calculations for the SS credit to reduce nonroof heat island effect can include contribution from tree shading at five years after construction. Although the LEED reference guides do not provide a recommended or required method for determining this square footage, 3D computer modeling programs provide new tools for designers to measure tree shade. Geographic location, date, and time are common features for rendering shadows in most 3D modeling programs.

Before going through this exercise, the real contribution of tree shading as calculated for LEED credits may be a mystery. After a few studies, tree shade can be part of a designer's visual estimating skills, and not a complex calculation.

1. Determine the dimensions of a typical shade tree at the required time from installation as required by the rating system credit. Typical dimensions of newly installed trees can be identified from field observations and nursery standards. Typical dimensions of the tree at a specific year after installation can be referenced from field observations, tree height, and canopy growth data, or interpolated based on a combination of information. Tree survey information can be used for existing trees.

2. Create a simple 3D model of the typical shade tree at the required year from installation in a 3D modeling program, such as Google SketchUp.

3. Insert the design linework into the 3D modeling program. Input topography if it will have a measurable impact on shaded area calculations.

4. Replace tree locations with the 3D model trees. Turn on shadows for the project's specific geographic location.

5. Repeat modeling and tree insertion for other major tree types.

6. Input the three times on the summer solstice date required by LEED calculations and create exports of each.

7. Use a computer-aided design (CAD) program to create a shade take-off on paving surfaces.

8. For reference in rough estimates, create some typical CAD blocks or typical shade square foot measurements per tree. A useful "back pocket" piece of data might be: in a particular region, a typical oak tree, south of paving, within six feet of paving edge will contribute an average of X square feet of shading.

This exercise can yield surprising results and has value for study even outside of LEED systems. Newly planted trees provide real shade with real-world dimensions. However, as calculated through the LEED rating system, shade is measured early in a tree's life cycle, and on the summer solstice—the time of year when a tree will provide the least shade. In many project layouts, strategies other than tree shading of paving are necessary to achieve the LEED credit. Based on typical dimensions, surface parking paved with black asphalt creates a particularly difficult hurdle for new trees alone to shade. With respect to nonroof heat island calculations, as with many other factors, existing trees provide a resource early in a project's life span that cannot be matched by small new transplants.

- Calculations will need to be completed to ensure that the requirements for compliancy have been met. The responsible party is encouraged to read the landscape architect's perspective on the previous page for some tips on calculating tree shading. Bear in mind that the shading from the building itself cannot be used in the calculations, but the shade from balconies, photovoltaic systems, and terraces can be included.

- The responsible team member will need to upload a site plan to LEED-Online, with the nonroof hardscape areas and strategies for compliancy properly labeled. If 50 percent or more of the parking will be undercover, a site plan should be uploaded showing the parking capacity and locations, as well as the SRI value of the parking area roof.

- *For LEED CI Projects:* As detailed in Chapter 4, compliancy with this credit (under SS Credit 1, Option 2, Path 4) should be evaluated prior to signing a lease. Should modifications be needed to comply, the lease should include these provisions. Some teams have found it more cost effective to shade the existing noncompliant hardscape areas as compared to replacing with a compliant material. If this determination was not addressed prior to signing the lease, the team should engage in a conversation with the building owner, base building civil engineer or architect, or facility manager to evaluate applicability and compliance and to determine if the site design needs to be modified.

SS Credit 7.2: Heat Island Effect—Roof

- Project teams should have determined this compliance path at the goal-setting meeting, as it could involve the implementation of a green roof. If the team is pursuing Option 1 and a green roof will not be installed, the architect will need to ensure the proper specification for the roofing material for SRI value based on the slope of the roof, as detailed in the LEED reference guides.

- Project teams are encouraged to research rebate opportunities for installing ENERGY STAR® or qualified roof products. Teams should refer to www.energystar.gov/index.cfm?fuseaction=find_a_product.showProductGroup&pgw_code=RO to determine qualifying products. The reference guide also has a listing of roofing products and the associated SRI value.

- The architect will need to provide a roof plan with the total applicable area calculated and associated slope(s). This applicable area does not need to include any mechanical equipment, photovoltaic panels, or any penetrations in the roof, such as skylights. The architect should also provide documentation of the roofing material(s), the emittance percentages, reflectance percentages, and SRI value(s).

- *For LEED CI Projects:* As detailed in Chapter 4, compliancy with this credit (under SS Credit 1, Option 2, Path 5) should be evaluated prior to signing a lease. Should modifications be needed to comply, the lease should include these provisions. If this determination was not addressed prior to signing the lease, the team should engage in a conversation with the building owner, base building architect, or facility manager to determine current compliance or if the roof needs replacement to capitalize on this opportunity and install roofing materials with high SRI values.

Project teams pursuing SS Credits 5.1, 5.2, and/or 7.2 need to address strategies to reduce the possibility of bird collisions with adjacent structures and glazed buildings. These strategies can include exterior shading devices, incorporating patterns within the glazing, and implementing visual markers such as differenti-ated materials, textures, colors, and opacity.

SS Credit 8: Light Pollution Reduction

- *Interior Lighting:* Project teams have the option to either have the nonemergency light fixtures auto-matically controlled or to provide shading devices for all exterior openings. If automatic controls are implemented, the responsible team member will need to upload the drawings showing the locations of the controls. If shading devices are installed, drawings are required showing the locations of the shading devices, how they are assembled, and that they are able to block at least 90 percent of the light. If the shading devices are automatically con-trolled, the sequence for operations or the building operation plan will need to be uploaded to LEED-Online.

- *Exterior Lighting (for LEED NC and CS projects):* Project teams will need to determine the lighting power density (LPD) for each application in order to establish the total power density for the pro-ject. They will then need to compare the LPD to ASHRAE 90.1–2007 to ensure that the project is in compliance (Figure 6.6).

- The lighting designer will then need to determine the lighting zone to determine the strategies to address the light distribution for precurfew and postcurfew conditions. The lighting zone is typi-cally determined by the population or density of an area. Project teams are encouraged to use the current U.S. Census data to support determination of the lighting zone, such as www.citydata.com.

It is important to determine the amount of time the light fixtures are operated to coordinate the energy consumption with the energy model for EA Credit 1, should the team pursue a performance based compli-ance path for energy performance. Projects with zero lot lines and/or minimal open space may find it chal-lenging to meet the requirements of this credit due to the maximum 0.1 footcandle at the site boundary.

- It is encouraged to engage a lighting professional to determine the appropriate solutions to comply with this credit, including the selection of the light equipment. This professional will need to coordi-nate with the electrical engineer, the architect, the civil engineer, and the landscape architect to verify locations and compliance of fixtures. A computer model is suggested to simulate the illuminance values and vertical light levels. Some lighting firms use a software called AGI32 from Lighting Ana-lysts, Inc., while those without much experience might look to the free lighting calculation software, Visual, at www.visual-3d.com. Project teams can also refer to www.darksky.org for a listing of manu-facturers and their approved fixtures to help com-ply with the requirements of this credit.

- These fixtures and controls will not only need to be included in the basis of design (BOD), but in the commissioning (Cx) activities as well.

- *For LEED CS Projects:* This credit applies to areas that are a part of the core and shell development, such as lobby and core circulation locations. Tenant spaces do not need to be included if no light fixtures will be supplied in those areas as part of the base building scope of work included in the LEED project boundary.

- *For LEED CI Projects:* As detailed in Chapter 4, compliancy with this credit (under SS Credit 1, Option 2, Path 6) should be evaluated prior to signing a lease. Should modifications be needed

Figure 6–6 The Utah Botanical Center's Wetland Discovery Point building at Utah State University in Kaysville was mindful of the nocturnal environment in which the center resides by providing very minimal exterior lighting and shielding any fixtures that would pollute the night sky. Photo courtesy of Gary Neuenswander, Utah Agricultural Experiment Station.

to comply, the lease should include these provisions. If this determination was not addressed prior to signing the lease, the team should engage in a conversation with the building owner, base building architect, or facility manager to determine current compliance for the interior space other than the tenant space and for the exterior lighting. If so, project teams should then continue compliant strategies within the tenant space and follow the documentation requirements listed above for automatic controls and/or automatic shading devices.

SS Credit 9: Tenant Design and Construction Guidelines (for LEED CS projects)

- The collective project team will need to prepare this document for future tenants to refer to for design and construction building specific best practices encouraging the incorporation of green building strategies. It is a good idea to collaborate with the developer's

LIGHTING DESIGNER'S PERSPECTIVE
The Role of a Lighting Designer on a Project Seeking LEED Certification

Faith E. Baum, IALD, LC, IES, LEED AP
Illumination Arts

A lighting designer should be included in the collaborative LEED effort from the outset of the design process. This ensures that the design team is aware of any potential lighting strategies that might impact other design choices or that can be addressed and implemented during the early design phases. It also allows the team to discuss possible adaptations in traditional mind-set about the lighting of the space. For example, reducing ambient light levels and adding supplemental task lighting may be a paradigmatic change for a company, but one that offers many benefits. From an aesthetic or architectural standpoint, it is a more holistic solution, making the space more visually interesting for occupants and visitors. From a functional standpoint, occupants have control over how much light they have on their task, making each person an active player in the lighting of their space. From an energy standpoint, this results in an overall reduction in energy consumption, realizing savings in operational costs and reducing the carbon footprint of the facility.

As far as LEED credits are concerned, the lighting designer has a limited but powerful area in which they can have an impact. The LEED for Commercial Interiors rating system offers up to nine points specific to lighting-related credits in the Sustainable Sites, Energy and Atmosphere, and Indoor Environmental Quality categories.

SS Credit 1 Option 2, Path 6: Light Pollution Reduction, provides two ways in which interior lighting can be controlled to satisfy this credit, either by reducing input power by at least 50 percent after regular business hours or by shielding the exterior openings of the building between 11 ~PM and 5 ~AM. Unfortunately, this is a building-wide requirement, making it difficult to achieve unless the building itself is trying to earn this credit or the tenant has control over the entire building.

> **SS Credit 1 Case Study:** The National Audubon Society intentionally sought out a building owner with a commitment to sustainability that matched theirs. However, achieving this credit was not feasible because of the number of tenants already in the building.

EA Credit 1.1: Optimize Energy Performance—Lighting Power can earn the project up to five points. After meeting the prerequisite of reducing connected LPD by 10 percent below ASHRAE 90.1–2007 (or local code, whichever is more stringent), every 5 percent reduction earns a point, up to 35 percent. Careful consideration of light levels, placement of lighting, lamp/ballast combinations and the use of task lighting can help the lighting designer achieve points on even the most challenging of projects.

> **EA Credit 1.1 Case Study:** At the Rockefeller Brothers Fund headquarters in New York, ambient light levels of 20–25fc were supplemented with decorative wallwashers between punched windows and task lights under cabinets and on desks, reducing the LPD by more than 25 percent and earning the project three points (Figure 6.7).

Figure 6.7. The lighting strategies at the Rockefeller Brothers Fund interior space in New York designed by Illumination Arts and FXFOWLE Architects include decorative wallwashers between the windows and task lights at each desk. This lighting strategy was able to reduce the LPD by more than 25 percent and earned the project three LEED points. Photo courtesy of FXFOWLE Architects and Eric Laignel.

EA Credit 1.2: Optimize Energy Performance—Lighting Controls allows for up to three points for daylight controls and occupancy sensors.

- Point 1: Installing daylight responsive controls in regularly occupied spaces within 15 feet of windows and skylights can be achieved in a variety of ways, some more costly than others. Typically, dimming ballasts are preferred to avoid the distraction of the lighting switching on and off, but step-dimming ballasts are a less expensive option that may have a faster return without creating that distraction. Sensors should be selected and located carefully to avoid light-level readings that are not relevant to the usable daylight in the space. Communication with the tenant about the effect of the daylight harvesting should be clear in advance to avoid surprises.

continued

EA Credit 1.2 Case Study: With the Rockefeller Brothers Fund project, linear direct/indirect luminaires near the windows were controlled with daylight sensors integral to the luminaires. In order for the light levels to be kept constant on the work surface, the light levels on the ceiling above each luminaire varied, depending upon the relationship between the luminaire, the windows, and the desk surfaces. From the perspective of daylight control, this was exactly as it should be, but it was important that the team understood the visual impact.

- Point 2: Installing daylight controls for 50 percent of the overall lighting load would work well in a building with a small floor plate or with skylights in the area beyond the 15-foot perimeter.
- Point 3: Occupancy Sensor control for 75 percent of the connected load can be achieved through a sophisticated system in open office areas and nonregularly occupied areas in addition to those required by code in enclosed spaces. For projects that consist largely of individually occupied spaces with full-height walls, this credit should be fairly simple to achieve, since occupancy sensors are required in these spaces by ASHRAE.

Indoor Environmental Quality (EQ) Credit 6.1: Controllability of Systems—Lighting has requirements for individual and group needs, both of which need to be met to earn the point. Individual lighting controls for 90 percent of the occupants is a natural task/ambient lighting solution. Under-cabinet lighting or desk-mounted task lights can achieve this, and with a manual switch to turn those lights on and an automatic shutoff to turn them off, the maximum energy savings will be realized. In multioccupant spaces, dimming can be used to adjust the lighting to meet group needs and preferences.

EQ Credit 6.1 Case Study: A simple downlight and wallwasher lighting solution was provided in the conference rooms at the National Audubon Society project (Figure 6.8). Both were separately controlled by dimmers, allowing the occupants to adjust the lighting to fit their needs and the task at hand.

EQ Credit 8.1: Daylight and Views—Daylight is not typically a credit over which the lighting consultant has much control, particularly for an interiors project. However, the designer can evaluate the available daylight and make recommendations about daylight harvesting and other ways in which daylight can be used to conserve energy and provide a comfortable working environment. Glare control should be considered as carefully as daylight harvesting in order to make the most of this "free" source of illumination.

EQ Credit 8.1 Case Study: The windows at the Rockefeller Brothers Fund site appeared to the interior designers to be too deeply recessed to provide adequate daylight to consider a daylight harvesting system. A visit by the lighting designer to the site found that the daylight penetrated the space sufficiently to justify such a system, saving the owner energy and earning one point under EA Credit1.2. Solar shades were recommended and implemented to ensure that direct sunlight and glare could be minimized and controlled.

Participation by a lighting consultant in LEED NC projects is more challenging, but offers similar efficiency and occupant controllability benefits. However, significant differences occur in the requirements to comply with the Light Pollution Reduction and Energy Optimization credits, as compared to the approach for LEED CI projects.

SSc8: Light Pollution Reduction has requirements regarding both interior and exterior lighting (where a CI project is required to address only the interior lighting. While the interior choices are similar to those in detailed in the LEED CI rating system, the

Figure 6.8. The lighting design at the National Audubon Society project in New York designed by Illumination Arts and FXFOWLE Architects includes simple downlights and wallwashers in the conference rooms where both were separately controlled by dimmers, thus allowing the occupants to adjust the lighting to fit their needs and the task at hand. These types of strategies helped to earn the project its LEED CI Platinum level certification. Photo courtesy of FXFOWLE Architects and David Sundberg/Esto.

exterior lighting requirements include specific allowances for the amount of light permitted at site boundaries and emitted at angles above nadir. These allowances are based on the type of "lighting zone" in which the site is located. A holistic approach to the site lighting is critical, with the location and selection of luminaires being key to meeting the requirements of this credit.

EAc1: Optimize Energy Performance refers to all sources of energy consumption, not just lighting, unlike the LEED CI rating system. While the lighting is not evaluated as a separate entity as it is for a CI project, reductions in connected lighting loads or LPD can reduce heating, ventilating, and air-conditioning (HVAC) requirements and help NC projects earn points toward this credit. With 19 points available, this credit has the largest opportunity to affect the desired certification level for a project. The lighting consultant can play a significant role in the collaboration with the owner and the design team, working together to achieve a common goal.

marketing department, as they may need the guidelines to attract future tenants. Start with an outline and expand from there; examples and benefits will help! Be sure to include references to the LEED for Commercial Interiors rating system and how the base building can help comply for tenants. Remember, these are required only to be guidelines for the tenants; it is up to the developer/owner to take it to next level and *require* tenants to comply.

The guidelines will need to address water use reduction; optimize energy performance for lighting power, lighting controls, and HVAC; energy use and metering, including measurement and verification, ventilation and outdoor air delivery, construction indoor air quality (IAQ) management, indoor chemical and pollutant source control, controllability of systems, thermal comfort, daylighting and views and commissioning; elimination or control of environmental tobacco smoke; and recommendations for and examples of sustainable strategies, products, materials, and services. When developing the guidelines, it might be helpful to think about the building standards and any information a tenant might need to be aware of for improvements. It is encouraged for the guidelines to supplement future lease agreements.

Water Efficiency

The WE credits and prerequisites that are typically addressed during these two phases of design include:

WE Prerequisite 1: Water Use Reduction (also LEED CI WE Credit 1 and LEED NC and CS Credit 3)

- Project teams will need to determine the full-time equivalent (FTE) number of occupants and transient occupants (reported as daily totals or FTE) to determine the baseline and design case water

consumption and therefore water savings. If the project includes a residential component, "the number of residents should be estimated based on the number and size of units in the project."[1] LEED-Online will assist with completing the usage calculations based on occupancy types. LEED CS projects may need to consult Appendix 1 in the BD+C reference guide for default occupancy counts. LEED-Online will help to ensure that these calculations are consistent for related credits.

- Water use and technologies shall be included in commissioning activities and therefore included in the project's measurement and verification plan. Calibration is required for projects that incorporate automatic sensors or flow valves.[2]

- Project teams are encouraged to refer to WaterSense to locate water-efficient products and programs. The owner, architect, and plumbing engineer should determine a strategy based on the project goals, which may include capturing rainwater to use for flushing. The responsible party (typically the mechanical/plumbing engineer) is required to specify efficient fixtures, fittings, and metering controls and complete the baseline and design case calculations to determine water savings. The responsible party will also need to upload the product data sheets listing the consumption rates, manufacturer, and model for each fixture and fitting. Water-efficient appliances and equipment, such as dishwashers, are not included in these calculations, but could be included in the calculations for teams pursuing exemplary performance.

- *For LEED CI Projects:* Project teams should have evaluated compliance prior to lease signing. If the tenant improvement project scope does not include restrooms, project teams will need to look at common areas of the base building to determine usage

LANDSCAPE ARCHITECT'S PERSPECTIVE
Educate Yourself, the Contractor, the Owner, and Landscape Maintenance Staff about the Project's Planting and Irrigation Approach

By Aiman Duckworth, ASLA, LEED AP
Landscape Designer and Associate at AECOM

Native plant palettes, meadows, reforestation, and planting without permanent irrigation have been established as standard components in a landscape architect's sustainable design and LEED project toolkit for benefits such as habitat creation, water use reduction, and improved water quality. Members of the project team, including the landscape architect, can be unfamiliar with the specifics of design, implementation, and maintenance of these landscape approaches. Even with mastery of the technical aspects of these landscape types, there are often complex cultural and aesthetic considerations beyond the requirements to achieve LEED credits.

A conceptually simple approach, such as planting native grasses and wildflowers instead of irrigated turfgrass, can make a strong contribution to achieving sustainability and LEED goals. Yet notions about "landscape" or "park" or "campus" can often include expanses of well-groomed and irrigated lawn or an invasive evergreen groundplane.

Clear communication with the owner, strong planting design, and thorough attention to installation and maintenance are keys to success when goals are for a habitat-focused and low-water-demand landscape. Take elements of surprise out of the design for the owner and stakeholders by developing a shared verbal and visual language for the project. Consider the following questions:

- What are the expectations for the landscape appearance through the seasons? Do these expectations differ among owner, resident, and visitor?
- How might sustainability or LEED goals influence the landscape's appearance?
- Is the owner familiar with landscapes similar to those proposed for the project? Should the design team tour some examples?
- What will a meadow, low-water-demand lawn species, rain garden, or reforestation look like at installation and until it matures? What will it look like through the seasons?
- Is a phased plant installation after the first growing season warranted?
- Could annuals or biennials be used for interest early in the landscape life cycle until perennial plants mature?
- What are the opportunities for visual interest other than mimicking "naturally occurring" successional landscapes?
- Is lawn more historically or programmatically appropriate than a native groundcover for all or portions of the project?
- If lawn is appropriate or desired, can it be concentrated in the most suitable and useful areas?
- Are there opportunities for low-water-demand lawn species and maintenance methods that reduce or eliminate fossil fuel use, chemical fertilizer, pesticides, and potable water use?

continued

The seasonal appearance of specific plant species in person can be difficult to fully represent and can push the limits of a typical plant photo board presentation. Collect time-lapse photos of meadows and other landscape types from installation to maturity, not just final marketing photos of landscapes in full bloom. These references provide a valuable tool that can keep a nonpermanent irrigation approach from being rejected early in design, or a meadow-in-waiting from being mown out of existence before establishment.

Also, remember the contractor and the maintenance crew. A naturalized landscape or preserved woodland does not mean "no maintenance." Even native and drought-tolerant species need attention for healthy establishment. Construction by definition creates disturbance, and new ecosystems in particular will react dynamically over time. The following questions can assist the process:

- Is the maintenance contractor familiar with the project's planting and irrigation approach?
- Is identification and responsible removal of invasive species part of the maintenance contract?
- Are there clear references of boundaries for different landscape maintenance zones?
- Are visual cues (such as edging, signs, grading) or physical barriers needed to protect young meadow shoots or tree saplings from mowers?
- What method of irrigation will be used in the establishment period for projects without permanent irrigation?
- What responsibilities do the contractor, owner, and maintenance staff take on for a temporary system that may be different than for a permanent system?
- Are resources available to operate a temporary system? If the owner thinks so, does the maintenance staff agree?
- Should a maintenance manual be included as part of the designer's services for the project?

Many recommendations for landscapes with sustainability and LEED goals fall under the category of good design. As intended by the rating systems, LEED certification goals can move the project team into slightly unfamiliar and more sustainable territory. Both landscape fundamentals and innovative approaches can guide the project to a successful outcome.

---

and consumption. Project teams are encouraged to collaborate with the building engineer/facility manager and owner to establish where water consumption is highest to assess potential options to reduce consumption and evaluate the impacts of each option. These options could include flow restrictors and reduced flow aerators on fixtures (where appropriate), faucet sensors and metering controls, and low-flow flush or waterless fixtures.

The responsible party (typically the plumbing engineer) is required to specify efficient fixtures, fittings, and/or metering controls and complete the baseline and design case calculations on LEED-Online to determine water savings and prove compliance with this prerequisite. The responsible party will also need to upload the product data sheets listing the consumption rates, manufacturer, and model for each fixture and fitting.

WE Credit 1: Water-Efficient Landscaping (LEED CI SS Credit 1, Option 2, Paths 7 and 8)

- Collaboration among the architect, mechanical engineer, landscape architect, and civil engineer is encouraged to determine the strategy once the project team determines the feasibility and goals. Owners and maintenance staff should be included in discussions to address their preferences, how the property will be used, and for maintenance considerations. Depending on the project's site and region, reduction strategies could include the combination of addressing native and adaptive plant species, density, and microclimate factors; high-efficiency irrigation systems; collecting rainwater; on-site or municipally supplied treated wastewater; and using nonpotable water delivered from the local municipality. "Groundwater seepage that is pumped away from the immediate vicinity of building slabs and foundations may be used for landscape irrigation to meet the intent of this credit."[3]

- Project teams are encouraged to create a site plan to include the "existing or planned structures, topography, orientation, sun and wind exposure, use of space, and existing vegetation."[4] This will help to conduct seasonal shadow studies of the vegetated areas to determine the best-suited plant species and the water use zones based on need. Soil studies should also be conducted to assess adjustments as necessary. Credit synergy strategies to align with SS Credit 7.1 should include shading of impervious areas. Remember, installing or using an existing well that collects groundwater to be used for irrigation does *not* meet the intentions of this credit. Although there are restrictions for the use of stormwater for indoor uses, there are not as many restrictions for reusing stormwater for exterior uses, such as irrigation. Teams are encouraged to research the restrictions to be aware of the opportunities for strategies available to pursue.

- The responsible party, typically the architect or landscape architect, will be required to complete the calculations to determine the potable water use reductions. They will need to determine a baseline water use rate for the project, as well as a design case water use rate, based on the proposed strategies for irrigation during the month of July. The responsible party will need to determine the major vegetated types included within the project and complete the water usage calculations for each using Table 1: Landscape Factors in the BD+C reference guide. These calculations are based on the landscape coefficient, species factor, density factor, and the microclimate factor for the vegetated areas included within the LEED boundary line. Remember, this boundary line must be consistent across all credits. Next, the declarant will need to determine the reference evapotranspiration rate as determined by the region, calculate the project-specific evapotranspiration rate, and then determine the irrigation efficiency using Table 2: Irrigation Types and Efficiencies from the reference guide. To complete the baseline case usage or total water applied (TWA), the responsible party will use the species factor, the density factor, and the irrigation efficiency. To complete the design case, the declarant will use the same microclimate factor and reference evapotranspiration rate and then will also need to include the controller efficiency, if moisture sensor–based systems are proposed, and/or the volume of reused water if collected rainwater, treated wastewater, or municipally supplied nonpotable water is to be used for irrigation needs.

- If your project site does not include any landscape plantings, the project may still be eligible. If the site vegetation is limited to planters and smaller garden areas and the square footage area for these areas is equal to at least 5 percent of the total site area, the project team can still pursue this credit.

- Once the calculations are completed to demonstrate reduction compliance, the responsible party will then need to compile a plan specifying the vegetation and irrigation system (if applicable) to be implemented. If an irrigation or rainwater capture system is to be implemented, product data including manufacturer and model numbers, should be collected and uploaded to LEED-Online.

- Project teams are encouraged to seek incentives, rebates, or grants available for installing high-efficiency irrigation systems and controls.

- *For LEED CI Projects:* Project teams should have evaluated compliance prior to lease signing. If the site does not comply, is the owner willing to install a rainwater-capturing system to use for irrigation? Is the owner interested in upgrading the irrigation system? What are the options to comply? What types of vegetation exist, and how much water do they require?

WE Credit 2: Innovative Wastewater Technologies (CI SS Credit 1, Option 2, Path 9)

- *For LEED NC and CS Projects:* As compared to this category's prerequisite, this credit refers to the amount of water leaving the site from flush fixtures to then be treated by the local municipality, therefore encouraging the implementation of efficient fixtures requiring less or no water to convey sewage. Collaboration among the architect, engineer, and owner is encouraged to determine the project goals, feasibility, and strategy. Project teams are encouraged to research local codes and laws for applicability and compliance regulations. A water

budget needs to be established for the assumed water consumption for end uses of nonpotable water in order to evaluate how other systems might be impacted and other trade-offs due to the proposed reduction strategies. Teams will need to decipher between the two compliance path options focusing on flush fixtures or treating the wastewater on site. Wastewater treatment typically requires a large amount of space and therefore is better suited for campus projects.

- In addition to selecting the appropriate flush fixtures, teams should also research opportunities for collected rainwater and stormwater, the supply of nonpotable water from municipalities (sometimes referred to as a purple pipe system), "treated and untreated greywater, and treated black water as sources of supply."[5] Teams should compare different systems as related to cost and environmental impacts of on-site treatment versus off-site supply. Teams should also evaluate the use of collected stormwater for this credit and for the previous credit that addresses irrigation needs, to determine which credit is more applicable and aligns with the project budget.

- During schematic design, the project team should determine the area required for treating wastewater on-site and a location for rainwater collection, if applicable.

- Once a strategy has been determined, the responsible party will need to design the treatment system and perform calculations to ensure compliance. Just as with the prerequisite, baseline and design case calculations will need to be determined based on occupancy. The baseline case used for the prerequisite will be used to show consumption for this credit as well. The baseline case is calculated by "totaling the annual volume of each fixture

ARCHITECT'S PERSPECTIVE
Mechanical and Architectural Coordination for Energy Efficiency

By Nathan Ogle, AIA, LEED AP
FFA

Figure 6.9. Villa Montgomery Apartments, a remediation project in Redwood City, California, by Fisher-Friedman Associates, earned LEED Gold certification under the LEED for NC rating system, for pursuing multiple Energy and Atmosphere credits including Optimize Energy Performance. Photo courtesy of FFA.

Villa Montgomery, a LEED Gold certified project, is a 58-unit building consisting of four stories of residential units and a landscaped courtyard above a podium with a management office, common room, retail space, and two levels of parking (Figure 6.9). The apartments are intended for low-income families and will carry long-term affordability restrictions, making

continued

them affordable to households earning from 20 to 50 percent of the area's medium income. The building is on an urban brownfield site, located on a major traffic artery in an area zoned for general commercial use, adjacent to a medium-density residential neighborhood and less than half a mile from the downtown district.

We began the design of this project with one goal in mind: energy efficiency and improving the efficiency of the total MEP system. Methods for doing this involved careful evaluation of individual mechanical components, waste reduction, peak demand analysis, usage of renewable energy systems, whole building analysis (e.g., daylighting, glazing, heating and cooling, thermal mass, natural ventilation, and programmable controls), and most importantly, understanding of the long-term life-cycle economics of the building systems.

The building employs a high-performance envelope, including a cool roof, insulated windows with low-E glass, and formaldehyde-free fiberglass insulation. The building's mechanical system is an innovative design with individual parts of the building heated and cooled by water source heat pumps, fed by a hydronic loop with efficient evaporative cooling integrated with the mechanical exhaust that is required for the garage.

The interrelationships of these strategies are complex, and careful analysis of their effects on one another is required to determine the best combination of the various choices available. Note that most of the preceding methods require close collaboration among the architect, the MEP engineers and the owners.

It is important to incorporate these considerations early, as changes are easier to accommodate in the onset stages, whereas changes to design, drawings, specifications, and compliance calculations are difficult to make later. It is possible for the mechanical designer to estimate the various relevant loads and climatic effects with reasonable accuracy with only the most basic information about the proposed building.

Also, it is very important to follow through after construction for commissioning, management, and maintenance. Measurement and verification of system performance is key to improvement in future design work, and the political value of a high-efficiency building is only increased by the existence of a data set that illustrates the systems are performing as efficiently as intended.

---

type and subtracting any nonpotable water supply."[6] The architect or plumbing engineer will also need to gather fixture and fitting data, including the manufacturer, consumption rates, and model numbers to upload to LEED-Online.

Energy and Atmosphere

The EA prerequisites and credits that are typically addressed during these two phases of design include:

EA Prerequisite 1: Fundamental Commissioning, and EA Credit 3: Enhanced Commissioning (LEED CI EA Credit 2: Enhanced Commissioning)

- For quality-control purposes, it is recommended to include a commissioning authority (CxA) as soon as possible, if not already, and satisfy Step 1 of the Cx process (as presented in Chapter 3). As stated earlier, it is beneficial to have the CxA attend the goal-setting meeting to have their input on the feasibility of goals

COMMISSIONING AGENT'S PERSPECTIVE
The Benefits of a Commissioning Agent

By Brian Fronapfel, PE, CEM, CBCP, LEED AP
ENERACTIVE Solutions

ENERACTIVE Solutions provided LEED commissioning services for the tenant fit-out of a commercial office building's first-floor area in Parsippany, New Jersey. The space was being renovated to serve as corporate administrative offices, encompassing approximately 12,800 square feet of floor area for use as general office space with user amenities including conference rooms, a kitchenette pantry, a staff lounge, and computer support rooms. The commissioning scope focused on the LEED elements of the energy systems, which were comprised of a network of terminal variable-air-volume boxes (fan powered with electric heat along the perimeter zones) providing ventilation and space conditioning through the adjustment of air supplied from a central core-and-shell air-handling unit. An individual Liebert split system conditioned the central server room, and lighting controls offered reduced energy consumption through the use of occupancy sensors in private offices, time-clock interfaces in common areas, and more advanced daylighting controls along all perimeter zones. The project was designed to, and certified as, a LEED Commercial Interiors project at the "Silver" level.

Our approach in this project, as with any successful commissioning project, held project team communication as paramount for an end result that would address all of the owner's concerns for timely, reliable, and efficient operation of the facility. In conducting the equipment testing as part of the construction phase, it became apparent that the pneumatic controls on the variable-air-volume terminal boxes were inadequate to provide proper operation. Numerous control boxes were only partially connected to the system, locations with bad pneumatic regulators and/or pneumatic-electric switches were identified, end caps were noted to be missing, and, in some locations, improper tubing was used, resulting in cracked end connections where the lines fell off the equipment within weeks after installation. In addition, several leaks were identified, where a large amount of control air was continuously draining from the system, reducing the line pressure below the minimum level required for proper unit operation. Through an approach of continual "punch list" generation and continual, collegial communication at regular construction meetings, the mechanical contractor was immediately and continuously notified of the conditions that needed rectification. As a result, a pneumatic technician was brought in to address all the issues and, after field verification by ENERACTIVE, the issues were marked as "closed" on the punch list and the systems operated as intended, with no impact to schedule, quality, or cost.

---

and determine the systems to be commissioned. The systems to be commissioned do not change from fundamental to enhanced Cx, but the team could be eligible for exemplary performance if the scope is expanded to include the envelope, water reuse systems, and/or fire suppression systems.

Teams are encouraged to refer to the National Institute of Building Sciences (NIBS) website (www.wbdg.org/ccb/NIBS/nibs_gl3.pdf) for information about commissioning exterior enclosures. During schematic design, the CxA can start the process of helping the owner to generate the owner's program requirements (OPR) and develop a Cx plan during design development to be updated during the project.

- The CxA may also be able to help the team research incentives available for constructing an energy-efficient building, helping the return on investment for the owner beyond the Cx scope by reducing change orders and improving the performance of the energy-related systems.

The Owner's Project Requirements (OPR)

Remember from the previous chapters that the goal of the eco-charette is to complete a LEED scorecard to ensure that the intentions of each of the prerequisites can be met and to summarize which credits are likely to be obtained and therefore will be pursued. After the eco-charette, the LEED coordinator should encourage the owner and the CxA to meet and develop the OPR to begin Step 2 of the Cx process. The LEED coordinator may sometimes be asked to supply a sample report or a questionnaire for the owner to complete to assist with the process. A questionnaire should be created, based on the following sections and topics of the report. With the completed LEED scorecard and the owner's responses to the OPR questionnaire from the CxA, the OPR is prepared and then distributed to the design team. Project teams are encouraged to refer to Appendix E to see a template for an OPR. The report should be broken down into the following sections to detail the intentions of the project:

1. General Requirements
   a. Include location and applicable codes

2. Owner and User Requirements

   a. Include the primary purpose, use, and intended size of the project.
   b. Include any pertinent history and future expansion or flexibility goals.
   c. Include the types of spaces to be included in the program.
   d. Include the construction and operation desired costs.

3. Environment and Sustainability Goals
   a. Include the LEED certification level desired.
   b. Include the LEED prerequisites to be addressed and the credits to be pursued.

4. Energy-Efficiency Goals
   a. Include the desired level of savings relative to ASHRAE 90.1–2007 or local energy code, whichever is more stringent.
   b. Include the level of commissioning.
   c. Include any preferred features, equipment, materials, or systems to be included.

5. Indoor Environmental Quality Requirements
   a. Include the operation and building usage, including occupancy schedules.
   b. Include the ventilation and thermal comfort goals, including temperature and humidity.
   c. Include IAQ strategies to be addressed, such as low-emitting products.
   d. Include occupant comfort and productivity strategies, such as controllability and acoustics.

6. Equipment and System Expectations
   a. Include budgetary and life expectancy goals
   b. Include any manufacturer, quality, or equipment preferences, including maintenance.

7. Building Occupant and Operations and Maintenance (O&M) Personnel Requirements

MEP ENGINEER'S PERSPECTIVE
The Benefits of the OPR and BOD

Kent D. Hoffman, PE, LEED AP
Principal at Schlenger/Pitz and Associates, Inc.

Since LEED certification is an integrative process, it is understood that the mechanical, electrical and plumbing design and construction components are affected, but to what extent? The LEED certification process not only directly impacts the efficiency and long-term costs associated with MEP systems, but the nature of the certification process itself enhances the ability of an MEP firm to provide its client with a higher quality of service.

One example of this positive impact is the development of the OPR and the BOD. When we began work on our first LEED project in 2003, much of what we learned was by trial and error. We initially treated the OPR and BOD as two items on a checklist that needed to be completed at some point before we could submit our documentation to USGBC for review. What we discovered over time is that, if we approach the *process* as intended by LEED, where the OPR and BOD are prepared, reviewed, and finalized in the initial stages of the project, the design process was actually made more effective for our client and was more efficient for the design team as well by eliminating erroneous assumptions on both sides.

I have found that the majority of "glitches" on projects are due to a lack of communication, rather than an error in computation. Most engineers have the ability to effectively solve technical challenges and problems, but we often fail to take the time to fully understand the owner's needs as they pertain to the building systems. We also may overlook the importance of adequately communicating our design intent to the owner. The result of these tendencies is that we run the risk of developing and installing systems that are insufficient and do not meet the owner's needs. Unfortunately, this can lead to a variety of challenges at a more advanced stage of the project when they cannot be as easily repaired, such as client dissatisfaction or even litigation. The OPR and BOD process helps to ensure that the proper communication between the owner and the other team members takes place in the early stages of the project when communication is most crucial and effective.

This process has proven to be so successful for our firm that we have now started to apply the principles on non-LEED projects. The feedback from clients has been overwhelmingly positive; many question why we have not utilized this approach all along, since it seems so logical to coordinate these issues in the beginning rather than to face challenges at the end. If the LEED process has a positive impact on your clients, it follows that you will be a design professional enjoying the fruits of continued success. And in today's difficult economy, that is a benefit that cannot be ignored.

---

a. Include O&M staff approach (i.e., full-time, 24 hours).
b. Include training expectations.
c. Include postoccupancy goals for system deficiencies.

The Basis of Design (BOD)

After the OPR is distributed, the design team will need to collaborate in order to develop the BOD to complete Step 2 of the process. This document is intended to address the systems and equipment to be commissioned. The document most likely will evolve during design and detail any assumptions and will therefore be project specific, but be sure to look at Appendix E for a sample BOD. According to the reference guide, the document should be broken down as follows:

1. Primary Design Assumptions—space use, regional conditions, occupancy, and include any information about salvaged and reused materials

2. Standards—codes and regulations

3. Narrative Descriptions—performance details of energy related systems to be commissioned

After the OPR and BOD are completed, the CxA is required to review the documents in order to satisfy Step 3 of the Cx process. It is the CxA's responsibility to ensure the two documents correspond to one another and are in sync.

The Commissioning Plan

Step 4 of the prerequisite required Cx activities includes the development and implementation of a Cx plan. The plan should be organized to address the requirements of the Cx team, including the owner, during each phase of the project specific to the approach, strategies, and schedule. The project team is encouraged to refer to the applicable reference guide for a list of the required components to be included in the Cx plan, including the expanded scope for EA Credit 3: Enhanced Commissioning, to ensure compliance, although each plan will be project specific. Generally, the plan will include the composition of the Cx team and the member roles, the OPR, the BOD, sampling rates for the systems to be commissioned, anticipated challenges, and a schedule of Cx activities.

EA Prerequisite 2: Minimum Energy Performance and EA Credit 1: Optimize Energy Performance

Project teams shall determine the compliance path appropriate for their project. Remember the concepts mentioned in Chapter 5, as the approach should be thought of holistically and efficiently with the triple bottom line budget in mind. Project teams should also be mindful of the point potentials for the different compliance paths for the credit, as those teams looking for more than three points, should pursue Option 1.

Site design should be initially discussed to address orientation and passive design features. Then think about the envelope and the building systems working together, not independently. It might also be beneficial for the team to refer to the EPA's Target Finder program and look at similar building types. The team should aim to reach a score of at least 80 for the project they are working on. Compliance paths 2 and 3 should be referred to when teams are looking for inspiration for measures to implement. These decisions will help determine the appropriate compliance path option to pursue for this prerequisite and the credit.

- *EA Credit 1, Option 1:* This is the best option for teams looking to evaluate the interactive benefits and impacts across all building systems and helps to estimate the return on investment (ROI) of different strategies. Should a team consider implementing a building automation system (BAS) or building management system (BMS), they will be able to include only the controls for energy reduction as part of energy modeling efforts and not any of the other compliance paths. This option is also best suited for project teams working with a district energy system.

- Project team members should become familiar with the sections of ASHRAE 90.1–2007 and the provisions included in order to understand the requirements for compliance and the performance alternatives. The standard is broken down into the following relevant sections:

  - Section 5: Building Envelope Requirements
  - Section 6: Heating, Ventilation, and Air-Conditioning Requirements
  - Section 7: Service Water Heating Requirements
  - Section 8: Power Requirements
  - Section 9: Lighting Requirements
  - Section 10: Other Equipment Requirements

- The team is encouraged to view the illustrated strategies in the referenced standard user's manual. For those familiar with the 2004 version of the standard, read through the new version, as there are a few changes to be aware of that are more stringent than the earlier version.

- If building information modeling (BIM) tools are not being used for the project, teams can start with simple energy modeling software, such as Google SketchUp, Ecotect, or Green Building Studio to get the ball rolling with design solutions, and target areas for energy savings can be identified. These target areas typically include space heating, space cooling, and lighting. Teams are encouraged to "plug-and-play" different components to find the best solution for the project. Be sure to give the energy modeler enough time to input the different features before rejoining the team to discuss. Chapter 7

will discuss the requirements for LEED in terms of modeling.

- Project teams implementing natural and/or passive ventilation strategies are encouraged to refer to the reference guide for compliance requirements, as this strategy will impact the energy modeling efforts.

- The standard also includes the energy cost budget method in Section 11 to give the project team the flexibility to exceed some of the prescriptive requirements should they plan on providing for energy cost-saving strategies in other areas. Teams should be cautious with this approach, as it typically is the number one mistake where teams should be using the performance rating method instead.

- Project teams need to be aware of the differences between process energy and regulated energy loads, as all energy-consuming systems will need to be accounted for in the model. The team should refer to Appendix G (a modification of Section 11) of the referenced standard to determine the estimated annual energy *cost* of the baseline and design cases by the means of whole-building energy simulation. The strategy with this compliance path is to reduce the total energy cost at least 10 percent to comply with the prerequisite for new construction projects (5 percent for major renovations) as compared to the baseline case. The baseline case is modeled with the same form but with different systems. The credit awards points for achieving at least a 12 percent reduction.

- To complete the lighting power calculations for performance-based compliance, the project team should determine which path to be utilized: the building area method or the space-by-space method. "Building area method calculations can be used only if the project involves the entire building or a single independent occupancy within a multi-occupancy building."[7] Project teams seeking a more flexible path shall look to the space-by-space method. Project engineers are encouraged to refer to the reference guide for some common mistakes when pursuing this compliance path.

- *EA Credit 1, Options 2 and 3:* If a prescriptive compliance path is to be pursued, the team needs to determine which option applies to their project type and size. Project teams should be aware that in order to comply with either of these options, the design solution must meet all of the requirements, as it is treated as an "all-or-nothing" situation in terms of LEED. Project teams also pursuing one or both of the EQ Credit 8: Daylight and Views credits, and pursuing either of these two EA options, are limited to the allowable glazing area and therefore could be challenged to meet the intentions of the EQ credits, as the window-to-wall ratio cannot exceed 40 percent.

  - For ASHRAE *Advanced Energy Design Guide,* the project engineer will need to determine the climate zone in which the project is located, in order to then establish the thermal performance of the "roofs, walls, slabs, doors, vertical glazing, skylights, interior lighting, ventilation, ducts, energy recovery, and service hot water."[8]

    - *For LEED CS Projects:* Projects must comply with all components of the *Advanced Energy Design Guide,* including those that may not be included in the base building scope of work resulting in the need for inclusion in a sales agreement or tenant lease(s).

- For Advanced Buildings™ Core Performance™, project teams will need to comply with Sections 1 and 2 to meet the requirements of the prerequisite and then will need to determine which sections will be complied with in order to pursue earning points for the credit. The guide is available for download from the Internet at Powells. com and provides a step-by-step approach to help project teams through the process of designing an energy-efficient project. The LEED coordinator is encouraged to monitor the progress with the checklist and keep the engineering team on schedule and focused. A separate checklist may be required to assign responsibilities and tasks to the applicable project team members, such as the lighting designer, mechanical engineer, and architect.

- *For LEED CS Projects:* If the scope of work does not include all of the components addressed by the referenced standard, the project team is then required to include only the systems controlled by the owner. LEED CS project teams can claim efficiency improvements based on the proposed strategies to be implemented by future tenants. Teams should consult the BD+C Reference Guide for more information.

- *For LEED CI Projects:* If the owner controls the applicable building systems and they are not included in the scope of work, these areas are exempt from the requirements of this prerequisite. Once the areas to be addressed are determined and included in the scope of work, the team will need to determine which compliance path they will use in order to document compliance for the prerequisite and the credits. Just like LEED NC and CS project teams, they have the option to pursue a performance-based or prescriptive-based approach. If the team pursues the prescriptive compliance path, an energy model is not required. Project teams pursuing a performance-based approach are encouraged to read the bullet points previously listed to review the simulation tasks and tips.

To meet the prerequisite requirements, the team will need comply with the mandatory provisions of the six sections listed previously for ASHRAE 90.1. Then the project team will need to also determine if the project will meet the prescriptive requirements of Sections 5.5 for building envelope, 6.5 for HVAC, and 9.5 for lighting, or the performance requirements of Section 11 of the referenced standard. The scope of work will need to reduce the connected LPD at least 10 percent below the reference standard and at least 50 percent of the rated power will need to be provided from ENERGY STAR–labeled appliances and equipment. Note that all of requirements of the prerequisite must be achieved in order to pursue certification.

The following credits are available to the team to optimize energy performance beyond the prerequisite requirements and seek points:

- *EA Credit 1.1: Lighting Power.* "This credit compares the installed interior lighting power with the interior lighting power allowance."[9] Remember, the prerequisite requires the project to reduce the LPD by at least 10 percent, whereas this credit requires a 15 percent reduction to start earning points. The lighting designer, or responsible party, is encouraged to determine the specific project footcandle levels for each space type within the project. Photometric studies can be used to evaluate the success of a lighting design and to adjust as required. Strategies could include indirect ambient lighting with an increased amount of task lighting. Specify-

ing energy-efficient fixtures with light-emitting diodes (LEDs) and compact fluorescent lamps (CFLs) and reducing the amount of incandescent and halogen lamps typically will help to lower the LPD. Note that daylight and occupancy sensors are *not* to be included in the LPD calculations, but can be included in the simulation if the team is pursuing the performance-based approach.

To complete the lighting power calculations, the project team should determine which path is to be utilized: the building area method or the space-by-space method. Teams that are working with a building type not listed in the reference standard and are seeking a more flexible path must look to the space-by-space method. Regardless of the path selected, teams are encouraged to download the compliance forms and calculation tools from the ASHRAE website to check the design strategy's compliance with the prerequisite and this credit. It might be necessary to proceed with both paths in order to determine which one is better suited for the project.

To determine the *lighting power allowance* when pursuing the building area method, it will be necessary to refer to Table 9.5.1 of the referenced standard to find the appropriate building type relevant to the project. The engineer or lighting designer would then multiply the listed number by the gross floor area to be lighted. The engineer would then need to compare this lighting power allowance to the total installed lighting power. To determine the *total installed lighting power,* the responsible party would need to determine the total watts of all of the lighting included in the scope of work and add them together.

To determine the lighting power allowance when pursuing the space-by-space method, it will be necessary to refer to Table 9.6.1b of the referenced standard to find the appropriate building space types applicable to the project and then list all of the applicable spaces with the coordinating gross lighted floor area and the allowable LPD as listed in the table. For each of the spaces, the responsible party will need to multiply the allowable LPD by the area of each space. The engineer would then need to compare this lighting power allowance to the total installed lighting power. To determine the total installed lighting power, the responsible party would need to determine total the watts for each of the space types and multiply by the coordinating square footage. Decorative and display fixture wattages can be excluded from these calculations but will need to be accounted for separately (refer to ASHRAE Section 9.6.2).

Regardless of the calculation method used, it is required to assume both fixtures in the calculations if two fixtures are required. This is typically applicable when ambient lighting is provided along with task lighting. Also, when determining watts for the fixtures, be sure to refer to ASHRAE Section 9.1.4.

• *EA Credit 1.2: Lighting Controls.* The team can pursue any of the three strategies offered to earn up to three points for this credit. The lighting designer is encouraged to coordinate with the architect and electrical engineer to determine "the illuminance targets of each major space type, the overall level of daylight and occupancy responsiveness desired, and information on the type of luminaires being considered of the space."[10] The credit offers a point for installing daylight controls for daylit areas and another for installing controls for 50 percent of the *lighting load* (not 50 percent of total fixtures). Another point is available for projects with occupancy sensors for at least 75 percent of

the connected lighting load (again load, not fixture count). Occupancy sensors are required as part of the ASHRAE 2007 requirements for spaces that are 5,000 square feet or larger; therefore, this strategy may already be required as part of complying with the prerequisite.

It is suggested for the team to determine if controls and sensors are appropriate for the spaces in the scope of work. Teams are encouraged to refer to www.wbdg.org/design/spacetypes.php to help them evaluate applicability. If occupancy sensors are appropriate, be sure to review the different types (i.e., passive infrared [PIR] detectors, ultrasonic and microwave emitters) to determine the type best suited for the project. Occupancy sensors typically have a payback of less than one year and are therefore encouraged to implement and pick up at least one point under the credit. If pursuing daylight-responsive controls, project teams are encouraged to weigh the triple-bottom-line values of a stepping approach as compared to implementing a dimming system, specifically to address the cost implications versus the possible distracting aspect for occupants.

To take advantage of credit synergies, project teams should design for independent controls for task lighting applications for EQ Credit 6.1: Controllability of Systems—Lighting. They also should be sure daylight-responsive controls comply with the provisions of ASHRAE 90.1–2007. The responsible party will need prepare a plan highlighting the daylit zones and indicate which light fixtures are intended to respond to each controller.

• *EA Credit 1.3: HVAC.* Project teams have the option to choose which compliance path they plan on pursuing to earn this credit, most likely to be the same path they choose to comply with the prerequisite. Project teams are encouraged to discuss strategies at design integration meetings to determine synergies, such as shading from vegetation, variable-frequency drive pumps, and variable-air-volume distribution systems that address varying demands, or high window placement to maximize daylighting opportunities. Coupling the efforts of EA Credit 1.1 will help this credit solution, as a lower LPD will result in a reduced cooling load. Be sure to encourage the team to weigh the triple-bottom-line values for the compliance path strategies to ensure that they align with the owner's requirements and project goals.

Option 1, Strategy 1: Equipment Efficiency aligns with three sections of the *Core Performance Guide* and requires the system to maintain minimum temperature and humidity ranges compliant with ASHRAE-55.

Option 1, Strategy 2: Appropriate Zoning and Controls, the project engineer will need to ensure that each solar exposure has a separate control zone. Each interior space that is separated by a full-height partition will need to be separately zoned as well. Private offices and other special-occupancy spaces are required to be equipped with active controls that can sense use and adapt the HVAC system in response to space demand. An active control can be an occupancy sensor or a carbon dioxide (CO_2) monitor and could correspond with a BAS to help regulate the airflow based on demand. For base buildings where the HVAC system is not capable of adapting to the space demand, project teams should refer to page 168 of the reference guide for required criteria. Note that the documentation requirements are the same for EQ Credit 7.1: Thermal Comfort—Design should the team also pursue that credit and take advantage of the synergistic effort for this compliance path.

Option 2: Comparison with ASHRAE 90.1–2007 corresponds with the design annual energy cost with the annual energy cost as depicted by the reference standard. If Option 2 is selected, project teams can look to the energy cost budget method or the performance rating method as detailed in Appendix G of ASHRAE 90.1 to determine end-use load components and prove compliance with this credit. Teams typically use an energy model when pursuing this compliance path option. Modeling can get a bit tricky for a tenant improvement project that is serviced by a larger building system. For example, multiple tenants can all tie into a centralized system, but the scope of work included in the LEED project boundary can be included only in the calculations for energy use and savings. Therefore, the modeler may have to model the whole system but then calculate the portion seeking LEED certification in order to document compliance.

- *EA Credit 1.4: Equipment and Appliances.* In order to comply with the prerequisite and this credit, the project team is encouraged to involve the office manager and owner to encourage a purchasing policy specifying ENERGY STAR equipment and appliances. They will need to look to ENERGY STAR when selecting products, such as refrigerators, office equipment, electronics, and commercial food service equipment, as HVAC equipment, lighting products, and building envelope materials are excluded from the calculations for both the prerequisite and this credit. The responsible party will need to gather product data for applicable products, including associated *rated power*, and consult with the electrical engineer to determine the energy use per day for the project space. The prerequisite requires the scope to include ENERGY STAR–labeled equipment for a minimum

MEP ENGINEER'S PERSPECTIVE
EA Credit 1: Optimize Energy Performance Compliance Paths

By William Amann, PE, LEED AP
President of M&E Engineers and Chairman for USGBC NJ Chapter

M&E Engineers was engaged to provide engineering services for the design of mechanical and electrical systems for a project in New Jersey. The building would be the new headquarters for a nonprofit environmental group, and achieving the highest practical LEED certification level was a goal. But being a nonprofit with limited funding, funding for design services was limited.

Figure 6.10 The existing basement wall of this renovation project in New Jersey was preserved due to the creative thinking of the design team. The team implemented geothermal technology and was able to earn LEED Platinum certification. Photo courtesy of M&E Engineers.

An old abandoned mill building was donated to the organization, which consisted of a stone foundation, walls, and a roof. The building was set into a hill, such that the south side was completely exposed, but the lower level was below grade on the north side.

Since the building was essentially just a shell, the renovation project was registered under LEED NC, version 2.1. The project scope included superinsulating the structure, using geothermal heat pumps, and adding solar photovoltaic panels. In order to achieve points under EA Credit 1: Energy Optimization, our plan was to follow the ASHRAE *Advanced Energy Design Guide for Small Office Buildings.* The project fit the criteria, and we would achieve four points, without having to spend time and money on an energy model.

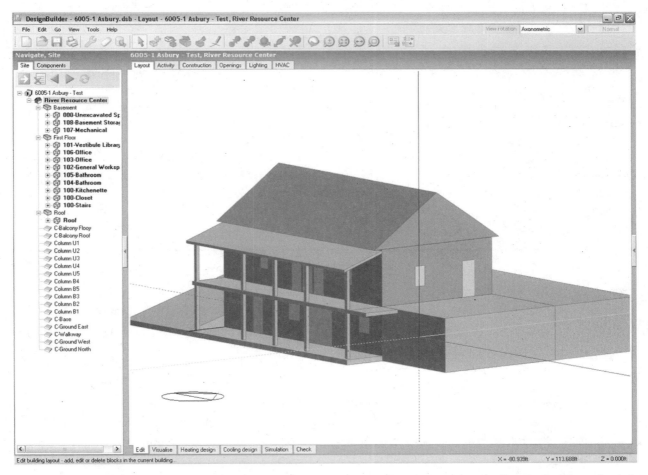

Figure 6.11. An eQuest energy simulation model helped the design team to develop the geothermal strategy, determine the proper insulation, and evaluate the benefits of the solar photovoltaic system for a LEED Platinum certified project in New Jersey. Image courtesy of M&E Engineers.

continued

To achieve the LEED credit, we just had to implement the recommendations listed in the ASHRAE design guide for Climate Zone 5. These recommendations included a minimum of seasonal energy efficiency ratio (SEER) of 13.0 for our heat pumps, and a maximum LPD of 0.9 W/ft², which we could easily achieve. It also provided specific R-values for the roof, walls, slabs, doors, and glazing, which were all higher than the values required in ASHRAE Standard 90.1, but were lower than what the architect was intending to specify. It all seemed very straightforward and easy, which is the intent of the energy design guides.

There was just one problem. According to the ASHRAE design guide, we needed to also insulate the below-grade walls with R-7.5 continuous insulation. Excavating the soil from the outside was out of the question from a cost standpoint. And inside the lower floor, the foundation wall was beautiful hand-laid stone that was one of the primary architectural features of the building (Figure 6.10). We needed to find another solution.

So while the budget was tight, we decided that the cost of insulating the walls could be redirected toward energy modeling. This did not cover the cost, so the remainder was provided pro bono. We created an energy model using ENERGY PLUS with DESIGN BUILDER for the input files. Unfortunately, DESIGN BUILDER did not allow us to model the geothermal system. So we created another model using eQUEST, which is a front end to the DOE-2 energy simulation engine (Figure 6.11).

The eQUEST analysis revealed that our superinsulated building with geothermal heat pumps would reduce the energy use by 48 percent compared to the baseline as defined by ASHRAE 90.1, Appendix G. This earned us 10 points under EA Credit 1, compared to the four that we would have achieved using the *Advanced Energy Guide.* The project has received Platinum certification with 58 total credits attempted, including 16 of the 17 possible points under Energy and Atmosphere.

---

of 50 percent of the rated power, while the credit requires at least 70 percent to start accruing points.

- *For Projects Seeking Performance-Based Compliance:* The responsible team member is encouraged to select a simplified or comprehensive computer simulation software package, such as SketchUp, DOE-2, or EnergyPlus, and begin a simplified energy model as early as possible to take advantage of the capabilities of the design tool. For the final simulation, they will need to establish the climate zone for the specific project and then calculate the energy use by type. They will need to

"maintain a list of energy end uses for the project (for both the baseline case and design case)."[11]

EA Prerequisite 3: Fundamental Refrigerant Management and for LEED CS and NC projects—EA Credit 4: Enhanced Refrigerant Management

- For the prerequisite, the project engineer shall only look to non-chlorofluorocarbon (CFC)-based refrigerants when evaluating new HVAC equipment and fire-suppression systems contained within the project's scope of work. This is typically easy to do, as CFCs have been banned as a refrigerant for new equipment. For major renovations or CI projects

MEP ENGINEER'S PERSPECTIVE
Refrigeration Compliance for LEED

By Christopher F. Zabaneh, LEED AP
Engineer of IBE Consulting Engineers

- EAc4 can be a tough credit to plan. Even when using less damaging refrigerants like R-410a or R-134a, the credit can only be confirmed possible once the systems are fully selected and entered into the LEED template.

- Size matters. The higher charge per ton of smaller split units is usually less likely to comply. Larger systems, such as central plant chillers, are usually no problem if new, and possible if much older. Beware of last-minute changes or swap-outs by the contractors, as this can make a difference. Swapping out computer room water-cooled fan coils for Split DX systems is common if the space runs outside chiller operation.

- Finally, *some* Green Building Certification Institute (GBCI) reviewers don't always pay attention to the arbitrary "Default Maximum Allowable Equipment Refrigeration Charge" in Table 4 in the reference guide and instead rely only on the LEED submittal template—but don't bet your certification on it.

- Though possible, this credit can't always be planned for, as the engineer responds to the changing needs of the client or the budget of the contractor.

---

with existing systems, the building owner should establish a phase-out plan to convert to a refrigerant that is more environmentally friendly.

- For NC and CS projects to comply with this credit, the mechanical engineer should look to avoid all refrigerants, use natural refrigerants, or select equipment that uses refrigerants with low ozone depletion and global climate change potential. Naturally ventilated buildings will automatically earn this credit. If refrigerants are used, the engineer will need to input the required equipment data on the credit submittal form to ensure that the calculated weighted average does not exceed 100. Teams are encouraged to refer to the Environmental Protection Agency's website to locate Significant New Alternative Policy (SNAP) for a list of ozone-depleting refrigerant alternatives. The project team will also need to design for a fire-suppression system that is not based on halon, CFC, and hydrochlorofluorocarbon (HCFC) refrigerant usage.

- The mechanical engineer will need to collect information from the manufacturer to prove the refrigerant required for the HVAC equipment specified. Additionally, to prove credit compliance, the engineer will need to provide product information for the fire-suppression system indicating the system does not use halons, CFCs, or HCFCs.

EA Credit 2: On-Site Renewable Energy (LEED CI SS Credit 1: Option 2, Path 11)

- The owner and architect should consult with the engineer to establish an assumption of expected energy use of the building to help determine the capacity requirements of the renewable energy source. Teams typically rely on the energy model for the project or the Department of Energy's Commercial Building Energy Consumption Survey (CBECS) for usage data. Once the estimated amount of energy is determined for the project, the teams will need to calculate the estimated cost based on the demand. The on-site renewable energy system will then need to supply energy equivalent to at least 1 percent of that cost in order to comply.

- Project teams should collaborate to evaluate the different eligible on-site systems available and appropriate for the project's region, including "photovoltaics, solar thermal, geothermal, wind, biomass, and biogas energy."[12] They should consult with the local utilities to inquire if there is an opportunity for net metering in order to supply power back to the grid at times of surplus. They should also research to find any applicable rebates and grants available.

- Project teams that implement an on-site renewable energy system, but the project does not utilize the system can be eligible to pursue this credit if renewable energy certificates are sold for 200 percent of the system's output.

- *For LEED CS and CI Projects:* – The base building will need to generate at least 2.5 percent on the building's energy consumption (based on cost) in order to earn this credit under the CI rating system. If occupying in a facility that pursued but did not earn LEED CS certification, notice that this credit requires only a minimum of 1 percent to comply, under the CS rating system.

- The responsible party will need to gather documentation for the energy source type and the backup energy source(s). They will need to calculate the total annual energy production in comparison to the total energy demand of the building. In addition, if any incentives were utilized to help offset the installation costs, the applicable documentation should be uploaded to LEED-Online as well.

EA Credit 5 (LEED CI EA Credit 3): Measurement and Verification

- *For LEED NC and CS Projects:* Project teams should inquire about the possibilities of implementing a BAS to help address the credit. If the system will be used, ensure that the team dedicates enough space for the monitors and equipment necessary for the system. Be sure to research incentives available for implementing the system along with submetering.

They are encouraged to reference International Performance Measurement & Verification Protocol (IPMVP), Volume III, to evaluate Options B and D to determine which compliance path they will pursue. For smaller projects that can isolate the main energy-related systems, Option B may be better suited and more cost effective, whereas Option D applies the measurement and verification (M&V) approach to the whole building. Option B includes isolating and metering the energy conservation measures (ECMs), such as HVAC or lighting systems. Teams pursuing Option D typically use the project energy model as a baseline, and then the team incorporates utility data analysis, spot metering, or permanent metering to track actual consumption.

The reference guide details the applications best suited for each option. Be sure to weigh the triple-bottom-line values of the approach to verify alignment with the owner's requirements and project goals. The costs will vary, based on the number and type of metering points and complexity of the system selected. Also listed in the reference guide are the following tasks for the team to focus on during design development[13]:

- Developing the energy model

- Specifying the number and types of meters

MEP ENGINEER'S PERSPECTIVE
Engaging an Engineer

By Kurt A. Scheer, PE, LEED AP
Associate at BDA Engineering

The process of a building's obtaining LEED certification is not tremendously complicated, yet requires all members of the team to understand this goal immediately. This involves the architect, engineer, owner, and contracting team. Traditionally, we were used to working with projects that look at LEED certification as a value-added service or simply a title, but this is becoming less prevalent, as more project teams fully understand the process that is required. An engineering consultant has a critical role in the overall process, as much can be gained within the EA category alone, as the current LEED NC version allows up to 19 points within this category. While some will look at this solely as the domain of the mechanical engineer, true success requires the other team members to contribute.

How well a building can perform, as it relates to energy, is a function of all its components, site orientation, and system selections, and therefore an effort of the entire team. Effective energy modeling can serve as a key tool to evaluate each of these items in a schematic design phase. It is here that a broad architectural engineering background and a holistic view of the building process is essential. The most successful projects have been those where we were granted the early opportunity to make sound design decisions, examine options, and model those proposals. At that point, evidence can be shown to help the design team make the final decisions. When this process is put forth, the end results are welcome and exceptional.

I was recently involved in a project that was an extensive renovation and addition of an existing multiple building site into a luxury hotel. The concept of "going for LEED" was not agreed upon until nearly 50 percent through the design process when the developer received a grant from the local Urban Redevelopment Authority, requiring LEED Silver certification. At this point, a budget was agreed upon, and the envelope, lighting, and mechanical systems were selected. I was essentially asked to model this building's energy performance to see what the result was, and it was no surprise that the result was less than desirable. While there were enough components to make this project a certified building, the EA credits did not meet the prerequisite. As the mechanical engineer, it was up to me to solve this dilemma. I proposed alterations to the envelope and minor changes to some of the building systems. This then created a scramble at the end to update documents and ensure that the project was within budget. Had this all been done in the early phases of the project, the results would have been substantially better, including a lower economic bottom line for the owner.

The approach to obtain a sustainable building project can at times appear complicated, burdensome, and unnecessary. This is not always the case, but when it does, it can be the result of one or more team members not being fully vested in the process. Each team member should take advantage of this opportunity to be involved and share his or her enthusiasm and understanding of the process. LEED is not a perfect protocol, but currently it is the only and best quantifiable means to measure a building's sustainable integrity.

continued

Taking a more active role in the design and construction process is not only beneficial for a LEED project, but also is beneficial for the professional development of the engineer as well. This provides an opportunity to interact with an array of team members, understand multiple disciplines and their role in the project, develop additional technical knowledge, and provide quality input as it relates to our specific project requirements and goals. The professional should never hesitate to welcome this opportunity that is often presented. Having a narrow view does little to help the project, as well as the individual.

Another critical component of any LEED project is building commissioning. My firm and I have also performed these services for nearly all of our projects, including those that have earned LEED certification. The value to the owner is exceptional, as a commissioning agent can add insight during the design process, construction, and post occupancy. Levels of involvement in these three phases can vary from project to project. There is seldom a case where commissioning does not result in the owner's receiving added benefit from not only the professional services they are purchasing, but also the system they will be living with for a long time. Again, a holistic approach is often critical to making this a worthy endeavor.

The basic theme of successful LEED projects is always the same: collaborate, collaborate, and collaborate. We have heard this many times before, but still it presents a challenge. For quite a while, the design process was a linear flow, from owner to architect to engineer. This approach does not work well in general, let alone for sustainable projects. The flow now needs to be circular, with all parties understanding the others' role and having one goal—a great project.

- Providing trending parameters for controls and applications

- Reviewing the design documents

- *For LEED CS Projects:* Project teams have the option of seeking two credits: Credit 5.1: Base Building Metering, and Credit 5.2: Tenant Metering. For Credit 5.1, the electricity-using systems must be measured by the means of metering or a BAS. If Credit 5.2 is to be pursued, the metering system needs to be expandable for tenants to be accountable for their usage in accordance with EA Credit 3: Measurement and Verification under the LEED CI rating system.

- *For LEED CI Projects:* Depending on the size of the tenant's space relative to the total building, project teams will look to either Case 1 or Case 2 as detailed in the ID+C reference guide. As mentioned in Chapter 4, smaller projects have the option to implement submetering equipment and/ or have the lease agreement reflect the tenant's obligation to pay for their energy costs outside of the base rent. For tenant spaces that occupy 75 percent or more of the total building area, continuous metering equipment will need to be installed for at least the 10 end uses as detailed in the reference guide. In either case, an M&V plan is required as detailed in IPMVP, Volume I. The reference guide lists the nine steps to create an M&V plan, five of which should be addressed during schematic design and design development. The first five steps are[14]:

Step 1. List all measures to be monitored and verified.

Step 2. Define the baseline.

Step 3. Estimate projected savings.

Step 4. Define the general approach.

Step 5. Prepare a project-specific M&V plan.

MEP ENGINEER'S PERSPECTIVE
Measurement and Verification for Large-Energy-User Projects

By Wayne Howell, PE
Principal at Clive Samuels & Associates, Inc

Implementing a measurement and verification (M&V) plan is an excellent way to ensure that the building systems are operating optimally and as designed. The M&V plan should be based on the best practices developed by the IPMVP. The plan should cover at least one year, but the most benefit will be derived from having a plan in place to monitor the building during its useful life. Subsequent energy usage verifications of predicted energy usage for facilities will become standard requisites to maintain certification levels.

M&V plans are useful for all building types, but large energy users or high-power-density projects, such as data centers, will reap greater benefits, as measurement and benchmarking are key steps to improving energy efficiency. Energy usage is measured and recorded against the baseline information. With this information, data center operators and information technology (IT) personnel can then monitor the impact of their efficiency efforts. When equipment changes are made, there will be a corresponding change in the amount of energy used. When no changes have been made and energy usage has increased, tracking this information will then provide an indication that the equipment is not functioning correctly and requires inspection.

A recent data center project, Emerson Corporate Data Center, was designed to meet Tier III reliability requirements. The data center uses Liebert CRAC and XD units for cooling and Liebert FDCs and PDUs for power distribution. All of these are monitored by a Liebert SiteScan system, which monitors the equipment—emergency generator sets, computer room air-conditioning (CRAC) units, FDCs, power distribution units (PDUs), automatic transfer switches (ATSs), the FM200 fire-suppression system panel, and even the under-floor leak detection system. This constant monitoring of vital building equipment lets building personnel know how the equipment is operating at all times, whether they are in the building or accessing the system from a remote location. Adding metering points to the system to monitor energy usage was easily accomplished, and the system is expandable for when the data center reaches its maximum server build-out in the future.

The M&V plan for the Emerson data center project serves three purposes. First, it tracks how efficiently the data center is operating by measuring real-time power consumption of equipment components and the aggregate whole-facility consumption. More importantly, it allows pinpointing of equipment that may be consuming more power than historical usage, indicating that the equipment may need possible servicing before adversely impacting the overall operation of the building. Finally, the M&V plan was used to meet the requirements of LEED Energy and Atmosphere Credit 5: Measurement and Verification to help the project earn a Gold certification from USGBC.

It is important to engage all of the project team members, as this credit involves contributions from many different disciplines, although the mechanical engineer is typically the responsible party for LEED documentation purposes. Project teams will need to determine which option of the IPMVP is most applicable to the project to develop the M&V plan. Option B is most appropriate for retrofits, where Options C and D should be evaluated for the different approaches for documenting savings, actual submeter data or estimated by the means of simulation.

Materials and Resources

The MR prerequisite and credits that are typically addressed during these two phases of design include:

MR Prerequisite 1: Storage and Collection of Recyclables

- The project team should establish easily accessible collection and storage areas for the project and size them appropriately according to minimum requirements listed in the reference guide. Teams should be aware of noise and odor impacts to adjacent spaces. Owners should be engaged to determine the signage to be implemented to encourage participation and avoid contamination, as well as to discuss the education of occupants, including the operations and maintenance staff, to ensure the program's ongoing success.

- Project teams should also research available recycling programs for the area in which the project is located. A local hauler should be engaged for input for accessibility and convenience and to find out if a commingled approach is available. Project teams that implement a comprehensive recycling program can seek an Innovation in Design credit.

- The architect will need to prepare a plan clearly delineating storage and collection areas. The owner should provide a narrative detailing the recycling policy for the building, including the area provided for supporting the recycling activities, accessibility, and frequency of pickups.

- *For LEED CS Projects:* Project teams should address the building's policy to include in the tenant guidelines for synergy with SS Credit 9.

MR Credit 1.1 Tenant Space—Long-Term Commitment (for LEED CI projects)

- The responsible party will need to obtain the signed lease agreement and locate the term language proving commitment compliance to upload to LEED-Online. It is recommended to complete these tasks as soon as possible to avoid scrambling when the team is ready to submit for a certification review with GBCI.

MR Credit 1: Building Reuse. Project teams pursuing either of these credits will need to ensure that the LEED project boundary line includes the entire building and not just the area contained within the scope of work.

MR Credit 1.1: Building Reuse—Maintain Existing Walls, Floors, and Roof (for LEED NC and CS projects)

- The project team will need to examine the existing conditions and then align them with the goals and requirements of the project's new occupant and/or use. The project team should coordinate with the structural engineer to determine the structural items to be salvaged and reused. During schematic design, the team should also engage a cost consultant to determine the cost savings related to the reuse. This will also help the team to evaluate strategies to pursue to increase the performance of the facility as well.

- The owner may be entitled to grants and incentives for preserving an existing building. The team should allocate this research task to the appropriate party to pursue and clarify.

- Remember, if the calculations prove that the project is not eligible to pursue this credit due to the inability to reach the required minimum reuse percentage thresholds, project teams can use the information to pursue MR Credit 2: Construction Waste Management, as long as the material is not included in both credits.

- The architect typically will ultimately be responsible for providing plans and elevations showing the area for all existing envelope and structural elements to be reused within the new design. He or she will then need to calculate the square footage of the structural elements to remain in comparison for the new elements to be incorporated during construction to complete the credit submittal template. These calculations can be time consuming, so ensure that enough time is dedicated to the effort.

MR Credit 1.2: Maintain 50 Percent Interior Nonstructural Elements (for LEED NC and CI projects)

- The architect will need to examine the existing conditions and then align them with the goals and requirements of the project's new occupant and/or use. The project team should evaluate nonstructural, fixed items to be salvaged and reused.

- The architect will ultimately be responsible for creating a plan showing the surface area for all existing finished ceilings and floors, interior and exterior walls, interior doors, and/or built-in casework to be

reused within the new design. Be sure not to include reused or salvaged furniture in the calculations for this credit, as it should be included in the next credit, MR Credit 3: Materials Reuse. He or she will then need to calculate the surface areas of the nonstructural elements to remain in comparison for the new elements to be incorporated during construction to complete the credit submittal template.

MR Credit 3 (LEED CI Credit 3.1): Materials Reuse

- During schematic design, project teams are encouraged to begin researching materials on- and off-site to be reused. Qualifying items fall under CSI Divisions 03 through 10 and Sections 31.60, 32.10, 32.30, and 32.90. Furniture may be included, but then must also be included in each of the remaining MR credits. Project teams pursing this credit are encouraged to visit www.planetreuse.com, a valuable resource to finding salvaged materials.

- Coordination is suggested between the owner, architect, and contractor. Remember, in order to comply, items salvaged on-site must take on a new use. Project teams should verify that the items to be reused do not contain any toxic substances. A cost consultant or expert may be required to help determine associated replacement costs to help with the calculations. It is best to determine an estimated budget up front to determine if compliance will be achievable.

- If the project requires demolition, project teams should assess the site for material reuse based on the extent of demolition, such as foundations, plantings, and pavings. Traditionally, many project teams have been able to crush existing slabs or foundations and reuse the material as fill for the

ARCHITECT'S PERSPECTIVE
The National Audubon Society: Selecting Environmentally Sensitive Materials

By Guy Geier, FAIA, FIIDA, LEED AP
Senior Partner, FXFOWLE Architects

The National Audubon Society has long been a leader in sustainable architecture. Between 1990 and 2008, Audubon's headquarters was located in a century-old building in lower Manhattan. At that time, it was considered one of the most energy-efficient, environmentally responsible office buildings in the country. In 2008, the nonprofit organization decided to move to a smaller, cost-effective space elsewhere in the city that could be designed and constructed with the highest sustainable standards and meet their current operational requirements. Located in a full floor of a former printing house near Greenwich Village, Audubon's new space offers high ceilings, full-height windows, and a large floor, which permits the entire staff to be on one floor.

FXFOWLE's design for Audubon's new headquarters was inspired by the organization's mission to "protect and restore vital ecosystems, and to ensure a healthy environment for people, wildlife, and the earth's natural resources." The headquarters functions as a model for their environmental mission and includes many innovative features, such as under-floor air distribution, open space planning to allow daylight penetration to the entire floor, energy-efficient systems, occupancy sensors and controls, high indoor environmental quality, and the use of recycled/reclaimed and locally produced materials. FXFOWLE ensured that sustainability was incorporated holistically throughout the entire project.

Audubon and FXFOWLE used a comprehensive approach to conserve and select environmentally sensitive materials for the organization's new headquarters and to reflect its mission. In addition to specifying drywall, carpet, and ceiling tiles with high levels of recycled content, reclaimed materials were used in two major components of the project: the barn siding that wraps around the interior core (Figure 6.12), and the raised-floor air distribution system.

The design team searched the New York tri-state area to find the precise wood for the wall covering behind the reception desk and around the core. Several factors guided the team's choice of wood: (1) its level of distress couldn't be too high, (2) it had to take stain well, and (3) it could not require too much millwork and resizing. All potential sources and wood suppliers within 500 miles were identified and reviewed, and the team looked at more than 20 different samples. In the end, the team selected and installed salvaged siding from a barn in upstate New York that had already been disassembled.

While the design team actively pursued the wood siding, the reclaimed floor system came about by a "happy accident." The project team identified a shuttered corporate data center that had a stockpile of the same floor system that the designers had specified. The recycled floor was installed in Audubon's headquarters at a savings of $50,000 to the client.

Figure 6.12. The National Audubon Society project in New York City by FXFOWLE earned its LEED CI certification by incorporating salvaged materials. Photo courtesy of FXFOWLE Architects and David Sundberg/Esto.

Both the reclaimed barn siding and the floor system contributed to the materials credit the project achieved under the LEED certification system.

The National Audubon Society continues its dedication to cost-effective, state-of-the-art technology, and a design that provides a healthy and productive work environment for staff and visitors, while minimizing its impact on the environment. Around the country, many Audubon centers have achieved LEED certification. The organization's leadership and collaboration with FXFOWLE for the New York City headquarters serves as a model for other businesses and organizations that sustainable design can be successfully and financially achieved without sacrificing aesthetic quality or vision, or going over budget. A true testament to the success of the project was scoring 48 points for LEED Platinum CI certification, making the National Audubon Society headquarters the highest-scoring CI project in the world.

new project; whereas the strategy is applicable directly to this credit. Project teams working with a brownfield project and looking to this strategy, need to ensure that these materials are safe to reuse.

- Remember, locally salvaged materials can also contribute toward earning MR Credit 5: Regional Materials.

- *For LEED NC and LEED CS Projects:* Reusing furniture may comply with this credit if the furniture is consistently included in the calculations for MR Credits 3 through 7. Therefore, project teams are encouraged to research where the materials to make the furniture were extracted, where the furniture was manufactured, if it contains any recycled content, or if it was manufactured with certified wood or any rapidly renewable materials. Also, in order to comply, the furniture to be reused must have been purchased at least two years prior to the relocation.

MR Credit 3.2: Materials Reuse—Furniture and Furnishings (for LEED CI projects)

- Project teams should inventory the existing furniture to determine the anticipated savings as compared to purchasing new. Project team members should determine if any repair is required to be sure to allot the necessary time. The design team should also approach suppliers for used items in lieu of purchasing new furniture needed for the new space.

- CI project teams are encouraged to prepare a preliminary furniture budget in order to determine the value needed to reach the 30 percent threshold. Teams are encouraged to aim higher than the minimum thresholds to compensate for changes down the road.

- For project teams using furniture with a salvaged component, be sure to read the Assembly Calculations section included in Chapter 9 to understand the approach and to assist with the documentation requirements for this credit.

- Remember, these reused items can contribute toward other MR credits. Therefore, project teams are encouraged to research where the materials to make the furniture were extracted, where the furniture was manufactured, if it contains any recycled content, or if it was manufactured with certified wood or any rapidly renewable materials.

MR Credit 4: Recycled Content

- Once the budget is established, project teams should evaluate the cost required in order to comply with this credit, as this credit is calculated as a percentage of total material costs, excluding labor and equipment. Therefore, "big ticket" items should be evaluated first to contribute toward earning this credit in a streamlined effort.

- The design team should look to materials with a higher postconsumer recycled content. For example, LEED NC and CS project teams should look to building envelope solutions with recycled content opportunities, as the envelope components will have a big impact on cost and therefore credit compliance. Engaging the engineers in a conversation to determine if the recycled content of the project's concrete can be increased with such products as Green Sense™ or fly ash would be beneficial as well. LEED CI projects should look to qualifying materials that will have a bigger impact on cost, such as acoustical ceiling tiles, gypsum wallboard, carpet, and metal studs, to include in the specifications. Websites such as www.greenwizard.com include databases for project team members to query to find manufacturers and products with eco-attributes and certifications.

- MEP equipment and fixtures do not comply, nor do any specialty items, such as elevators.

- *For LEED NC and CS Projects:* Remember, including Division 12 items is optional, but required if included in any MR credit 3 through 7. LEED-Online will help to ensure that the same total material cost is used consistently across credits.

MR Credit 5: Regional Materials

- Once the budget is established, project teams should evaluate the cost required in order to comply with this credit, as this credit is calculated as a percentage of total material costs, excluding labor and equipment. It is essential to remember the requirements for this credit; just because a material is purchased within 500 miles of the project site, does not imply compliance. In order to be eligible to contribute toward earning this credit, a material would also need to be manufactured locally, at a minimum for LEED CI projects, whereas LEED NC and CS projects require the raw materials to be extracted within 500 miles, as well as manufactured.

- A proactive design team should look to materials with the largest impact on the budget that can be locally sourced, such as structural members. MEP equipment and fixtures do not comply, nor any specialty items, such as escalators. It is best to start this exercise early and to aim higher than the intended percentage threshold to ensure compliance.

- *For LEED NC and CS Projects:* Remember, including Division 12 items is optional, but required if included in any MR credit 3 through 7.

MR Credit 6: Rapidly Renewable Materials (for LEED NC and CI projects)

- Once the budget is established, project teams should evaluate the cost required in order to comply with this credit, as this credit is calculated as a percentage of total material costs, excluding labor and equipment. It is best to start this exercise early and to aim higher than the intended percentage threshold to ensure compliance.

- The design team should look to materials that could be composed of rapidly renewable materials, such as flooring solutions, window treatments, or millwork. MEP equipment and fixtures do not comply, nor do any specialty items, such as elevators. The benefits and trade-offs should be evaluated for applicable products. For example, bamboo can also qualify a Forest Stewardship Council (FSC)-certified, but is sensitive to humid climates and may warp if not acclimated properly. Cotton insulation typically is more expensive than fiberglass batt insulation, just as linoleum is more expensive than vinyl, and wool carpeting costs more than nylon solutions.

- *For LEED NC Projects:* Remember, including Division 12 items is optional, but required if it is included in any MR credit 3 through 7.

MR Credit 7 (LEED CS MR Credit 6): Certified Wood

- Once the budget is established, project teams should evaluate the cost required in order to comply with this credit, as this credit is calculated as a percentage of total new wood material costs, excluding labor and equipment. Just as suggested previously with the other MR credits, it is best to start this exercise early and to aim higher than the intended percentage threshold to ensure compliance.

- The design team should look to "structural and general dimensional framing, flooring, sub-flooring, wood doors and finishes"[15] for opportunities to comply. Remember, the more wood used, the more challenging and possibly expensive this credit becomes. Be sure to evaluate wood species and grades to determine the strategy and approach to comply and budgetary impacts.

- Project teams should research suppliers to determine availability. If possible, these suppliers should be presented to the contractor or bidders to encourage coordination for pricing. The owner may want to purchase these materials early if availability is a concern.

- *For LEED NC and CS Projects:* Remember, including Division 12 items is optional, but required if it is included in any MR credit 3 through 7.

Indoor Environmental Quality

The EQ prerequisites and credits that are typically addressed during these two phases of design include:

EQ Prerequisite 1: Minimum Indoor Air Quality Performance, and EQ Credit 2: Increased Ventilation

- Project teams should research local codes to identify the requirements for outside air delivery and then compare them to ASHRAE 62.1 – 2007, to determine which is more stringent to ensure that the selected ventilation system meets the requirements of this prerequisite. Most likely ASHRAE 62 is more stringent, but the additional requirements will not typically have any cost implications to comply with the prerequisite. Project teams should determine which ventilation strategy is appropriate for the project: mechanical, natural, or mixed mode. This decision is typically driven by the climate conditions and the size, type, and use of the project. Natural ventilation strategies can improve the economic bottom line, as the need for mechanical equipment and operational expenses are both reduced.

- Spaces with a shorter slab-to-slab height may want to look to displacement ventilation strategies, such as a raised access floor with under-floor air distribution to reduce the need for ducting. Project teams can also look to demand-controlled ventilation systems if they are also pursuing EQ Credit 1: Outdoor Air Delivery Monitoring and seeking strategies to minimize cost increases. Project teams will need to evaluate the impacts on energy efficiency to determine the right balance for the project.

- To meet the requirements of the prerequisite, the selected ventilation strategy will determine the standard to reference for the chosen compliance path, although both compliance path options may need to be adhered to for the same project. Mechanically ventilated buildings and mixed-mode spaces will need to follow Case 1, while naturally ventilated spaces follow Case 2. If any portion of a building is naturally ventilated, that portion must follow Case 2, even though the rest of the building is mechanically ventilated and following Case 1.

- For credit compliance, project teams working with a mechanically ventilated space will need to increase the ventilation rate by 30 percent as compared to ASHRAE 62.1–2007. They will need to look to Section 6 of the referenced standard to determine if they will proceed with the ventilation rate or the IAQ procedure. Teams working with naturally ventilated buildings also have two compliance methods to choose from: they either refer to Chapter 2 of the Chartered Institution of Building Services Engineers (CIBSE) Applications Manual 10–2005 (AM10), "Natural Ventilation in Non-Domestic Buildings" for a prescriptive approach, or they will need to document the room-by-room airflow rates using a macroscopic, multizone analytic model. This modeling exercise should be started early to ensure the most effective design and proper opening sizes. Be advised that it is much more difficult to achieve the requirements of this credit with a naturally ventilated building.

- *For Mechanically Ventilated Projects:* Project teams will need to determine the occupancy of the project, as the requirements of the referenced standard are based on the project's size, occupancy count, the occupant's intended activities, and the ventilation system. Calculating these factors should help to avoid oversizing the mechanical equipment. Project teams are encouraged to evaluate the opportunities to implement energy recovery systems and economizers to balance the energy performance and compensate for the increase in air changes. The mechanical engineer should continue to run ventilation rate calculations to ensure compliance. He or she will be able to use the same calculations completed for EQ Prerequisite 1 to comply with this credit if working with a mechanically ventilated building.

  - For project teams also pursuing EQ Credit 5: Indoor Chemical and Pollutant Source Control, note the Minimum Efficiency Reporting Value (MERV) filter requirement of 13, as this type of filter typically impacts fan and duct sizing.

- When determining outdoor air intake locations, teams should avoid locations with possible contaminants. These locations can include "loading areas, building exhaust fans, cooling towers, street traffic, idling vehicles, standing water, parking garages, sanitary vents, waste bins, and outside smoking areas."[16]

- *For LEED CS Projects:* Project teams that do not know the occupancy counts should refer to ASHRAE Table 6–1 for the default occupancy counts to use. The mechanical engineer will need to create a chart describing the different space types and expected uses to upload to LEED-Online.

- *For LEED CI Projects:* Existing HVAC systems or space that is naturally ventilated are incapable of supplying the required amount of ventilation and therefore cannot comply with this prerequisite. The declarant will need to "document the space and system constraints that make it not possible, complete an engineering assessment of the system's maximum cubic feet per minute (cfm) capability toward meeting the requirements of ASHRAE Standard 62.1–2007 (with errata but without addenda), and achieve those levels, with a minimum of 10cfm per person."[17]

EQ Prerequisite 2: Environmental Tobacco Smoke (ETS) Control

- *For LEED NC and CS Projects:* Owners shall determine the compliance path for this prerequisite. Will smoking be permitted within the building? Will there be a designated location for smoking on-site? If smoking will be allowed within the building, project teams will need to coordinate to ensure that the spaces are separately exhausted with impermeable deck-to-deck partitions and are negatively pressurized in comparison to adjacent spaces. If smoking will not be allowed within the building, but allowed on-site, the project architect, owner, civil engineer, and landscape architect will need to collaborate in order to designate a space at least 25 feet away from the building entrances, operable windows, or any outdoor air intakes. Projects with a residential or a hospitality component shall refer to the BD+C reference guide for additional information.

- Encourage collaboration among the team members to ensure that the smoking-related requirements are included in the OPR and BOD to comply with EA Prerequisite 1: Fundamental Commissioning.

- Coordination is suggested with the facility manager or owner to develop a smoking policy for the building and site, including locations of permissible smoking areas. The owner, the facility manager, and the tenant (if a LEED CI project) should then sign the policy and upload it to LEED-Online. Project teams also need to address signage for the building and site to align with the policy provisions.

- *LEED CI Projects:* Project teams will need to verify the smoking policy with the building owner. As stated in Chapter 4, it is best to select a building that prohibits smoking within the building. If smoking is allowed, project teams will need to design for a separate ventilation system from the rest of the building. If smoking is not permitted within the building and an exterior designated space is provided, ensure that this location is at least 25 feet away from the building entrances, operable windows, or any outdoor air intakes.

EQ Credit 1: Outdoor Air Delivery Monitoring

- When designing the ventilation systems, project teams should implement airflow sensor devices to monitor the ventilation rate, as well as CO_2 monitors. The project's mechanical engineer can choose to either use multiple monitors in occupied spaces that use measured concentration, or for projects with limited airflow monitoring capabilities, they can choose to use differential CO_2 monitoring. With the former approach, an alert must be signaled if the concentration exceeds the set point by 15 percent; with the latter approach, the units must be able to provide more "outside air if the CO_2 delta between the spaces reaches or exceeds 530ppm."[18]

- Coordination between the architect and mechanical engineer is encouraged for overall system design and for sensor placement, as well as intake locations. There needs to be a clear understanding of qualifying densely occupied spaces, as not all conference rooms are applicable. Note that designing a centralized system or implementing a building automation system or demand control ventilation can achieve this credit in a cost-effective manner by minimizing ducts, providing for automatic responsiveness, and conserving energy.

- Encourage collaboration with the CxA to ensure that the monitoring and alarm devices are included in the Cx plan in order to comply with EA Prerequisite 1: Fundamental Commissioning.

- Remember, fan tracking, building pressurization measurement, or other air balance control strategies do not meet the intentions of this credit as a means of monitoring outdoor airflow. Therefore, it could be worthwhile to research incentives or grants that may available from the local utility providers for installing sensors and/or monitors.

- *For LEED CS Projects:* Project teams should consider providing means for the tenants to monitor the CO_2 levels within their space, which in turn could also help a tenant seeking CI certification earn points.

- *For LEED CI and NC Major Renovation Projects:* If the tenant space or addition is connecting to an existing HVAC system, the project team will need to address how the monitors will interact with the existing system as a whole, including automation.

EQ Credit 3.1 (LEED CI EQ Credit 3): Construction IAQ Management Plan— During Construction

- Although this is a credit to be submitted after substantial completion for a construction-side review, design teams should ensure that the mechanical systems can support the desired MERV filter to be specified (minimum of MERV 8 required, but 13 may be needed if the team is pursuing EQ Credit 5 as well). Project teams will need to ensure that the desired MERV filter is listed in the specifications. The next chapter will detail the additional information to be listed in the specifications.

EQ Credit 3.2: Construction IAQ Management Plan—Before Occupancy (for NC and CI projects)

- Typically, this credit is pursued by project teams also pursuing EQ Credit 3.1 and the suite of EQ Credit 4, but it is not required to do so. It is encouraged to verify with the mechanical engineer that the required air volume for a flush-out will be possible with the HVAC system designed and to estimate the time needed to deliver the required 14,000 cubic feet per square foot. If the project is naturally ventilated, temporary fans and equipment typically are required to meet the intentions of this credit. Although this credit is submitted after substantial completion, just as with the previous credit, design teams should ensure that the specifications address the requirements and options. The next

chapter will detail the additional information to be listed in the specifications.

EQ Credit 4: Low-Emitting Materials

- Project teams should research materials and products that will be used inside the weatherproofing of the space to comply with these credits. They should focus their efforts on applicable finishes, such as paints and flooring systems. EQ Credits 4.1 and 4.2 are eligible for the VOC budget methodology should a product surpass the maximum VOC level. If teams pursue this option, they will need to document the average VOC level of all applicable products utilized on the job site does not exceed the maximum total content allowed. LEED 2009 has changed the requirements for EQ Credit 4.3, to ensure that project teams install low-emitting finishes for 100 percent of the finished floor area. Beware, EQ Credit 4.4 is an "all-or-nothing" credit, as it requires products to comply in order for the team to be eligible to earn the credit.

- LEED CI projects have the opportunity to address systems furniture and seating under this credit, while LEED NC and CS can address their furniture procurement strategy as an ID credit. As mentioned previously, project teams are encouraged to use the Internet to find websites, such as www.greenwizard.com, to locate applicable materials and products with applicable certifications, such as FloorScore® and Greenguard™. For furniture selection, it may just be easier to visit the Greenguard website for a list of compliant products to select from otherwise documentation will be needed to prove compliance with Option 2: the EPA's Environmental Technology Verification (ETV) testing or Option 3: other third-party testing based on American National Standards Institute (ANSI)/ Business and Institutional Furniture Manufacturer's

Association (BIFMA) standards M7.1–2007 and X7.1–2007. If not pursuing EQ Credit 4.5 or the ID opportunity with Option 1, project teams are encouraged to visit the Scientific Certification Systems (SCS) Indoor Advantage Gold website for a list of tested furniture that will typically comply with Option 3. Remember, occasional furniture is not included in the compliance requirements for this credit, as only systems furniture and seating are addressed. When using products that are Greenguard certified for EQ Credit 4.3 compliance, be sure to use the Greenguard for Children and Schools program, as the generic standard does not meet the credit requirements. Project teams should download the reference guide errata from the USGBC website, as some of the volatile organic compound (VOC) content level thresholds have been updated.

EQ Credit 5: Indoor Chemical and Pollutant Source Control

- Project teams should engage the owner to determine which type of entryway system is preferred and appropriate for the climatic region in which the project resides.

  - *For LEED CI Projects:* Remember, if the tenant space does not have direct access to the exterior, the entryway system requirement may be waived.

- Project teams should then determine if there are any areas with hazardous gases or chemicals, and if so, these areas should not be located next to regularly occupied areas but should be located near exterior walls to reduce the amount of additional ductwork, or stacked vertically to be efficiently exhausted. These spaces will need to be separately exhausted with deck-to-deck

partitions or hard lid ceilings. Remember, this requirement applies not only to lab spaces, but also to high-volume copy areas, print and fax areas, and battery backup unit storage rooms, such as uninterrupted power supply (UPS), as well.

- Project teams will then need to determine if any areas will be used for chemical mixing, and if so, these chemicals will need to be separately drained.

- Mechanical systems will need to be designed for MERV 13 filters or better.

- Hazardous liquids will need to be properly stored and disposed of, although compliance requirements are a bit vague, project teams should therefore seek additional information from GBCI if necessary.

EQ Credit 6.1: Controllability of Systems— Lighting (for LEED NC and CI only)

- The goals for lighting controllability, and not necessarily lighting controls, should be addressed in the OPR and BOD to ensure that they are carried throughout the design and construction activities. Although not required, an overall successful strategy will address *both* lighting control *and* controllability.

- Project teams are encouraged to engage a lighting designer to focus on a task-oriented approach for the project that addresses ergonomics and glare control. Coordination between the lighting designer and architect should address the intended purpose of the spaces, the ceiling finishes, and the ceiling heights to optimize the success of the design. Project teams should plan for ceiling heights at least 9½ feet, with the ceilings finished in the lightest color possible.

- For open-plan work areas and offices, project teams shall make provisions for task lighting to ensure that at least 90 percent of the occupants have access to control the lighting in their workspace. Multioccupant spaces will also need to have controls to allow flexibility to meet the needs of the group, such as audiovisual presentations and meetings. Light fixtures with dual capabilities of downlighting and general illumination that can be switched separately are ideal. The idea is to implement override switches for a combination of dimmers, occupancy and daylight sensors for multioccupant areas, and individual adjustable task lighting for single-occupied spaces, but it could be as simple as plug-in lamps at open-plan workstations and on/off switches for shared, multioccupancy spaces. Glare control should be addressed with light fixtures, as well as daylighting strategies, regardless of the credit strategy.

- As the drawings are developed, coordination is also encouraged with the electrical engineer to ensure that the circuitry is correct and the power requirements are addressed. A floor plan, including furniture arrangements, will need to be prepared depicting the location, zone, and type of lighting controls that are to be implemented.

- *For LEED CI Projects:* Project teams should take advantage of credit synergies as related to lighting systems. They should be sure individual controls comply with the provisions of ASHRAE 90.1–2007.

EQ Credit 6.2 (LEED CS EQ Credit 6): Controllability of Systems—Thermal Comfort

- Project teams will need to address this credit as early as possible, as there are few feasible ways to meet the requirements, so planning is critical for success. In order to supply individual thermal comfort controls for at least 50 percent of the occupants, project teams with a hybrid approach or that are mechanically ventilated are encouraged to evaluate the implementation of a raised access floor in order to distribute under-floor air with individual controllable diffusers. Another option is to implement heating radiators or radiant panels with individual temperature controls. Project teams with a naturally ventilated building need to evaluate the location of windows and the quality of the outside air. Compliancy will be based on the occupant's ability to adjust at least one of the environmental thermal comfort factors of ASHRAE 55 -2004: air temperature, radiant temperature, relative humidity, or air speed.

- *For LEED CS Projects:* Naturally ventilated buildings will have an easier effort for compliance with this credit as opposed to base buildings that are mechanically ventilated or ventilated by the means of a mixed-mode approach due to the lack of the ability to finish the interior spaces. Although the scope of work may not include the completion of the tenant spaces, the base building mechanical system needs to be expandable in order to achieve the requirements of the credit in order to comply.

EQ Credit 7.1: Thermal Comfort—Design (LEED CS EQ Credit 7)

- Project teams will need to refer to ASHRAE 55–2004 in order to confirm compliancy with this credit based on the ventilation system to be implemented. In addition to the four environmental factors previously listed, project teams will also need to address the two personal factors of thermal comfort as defined by the reference standard. Therefore, the team will need to account for the environmental factors, as well as the metabolic rate and clothing personal factors. For mechanically ventilated spaces, the key

RAISED-ACCESS FLOOR MANUFACTURER'S PERSPECTIVE
Under-Floor Air Distribution System Contributions to LEED Certification

By Scott Alwine, LEED AP
Marketing Manager at Tate Access Floors

The greatest contribution toward LEED certification using an access floor system is by incorporating under-floor air distribution (UFAD) (Figure 6.13). A UFAD system delivers increased ventilation effectiveness, improved thermal comfort, and controllability of the systems, while optimizing energy performance. In addition, many access floor manufacturers use recycled content in their products to contribute toward earning even more credits. All of these features can contribute toward achieving points in the following three categories of the LEED rating systems: Energy and Atmosphere, Materials and Resources, and Indoor Environmental Quality.

The UFAD system works by delivering fresh conditioned air directly to the occupied zone. As the air is delivered from the floor, natural convection pulls the air through the six-foot occupied zone toward the return in the ceiling. The one-directional airflow of the system increases ventilation by providing higher levels of outdoor air to the occupied zone and replacing the contaminated air rather than circulating it back down through overhead vents.

Although energy performance is determined by calculating demand for all of the building systems in conjunction with the determined envelope, incorporating UFAD systems can contribute to reducing demand. Energy performance is improved by reducing fan power due to lower static pressure requirements, and by using warmer cooling temperatures (62–65°F), which enable longer use of economizer hours.

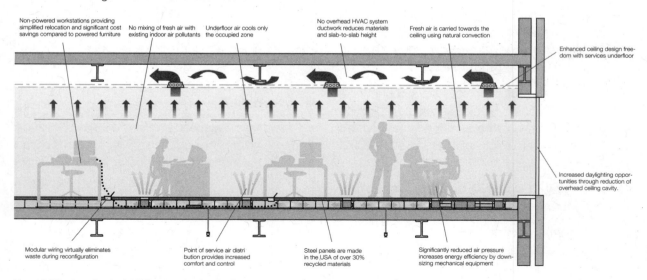

Figure 6.13.   A section to detail the strategy of under-floor air distribution (UFAD).Image courtesy of Tate Access Floors, Inc.

The UFAD attributes further help to improve indoor environmental quality by reducing fan noise, improving air quality and thermal comfort capabilities, and allowing for greater daylighting opportunities. Fan noise or air whistle is reduced due to the reduced amount of pressure utilized in a UFAD environment. Air quality is improved by the one-directional flow of air, avoiding mixing and recirculating air. Thermal comfort is also improved by placing air diffusers in close proximity to each person, enabling them to control the amount and direction of airflow in their area. Daylighting opportunities can be improved by the ability to reduce the amount of plenum space needed for ductwork and cabling overhead and shifting

Figure 6.14 Utilizing a raised-access floor and focusing the air distribution and cable runs at the floor level allows the project team to capitalize on increased ceiling heights and daylighting opportunities. Image courtesy of Tate Access Floors, Inc.

continued

those components to the floor, reducing the amount of space required for service distribution, allowing for higher ceilings and more open indoor space.

In addition to the recycled content used in a raised-floor system (Figure 6.14), manufacturing facilities are located within the United States offering many projects the ability to apply the access floors toward MR Credit 5: Regional Materials. Using a salvaged raised-access floor system may help to earn another MR credit, as raised floors can last beyond the lifetime of a building. While this may be applicable for a LEED NC, CS, or CI project now, project teams in the future may be able to disassemble the system in an existing building and reuse it in a new one.

While many LEED benefits come from implementing UFAD, managing wires and cables under an access floor may qualify for ID credits. Placing wires and cables under the floor reduces materials by eliminating vertical runs and saturation wiring. Termination boxes are placed only where they are needed, reducing the number of outlets. Using modular connectors can encourage reuse during reconfiguration by using the termination plugs to disconnect, move, and reconnect the wires instead of abandoning them and running new wires.

---

is to utilize the load calculation methods to ensure that the HVAC is not oversized but still meets the needs of the occupants. Whichever ventilation strategy is utilized, the approach should align with both the OPR and BOD.

EQ Credit 7.2: Thermal Comfort—Verification Lighting (for LEED NC and CI)

- The owner shall be engaged to develop a survey based on the strategy of the previous credit to be delivered after occupancy. This can be conducted in-house if the owner has the resources, or a third party can be hired to perform the postoccupancy survey, such as the University of California–Berkeley's Center for the Built Environment (CBE). The survey should ask occupants to rank their satisfaction on a seven-point scale and should include questions about the weather conditions at the time of the survey (including season), activity level prior to taking the survey, clothing type, and the occupant's tasks performed in the space to provide a thorough understanding of the conditions in the

space the occupant occupies. A plan for corrective action will also need to be developed and implemented should the survey results indicate that more than 20 percent of the occupants are not satisfied with the thermal environment. These efforts should be completed and uploaded to LEED-Online as soon as possible, as they are not dependent on the completion of the construction documents.

- Project teams will also need to implement a permanent monitoring system to ensure the occupants' comfort as detailed in the previous credit, although performing periodic testing with handheld meters is also acceptable. The system will need to monitor air temperature and humidity for occupied spaces at a minimum. A list of the sensors, setpoints for each zone, and the alarm trigger values will be needed for compliance purposes.

EQ Credit 8: Daylight and Views

- Project teams are encouraged to engage a lighting designer to be responsible for EQ Credit 8.1:

Daylight. Although there are four compliance path options for the credit, developing a computer simulation is best advised, as it allows for the most flexibility when designing as compared to waiting until the space is constructed to verify compliance.

- For both credits, coordination is encouraged among the lighting designer, architect, civil engineer, interior designer, mechanical engineer, and electrical engineer to ensure a successful and compliant holistic strategy, taking into account building orientation, envelope selection, energy demands, lighting requirements, sensors and controls, thermal impacts, window locations, furniture arrangements, and glare control. Once the goals are established, they should be incorporated into the OPR and BOD.

- The most important factor for teams to address is consistently across all compliance path options for this credit: glare control. This strategy is important to address because avoiding it can hinder the productivity and comfort of the building occupants. Solar heat gain is another factor for teams to consider and address, as it directly impacts energy efficiency. Different types of glass perform in different ways, depending on how much light is reflected, absorbed, and transmitted. Transmitted light, or T_{vis}, and the amount of light absorbed impacts solar heat gain. For daylighting purposes, it is best to select glazing with a high T_{vis} to allow for the greatest amount of incident light to pass through the glazing. Therefore, project teams are challenged to find the balance between solar heat gain and T_{vis}. Project teams can also incorporate overhangs, light shelves, and light wells to help to reduce cooling loads.

- *For EQ Credit 8.1:* All project teams can choose whether to pursue a performance-based or a prescriptive-based compliance path, similar to pursuing the energy performance prerequisite and

credit within the EA category. The performance-based option includes a computer simulation demonstrating footcandle (fc) levels between 25 and 500 provided by daylight for the applicable spaces. The prescriptive path involves completing calculations to show compliance depending on top-lighting daylighting zones (using skylights) and side-lighting daylighting zones (using windows or glass doors). Top-lighting daylight strategies must include skylights with a minimum 0.5 visible light transmittance (VLT) for at least 3 to 6 percent of the roof area, and the distance between the skylights must not be more than 1.4 times the ceiling height. Only glazing areas 30 inches above the floor can be included in side-lighting daylight calculations. In this zone, the window-to-floor ratio (WFR) multiplied by the VLT must be between 0.150 and 0.180 in order to comply with the requirements of this option. A third option is available for teams wishing to wait until the space is constructed in order to measure the actual light levels in the applicable spaces, and a fourth option can be pursued to show compliance with this credit by combining of any of the three other options.

- *For EQ Credit 8.2:* Whereas with EQ Credit 8.1 the idea is to increase the daylight measurements within the space, the goal for this credit is to increase the view to the outdoor environment. So, although they can work in tandem, it is critical to be mindful of the seated environment to achieve this credit. Therefore, project teams should be cognizant of low-height furniture and partitions and incorporate interior glazing to allow more occupants to have access to exterior views.

- The responsible party will need to generate floor plans, sections, and elevations to show glare controls measures for EQ Credit 8.1: Daylight and the lines of sight for EQ Credit 8.2: Views.

LIGHTING DESIGNER'S PERSPECTIVE
Benefits of Computer Daylight Simulation

By Magdalena L. DiDomenico, LC, LEED AP
MAG-Lighting Design, LLC

Because we tend to spend more than 90 percent of our time indoors, providing occupants with a healthy and pro-ductivity-boosting connection to the outdoor environment is one element to achieve within the EQ category of LEED. Each of the LEED rating systems awards a team's effort to design a space providing an adequate amount of daylight by allotting up to two points under EQc8.1: Daylight and Views—Daylight credit, including exemplary performance opportunities.

Although there are four different methods to achieve this credit (simulation, prescriptive, measurement, or a combi-nation of all of the above), our practice found the most beneficial approach was option 1—simulation. The ability to quantify the amount of natural light penetrating the building by generating a computer model of the designed spaces became a great cost-saving tool for many projects. Allowing the lighting designer to perform computer calculations before the building construction can result not only in delivering fundamental evidence to save funds at a later phase of the project (e.g., construction cost savings can be predicted by testing different light shelves and shading device designs) but also in revealing changes for design improvement. The capability to test variables (e.g., transparency of different glazing options and the reflectance value of surfaces) made this tool much more versatile to the project team than other options.

Incorporating electrical lighting into a computerized daylight analysis can also have an impact on the daylight-harvesting system design. Appropriate design of the daylight-harvesting system can significantly reduce the demand on the cooling or heating systems, thus significantly impacting the overall building energy performance.

Although EQ Credit 8.1 requires performance of a daylight study for September 21 at 9 AM and 3 PM in clear sky condi-tions, our practice found it beneficial to the client to illustrate a full spectrum of computer analyses for other solar alti-tudes, analyzing solar patterns throughout different day times and under different sky conditions (e.g., vernal [spring] equinox—around March 21; and winter and summer solstices—around December 21 and June 21). This further analysis was able to provide our clients with greater insight for expectations after occupancy.

- *For LEED CS Projects:* Since the tenant spaces are not a typical part of the scope of work, the base building team will need to demonstrate the tenant's capability to comply based on the floor plate design and window placement.

Innovation in Design

Project teams should start to research strategies to pursue to meet the intentions of this category. Teams are encouraged to consult the USGBC website for a summary of previously approved strategies, including the LEED Pilot Credit Library. They should also refer to the reference guides to research opportunities for exemplary performance or to find a credit from another rating system to pursue. The project administrator shall assign the LEED AP on the project the applicable ID credit on LEED-Online for them to upload their credential certificate proving compliance.

Regional Priority

If a project is not yet registered, project teams shall refer the USGBC website to download the spreadsheet for the state in which the project resides to discover which six opportunities are established for the project's zip code. They are encouraged to compare to the project's scorecard to determine if any opportunities align with the six available. When a project is registered, LEED-Online will indicate the available RP credits specific to the project, as shown on the Scorecard tab.

Preliminary Specification Review

The LEED coordinator is encouraged to review the project specifications at the end of the Design Development phase to ensure that the team is on the right path. Quality assurance language is recommended to be included in the Division 1 specifications, especially if the project is seeking the contractor to provide a separate LEED coordinator during construction (possibly as a subcontractor to the general contractor). In this case, sample language might include the following:

1.1 Quality Assurance
    A.   Construction LEED Coordinator Qualifications: A firm or individual experienced in

the evaluation of materials and products for compliance with LEED requirements, and experienced in the documentation of construction related activities for compliance with LEED requirements.

    1. LEED Coordinator: <Enter contact information> or The construction LEED Coordinator shall be a LEED Accredited Professional.

    2. Basis of Qualifications: Organization with LEED Accredited Professionals on staff and has LEED-certified project experience.

    3. Preconstruction Meeting: Within <30> days of award of contract and prior to commencement of work, schedule and conduct a meeting with owner and architect to discuss all LEED requirements, including proposed methods for material attribute tracking, construction waste management (defined in Division 1 Section "Construction Waste Management") and the required construction indoor air quality (IAQ) management plan.

    B.   LEED Coordination Conference: Conduct a LEED coordination conference at project site prior to the commencement of major construction activities with all major contractors and subcontractors present. Conduct the coordination conference to comply with requirements in Division 1 Section "Project Coordination."

It is advised to be sure to also include the following sections in Division 1 to address the environmental goals and requirements of the project, including the development of LEED action plans. Project teams can look to resources such as Masterspec® as published by ARCOM for the American Institute of

ARCHITECT'S PERSPECTIVE
N20–HDR-CUH2A's New Second Office

By Simon Trumble, AIA, LEED AP, Senior Project Designer
and Jorge Rodriguez, AIA, LEED AP, Studio Design Leader
HDR-CUH2A a division of HDR architecture

The new Washington office of HDR-CUH2A, designed by the firm itself, aims to clearly represent the direction and intention of the firm ideals. This 12,500-square-foot, 50-person office space designed with the intention to achieve silver certification under the LEED for Commercial Interiors rating system will be among the first offices within the company to become certified. HDR-CUH2A has professed a commitment to LEED, making it part of its core values and business model. The design of this space represented a great opportunity to provide itself with the same design process and level of attention to concept, detail, and execution that the company has rendered consistently to its clients.

The design process for this new office started by maintaining its location within a walking distance to the Metro train system and a dense network of public transportation options, and it continued by challenging assumed preconceptions of our own spatial and personal needs, establishing measurable goals of the users, and understanding particular physical constraints of the selected property. The design process itself aimed to maintain the most open level of discussion among the group, yet operating in an efficient decision-making process. In this instance, the design process started with a programming session and an in-house visioning session, in which participants were asked to represent, using a preselected set of images from a card deck, their emotional response to the image and the association they envisioned between image and desired project goal. Out of this visioning process emerged several design goals: to create a series of spaces that enhance the collaborative culture espoused at HDR-CUH2A; to have an environment that expresses and celebrates the knowledge, expertise, and enterprise of the individuals that make up the company; and, finally, to invest in an environment that tangibly elaborates the company commitment to environmental stewardship.

The open office environment uses extensively exposed materials and systems (Figure 6.15), characterized by simple articulations and minimal processing and joinery of sustainable materials, from recycled paper-stone countertops, ultra-low VOC paints and adhesives, recyclable carpets, formaldehyde-free medium-density fiberboard (MDF) cabinets to reclaimed teak flooring, throughout. The L-shaped open work spaces are arranged linearly along a spine to allow people to face each other and communicate more effectively. The collaborative culture is furthered through the use of a mixture of teaming spaces with ranging scales of intimacy. These spaces, such as conference rooms, huddle rooms, and teaming areas, have writable surfaces and are located within a few feet of any desk within the office. The end result is a continuous environment open to the exterior glazing (Figure 6.16), allowing views to the outside and natural light to fill the majority of the space. In fact, the only spaces without natural light are in the office shower, the storage rooms, print room, and kitchenette. The print room and kitchenette, in spite of being centrally located, still maintain views to the exterior. This abundance of natural light filling the environment has allowed a 16 percent reduction in lighting levels over ASHRAE 90.1. The zoned environment is fully controlled via occupancy sensors and can be switched centrally from multiple locations throughout the office.

Figure 6.15. The offices of HDR-CUH2A in Washington were designed with the workstations closest to the windows and the private offices at the core. Photo courtesy of Jayanath Ranaweera

The final results, through the deft use of space, light, and material, have challenged preconceived individual notions of office and redirected it into a more common cultural value, one of sustainability, environmental stewardship, collaboration, and ultimately mutual pride in this organization. Although this Commercial Interiors office project has not yet finished the LEED evaluation process, and there is the expectation to achieve a LEED Silver rating, the effort given to selecting materials, familiarizing the contractors, and coordinating the paperwork has been very comprehensive and as such very time consuming. Many hours were invested in evaluating materials documenting its installation and providing the graphic as well as paper material backup to fulfill the LEED application requirements. Our expectation is that in the future, this will become easier and more familiar to the building and materials supply community. At the moment, this is still an emerging field and requires a high level of effort and focus on the goal that must not be averted by all three parties—owner, architect, and builder—in order to achieve the highest LEED ratings possible.

continued

Figure 6.16 The open-plan work area at HDR-CUH2A offers access to views of the outdoors and takes advantage of naturally supplied daylighting. Photo courtesy of Jayanath Ranaweera

Architects, www2.buildinggreen.com/guidespecs, or a specification writing consultant for samples of the following sections:

- Construction Waste Management
- Sustainable Design Requirements (including IAQ requirements)
- Commissioning Requirements

Project teams looking for a more all-encompassing approach to specification can look to the Federal Green Construction Guide for Specifiers at www. wbdg.org/design/greenspec.php.

A project-specific LEED scorecard should follow the Sustainable Design Requirements section to summarize the goals of the project. It is also critical to include language in the rest of the divisions to reference the environmental goals during construction, such as MR Credits 2 through 7 and EQ Credits 3 through 5. The submittal requirements for proper review shall be referenced throughout the manual, including the applicable LEED credit and required data to be included in the submittal, such as cost, recycled content, and/or VOC content. Quality assurance language should also address requirements as related to LEED goals, such as the extraction, processing, and manufacturing of applicable products within 500 miles of the project site.

It is best to advise the design team to avoid a mixed specification approach and not combine a descriptive or prescriptive specification and a performance-based specification. For example, ceiling tile can be specified based on its size and finish, which may conflict with the recycled content or manufacturing location impacting its contribution to earning MR Credits 4 and 5.

Should the project not require a separate LEED coordinator during construction, the specifications should be clear to identify roles and responsibilities to avoid confusion and incorrect bidding.

The next chapter will discuss additional specification inclusions as the project enters into the Construction Documents phase of design.

In Summary

A LEED coordinator will be quite busy at the commencement of the project to help establish the environmental goals for the project with the rest of the team. During the Schematic Design phase, the LEED coordinator is heavily involved with the design of the conceptual features of the project as they take shape due to the environmental goals, such as orientation and footprint. Parking requirements are determined, FTE calculations are completed, and reuse strategies are evaluated. During the Design Development phase, the coordinator may see a bit of a calm as the design team is diligently fulfilling the programming requirements and therefore possibly also a *reduction* in design integration meetings. The coordinator is encouraged to use this time to ensure that LEED-Online is ready for the team, project details have been entered, and all the prerequisites and credits have been assigned to the appropriate team members, and submit any credit interpretation requests (CIRs), if necessary. Typically, during the Design Development stage, the specialized consultants, such as lighting designers and acousticians, are brought onboard. The LEED coordinator should ensure that these consultants are invited to the design integration meetings and are informed of the project goals.

chapter 7

Construction Document Phase

By Melissa Muroff, Esq.
Principal of Roofscapes, Inc.

The green roof designer bears the responsibility of incorporating quality assurance provisions into the specifications to assure that contractor bids reflect the design intent. Specifications should include criteria for specific properties critical to the performance of green roofs (Figure 7.1). Standardized and accepted methodologies (e.g., American Society for Testing and Materials [ASTM], German Landscape Research, Development and Construction Society [FLL], Test Methods for the Examination of Composting and Compost [TMECC], Measurement Systems Analysis [MSA]) for measuring these properties should be cited in green roof specifications. Prospects for success of green roofs will be improved if they comply with recommendations made in standard guides, the most completed of which is the German FLL *Guidelines for the Planning, Construction, and Maintenance of Green Roofing.* Similar American guidelines are under development by ASTM and the American National Standards Institute (ANSI).

Green roof specifications serve as the vehicle for enforcing the assuring quality installations. The specifications can include provisions requiring the following:

- Leak detection, repair, and restoration
- Coordination of the roofing and green roofing details, shop drawings, scopes, and construction sequence
- Proof of green roof installer's qualifications
- Guarantee of plant viability and coverage
- Guarantee of the performance of all green roof components
- Guarantee of the green roof's stormwater performance

continued

Figure 7.1 The green roof at Diamond Beach Condominium in Long Branch, New Jersey, has a 6.5-inch deep unirrigated dual media assembly. Photo courtesy of Roofscapes, Inc.

- Guarantee of the green roof dead load

- Performance test data for the green roof media

- Sufficient maintenance during the period during which the plants are establishing

Green roof maintenance should not be overlooked or undervalued. The green roof typically is the one building component that improves—rather than degrades—with age. Admittedly, almost any roofer or landscaper can install a green roof well enough so that it meets expectations on day one. The mark of an exceptional green roof design and installation team, however, is a green roof that continues to thrive and mature 5, 10, and 20 years later (and beyond). Although considerable maintenance may be required during the first two to three years when the plants are establishing, low-maintenance sedum groundcover green roofs require as little as two to three man-hours per 1,000 square feet per year after the establishment period. For these roofs, a little well-timed maintenance in the spring and fall seems a reasonable cost to preserve this unique investment that will last many decades. Alternatively, even after the establishment period, herbaceous perennials, shrubs, and trees on green roofs will require the same amount of maintenance on a roof as they do on the ground; so the customer's expectations should be managed accordingly.

As mentioned in the previous chapter, the Design Development phase may be very hectic for the design team, while the Leadership in Energy and Environmental Design (LEED®) coordinator must patiently await documentation progress and development. The Construction Document phase brings the coordinator back into the hot seat, as the team is gearing up for a design-side certification review with Green Building Certification Institute (GBCI). This chapter focuses on the critical tasks to be completed during the Construction Documents phase in order to submit for a design review after the plans and specifications are submitted for permit review. Remember, it is critical to keep the team focused and on point with LEED documentation requirements during this phase, because once the construction documents are issued for permit, the consultants are typically assigned to another project quite quickly. To help simplify the discussion of the tasks to be completed, commissioning (Cx) and energy simulation modeling is discussed separately followed by a construction document and specification review, ultimately leading up to a documentation review on LEED-Online to submit for the design review.

Commissioning

By this phase of the project, the owner's program requirements (OPR) and basis of design (BOD) should have been reviewed, and the Cx plan should be generated and implemented as discussed in the previous chapter. Step 5 of the required Cx activities stipulates the Cx activities must be incorporated into the CDs. As previously stated, it is strongly suggested to include a separate commissioning section in the Division 1 specifications to detail the commissioning authority's (CxA's) role and the responsibilities of the contractor during construction, as the two will need to work together. The mechanical and electrical divisions should also include Cx notes, as these systems are included in the Cx plan. It is important that the bidding subcontractors understand the Cx process and how their involvement maybe required during functional testing. As the CxA is typically hired by the time the documents are issued for bid, the specification should clarify that the contractor is not responsible for hiring a CxA. If the team is not pursuing Energy and Atmosphere (EA) Credit 3 for LEED for New Construction and Major Renovations™ (NC) and LEED for Core & Shell™ (CS) (EA Credit 2

MEP ENGINEER'S PERSPECTIVE
Energy Modeling Pitfalls

By Aaron Dahlstrom, PE, LEED AP
In Posse LLC

Energy modeling is the art and science of simulating the energy performance of buildings using models. Within the context of LEED for New Construction, there are three main reasons for conducting energy modeling: optimizing a building's energy-related design; estimating the contribution of energy-efficiency features as part of the LEED certification process; and calibrating a model to postoccupancy energy bills to verify the performance of the energy-efficiency features.

Energy modeling for LEED submission is often calculated with powerful third-party tools, including DOE-2, Trane Trace, and EnergyPlus. Engineers and architects who enter the world of energy modeling can find themselves bewildered, or worse, can find their LEED submission rejected because they are unfamiliar with the complexity of energy modeling inputs, software defaults, and the synergistic interactions between systems. A number of principles and tools will help a savvy learner avoid the most common pitfalls of LEED energy modeling. The main tools that help such a learner include reasonable expectations, informed intuition, knowledge of the required protocols, and familiarity with common mistakes.

Having reasonable expectations regarding the results can fundamentally assist accurate energy modeling. Energy modeling includes a host of default assumptions, starting with the weather data used to test the building's thermal performance. This data is processed based on historical climate measurements to represent long-term weather trends. Thus, for buildings with strong exterior load dependencies, it is unreasonable to expect average weather data to accurately predict specific performance in any given actual year. Similar averages exist for HVAC equipment performance curves. While modelers may customize equipment performance using full-load efficiency factors from the manufacturer, few models modify the default "part-load" performance curves, which specify the amount of energy used on non-peak-load days. Similar averages and defaults are included for equipment control sequences, lighting use profiles, office equipment use profiles, and so on. Thus, unless carefully calibrated to inputs measured at the building scale, energy models can be expected to provide general comparisons among different choices, but should not be expected to provide a specific budget for any given year's energy use.

Another crucial tool for accurate energy modeling is a strong intuition regarding how building energy systems should function, independent of model results. For example, LEED requires that all "software warnings and errors" be explained as part of the LEED submission. On a recent project, an energy recovery system generated a warning that the coils were gathering ice through a significant part of the winter. Our intuition was that there was an error in an internal source of humidity (moisture gain from people or a process load). When the model was investigated, the intuition proved correct, and the warning was eliminated prior to submission to the certification body. Intuition will also lead modelers to examine the relative energy use of heating, ventilating, and air conditioning (HVAC) versus domestic water heating versus lighting and equipment. For example, standard office buildings rarely have high domestic water-heating loads producing results that do not match this expectation requiring further review. Finally, intuition can help modelers validate that the addition of energy performance features is generating the results they expect. While a cool roof may significantly reduce air-conditioning load in an office building, its percent contribution will be greatly reduced in a high-internal-load manufacturing facility.

Third, awareness of the requirements of the referenced protocols can help to generate accurate simulations. The *LEED Reference Guide for Building Design + Construction* (BD+C) includes a number of specific instructions regarding model performance—for example, process loads are required to make up at least 25 percent of the baseline energy cost, unless specific documentation is provided showing all of the actual process loads planned for the building. This may impact buildings, such as K–12 schools or multifamily residential buildings that often have low process uses. Modelers will need to address this requirement to avoid the LEED certification authority's rejecting the submission. In addition, the rating system references American Society of Heating, Refrigerating, and Air-Conditioning Engineers (ASHRAE) 90.1, an independent energy performance standard for buildings. The standard contains a large number of specific prescriptions, which LEED reviewers are relatively thorough with enforcing. For nonmodelers, a familiarity with some of the basic language of the standard, such as the names and number designations of HVAC system types, can help check model submissions so typos do not cause a project to receive special scrutiny from reviewers. For modelers, the ASHRAE 90.1 user's manual offers a wealth of guidance and example cases for the difficult cases. For example, it details what envelope requirements apply to a major renovation that modifies windows but not wall insulation and how elevator energy use should vary across an average day.

Finally, familiarity with common mistakes others have made will aid in modeling success. The BD+C reference guide includes a tabulation of mistakes that reviewers have often flagged on past projects. For example, many modelers have neglected the fact that the ASHRAE window performance allowances refer to the overall performance of the entire assembly, including the window frame, rather than specifically to the glazing only. Another common error is to neglect to include all the energy uses inside the building, including items such as elevators and exterior lighting. New modelers are encouraged to review the common mistakes list within the BD+C reference guide, and cross-reference the applicable ASHRAE texts to be sure that their models are not making mistakes with these common problem areas.

LEED and energy modeling offer opportunities for improvements in building science and modeling physics to inform high-performing buildings in this generation and for years to come. Engineers, architects, and modelers savvy with energy modeling efforts understand that bringing all their intuition, reasoning, and knowledge about the standards results in the production of high-quality modeling outputs.

---

for LEED for Commercial Interiors™ [CI] projects): Enhanced Commissioning, a CxA can be engaged anytime prior to the equipment installation. The specifications should include this approach, if appropriate.

If the project team is pursuing EA Credit 3 (EA Credit 2 for CI projects): Enhanced Commissioning, the CxA will need to review the construction drawings and specification prior to midconstruction document phase. This review ensures the owner's requirements and BOD are consistent with the documents to be issued to the contractor for construction. This review completes Step 6 of the commissioning activities.

Whole-Building Simulation

Project teams that started with simple modeling software will need to choose which energy modeling software to use for LEED documentation purposes. The Department of Energy's DOE-2 program is the most widely used software but is text based, and therefore is typically paired with a "front-end" software for graphic interfaces. Some teams prefer to use EnergyPlus, as it combines DOE-2 and another Department of Energy software, Building Loads Analysis and System Thermodynamics (BLAST). Other teams utilize VisualDOE, the Windows-based interface to DOE-2. eQuest is another DOE-2 interface and is also qualified for calculating tax deductions for commercial buildings under the Energy Policy Act (EPAct 2005). For teams in California, eQuest and EnergyPro compete for use, as they were both designed to comply with the state's Title 24 energy code.

There are also some other modeling tools that are not best suited for whole-building simulation applications. Trane has developed a Windows-based version of TRACE 600, which is best used as an equipment-sizing tool but not necessarily for energy simulation. Readers, beware—at the time of printing, this software is not compatible with ASHRAE 90.1–2007, but only the 2004 version of the reference standard and therefore not applicable for LEED rating systems, version 3.0. System Analyzer can be coupled with TRACE to allow a more detailed analysis. Carrier's HAP software is also best used for sizing. ENER-WIN is available for large commercial building projects but not intended to study changes in HVAC systems.

In addition to the project type, size, and systems, a project team should be aware of what the documentation requirements are for the purposes of LEED, to help them select the appropriate simulation software.

As mentioned in the previous chapter, all of the building energy components will need to be included in the model. Energy saving reductions are not allowed to be calculated using the energy cost budget method. Process energy loads shall be modeled the same for both the baseline and design cases. Reductions in plug loads are not accounted for in the model, as those are addressed separately using the exceptional calculation methodology. These calculations are required in addition to the energy model. Project teams should see reference to exceptional calculation methodology in ASHRAE 90.1. Exceptional calculation methodology will also need to be used if the process energy loads differ for the baseline and design cases or if the model cannot calculate specific situations for the project. If project teams pursue this method, they will also need to submit all assumptions made for the baseline and design cases.

The reference guide details the requirements for the different components to be addressed by simulation. For example, a project's schedule of operations does not change from the baseline case to the design case, although the baseline case has to be modeled at least four times, according to the reference standard's Table G3.5.1(a), to address orientation and solar heat gain coefficients. Simulation requirements for the building envelope, lighting systems, HVAC systems, process energy, energy rates, and service hot water systems are also described in the reference guide and therefore should be reviewed by the project team. Projects with natural ventilation strategies are evaluated on a case-by-case basis. For projects with on-site renewable energy systems and/or site-recovered energy costs, the associated cost savings are not included in the proposed design case, and therefore the team would need to pursue the performance rating method detailed in Appendix G of the reference standard. NC and CS teams are encouraged to refer to pages 275–276 of the BD+C reference guide for a list of common mistakes when pursuing Option 1.

Specification and Plan Review

At the end of the Design Development phase, the specifications should be reviewed to ensure that the team is on the right path and including the required language addressing LEED requirements. When the construction documents are 90 percent completed, they are typically submitted to the owner for a review prior to submitting for permit review and/or issued for bid. It is at that time the LEED coordinator should also review the documents to ensure the LEED strategies are included and clarified. Most projects fail to keep the efforts continued through construction in order to earn certification; hence the reason there are more registered projects than certified. The most common mistake typically comes down to misunderstandings about responsibilities during construction. Here, the main LEED categories are listed with the prerequisites and credits that are typically addressed in the construction drawings and specifications with key information to verify and confirm:

Sustainable Sites (SS)

- **SS Prerequisite 1: Construction Activity Pollution Prevention (for NC and CS projects).** Although this prerequisite is not eligible for a design-side review, the LEED coordinator should review the erosion and sedimentation control (ESC) plan. Verify that the introduction includes the standard followed for compliance and that the temporary and permanent control measures are listed. The specifications should clarify who is responsible for the verification and inspection

of the control measures. There are three options by which to prove compliance, so it is critical to assign responsibility. The options include dated photographs, a written report, or an inspection log. In any case, a plan for corrective action should be developed and implemented if needed, especially after rain events.

- **SS Credit 4.1 (LEED CI SS Credit 3.1): Alternative Transportation—Public Transportation Access.** Ensure there is pedestrian access to the bus stops or rail station and that they fall within the credit's distance limits.

- **SS Credit 4.2 (LEED CI SS Credit 3.2): Alternative Transportation—Bicycle Storage and Changing Rooms.** Verify that the correct amount of showers and bicycle racks are indicated on the plans and that they are not located more than 200 yards from the building entrance. Zero-lot-line projects will need to incorporate bicycle storage on the sidewalks with appropriate signage reserving the racks for occupant usage.

- **SS Credit 4.3: Alternative Transportation-Low-Emitting and Fuel-Efficient Vehicles–** Ensure the correct amount of preferred parking spaces or refueling stations are provided (depending on compliance path). If preferred parking will be provided, verify the spaces assigned are the closest to the building entrance(s).

- **SS Credit 4.4 (LEED CI SS Credit 3.3): Alternative Transportation—Parking Capacity.** Verify that the site plans indicate the accurate amount of parking and the preferred parking spaces. Be sure the team did not double count the preferred parking along with the requirements of the previous credits.

- **SS Credit 5.1: Site Development—Protect or Restore Habitat.** Ensure that the plans and specifications detail construction entrances, staging areas, and site disturbance setbacks to protect and preserve existing natural areas. Although not typically noted on drawings to be issued for permit/construction, be sure to verify a consistent LEED project boundary across all credits. Project teams are encouraged to include compliance with this credit's requirements in the contract agreement with the contractor, as implementation is critical to achieving the credit.

- **SS Credit: Stormwater.** Verify that the stormwater management strategies are included in the specifications and clearly noted on the plans with the strategy linked to the coordinating area.

- **SS Credit 7.1 (LEED CI SS Credit 1, Option 2, Path 4) Heat Island Effect—Nonroof.** Ensure that the specifications address high solar reflectance index (SRI) paving materials (Figure 7.2), or for major renovations and tenant improvement projects, the specifications and drawings require the construction team to clean the existing weathered gray concrete hardscape areas and define the minimum goal for the SRI value.

- **SS Credit 7.2: Heat Island Effect—Roof.** Verify that the specified roofing material's SRI value is consistent with the requirements of this credit.

- **SS Credit 8.1: Light Pollution Reduction.** Ensure that there is a light fixture schedule on the lighting plan(s) with specifications, such as wattage, ballasts, controls, and cover for cutoff. Double check to verify that the interior light controls are indicated, as well as any window shades. Be sure to verify that interior light fixtures do not spill a cone of light more than 50 percent to the exterior at any envelope openings.

Water Efficiency (WE)

- **WE Prerequisite 1: Water Use Reduction (also LEED CI WE Credit 1, LEED NC and CS Credit 3, Credit 2: Innovative Wastewater Technologies, and CI SS Credit 1, Option 2, Path 9).** Ensure the proper fixtures are indicated on the plans and in the specifications to achieve the minimum requirements and/or desired water reductions better than the reference standard.

- **WE Credit 1: Water Efficient Landscaping (CI SS Credit 1, Option 2, Paths 7 and 8).** Ensure that the correct irrigation system is specified or that the vegetation is appropriate for the desired compliance path.

Energy and Atmosphere (EA)

- **EA Prerequisite 1: Fundamental Commissioning, and EA Credit 3: Enhanced Commissioning (LEED CI EA Credit 2: Enhanced Commissioning).** Verify that the Cx scope is included and addressed accurately in the Division 1 specifications, as well as the mechanical and electrical divisions clarifying responsibilities, such as prefunctional testing.

- **EA Prerequisite 2: Minimum Energy Performance, and EA Credit 1: Optimize Energy Performance.** Ensure that the drawings and specifications include the building systems that coordinate with the strategies being pursued in the energy model. The more detailed the documents are, the less chance for nonconformity and mistakes.

- **EA Prerequisite 3: Fundamental Refrigerant Management, and Credit 4: (for NC and CS projects).** Verify that the correct equipment is specified and meets the strategy for compliance.

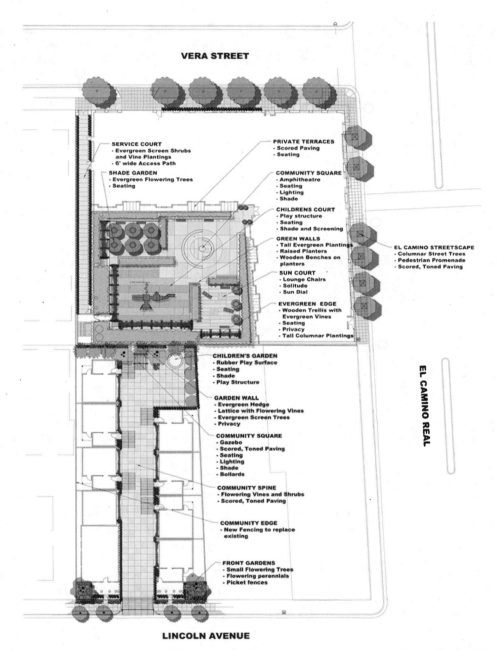

VERA STREET

SERVICE COURT
- Evergreen Screen Shrubs and Vine Plantings
- 6' wide Access Path

SHADE GARDEN
- Evergreen Flowering Trees
- Seating

PRIVATE TERRACES
- Scored Paving
- Seating

COMMUNITY SQUARE
- Amphitheatre
- Seating
- Lighting
- Shade

CHILDRENS COURT
- Play structure
- Seating
- Shade and Screening

GREEN WALLS
- Tall Evergreen Plantings
- Raised Planters
- Wooden Benches on planters

EL CAMINO STREETSCAPE
- Columnar Street Trees
- Pedestrian Promenade
- Scored, Toned Paving

SUN COURT
- Lounge Chairs
- Solitude
- Sun Dial

EVERGREEN EDGE
- Wooden Trellis with Evergreen Vines
- Seating
- Privacy
- Tall Columnar Plantings

EL CAMINO REAL

CHILDREN'S GARDEN
- Rubber Play Surface
- Seating
- Shade
- Play Structure

GARDEN WALL
- Evergreen Hedge
- Lattice with Flowering Vines
- Evergreen Screen Trees
- Privacy

COMMUNITY SQUARE
- Gazebo
- Scored, Toned Paving
- Seating
- Lighting
- Shade
- Bollards

COMMUNITY SPINE
- Flowering Vines and Shrubs
- Scored, Toned Paving

COMMUNITY EDGE
- New Fencing to replace existing

FRONT GARDENS
- Small Flowering Trees
- Flowering perennials
- Picket fences

LINCOLN AVENUE

Figure 7.2 Villa Montgomery Apartments in Redwood City, California, by Fisher-Friedman Associates, earned LEED Gold certification under the LEED for NC rating system, for implementing a sustainable approach for the hardscape areas and creating over 11,000 square feet of open space for the residents to enjoy. Photo courtesy of FFA.

LANDSCAPE ARCHITECT'S PERSPECTIVE
Design Water as One System

By Aiman Duckworth, ASLA, LEED AP
Landscape Designer and Associate at AECOM

Water has many first names: rain, storm, potable, grey, black, process, and so on. Ultimately, water is one precious resource, and designers can best serve a project by approaching the water cycle of a project as one cohesive system. As multiple disciplines typically create the final LEED documentation for different water-related credits, innovative opportunities can be lost in the fragmentation. Create a water cycle design for the project in the Conceptual Design phases, with collaboration among the landscape architect, irrigation engineer, architect, civil engineer, mechanical/electrical/plumbing (MEP) engineer, and ecosystem specialist. Account for the path and changes of all water entering and leaving the site.

If the building(s) were missing from drawings in the design process, there would surely be disconnections in the project. Yet water typically finds representation in design dialogue only as pipes, topography, or calculations that can easily be the focus of only one team discipline. The water cycle design can also be represented graphically as a simple two-dimensional flow diagram, or a three-dimensional illustration of volumes of water at various stages and locations on-site. Appropriate team members can then develop volumes and flows corresponding to the project water budget. A water cycle design graphic provides a shared representation that all team members can reference. It can help ensure that no opportunities are left out to limit disruption and pollution of water systems because of lack of dialogue between disciplines.

- **EA Credit 1: Optimize Energy Performance (for LEED CI projects).** Ensure that the correct type and number of controls, sensors, wiring, equipment, fixtures, and pipe insulation are specified in the documents and in the correct place, and coordinate with the calculations proving compliance with LEED requirements.

  - *EA Credit 1.2, Strategies 1 and 2:* Be sure the lighting plan(s) indicates which daylight sensor coordinates with the appropriate/applicable light(s).

  - *EA Credit 1.2, Strategy 2:* Be sure to verify the daylight sensor controls are within 15 feet of windows or skylights and that the specifications clearly outline the responsibility of calibration, training, and verification.

- *EA Credit 1.3:* Verify that the efficiency ratings are noted in the specifications and/or equipment schedules for the applicable equipment. For Option 1, review the drawings to ensure the zones are noted correctly and coordinate with the appropriate controls. The specifications should be reviewed to ensure that the controls are correctly described.

- *EA Credit 1.4:* Verify the correct equipment is listed in the appropriate schedule.

- **EA Credit 2: On-Site Renewable Energy (LEED CI SS Credit 1, Option 2, Path 11).** Ensure that the on-site renewable system is included in the specifications and drawings with associated bracing and anchors as required by code. Be sure the Cx aspects are covered in the specifications.

- **EA Credit 5: Measurement and Verification.** Review the meter placement in the drawings, and if a building automation system (BAS) is to be used, ensure that there is room dedicated for all of the necessary equipment. Ensure that the specifications address the commissioning of the BAS, if applicable.

Materials and Resources (MR)

- **MR Credit 1.1: Building Reuse, Maintain Existing Walls, Floors, and Roof (for LEED NC and CS projects).** Ensure that the CDs indicate which areas are to be protected and preserved and instructions for restoration during demolition and construction phases. Verify that the areas do not include any hazardous materials, unstable envelope components, roofing materials, window assemblies, or doors for the purposes of LEED compliance.

- **MR Credit 1.2: Maintain 50 Percent Interior Nonstructural Elements (for LEED CS and CI projects).** Specifications should identify the measures during demolition and construction to preserve the elements to be reused. Drawings should also indicate which areas are to be protected and preserved and instructions for restoration during demolition and construction phases. Verify that the areas do not include any hazardous materials or exterior walls or doors for safety and compliance purposes.

- **MR Credit 2: Construction Waste Management.** Be sure to review the Division 1 specifications to ensure that the waste diversion goals are addressed and identify the responsible party to develop and implement a construction waste management plan. The specifications should also address on- and/or off-site sorting strategies to comply for different material types.

- **MR Credit 3: Materials Reuse.** Construction documents and specifications should identify items on-site to be reused and should detail the procedures in order to salvage them or what their intended new use is. For items to be salvaged from off-site, the specifications should provide information to the contractor in order to locate the sources.

- **MR Credit 3.2: Materials Reuse, Furniture and Furnishings.** Project teams are encouraged to read the Furniture section in Chapter 8 for guidance, as furniture is typically omitted from the contractor's scope of work and is therefore not included in the specifications. If the furniture procurement is included in the contractor's scope, confirm the specifications clearly define the salvage requirements in Divisions 1 and 12.

- **MR Credit 4: Recycled Content, MR Credit 5: Regional Materials, and MR Credit 6: Rapidly Renewable Materials.** Division 1 specifications should include goals to inform the contractor and encourage conversations with suppliers and subcontractors during the preconstruction or the bidding process. The other applicable divisions, such as 3 through 10, should also define the requirements to meet these credits. The specifications should also address the documentation requirements to comply with each credit. Be sure the responsibility for tracking the materials for compliance contributions is clearly defined as well.

- **MR Credit 7: Certified Wood.** Specifications should list Forest Stewardship Council

(FSC)-certified vendors, chain-of-custody (COC) requirements, and the FSC website as a resource. The website should be listed for the contractors to refer to for COC documentation requirements. Specifications should also outline and explain the line-item approach for listing all new wood materials purchased for the project for LEED documentation purposes.

Indoor Environmental Quality (EQ)

- **EQ Prerequisite 1: Minimum Indoor Air Quality Performance and EQ Credit 2: Increased Ventilation.** For mechanically ventilated projects, ensure that the specifications include the intended Minimum Efficiency Reporting Value (MERV) filter requirements. Review the mechanical equipment schedule and plans to ensure that outside air is delivered to the appropriate areas. For naturally ventilated projects, be sure all floor areas are within 25 feet of an operable window and that the windows are sized to be 4 square feet per 100 square feet of floor area. If there are any areas outside of the 25-foot maximum distance to an operable window, verify that those spaces are designed to receive mechanically supplied outdoor air and have exhaust provisions.

- **EQ Prerequisite 2: Environmental Tobacco Smoke (ETS) Control.** Projects that do not allow any smoking on site are best situated for compliance. If smoking will be allowed within the building, review the partition schedule to ensure that the dedicated spaces are separately exhausted with impermeable deck-to-deck partitions and are negatively pressurized in comparison to adjacent spaces. Be sure to verify that areas for potential air leakage are addressed. If smoking will not be allowed within the building but allowed onsite, verify that an exterior space

has been designated at least 25 feet away from the building entrances, operable windows, or any outdoor air intakes. If working with a residential component and blower-door tests are required, verify that the details are addressed in the specifications. Regardless of the smoking policy, be sure signage is included in the scope to identify designated areas and/or the no-smoking policy.

- **EQ Credit 1: Outdoor Air Delivery Monitoring.** Confirm that the mechanical engineer indicated the sensor locations on a floor plan and included the devices in the mechanical equipment schedules. Verify that carbon dioxide (CO_2) monitors are detailed to be installed between three and six feet above the finish floor and that CO_2 monitors are indicated in all densely occupied areas. If CO_2 sensors are intended to be compared to outdoor CO_2 levels, outdoor monitors must be indicated on the plans as well.

- **EQ Credit 3.1: Construction Indoor Air Quality (IAQ) Management Plan—During Construction.** Verify that the specifications address filtration media, installation timing, compiling an IAQ management plan clarifing the photograph requirements, and the Sheet Metal and Air Conditioning Contractors' National Association (SMACNA) guidelines including: the wrapping of ductwork for delivery and installation, and the protection of absorptive materials. Be sure responsibilities are clearly defined, including the plan and monthly reports, and completing the LEED credit submittal template. While reviewing the specifications, be sure the smoking policy is addressed and the maximum VOC limits for compliance with low-emitting EQ Credits are included.

- **EQ Credit 3.1: Construction IAQ Management Plan—Before Occupancy.** Verify the specifications list the requirements for either a flush-out or air quality testing and who is responsible for completing these tasks.

- **EQ Credit 4: Low-Emitting Materials.** Verify that the Division 1 specifications include the VOC requirements applicable for the project, depending on the credits the team is pursuing. Additional requirements should be listed throughout the other divisions to ensure compliance. For example, if the team is pursuing EQ Credit 4.2: Paints and Coatings, Division 9 Painting should include the VOC limits of the different specified paint products, such as flat paints to comply with Green Seal Standard 11. Be sure to address EQ Credit 4.4, as it restricts the use of urea formaldehyde for all composite materials such as plywood, door cores, and millwork substrates. The specification writing resources in the previous chapter details the suggested language to include.

- **EQ Credit 5: Indoor Chemical and Pollutant Source Control.** Review the ground-floor plan to ensure that the main entry way systems are at least 10 feet in the direction of travel (Figure 7.3), and if rollout mats are to be used, that the mats meet the parameters described in the applicable reference guide. The door and partition schedules should also be reviewed to verify that there is a self-closing door specified and deck-to-deck partitions for hazardous material use areas. If deck-to-deck partitions are not specified, check the ceiling plan to verify if a hard lid ceiling is planned instead for any chemical areas. In any case, be sure the areas are separately exhausted with no air recirculation. Also, verify that any uninterruptible power supply (UPS) machines and/or battery banks are segregated, and confirm that the storage and containment of hazardous liquids has been planned for and is not located near any outdoor air intake locations.

- **EQ Credit 6.1: Controllability of Systems, Lighting (for LEED NC and CI projects).** Review the plans to ensure that the location and type of controls are noted and verify that the specifications detail the control requirements to ensure they are included in the bid and installed during construction. For example, the National Audubon Society project was able to earn the highest level of LEED certification due to the project team's diligent effort to include controls, sensors, and adjustable task lighting (Figure 7.4). Be sure the lighting system is included in the commissioning scope if it is addressed in the specifications.

- **EQ Credit 6.2 (LEED CS EQ Credit 6): Controllability of Systems—Thermal Comfort.** For mechanically ventilated spaces, verify the location of comfort controls in single-occupied spaces and that each multioccupant space has independent comfort controls. Review for coordination with the BAS. For naturally ventilated spaces, review the window schedule to ensure proper specification. For mixed-mode projects, verify coordination among the windows, sensors, and the BAS to increase efficiency.

- **EQ Credit 7.1: Thermal Comfort, Design (LEED CS EQ Credit 7).** Ensure that the specifications address ASHRAE 55 requirements, operations and maintenance (O&M) manuals, and clarify the declarant's responsibility for this credit.

- **EQ Credit 7.2: Thermal Comfort, Verification Lighting (for LEED NC and CI projects).** Verify that the permanent building monitoring system is included in the CDs and specifications.

Figure 7.3 Implementing grate entryway systems, such as this one at the Waterfront Tech Center in Camden, New Jersey, contributes to earning EQ Credit 5: Indoor Chemical and Pollutant Source Control. Photo courtesy of Stephen Martorana, LEED AP BD+C of the New Jersey Economic Development Authority.

LEED-Online Documentation Review

Once the plans and specifications are finalized, the LEED coordinator will need to motivate the design team to complete the LEED submittal templates and upload all of the supporting documentation to LEED-Online. The LEED coordinator will need to be diligent to review all of the templates and documentation in a timely manner just in case further information is needed from the team. Remember, the design team members may be assigned to a new project, so the more time that passes after permit review, the more challenging it may be to receive a response, which will ultimately delay the submission to GBCI for certification review. Therefore, it is recommended to complete any prerequisites or credits, such as EQ Prerequisite 2: Environmental Tobacco Smoke (ETS) Control, that can be completed prior to the completion of the CDs to leave time to address the others in order to submit shortly after CDs are issued.

Figure 7.4 The lighting design at The National Audubon Society project in New York, designed by Illumination Arts and FXFOWLE Architects, includes sensors and adjustable task lighting at the workstations. These types of strategies helped to earn the project its LEED CI Platinum level certification. Photo courtesy of FXFOWLE Architects and David Sundberg/Esto.

The LEED coordinator also needs to ensure that the project information forms provided on LEED-Online are completed prior to reviewing the uploaded information from the design team, as the team will need the information from the forms in order to complete the credit submittal templates. Therefore, completing them early will not cause any delays and will allow for time to review documentation prior to the certification review submission. These forms include information such as: conformity to the minimum program

requirements (MPRs); project summary details, such as the project's gross square footage and total project budget; occupant and usage data, such as full-time equivalent (FTE) values; schedule and overview documents; and any previously LEED certification details.

Although the CDs and specifications to be submitted for permit review and ultimately delivered to the construction team were reviewed, the LEED coordinator will still need to review the documentation uploaded to LEED-Online for accuracy, consistency, and completion. The coordinator will need to review the submittal template and supporting documentation the design team has uploaded for every prerequisite and credit the team is pursuing. It is important to ensure that the documentation proving compliance is clear, concise, and directly conveys the strategies meeting the requirements for each prerequisite and credit. For example, to show compliance with SS Credit 4.1: Public Transportation Access (SS Credit 3.1 for CI projects), the responsible party will need to upload a plan with the location of the bus stop(s) or rail station and the building entrance. The path and the distance should be clearly noted on the plan (perhaps in a bold color while the background is black and white) to make it clearly understood by the reviewing party. The strategy must also be consistent with the narrative on the credit submittal template with the supporting documentation files listed correctly. Remember to submit only the required documentation as miscellaneous and/or irrelevant information should be omitted from the uploaded supporting documentation, such as landscaping or grading information for a plan documenting compliance for parking capacity. The GBCI review team will request additional information if necessary. It is best to be thorough but lean, as overwhelming the review team with irrelevant, abundant, or superfluous information is not the right approach.

For each prerequisite and credit, the LEED coordinator is encouraged to confirm whether the streamlined path or full documentation path is appropriate and correct. Remember, the streamlined path requires the licensed professional to sign the license profession exemption (LPE) form located on the LPE tab within LEED-Online for applicable credits. If any tables or schedules were completed, the LEED coordinator shall ensure that all the quantities and such are filled in correctly. Some prerequisites and credits require narratives; therefore, be sure to note if any are missing and, if not, read through them all to ensure accuracy, relevance, and thoroughness. Sometimes, it is best to pretend to be the actual reviewer. Are you overwhelmed with the information as you read through it? Is some supporting information difficult to read? Is the documentation uploaded so that it is readable, or does it need to be rotated? Are shower locations and quantities highlighted? Are the roofing materials and slopes clearly noted? Is the strategy clearly defined and understood? Here, the main LEED categories are listed with the prerequisites and credits that are typically addressed during the design side certification review to verify and confirm prior to submission.

Sustainable Sites

- **SS Credit 1: Site Selection.** For NC and CS projects, if the site complies, a submittal template will need to be completed. If portions of the site do not comply, a narrative will be required describing the intent to preserve the sensitive areas to be reviewed based on special circumstances. The responsible party should also upload detailed site plans depicting the sensitive areas not to be disturbed. Be sure the plan is cleaned up of any irrelevant information to clearly show complying strategy.

For CI projects, documentation requirements will vary, depending on the path(s) pursued. Tenants that lease within a LEED-certified building and are pursuing Option 1 will need to upload the LEED certification and final scorecard for the base building (regardless of the rating system it was certified under). For Option 2, project teams can pursue the LPE compliance path or should refer to the

GBCI REVIEWER'S PERSPECTIVE
Top Five Tips for Submitting a LEED Project to GBCI

By Martin Mechtenberg, Assoc. AIA, LEED AP
Principal at EmpowerDesign Studios

1. **Consistency is key.** Provide clear, consistent project information across all credit submittals. This includes project boundaries, square footage information, FTE numbers, spaces claimed as regularly occupied or multi-person, materials used and product costs. Credits are cross-referenced, so a mistake in one can lead to a request for clarification in a related credit even if your submittal for that credit was perfect. Before uploading the final project, make a list of key information and go over the application one more time, looking for any areas where conflicting data has been provided.

2. **A needle in the haystack.** Highlight important information in the materials provided to support a credit submittal. For example, if you are submitting 12 pages of mechanical drawings in support of EQc5, clearly mark the location of the rooms and entrances that are relevant to the credit submittal. This will help the reviewer quickly find the important information, and decreases the likelihood of an oversight or misunderstanding.

3. **Out of many: one.** Consider combining files when uploading supporting documentation to LEED Online. Multiple files that each contain an important bit of information can be difficult to review. Combining key files together into a single, well-marked document can make the review process quicker and less prone to error.

4. **Check your standards!** Ensure that you are following the correct referenced standard for each credit reviewed, per the rating system. For example, if ASHRAE 90.1 2007 is the required standard, make sure your team doesn't use ASHRAE 90.1 2004 instead. Make sure any supporting documentation you upload follows the correct standard too – especially if it's coming from a vendor, contractor or outside consultant.

5. **A second set of eyes.** When the application is complete and ready to be submitted, consider having a third party review it for clarity and consistency. Sometimes a fresh review by someone not directly involved with the application will quickly notice an oversight or error that could save a credit from denial—and save you work in the long run.

---

coordinating credit listed below for documentation requirements. Path 4 requirements can be found in Chapter 10. Project teams should note that some credits may be more time consuming than others, as documentation may be needed from the other tenants and not just the building owner, such as Light Pollution Reduction, Path 6.

- **SS Credit 2: Development Density and Community Connectivity.** Verify that the correct information and supporting maps and schedules have been uploaded and clearly delineate

compliance. Since the submittal template on LEED-Online tabulates the density radius, the template should be checked to ensure that it suggests compliance. For either option, a licensed professional can complete the submittal template by using the LPE form and avoid completing the calculations, but they should be confident that the project complies, as their license could be in jeopardy. For Option 2, if any of the basic services do not exist but are planned, the responsible party will need to upload a lease agreement or a letter from the owner indicating that the services will be provided by the time the project is occupied. Remember, only 2 of the 10 basic services are allowed to be projected.

- **SS Credit 4.1 (LEED CI SS Credit 3.1): Alternative Transportation—Public Transportation Access.** Ensure that the pedestrian access distance from the building entrance is compliant with the requirements of the credit. The route should be highlighted and the distance clearly noted. If the team is pursuing an Exemplary Performance point under the Innovation in Design (ID) category, review the comprehensive management plan for completion and accuracy *or* verify the ridership data for the bus, rail, or other compliant public transportation method. Remember, the goal of the transportation management plan is to reduce single-occupancy-vehicle commuting.

- **SS Credit 4.2 (LEED CI SS Credit 3.2): Alternative Transportation—Bicycle Storage and Changing Rooms.** Verify that the correct showers and bicycle racks are shown on the site plan uploaded to LEED-Online. Remember, miscellaneous and irrelevant information should be omitted from the plan and the relevant areas should be highlighted. Be sure the submittal template information is correct and aligns with the supporting plans. Be sure to include signage declaring that bike racks are reserved for occupant usage, if applicable.

- **SS Credit 4.3: Alternative Transportation-Low-Emitting and Fuel-Efficient Vehicles –** Ensure the correct amount of preferred parking spaces or refueling stations are noted on the uploaded plan (depending on compliance path). If preferred parking will be provided, verify

the spaces assigned are the closest to the building entrance(s). Be sure the credit submittal template indicates the correct compliance path and the supporting documentation is listed.

- **SS Credit 4.4 (LEED CI SS Credit 3.3): Alternative Transportation—Parking Capacity.** Review the uploaded site plan to verify the parking capacity for the project; for NC and CI projects, be sure the preferred parking spaces are clearly noted. Check the accuracy of the LEED submittal template and that the owner has confirmed the correct compliance path option.

- **SS Credit 5.2: Site Development—Maximize Open Space.** Ensure that the owner has signed the credit submittal template declaring that the open space will remain for the life of the building. The LEED coordinator should also review the site area versus open space calculation to ensure compliance. The responsible party should have uploaded a site plan with the open space (and green roof space, if applicable) and pedestrian-orientated hardscape clearly notated along with the calculation demonstrating compliance.

- **SS Credit 6.1: Stormwater Design—Quantity Control.** Verify that the best management practices (BMPs) are indicated on the site plan and that there is a notation of the site areas they coordinate with. The civil engineer is typically responsible for the calculations and therefore should be responsible for completing the credit submittal template.

- **SS Credit 6.2: Stormwater Design—Quality Control.** The LEED coordinator needs to verify that the treatment strategies are included in the uploaded plans and the credit submittal template is

LEED-NC 2.2 Submittal Template
SS Credit 8: Light Pollution Reduction

design

Lighting Power Density Tabulation Exterior Site Areas

Location ID	Units	Area OR Length	Actual LPD	ASHRAE Allowable LPD	LEED Allowable LPD	
Parking Lot	W/sf ▾	115,020	.054	.15	.12	CLEAR
Front Walkway	W/sf ▾	5,894	0	.2	.16	CLEAR
Central Walkway	W/lf ▾	196	0	1	.8	CLEAR
Main Entry	W/lf ▾	7	0	30	24	CLEAR
Office Entry	W/lf ▾	3	0	20	16	CLEAR
Back of House Entries	W/lf ▾	30	26	20	16	CLEAR
Back Walkway	W/lf ▾	245	1.5	1	.8	CLEAR
	▾				0	CLEAR

Figure 7.5 A partial example of a completed credit submittal template for SS Credit 8: Light Pollution Reduction for the Hannaford project in Augusta, Maine, by Clanton & Associates. Image courtesy of Clanton & Associates.

completed accurately. BMPs will need to be listed with the expected result of the strategy. A list of the nonstructural and/or structural control measures will need to be provided, as well as the expected annual rainfall, and how the measures treat the rainfall to meet the intentions of the credit by the TSS removal performance. If a local standard was used to plan the strategies, the civil engineer should refer to this standard and include the approach in the narrative on the credit submittal template.

• **SS Credit 8.1: Light Pollution Reduction.** By the end of the Design Development phase, the team should have finalized the desired light levels and the light distribution for site distribution. The

credit submittal template should be completed confirming that the credit requirements were adhered to. For projects with exterior luminaries, the lighting power densities (LPDs) need to be tabulated. Figure 7.5 includes an example of a completed table listing the LPDs for different exterior locations.

The responsible party should prepare interior lighting plans showing the locations of controls and/or shades. If shades will be used, the cut sheets of the product should be uploaded to LEED-Online clarifying that they prohibit at least 90 percent of light from passing through. For either option, a sequence of operations needs to be uploaded as well.

For the exterior light fixtures selected, the responsible party will need to collect the applicable cut sheets and upload them to LEED-Online, along with the photometric site plan and a site lighting plan. If a team is challenged with local ordinances that are stricter than the requirements to comply with this credit, a narrative will need to be written describing the approach, including the areas not in compliance due to the overruling by the municipality. The following includes a sample of a required narrative and an optional narrative courtesy of Dane R. Sanders, PE, LEED AP, Principal of Clanton & Associates, Inc. These narratives were used to demonstrate compliance for this credit for the Hannaford Bros. project in Augusta, Maine:

Required Narrative

Luminaires around the site perimeter were specified with an optical system that minimizes light distributed behind the pole. Where possible, perimeter lighting poles were mounted in landscape islands to increase the distance from the property line. This strategy resulted the following maximum values at the property line: Horizontal Illuminance (max) = 0.2 fc, Vertical Illuminance (max) = 0.2 fc. At 15′ beyond the property line: Horizontal Illuminance (max) = 0.0 fc. All outdoor luminaires are IESNA full cut-off classification, resulting in zero lumens emitted above 90-degrees from nadir.

Optional Narrative

The lighting within the entry drives was removed from the LEED calculation because this lighting is required by the Department of Transportation in the State of Maine. The requirement, "Pursuant to the provision of 23 M.R.S.A. § 704-A and Chapter 305 of the Department's Regulations," states, "Overhead lighting shall be provided, if not existing, to illuminate the intersection. Overhead lighting shall have an average of 0.6 to 1.0 foot candles, with the maximum to minimum lighting ratio of not more than 10:1 and an average to minimum light level of not more than 4:1."

Water Efficiency

- **WE Prerequisite 1: Water Use Reduction (also LEED CI WE Credit 1 and LEED NC and CS Credit 3).** The declarant will need to upload the fixture cut sheets noting the manufacturer(s), model numbers, and flush or flow rates. The credit submittal template will need to be filled in to calculate the baseline case and the design case to determine the water reduction percentage verifying compliance. This not only includes the fixtures, sensors, and aerators, but any captured or reused water as well.

- **WE Credit 1: Water Efficient Landscaping (CI SS Credit 1, Option 2, Paths 7 and 8).** The credit submittal template should be reviewed for accuracy. Calculations will need to be completed for both the baseline and design cases on the credit submittal template. Verify that the values are consistent for the landscape area, the microclimate factor, and the evapotranspiration rate for both the design and baseline cases. The baseline case uses sprinklers for irrigation delivery, assumes irrigation efficiency controls are not used, and does not include nonpotable water. If temporary irrigation is used, the landscape architect will have to sign the credit submittal template confirming that the system will be removed after one year or after the plantings have been established. If the project is only installing planters, the template declarant will need to provide the square footage of the planters and the gross land area contained within the LEED project boundary line. The LEED coordinator should verify that the landscaping plans have been uploaded to LEED-Online, and if the strategy includes controllers or moisture sensors, the product documentation should be uploaded as well and noted on the credit submittal template. If nonpotable water is to be used to irrigate the property, plumbing plans and/or quantity calculations will also need to be uploaded.

- **WE Credit 2: Innovative Wastewater Technologies (CI SS Credit 1, Option 2, Path 9).** Prior to filling out the credit submittal template for this credit, the template will need to be completed for WE Prerequisite 1 as LEED-Online pulls information from one credit to another to ensure consistency, such as FTE calculations and fixture consumption. Project teams are therefore encouraged to use the calculation features of LEED-Online during the design process to ensure compliancy. Once the template is completed, the LEED coordinator should verify the cut sheets for the fixtures have been uploaded to LEED-Online including the manufacturer, model number, and water consumption rates. If stormwater is to be used for indoor flushing, the responsible project team member will need to upload information of the system and its contribution to meet the flush requirements for compliance.

Energy and Atmosphere

- **EA Prerequisite 2: Minimum Energy Performance and EA Credit 1: Optimize Energy Performance**

  - *For NC and CS Projects:* This prerequisite is eligible for LPE compliance, should the declarant be licensed. If pursuing Option 1, the project team may wish to wait to submit for a construction side review instead of a design side review,

as strategies may change. When the team decides to submit for a certification review, be sure to verify that the loads not met is less than 300 hours on the credit submittal template to avoid any review issues. It is important to also verify that the process loads are at less than 25 percent, and if not, the team will need to upload documentation declaring the loads are suitable. Teams are encouraged to collect all equipment cut sheets and upload to LEED-Online along with coordinating schedules.

If pursuing Option 2, the submittal template does not detail the documentation requirements for the prescriptive strategies specific to the project, but only requires the engineer to sign the form declaring compliance and to submit a checklist of requirements and supporting documentation proving compliance. A narrative is also required on the submittal form. The documentation requirements for the prerequisite and the credit are the same, therefore there is no additional work required for the project team to pursue the credit once documentation is uploaded to LEED-Online for the prerequisite.

If pursuing Option 3, the responsible party will need to provide documentation proving compliance with each of the steps in Sections 1 and 2 of the *Core Performance Guide* for the prerequisite. In order to comply with the credit, at least three of the strategies listed in Section 3 need to be implemented and documentation provided proving compliance. Some strategies such as cool roofs, night venting, and commissioning more sustainable features do not contribute to earning this credit. Documentation examples include: sections, specifications, and engineering drawings, including electrical and mechanical plans.

Project teams will also need to determine the ENERGY STAR® rating with the EPA's Target Finder tool and upload the score to LEED-Online.

- *Prerequisite for LEED CI Projects:* Ensure that the submittal template and ASHRAE compliance forms are completed and signed by the responsible party. To show compliance with the LPD requirements, teams may use the DOE's COMcheck software. Verify that the list of equipment and appliances meets the 50 percent minimum for rated power.

- **EA Prerequisite 3: Fundamental Refrigerant Management and Credit 4: (Credit for NC and CS projects).** If refrigerants are used, ensure that the calculated weighted average does not exceed 100. This may require some effort from the manufacturer to obtain the necessary information for the refrigerant utilized, such as refrigerant charge, ozone depleting potential (ODP) and global warming potential (GWP). The refrigerant leakage rate is always assumed to be 2 percent, while the end-of-life refrigerant loss is assumed to be 10 percent. LEED CS projects can pursue the alternate compliance path if future tenants will be responsible for compliance. In either case, verify that the template is signed and completed correctly.

- **EA Credit 1: Optimize Energy Performance (For LEED CI projects).** Ensure that each of the credit submittal templates and ASHRAE compliance forms are completed and signed by the responsible party. To show compliance with the LPD requirements, teams may use the DOE's COMcheck software. Verify that all

documentation proving compliance is uploaded and oriented correctly.

- *EA Credit 1.2, Strategies 1 and 2:* Be sure the lighting plan indicates which daylight sensor coordinates with which light(s). For EA Credit 1.2, Strategy 2, ensure the calculations were based on lighting load and not total light fixtures.

- *EA Credit 1.3, Option 1, Strategy 1:* A summary of the heat, cooling, and fan sizing load calculations should be uploaded to LEED-Online to prove the requirements of Section 1.4: Mechanical System Design have been met. To document Section 2.9: Mechanical Equipment Efficiency compliance, the template needs to be signed declaring that the project is in compliance with the efficiency requirements of the referenced standard. The zoning requirements should also be confirmed on the template, and review the narrative describing the HVAC system for the building (if applicable) and the tenant space. The description should include the control logic, the reasoning behind the zone determination, and the expected energy savings per control. To prove that the project meets the requirements of Section 3.10: Variable Speed Control, the template requires the engineer to provide the variable speed fans and pumps that are included in the scope of work, where they are located, and that the wattage demand is at least 50 percent of the design flow.

- *EA Credit 1.3, Option 1, Strategy 2:* The project engineer should compile a list of HVAC controls and sensors, and complete the submittal template to detail the assumed energy savings for each control and zone distribution reasoning. If Option 2, the cost budget approach, is being pursued, the responsible party will need to list the energy end uses with the correlating peak demand and cost, as well as list the baseline costs by energy type.

- *EA Credit 1.4:* Ensure that the template includes all of the eligible equipment and appliances and the ENERGY STAR label applicability, and that the coordinating rated power data is correct.

- **EA Credit 2: On-Site Renewable Energy (LEED CI SS Credit 1, Option 2, Path 11).** Verify that the correct compliance path to determine the average energy consumption credit submittal template is selected and the coordinating data is inputted correctly as well.

Materials and Resources

- **MR Prerequisite 1: Storage and Collection of Recyclables.** Ensure that the owner has completed the submittal template correctly (including the narrative) and has signed the form indicating compliance. Floor plan(s) also need to be uploaded, demonstrating that the collection and storage areas are accounted for with the areas clearly delineated.

- **MR Credit 1.1: Tenant Space—Long-Term Commitment (for LEED CI projects).** Verify that the owner has completed the submittal template correctly, signed the form, and uploaded the lease documentation proving compliance. Be sure to highlight the relevant information within the lease to make it easier for the review team.

Indoor Environmental Quality

- **EQ Prerequisite 1: Minimum Indoor Air Quality Performance, and EQ Credit 2: Increased Ventilation.** For mechanically ventilated buildings, ensure that the outside air calculations are separated from any naturally ventilated areas and all regularly occupied areas are listed on the submittal template. Ensure that the calculations prove the air rates meet or exceed the ASHRAE standard and review the narrative. For naturally ventilated projects, confirm compliance with the applicable path pursued and review the narrative. Review supporting documentation for accuracy and clarity and ensure that the supporting documentation is listed on the credit submittal template.

- **EQ Prerequisite 2: Environmental Tobacco Smoke (ETS) Control.** Verify that the correct compliance path is chosen on the LEED submittal template and the appropriate plans with dedicated areas indicated, are uploaded to LEED-Online and demonstrate compliance.

- **EQ Credit 1: Outdoor Air Delivery Monitoring.** This credit is eligible for an LPE path for LEED CI projects, should the licensed engineer verify compliance and sign the credit submittal template and complete the LPE form, therefore eliminating the need to upload any supporting documentation. Should the team pursue NC or CS certification or the LEED CI responsible party not be eligible for the LPE path, calculations, floor plans with sensor locations, details of airflow measurement devices in non–densely occupied areas, and a list of densely occupied areas will all need to be uploaded to LEED-Online, along with the completed credit submittal template for mechanically ventilated projects. For naturally ventilated spaces, the responsible party would need to upload floor plans depicting the windows, zones, and CO_2 sensor locations, along with the signed credit submittal template indicating compliance.

MANUFACTURER'S PERSPECTIVE
A Manufacturer as an Owner Pursuing LEED

By Julie Smith of Haworth

From an owner's perspective, Haworth Inc., a global design and manufacturing company for office furniture and interior architecture, is in a unique position. The company's architecture and design customers are increasingly savvy and require

Figure 7.6 One Haworth Center in Holland, Michigan, addresses such factors as daylighting, views, and low-emitting material selections to bring value to the indoor environmental quality, helping the project to earn LEED Gold certification. Photo courtesy of Haworth Inc.

sustainable office furniture products in bids. In response, Haworth has expanded its product base to include sustainable interior architecture elements, such as raised-access floors and moveable walls. Potential clients look to purchase from companies that practice and implement sustainable practices internally, such as manufacturing procedures and operating green facilities, and those that are LEED certified. So, when Haworth started its own green building project, expectations were high. Opened in 2008, Haworth's complete renovation of its global headquarters delivered, with many sustainable elements such as a 45,000-square-foot green roof and a three-story, 35,000-square-foot glass atrium (Figure 7.6). More importantly, Haworth achieved its goal of making design choices that both enhanced sustainability objectives *and* power-fully demonstrated that a sustainable space can be beautiful and efficient, as well as inspiring to the mind and spirit.

For Haworth, there are two examples that best illustrate the LEED certification and overall green building experience. The first is a dedication to the triple bottom line—people, planet, and profit. Haworth believes that, in order to be truly sustainable, decisions must benefit the environment and make business sense. This was put to the test in making an on-site renewable power generation decision when a photovoltaic system was explored. But, with a facility located in Holland, Michigan, one of the cloudiest places in North America, and the cost and effectiveness of the technology not as advanced as it could be, Haworth decided not to pursue the system with this project. Instead, the company opted to purchase renewable energy credits. In fact, in 2010, the Haworth HQ project received LEED Gold certification and repre-sents the first time carbon credits from a renewable energy project (from the CarbonNeutral Company) used to achieve green power credits instead of on-site renewable energy credits.

Another example of Haworth's green building and LEED certification experience occurred during the deconstruction phase. With a vital Turner Construction partnership, Haworth set a goal to recycle as much waste as possible. In a typi-cal renovation, only 20 to 30 percent of waste is recovered and, under the LEED rating system, up to two points can be earned for recycling or salvaging up to 75 percent of the construction waste. The Haworth global HQ project far exceeded the benchmark by diverting over 97 percent of waste. Creative reuse and recycling included: local schools and charitable organizations shopping the building to identify and remove usable materials and furnishings; carpet tiles cleaned and sanitized for resale; hydraulic elevator fluid treated and reused; and all waste window glass combined with concrete dust to construct new concrete block.

- **EQ Credit 5: Indoor Chemical and Pollutant Source Control.** Regardless of the rating system, this credit is eligible for LPE compliance path. Should the team opt not to pursue the LPE approach, the responsible party will not only need to complete the credit submittal template, but also is required to prepare and upload supporting documentation proving compliance with each of the four requirements of this credit. The credit submittal template requires the entryway system product information to be listed, the chemical and hazardous material locations to be listed, and the installed filtration media product details to be listed. Supporting documentation will need to coordinate with the credit submittal template, locating the rooms containing chemicals and/or hazardous gases, noting the separation of the locations, and indicating the exhaust system(s). Note that although this is a design credit, it is required to be signed by the contractor. If the contractor is not on board when the project administrator issues for a design-side review and sign off on this template, this credit will need to be deferred for review until after substantial completion.

- **EQ Credit 6.1: Controllability of Systems, Lighting (for LEED NC and CI projects).** Review the credit submittal template to ensure that the occupancy types are listed, with the coordinating lighting control type(s) provided. Confirm that the uploaded supporting documentation is noted on the credit submittal template and includes floor plans with furniture arrangements that depict the location, zone, and type of lighting controls that are to be implemented during construction.

- **EQ Credit 6.2 (LEED CS EQ Credit 6): Controllability of Systems—Thermal Comfort.** This credit is eligible for a streamlined path by the LPE for CI projects. If the licensed engineer signs the credit submittal template, the thermal comfort control table is not required to be completed for all regularly occupied areas. For NC and CS projects, the declarant will need to complete the table requiring occupancy types, quantities, thermal comfort control types, and a thermal comfort control description for each space within the project to verify compliance. If the LPE path is not pursued, supporting documentation will also need to be uploaded. The supporting documentation for this credit includes plans noting the location and type of thermal comfort controls to coordinate with the table on the credit submittal template, and the thermal comfort control schedules should also be uploaded. The declarant will also need to verify the type of ventilation for the project and the coordinating credit requirements on the template.

- **EQ Credit 7.1: Thermal Comfort, Design (LEED CS EQ Credit 7).** Although this credit is eligible for a design side review, it should not be submitted until after construction, due to the supporting documentation requirements; although the mechanical engineer should still complete the credit submittal template and upload as much of the supporting documentation as possible. The contractor will sign the template, but it is best if the mechanical engineer completes the ASHRAE 55 6.1.1 input factor data, document the operational procedures, and select the calculation method best suited for the project. The engineer will have three options from which to choose: predicted mean vote/predicted percentage of dissatisfied (PMV/PPD) calculation, ASHRAE comfort tool, or a psychometirc comfort zone chart from ASHRAE 55.

- **EQ Credit 7.2: Thermal Comfort—Verification Lighting (for LEED NC and CI projects).** Some project teams assign this credit to the CxA, as they will be a part of the postoccupancy survey exercise for corrective action. No matter which team member is assigned as the declarant, the corrective action plan and thermal comfort survey should both be uploaded and reviewed, as well as the completed credit submittal template.

- **EQ Credit 8.1: Daylight and Views—Daylight.** Confirm that the credit submittal template is completed with the required information, such as visible light transmittance (VLT) values and a list of the regularly occupied space meeting the credit requirements. Verify that the minimum and maximum required footcandle levels are achieved. Confirm that the square-footage calculations for daylight areas and total regularly occupied areas are accurate. Confirm that the supporting documentation, including simulation data for

Option 1, calculations for Option 2, and/or floor plans and sections showing glare control devices have been uploaded to LEED-Online. If pursuing Option 3, this credit will need to be deferred for a construction review in order to gather daylight measurement values for compliance purposes.

- **EQ Credit 8.1: Daylight and Views—Views.** Verify that the regularly occupied space calculations are completed correctly, as fixed items can be removed from the square-footage calculations. The floor area with a direct line of sight will need to be calculated and could include passing through two interior glazing areas but not through walls taller than 42 inches or solid doors. Be sure this value is entered on the credit submittal template. A floor plan will need to be uploaded depicting the areas with access to exterior views as compared to areas without access. Sections will also need to be uploaded to LEED-Online confirming the direct line of sight from a seated height and therefore should include furniture as well. CS projects will need to provide a suggested floorplan layout proving the opportunity is available for future tenants.

Innovation in Design and Regional Priority

The LEED coordinator should review each ID and RP credit completed for a design review prior to the submission to GBCI. Always review the credit submittal templates and ensure that they are signed. Verify that any required supporting documentation is also uploaded, noted on the credit submittal template, and clearly depicts the strategy and compliance. Remember, it is best to orient the documentation so that it is legible once opened and does not need to be rotated. All key information should be highlighted to draw the reviewer's attention to important concepts.

Submitting for a Design Review

After all of the documentation has been reviewed, the project team administrator will submit for a design review with GBCI. A design review fee is required at the time of submission. An email should be received indicating that the project has been submitted and LEED-Online will indicate the project is under review. The review period typically will take 25 business days, but can depend on the demand for certification reviews at the time of submission or holidays. After the initial review is completed, a report summary will be available to download from LEED-Online summarizing the prerequisites and credits that were submitted for review and are expected to be awarded with an indication of "anticipated." The review team may also require clarification and/or additional documentation from the project team and is typically very clear on what additional information is required to be submitted by the means of a "Technical Advice" note provided for any applicable prerequisite and/or credit; these will be denoted by "pending," as described in Chapter 1. LEED-Online will revert back to the Design Application phase if such information is required for clarification granting the team 25 business days to respond. At this time, the project team administrator should compile a checklist for each prerequisite and credit that requires clarification and assign each one to the responsible team member(s) along with a deadline for completing the task. Once the clarification information is submitted, the review team should respond within 15 business days with final design review comments and moving the project along to the Construction Application phase. If the team received indication that a prerequisite or credit was denied and therefore will not be awarded, they have the opportunity to submit for a design appeal for an additional fee. If the appeal is submitted, the project will move into the Design Appeal phase. Project team members will have the opportunity to submit documentation to be reviewed and should receive review comments with 25 business days after the appeal fee has been paid and processed. To avoid issuing an appeal, it is best advised to submit as much clarifying information as possible during the Design Review phase.

Next Steps

Typically, the CDs are issued for permit review and bid, and the design review application is in process. During this time, teams are encouraged to start the application process for any rebates and incentives. It is also an appropriate time to host a prebid conference with the bidding general contractors and subcontractors, if applicable to the project type. Be sure to read the bid review section in the next chapter for more information concerning the contractor selection process.

Prebid Conference

Review environmental goals and the LEED scorecard, thoroughly clarifying the scope during construction. This will clarify the importance of specifications for substitution purposes. For example, the requirements of SS Credit 5.1: Site Development, Protection, or Restore Habitat should be detailed to ensure that the bidders have an understanding of the site limitations and do not plan to level the site. SS Credit 7.2: Heat Island Effect—Roof should also be mentioned, as the roof material's SRI value is critical to earning the point. SS Credit 8: Light Pollution Reduction is another critical credit to be mentioned, as light fixtures cannot be substituted for fixtures without shielding or that do not align with wattage specifications, and window shades cannot be substituted that allow more than 50 percent of light to pass through. Review the importance of water consumption rates for flush and flow fixtures. If occupancy sensors are included in the scope, be sure to go over the EA credit requirements. If there are any materials to be reused and salvaged, it is critical to mention this goal, as it impacts pricing, staging, and/or scheduling. Be sure to review MR Credits 2 through 6, as the determination of vendors most likely will be impacted, and possibly pricing and scheduling. Make a point to discuss the requirements for compliance with EQ Credits 3.1 and 3.2 for SMACNA adherence and/or if a flush out or air quality testing is preferred. Also, be sure to review the MERV filter requirements, as they often are omitted from bid inclusions.

Roles and responsibilities should also be addressed, especially concerning indoor air quality, commissioning, LEED documentation, construction waste management, and erosion and sedimentation control measures. Progress meetings and scheduling should be addressed, specifically referencing the intended LEED certification review submission for documentation purposes.

ENGINEER'S PERSPECTIVE
Experiences of Gaining LEED Certification

Scott Bowman, PE, LEED AP BD+C
KJWW Engineering Consultants

Following are some comments related to the submittal and review process of KJWW, and me personally, as we have helped to earn certification for our projects. Most of these comments relate to submissions for LEED NC v2.2, with some reflection of the change from U.S. Green Building Council (USGBC®) review to GBCI.

Commissioning Documentation, EA Prerequisite 1 and Credit 3

Our firm tends to probably overdocument Cx, but since the information is developed electronically anyway for the owner, we feel it is better to upload everything to avoid any question in the mind of the reviewer. Sometimes that means information is shown in two ways. For example, we always upload a file that is noted as the final commissioning plan, a requirement of the LEED template for EA Prerequisite 1. That same plan shows up in the final Cx report as well. To date, we have never had a reviewer question our Cx submissions, either for the fundamental prerequisite or EA Credit 3: Enhanced Commissioning.

Also, sometimes the process requires a little creativity to address all requirements of the LEED submittal template. For example, LEED requires a CxA to show how commissioning has been included in the project requirements, in addition to the Cx plan. Normally, this is where we would submit the Cx specifications. However, in many design/build projects, there is not a specification! Typically in these types of projects, the construction manager has separate contracts that include a requirement to assist in LEED certification, of which Cx is a requirement. To show compliance, we have the CM write a letter stating how the Cx plan is used as the project requirements of all the parties in the project, and we have received no comments to date.

Minimum Indoor Air Quality Performance EQ Prerequisite 1 (ASHRAE 62.1)

Sometimes form is more important than content. ASHRAE 62.1 is a complex standard when applied to variable air volume systems. We have developed an internal design tool that is used by our engineers to manage this process as we design systems. This tool has a summary page that shows the compliance with the standard and lists the required ventilation rates and minimum set points for all the terminal air boxes. We have submitted this tool a few times, and there has always been a question from the reviewer asking us to show how we complied. Since we felt our tool showed this compliance, we were somewhat at a loss on how to address this question any more clearly. One of our engineers then developed a tab in our tool that specifically emulates the table that is shown in the LEED reference guides. This has the same information, just presented in a form that is referenced by LEED. We have not had that same question from a reviewer since we started using this method.

Also, our normal schedules for air-handling units have a column for ventilation air. We normally include a copy of this schedule to show the quantity for each unit and how it matches the compliance tool output and felt that complied with the LEED requirement. However, the LEED template specifically asks for the units and ventilation rates to be in the narrative portion of that document. Again, the information is there, but in this case they specifically want it shown in the template. Details are important!

Thermal Comfort Design EQ Credit 7.1 (ASHRAE 55)

The method of showing conformance to EQ Credit 7.1: Thermal Comfort—Design, has changed over time as the rating system versions have been updated, and as the review shifted from USGBC to GBCI. Earlier compliance was shown (and accepted) with only a short narrative and a declaration by the engineer of record stating conformance with ASHRAE 55, whereas now more narrative was required with the affirmation. We therefore started uploading the results of an internal spreadsheet tool we developed that helped us confirm ASHRAE 55 compliance.

Recently, we have uploaded a much longer narrative with specific information on outdoor design conditions, interior design criteria and assumptions, a general system description (with emphasis on how air and any radiant heat are configured), air velocities design criteria, and controllability. We also include prints of our internal ASHRAE tool. Specifically, be sure to include information on activity rates, anticipated clothing, air velocity, and radiation. ASHRAE 55 is more than just temperature and humidity, and GBCI is looking for a more detailed understanding of how ALL criteria have been addressed in the project.

PART 3 THE CONSTRUCTION PHASE

chapter 8

Coordination with the
Construction Team

This book is intended to serve as a resource for teams through the Leadership in Energy and Environmental Design (LEED®) certification process, during both design and construction. Up until this point, the tasks detailed have been associated with the design phases of a project, where now we focus on those to be addressed during construction. These construction related topics are limited to tasks wrapped around LEED and therefore details about general construction, such as risk management, bonding and insurance requirements, and contract agreements are omitted. It does, however, speak to documentation management, indoor air quality (IAQ) guidelines, construction waste management, and commissioning (Cx), as a means to guide teams through the tasks required for projects seeking LEED certification (Figure 8.1). The key to success is driven by a proactive, team-oriented approach and steers clear to avoid

Figure 8.1 Coordination of the construction activities to align with LEED requirements was critical to the success of The Utah Botanical Center's Wetland Discovery Point project, at Utah State University in Kaysville. Photo courtesy of Gary Neuenswander, Utah Agricultural Experiment Station.

a reactive approach which typically takes more time, costs more money, and can produce an unhealthy environment for construction workers and building occupants.

Bid Review

Depending on the type of contractual approach for the project, the project may or may not be "put out to bid" to multiple general contractors. For those that do, project teams have a number of ways to approach the contractor selection method:

- Qualification based

- Price based

- Best value

Depending on the complexities of the project, such as if a building management system (BMS) is specified and the team is pursuing the Energy and Atmosphere (EA) Credit for Measurement and Verification, along with outdoor air delivery monitors and sensors, it is suggested to pursue a qualification-based approach to select an experienced and skilled construction team as a large range of coordination is required to ensure each of the components are addressed accurately. Most projects are typically price based, as the economic bottom line tends to be the primary driver. For teams pursuing LEED projects, the best value approach is not typically pursued for selecting a contractor unless it is a publicly funded project.

Understanding the intentions of the bidding exercise and the selection approach will help to determine the appropriate contractor for the project. It is important to review the bids to ensure the goals of the project are kept intact and critical items were not omitted. If the contractor is responsible for engaging a LEED consultant to manage the construction documentation efforts, be sure to review the qualifications of the team prior to selection.

Although each project is unique and will pursue different credits, there are a few general tips for reviewing bids in terms of LEED. LEED or not, when reviewing any bid, it is critical to look for substitutions and/or omissions.

Similar to the approach in the rest of this book, it is best to start with the Sustainable Sites (SS) category and work your way through the scorecard, finishing with Innovation in Design (ID) and Regional Priority (RP) categories. The key is to verify LEED certification–dependent items are accounted for. For example, be sure to confirm exterior light fixtures have not been substituted and that the interior lighting controls or the window coverings were not omitted. Verify the green roof assembly has not been substituted and make sure the mechanical subcontractor included the correct Minimum Efficiency Reporting Value (MERV) filters during construction and prior to occupancy. Verify the outside air delivery monitoring, sensor, and alarm devices are included in the bid. Confirm the waste and IAQ construction management approaches and verify the compliance path intended for flush-out or air quality testing to be sure the schedule is accurate. If testing is intended, are the right number of tests, based on the size of the project, included in the bid? Ensure that the commissioning (Cx) scope is understood and there are no overlaps of responsibilities that would result in an increase of fees. Most importantly, it is critical to verify that the materials cost is in line with the estimates developed during design, as this is the basis of compliance with Materials and Resources (MR) credits.

GENERAL CONTRACTOR'S PERSPECTIVE
Compliancy with LEED during Construction

By Easy Foster, CPC, LEED AP
Duratech LP

In an effort to disclose some lessons learned as the general contractor working on projects seeking LEED certification, we offer the following tips to other contractors:

1. During the preconstruction process, it is imperative that all parties be aware of the level of certification the project is targeting. Each item can have an impact on the costs, and all parties need to be aware of what items will drive up the budget and the potential return on investment (ROI) of the item. Subcontractor and manufacturer feedback during the initial budgeting stages can be very beneficial.

2. Carefully review submittals and ensure the products align with achieving particular LEED credits such as local/ regional materials, low-emitting materials, and recycled content. Maintain real-time records of all products purchased and track for applicability to contributing to LEED credits. It is true that most the documentation required can be researched after the fact, but it is always best to manage the documentation process as an ongoing effort during the preconstruction and construction phases.

3. Accurately record all material costs separately from those dealing with labor or overhead. Require subcontractors to supply this information on their schedules of values and for every change during the course of construction.

4. Keep a map for quick and easy access, with a circle indicating the distance limit for the procurement of materials that are harvested and fabricated within 500 miles to comply with MR Credit 5. This will make it easier to determine which suppliers fall within the required range.

5. Make sure certified wood comes with all the appropriate chain-of-custody documentation from all points of distribution. This is critical in tracking and proving the procurement and installation of certified lumber products.

6. Finding a waste-hauling company that will supply the documentation as to where a project's waste actually went, and getting the information in a timely manner is critical for LEED compliancy for the MR credits. Finding capable subcontractors able to deliver the appropriate documentation was a challenge years ago but has since become better aligned with the requirements. Selecting the compliance path for these credits depends on the space available on a project site to dedicate for containers, as well as the effort to manage the disposal process to keep disposal items and materials separated. In order to meet the requirements for on-site collection and separation, the dumpsters would need to be clearly marked for the different material and someone dedicated to enforce the policy. This construction waste management effort to comply would differ than a conventional type project where there would only need to be space for one or two containers, not six.

7. Ensure documentation of the project and getting in the habit of taking pictures on a daily basis. Take lots of pictures and label each one for its importance and applicability to LEED. Take pictures of the site before and after temporary protections are installed. Pictures of mechanical/electrical/plumbing (MEP) details can be crucial to document protections and installation techniques.

8. Install signs prohibiting the use of tobacco products on the property at an early stage to avoid problems as the building is enclosed.

continued

9. Keep a stormwater pollution protection plan (SWPPP) in place and avoiding mishaps for this prerequisite in the SS category. We would recommend inspecting the SWPPP controls daily to make sure that they are in place and operational to ensure compliancy.

10. In order to address compliancy with the Sheet Metal and Air Conditioning Contractors' National Association (SMACNA) Guidelines for EQ Credit 3.1, we would recommend avoiding any early deliveries of ductwork and heating, ventilating, and air-conditioning (HVAC) equipment to the project by working closely with the mechanical subcontractor on scheduling. This item is extremely important to not only avoid contaminates to infiltrate the duct or equipment, but also keeping equipment as pristine as possible. Once the ductwork is delivered, it is equally important to keep all of ductwork and equipment openings covered after installation, to keep contaminates out. The on-site superintendent should ensure that the building remains as clean as possible when the building is enclosed, especially at start-up operations. The construction team also needs to monitor the air filters, so that they get changed as needed. Team members should also avoid activities that create dust when HVAC equipment is in operation.

11. Meet often and consistently with commissioning agents to ensure that all procedures are in line with the design intentions, including the owner's project requirements (OPR) and basis of design (BOD).

12. Instruct cleaning personnel to use or engage in a cleaning contract that will employ the use of certified cleaning products to avoid contaminating the project site.

Furniture

Furniture is typically not included in the project manuals and specifications, as it is not part of the contractor's scope of work, but this does not imply it is not to be included in the LEED scope of work during construction. Owners most likely will require assistance compiling specifications in order to distribute to local dealers. These specifications should reference LEED requirements just as with the construction specifications. The previous chapter provided some resources to help develop the specification language as it is best advised to start this process early, as some items may require a longer lead time due to the sustainable requirements. This also leaves time for testing to comply with Indoor Environmental Quality (EQ) Credit 4.5 for LEED for Commercial Interiors™ (CI) projects or LEED for New Construction and Major Renovations™ (NC) and LEED for Core & Shell™ (CS) projects pursuing an Innovation credit. Remember, LEED NC and CS project teams have the choice to include furniture in MR credit calculations, but if it is included for one credit, it must be included for all. CI projects are required to include furniture in all of the MR credit calculations.

Training the Construction Team

Prior to the commencement of construction, it is advised for the LEED coordinator to pull the construction team together for a training exercise. This meeting may need to be conducted a couple of times, as not all of the subcontractors are hired at the onset of construction. Although mechanical and electrical equipment is not included in most of the MR credits, the subcontractors should attend the meeting, as they will need to coordinate with the commissioning agent (CxA) and will need to be aware of on-site construction waste management requirements and SMACNA guidelines for EQ credit compliance.

As more and more projects are designed and constructed to LEED standards, expectations and responsibilities are better managed, but it is still encouraged to bring everyone together to ensure that there is a thorough understanding of the project goals, as they differ from one project to another. It is a good idea to have everyone meet in person as it allows them to establish a rapport with one another, as the key is to encourage a team environment with open communication. The following is a suggested list of topics to be presented at the training meeting:

- **What Is LEED and Why Is It Important?** – Typically, a slide show presentation works best to give a visual representation of what green buildings look like as compared to the perception. It is also a good idea to present a process or timeline of efforts that have already taken place and what needs to be focused on during construction. This typically solidifies the importance of the goals.

- **Responsibilities and Documentation.** Who is responsible for what? What will the LEED coordinator be responsible for? What about the contractor, the mechanical subcontractor, the waste hauler, or the drywall contractor? The success of certification during construction is based on the performance of the team as a whole. Remember from Chapter 3 to prequalify the subcontractors to ensure success.

- **Material Tracking.** It is critical to describe the information necessary for the submittal review process, such as volatile organic compound (VOC) levels and postconsumer and preconsumer recycled content. Be sure to clarify the difference between a reused product versus a recycled product.

- **Construction Indoor Air Quality (IAQ) and SMACNA Guidelines.** – Be sure to discuss the SMACNA guidelines with the contractor and the mechanical subcontractor, as well as MERV filter requirements and the protection of absorptive

materials. Where will materials be stored? Be sure to monitor the delivery of materials and not to conflict with activities that might cause damage. Include the five SMACNA strategies in the presentation, including examples. Print a one-page display of the strategies to be implemented and post around the site as a reminder. It might also be helpful to show a template for the documentation submittal such as the one included in Appendix G. Be sure to address the smoking policy on-site and ensure that the team is aware of the protection of the ductwork for delivery and installation prior to use. If the team is also pursuing EQ Credit 3.2, be sure to address the flush-out or air quality testing compliance paths (whichever pertains to the project).

- **Construction Waste Management.** Be sure to have the waste hauler attend the meeting and review the strategy to be implemented. Will the waste be collected in a commingled fashion or be sorted on-site? If on-site, who will monitor the waste containers? Who will make signs declaring which container is dedicated to which type of waste? Where will the containers be located? Be sure to address recycling efforts for waste generated in the construction trailers, as well. Achieving success can sometimes cause the need for "dumpster diving" to sort waste from inappropriate containers—seriously!

- **Commissioning.** Be sure to encourage a team-oriented environment, as the CxA is meant to work in tandem with the rest of the team. Remember, the CxA can save the subcontractors from call-backs after occupancy and therefore save them time and money, so it is a good idea for them to work together and not against one another. Therefore, not only is it important to discuss the role and responsibilities of the CxA, but to also have him or her attend the training session as well.

OWNER'S PERSPECTIVE
The Importance of Collaboration

By David Anderson
Director of the Utah Botanical Center, Utah State University

LEED certification was an important goal for development of the Wetland Discovery Point building (Figure 8.2). The LEED Platinum goal was established at the onset of the project. Although an aggressive objective, we were able to achieve the environmental goals of the university because we launched the initiatives early (Figure 8.3).

The most important recommendation for other groups is to assemble a project team that is highly aware of the LEED process and its inherent pitfalls. Selection of an enlightened and dedicated architectural team is critical. We would *not*

Figure 8.2 The Utah Botanical Center's Wetland Discovery Point project, at Utah State University in Kaysville, earned LEED Platinum certification for its efforts to create biodiversity. Photo courtesy of Gary Neuenswander, Utah Agricultural Experiment Station.

Figure 8.3   The Wetland Discovery Point building at Utah State University utilizes a trombe wall to capture heat from the sun, as well as radiant heat flooring to increase the energy efficiencies of the project. Photo courtesy of Gary Neuenswander, Utah Agricultural Experiment Station.

have been successful had we not had a group of attentive and watchful professionals who carefully watched the design and construction phases. On several occasions the architects identified and worked through challenges with the general contractor and subcontractors. For example, because we had someone dedicated to the process, they were monitoring the construction waste management from the beginning and were able to detect an error early in the process. Due to this error, we "lost" percentages for some material that was improperly handled. To rectify the situation as quickly as possible, the project team met to discuss how to improve handling the construction waste generated on the job site better. This early collaboration during construction resulted in the project's achieving two points under MR Credit 2 for Construction Waste Management, as we were able to achieve 87.66 percent of project waste diverted from landfills. Had the problem gone unnoticed, the mismanagement of construction waste would have cost us points in the LEED certification process.

- **Schedule of Values.** This is especially important for CI projects, as no default value is allowed for calculating compliance. Regardless, the LEED coordinator will need the total material costs for the project in order to determine the critical materials for compliancy and to track progress during construction.

The LEED Implementation Plan

The LEED coordinator may be able to couple the training exercise with the preconstruction meeting to review the LEED implementation plan as a means to streamline the efforts and time on site. Most requests for proposals (RFPs) issued by government agencies require a meeting to discuss the LEED implementation plan, whereas some commercial projects will only require the plan to be completed without a meeting with the team. The LEED implementation plan typically includes the following three action plans that will provide the team an indication of credit compliance during construction. Typically, the plan is required to be submitted within 30 days of receiving the notice to proceed. Obviously, these details can differ from project-to-project especially a project with the same LEED coordinator on the team during design and construction hired by the owner, and not the contractor. Therefore, the following information may not be applicable to all projects, but is included for those projects where it is required.

Action Plans

The LEED coordinator during construction will typically be responsible for creating the following three action plans and corresponding credits in accordance with the specification requirements and submitting to the team for review and approval. Bear in mind, a contractor can sub this scope out to a construction side

LEED coordinator. The goal is to create these plans in a timely manner and lay the groundwork for responsibility for documentation purposes. This chapter will help with compiling the reports, while the next chapter will help with the details of each to be addressed throughout the construction phase to prepare for a final certification review with Green Building Certification Institute (GBCI).

- Materials Tracking Action Plan to address the following credits:

  - MR Credit 4: Recycled Content

  - MR Credit 5: Regionally Extracted, Processed and Manufactured

  - MR Credit 6: Rapidly Renewable Materials (for NC and CI projects)

  - MR Credit 7: Certified Wood (MR Credit 6 for CS projects)

  - EQ Credit 4: Low-Emitting Materials

- Construction Waste Management Plan to address the following credit:

  - MR Credit 2: Construction Waste Management

- Construction IAQ Management Plan to address the following credits:

  - EQ Credit 3.1: Construction IAQ Management Plan—During Construction

  - EQ Credit 5: Indoor Chemical and Pollutant Source Control

Materials Tracking Action Plan

The Materials Tracking Action Plan typically addresses the requirements to comply with each of the associated credits listed previously and, therefore should most importantly clarify which credits the team is

WASTE CONSULTANT'S PERSPECTIVE
Construction Waste Recycling: Where the Real World Meets LEED

By Wayne DeFeo, LEED AP
Principal of DeFeo Associates

LEED Accredited Professionals (APs) need to understand that there are a number of variables that must be taken into account when planning for the recycling of construction and demolition (C&D) waste. Notwithstanding that, in theory, it is possible to recycle nearly every component of a construction project, there are a number of real-world impacts that can interfere with achieving a near-zero waste stream. In other words, theory is a wonderful thing, but reality and theory often do not meet eye to eye.

The primary debate for recycling of C&D waste is whether to source separate or to commingle the materials being recycled. Purists would require that we source separate all materials. Others would say to never waste time on source separation when there are a number of facilities that can break the waste stream down into marketable parts. True source separation requires that the job site have multiple containers for the multiple materials that can be removed from the site. This means that you need containers for wood, metal, drywall, and so on. The alternative method utilizes a commingled approach. In this approach, all of the material from the site is commingled into a single container. The load is then taken to a materials recovery facility (MRF) that utilizes mechanical equipment to separate the mixture into marketable parts.

In reality, the best approach is often a blend of source separation and commingling. The determining factors in establishing whether to source separate or commingle include:

1. The composition of the materials in the mix (this requires an on site review)
2. The cost of disposal as solid waste versus the cost of recycling (Do you pay $50/ton for disposal or $50/ton for recycling?)
3. The proximity and availability of recycling locations to the job site (travel costs money)
4. Site constraints (the amount of room available to store materials on site)
5. LEED goals and objectives (Platinum projects must achieve the highest recycling rates)

In a recent LEED project, we established that the largest single component of the C&D stream was heavy metal. Accordingly, source separation of the metal was determined to be both cost effective and appropriate as a means of maximizing recycling. However, the remainder of the C&D stream was best handled through a commingled approach utilizing an MRF. In this case, "best handled" was determined by a careful analysis of items 2 through 5. Three separate MRFs were reviewed, and the MRF most capable of removing the greatest percentage of recyclable material was selected after the completion of a cost analysis comparing disposal to recycling. Although there were no site constraints involved, the labor costs would have been prohibitive from the client's point of view. Thus, complete source separation was eliminated. The

continued

result: a recycling rate of 82.7 percent with the project meeting the financial needs of the client. In addition, the project exceeded its design goals and achieved a LEED Silver rating.

In two other projects, the decision as to whether or not to source separate or commingle the materials was determined by site constraints. In both of these projects, it would have been physically impossible to add containers to the project location; thus, we had a limiting factor that trumped all others. Notwithstanding these constraints, both projects achieved recycling rates in excess of 86 percent. How? By careful audits of the proposed MRFs and continuous project management.

---

pursuing and are relevant to construction activities. The requirements for compliance should follow each of the credits to ensure a thorough understanding by the construction team. The strategy should be defined for MR credit compliance, including a list of contributing materials and products. The requirements should include the VOC limits for the applicable materials and products for the applicable coordinating EQ Credit 4 credits. The tracking methodology and reporting requirements, such as calculations, certifications, and material safety data sheets (MSDS), should also be defined. An example of the different forms to be used should be included, such as the form for the subcontractors and vendors to complete with each submittal and the comprehensive form that will be used to track all of the materials.

The Construction Waste Management Plan

The Construction Waste Management Plan typically addresses the C&D waste diversion strategies. It should include the project information and an executive summary, and most importantly, the plan should define a strategy to generate less waste during demolition and construction, not just how to divert the waste from landfills. Each of the following should be addressed:

- Waste management goals

- Waste prevention planning

- Communication and education strategy

- Implementation plan

- Evaluation plan

- Anticipated project waste materials, disposal, and handling

- Monthly reporting

- Final reporting to LEED-Online

- Sample construction waste calculator

The Construction IAQ Management Plan

The Construction IAQ Management Plan typically addresses the protection of absorptive materials and SMACNA guidelines in the following five areas: HVAC protection, source control, pathway interruption, housekeeping, and scheduling. The report should include a description of each of the requirements and prescribes practices and strategies to be implemented for compliance. If the team is pursuing EQ Credit 3.2, the plan should also address flush-out procedures or air quality testing, depending on which compliance path the team plans on pursuing.

The plan can also include sample signage to be displayed on-site and a checklist to be completed by the contractor once a week. If the team is pursuing EQ Credit 5 as well, the plan should note the MERV 13 filter requirement to be adhered to prior to occupancy. Chapter 9 discusses the details of the tasks to be completed. Appendix F includes a sample IAQ management plan for project teams to reference when creating their own.

Tasks during Construction

In addition to the monthly reports described previously and that are detailed in the next chapter, there are other tasks that need to be addressed by the LEED coordinator during construction (Figure 8.4). For example, EA Credit 6: Green Power for NC and CS Projects, and EA Credit 4 for CI projects is typically kept as a "last-minute" credit, as it does not

Figure 8.4 It is highly encouraged to visit the construction site often to verify the compliance of construction-side credits.

require any effort specifically during design or construction. During construction, the LEED coordinator, the electrical engineer, or the owner is typically responsible for obtaining quotes from a Green-e certified provider. They have the option to choose either to estimate the energy consumption of the building (or tenant space for CI projects) by the means of EA Credit 1 (EA Credit 1.3 for CI projects) calculations or by the U.S. Department of Energy's Commercial Buildings Energy Consumption Survey (CBECS) database. Note that this credit is based on actual consumption, not on cost, as with EA Credit 2: On-Site Renewable Energy (SS Credit 1, Option 2, Path 11 for LEED CI projects).

The following tasks also need to be continually addressed during construction and should be verified by visiting the site and performing inspections (Figure 8.4):

Erosion and Sedimentation Control (for NC and CS Projects Only)

The project team will need to determine the appropriate compliance path in order to comply with SS Prerequisite 1: Construction Activity Pollution Prevention. During design, the civil engineer (or others) developed an erosion and sedimentation control (ESC) plan to be implemented during construction. The plan details temporary and permanent control measures to be administered. The responsibility for frequent inspections of the controls, especially after rainfall, needs to be assigned. This responsible party will need to keep track of the controls during construction by the means of an inspection log, dated photographs, or a written report. This documentation will be uploaded to LEED-Online after construction in order to prove compliance.

Construction Staging Areas (for NC and CS Projects Only)

If the project team is pursuing SS Credit 5.1: Site Development—Protect or Restore Habitat, it is a good idea to mark off the site with flags, barriers, and signage to delineate areas to be preserved and not disturbed during construction. The contractor should ensure that all subcontractors are aware of the limit site area and compliance criteria with weekly reminders at progress meetings. It is also advised to assign someone the responsibility to take time-stamped pictures multiple times during construction showing compliance just in case the project is audited.

Commissioning

Although the commissioning authority is involved during the design phase, his or her scope becomes more intensive during construction. The CxA can be expected to attend some of the construction progress meetings, and if EA Credit 3 is being pursued, the CxA will be a part of the submittal review process, completing Step 7 of the required tasks.

The CxA will need to work with the contractor and subcontractors to determine responsibility and to schedule the monitoring of the installation and calibration of the applicable systems. These installation inspections may also be referred to as prefunctional inspections, as the equipment will be monitored during start-up. This initial inspection is to correct any issues prior to the systems performance testing.

After the applicable equipment has been installed, programmed, and balanced, the CxA will work with the subcontractors to conduct the systems performance

GENERAL CONTRACTOR'S PERSPECTIVE
LEED during Construction

By Michael J. Parnell, LEED AP
Senior Project Manager at Hunter Roberts

Our client's goal was LEED Silver, and at the time of project inception, that goal appeared to be a stretch given our client's overall project budget. But the LEED design and construction process does not have to be handcuffed by budgetary constraints. It is a process geared toward innovative thinking and careful management of construction operations. You must think outside of the box, review each potential point, and come up with ideas as to how each point could apply to your project, and together find ways to make those "potential" points a reality. Be creative, work with each other, and you will find that building "green" not only enhances the operational performance and occupancy wellness of the space, but also fosters a better working relationship among project team members by creating a common goal and purpose for the project.

Our project team did just that, and by working together and making small modifications where possible, we were able to not only attain the client's goal of Silver, we secured enough points for LEED Gold certification. An example of this is that the original design called for "select" wood planking for an exposed ceiling, but by the architect's permitting more knots in the wood, we were able to purchase 100 percent certified wood from a renewable forest, and therefore able to achieve an Exemplary Performance point for 95 percent certified wood. A small concession such as this allowed for two LEED points where we would not have achieved any in the original design.

testing, also known as functional performance testing, as part of Step 8 of the required Cx activities. For example, this will typically include the lighting controls to be tested for functionality during the different modes and for sequencing accuracy and verification that the coordinating light fixtures are connected to the correct sensor. This step also includes the confirmation of outside air delivery rates of the mechanical system. Carbon dioxide (CO_2) sensors should be verified to ensure correct installation in the proper locations and that the monitors coordinate with the proper alarm setpoints. MERV filter confirmation will ensure compliance with EQ Credits 3.2 and 5. Sequencing will be tested for all equipment including "startup, shutdown, capacity modulation, emergency and failure modes, alarms, and interlocks to other equipment."[1] Step 8 concludes with the evaluation of the testing and comparison with the OPR and BOD, with the results reported to the owner to ensure that any necessary corrections are implemented to resolve any problems and defects. The key objective is to ensure that energy use is not excessive and the systems are working in a collective manner.

Step 9 requires the CxA to develop a systems manual and is required only if the team is pursuing EA Credit 3 (EA Credit 2 for CI projects). The manual should indicate that all of the systems that were commissioned will be in addition to all of the operations and maintenance (O&M) manuals submitted by the contractor. The manual will typically address operational matters more than maintenance issues and will be project specific, as the system interactions will be addressed as well as the project BOD is included. According to the LEED BD+C reference guide, the systems manuals should also include the following[2]:

- System single-line diagrams
- As-built sequences of operations, control drawings, and original setpoints

- Operating instructions for integrated building systems
- Recommended schedule of maintenance requirements and frequency, if not already included in the project O&M manuals
- Recommended schedule for retesting of commissioned systems with blank test forms from the original commissioning plan
- Recommended schedule for calibrating sensors and actuators

chapter 9 Monthly Reports

Material Tracking: Getting Started

Building off of the efforts completed during each of the design phases and after writing the Leadership in Energy and Environmental Design (LEED®) action plans as described in the previous chapter, the material tracking process begins with an evaluation of the schedule of values for the project. In order to start reviewing products and materials, the LEED coordinator will need to set up the monitoring and reporting spreadsheets in order to document the contributions and progress toward achieving compliance. Appendix G provides sample forms in order for project teams to create their own. It is the assigned team member's responsibility to collect the documentation, review each material, and log the compliant data in the spreadsheets to submit collectively in a monthly report. If noncompliant materials or products are issued for submittal review, it is the same team member's responsibility to follow up with the subcontractor or contractor to verify a replacement product. The spreadsheets will be used to issue monthly progress reports to the team and ultimately at the end of construction to complete the applicable Materials and Resources (MR) and Indoor Environmental Quality (EQ) credit submittal

templates. Remember, success during construction is achieved by assigning responsibilities, holding individuals accountable, keeping up with the documentation, and maintaining open lines of communication.

After the spreadsheets are set up for the project, the responsible team member will need to determine the total material cost for the project. This will need to be determined using either the default value (an option only for LEED for New Construction and Major Renovations™ [NC] and LEED for Core & Shell™ [CS] projects) or the actual material cost excluding labor and equipment. Once the value is determined, it will need to be entered into the spreadsheets and will be used to track the credit compliance during construction. The actual value is confirmed at project completion. Therefore, it is important to clarify this to all team members to set the expectations for the monthly progress reports to follow.

Some manufacturers have online calculators to help the responsible team member determine the applicable LEED relevance contributing to MR and EQ credits. For other products, including a sample material data reporting form to give to the subcontractors to use during the submittal review process will give the subcontractor an idea of the type of documentation required and should summarize the information in one place for each submittal. It may be helpful to compose a letter to the general contractor to provide the intent of the material data reporting form and all of the components addressed on the form, such as material reuse, recycled content (including an explanation of differences of postconsumer and preconsumer recycled content and a list of common materials with recycled content), regional materials, rapidly renewable materials, certified wood, volatile organic compound (VOC) content (including a clarification of no added urea-formaldehyde), and flooring systems. This will also help the contractor to explain the form to the subcontractors, especially those who were not able to attend the pre-construction training session.

It is strongly encouraged to develop the reporting forms, the explanation letter to the contractor, and the monitoring and reporting spreadsheets as soon as the notice to proceed is received. This way, when the first submittal is issued for review, the material data reporting form should be included and completed by the subcontractor and there are no delays in the actual review process or document compliance, and to then issue the submittal back to the contractor. Remember, the monitoring and reporting spreadsheets are intended to track the materials and are to be submitted collectively to the team as a monthly report summarizing the progress.

Total Material Cost for MR Credits

In order to complete the monthly reports and track materials, the construction team will need to release the schedule of values in order to determine the total material cost for the project. Depending on the rating system being pursued, project teams may have an option when determining the cost to base compliance on.

While NC and CS project teams have the option to calculate the actual material cost of the project, excluding labor and equipment, CI project teams are required to pursue this calculation. This actual material cost will need to be determined for CSI Divisions 03 through 10, 31, and 32. Section 31.60.00 Foundations is used from Division 31, and for Division 32, Sections 32.10.00 Paving, 32.30.00 Site Improvements, and 32.90.00 Plantings are to be used if applicable to the project scope. For NC and CS projects, it is a bit easier, as the teams have the option to use a default 45 percent value of the total construction cost for the material cost for the calculations. It does not matter if the team chooses to use the actual cost instead of the default material cost, just as long as the value is used consistently across all MR credits. Identifying the actual cost can be quite time consuming, so it is encouraged to start the effort early. Therefore, only NC and CS project teams with a low material cost (as compared to labor) should pursue the actual total material cost compliance option.

The overall goal to comply with MR Credits 3 through 7 is based on a percentage of total material cost. Therefore, it is encouraged to track building materials with a higher dollar amount to avoid tracking frivolous items that will have little impact contributing to earn credits. Project teams should determine the critical items early in the construction process to ensure that the "right" materials are purchased.

OWNER'S PERSPECTIVE
Procurement Strategies

By Steve Martorana, LEED AP BD+C
New Jersey Economic Development Authority

Figure 9.1   The Waterfront Tech Center, Camden, New Jersey, a LEED Gold certified CS and CI project. Photo courtesy of Stephen Martorana, LEED AP BD+C of the New Jersey Economic Development Authority.

continued

With each of my five LEED CI projects, achieving the MR credits for recycled content and regional materials has played a considerable role in earning certification (Figures 9.1 and 9.2). In our region, it has been relatively easy for us to achieve over 30 percent recycled content and over 40 percent for materials manufactured regionally. This not only achieves the LEED credit, but also has resulted in obtaining innovation points for Exemplary Performance. Much of this is attributable to assuring that the architect and construction manager (CM) have a clear understanding of the project goals. As project administrator, I have worked with our CM and subcontractors to ensure that materials are procured at the right price, while keeping the goal of LEED certification in mind.

We have seen major differences in the manufacturing location and amount of recycled content in gypsum board and ceiling tiles, as both play an important part in the recycled content and regional material calculations for a project seeking

Figure 9.2 The Biotechnology Development Center in North Brunswick, New Jersey, a LEED Silver CI project. Photo courtesy of Stephen Martorana, LEED AP BD+C of the New Jersey Economic Development Authority.

LEED CI certification. For example, we were able to work with a subcontractor to purchase gypsum board through a local plant versus a plant over 500 miles away from the site. By doing this, we also realized the local manufacturer's products contained a recycled content of 5 percent postconsumer/95 percent preconsumer versus 3 percent postconsumer/3 percent preconsumer for the product manufactured more than 500 miles away. Achieving a high recycled content from a local plant assists when trying to get credit for materials extracted and manufactured locally, versus sourcing virgin gypsum from overseas. Additionally, I have worked with our manufacturer representatives for ceiling tiles and was able to get our specified tile from a Pennsylvania plant, which is within 500 miles of our project sites, as compared to the same tile manufactured at a Florida plant, for no additional cost. We have also specified that the ceiling tile be their high-recycled-content version for a minor upcharge. Purchasing and installing high-recycled-content materials sourced from local manufacturers gave our project teams the opportunity to use the same material to contribute to more than one credit, thus helping us earn higher levels of certification. These are a few simple examples that show how making smart decisions in procurement can ensure that you obtain exemplary percentages for recycled content and regional materials, which can significantly contribute to your overall LEED points.

Assembly Calculations for MR Credits

Project teams may be presented with a building component assembled with multiple materials. For example, each of the different materials could be manufactured with different environmental impacts, such as extraction and processing locations, and they can contain different amounts of postconsumer recycled content, preconsumer recycled content, or none at all. In this particular case, the team would need to evaluate the assembly recycled content of the component. It does not matter if the assembly consists of multiple materials (think concrete) or multiple subcomponents (think furniture). To calculate compliance with MR Credit 4: Recycled Content, teams would need to divide "the weight of the recycled content by the overall weight of the assembly."[1] For example, if window assemblies were evaluated, the frame would most likely have a different recycled content than the glass itself. The weight of the frame would need to be determined versus the weight of the glass, and then tallied with proportionate value of different types of recycled contents in order to determine the overall recycled content value of the assembled material. For assembly products with different recycled content values, the recycled contents

have to be broken out and multiplied by the cost. For example, if a toilet partition has 30 percent preconsumer and 10 percent postconsumer recycled content values, and is worth $10,000, the responsible party would perform the following calculations:

Preconsumer value of 30 percent:
$$\$10,000 \times 30\% \times 0.5 = \$1,500$$

Postconsumer value of 10 percent:
$$\$10,000 \times 10\% = \$1,000$$

Total product value contributing to MR Credit 4:
$$= \$2,500$$

The same concept can be applied to other MR Credits, such as Material Reuse, Regional Materials, Rapidly Renewable Materials, and Certified Wood. For example, if the project team purchased a conference room table with a salvaged base and a new glass top, the weight of the base would need to be determined as a percentage of the table as a whole. If the base weighed 75 percent of the total assembly, 75 percent of the assembly cost could be used toward MR Credit 3 and possibly MR Credit 5 if the base was salvaged locally. Therefore, it may be necessary to have the manufacturers provide their product's assembly information categorized by weight.

MANUFACTURER'S PERSPECTIVE
A Manufacturer's Approach to LEED

By Melissa DeSota, Steelcase, Inc.

As a manufacturer of products that contribute to LEED points, we recognize that our obligation to customers, architects, and designers is to help them understand *how* and *where* our products may contribute to a LEED project. We do this in several ways—education, accessible and understandable tools and documentation, and experience.

Education is particularly important. Understanding the fundamentals of green building is critical to defining sustainable design goals and delivering on them. We've worked with internal practitioners and third-party green building experts to develop a number of tools, like white papers and sustainability courses.

The second way we help is to provide accessible, succinct information required by LEED. Providing this LEED documentation for projects requires us to streamline and consolidate a diverse collection of information from sources across our company. We pull LEED data from product development, marketing groups, suppliers, and more, and incorporate it all into one document summarizing each product. This primary document, called a "product environmental profile," provides the LEED AP all of the data needed to understand and verify the furniture contribution (Figure 9.3). In the spirit of full transparency, these "profiles" reside on our Steelcase website for access by anyone, 24/7.

Recycled Content Summary

Total Weight (lbs)   589.1 - BIFMA Typical Open Plan Workstation

Recycled Content (lbs)	252.7	Recycled Content	42%
Post Consumer (lbs)	94.6	Post Consumer	16%
Pre Consumer (lbs)	158.1	Pre Consumer	26%
Recyclable Content (lbs)	418.0	Recyclable Content	71%

Disclaimer

Numbers may vary based on model and options selected. Calculations of recycled content are based on data provided by suppliers and other available information. This data may include industry averages, ranges or other broadly based information. Steelcase makes conservative assumptions when compiling this information to provide the most accurate recycled content calculations possible but variability in market conditions or manufacturing processes may result in higher or lower content. This document will be reviewed and updated periodically and is subject to change without notice.

Figure 9.3 A portion of a product environmental profile for Steelcase's Montage workstation product detailing product's recycled content. Image courtesy of Steelcase, Inc.

Figure 9.4 The Steelcase, Inc. WorkLab™ in Grand Rapids, Michigan, earned LEED platinum certification, making it the first showroom in the office furniture industry to achieve the highest ranking available. The Steelcase WorkLab is a brand experience center for design professionals and customers that demonstrates the newest Steelcase products in a variety of workplace settings. Photo courtesy of Steelcase, Inc.

Steelcase also builds to LEED standards. We recently received Platinum certification for our WorkLab™ in Grand Rapids, Michigan, making it the first showroom in the office furniture industry to achieve the highest ranking available (Figure 9.4). Building sustainable spaces is one piece of our overall corporate sustainability strategy. We also view it as a critical opportunity to test our own processes and the effectiveness of our service delivery relative to LEED. It helps us know how we can improve the sharing of understanding, information, and documentation.

Material Tracking: Documenting MR Credit 1: Building Reuse

Responsibility typically falls on the design team to complete the calculations and upload the supporting documentation for this credit. The credit is not allowed to be submitted for a design review, as the intended conditions may change during construction. Therefore, during construction, when the envelope or nonstructural interior components to remain are indeed preserved and reused, documentation and calculations should be completed to coordinate with the conditions on-site. The responsible party will need to prepare plans and elevations that clearly denote components to be reused to upload as supporting documentation proving compliance.

Material Tracking: Documenting MR Credit 3: Materials Reuse

Project teams may need to engage a cost estimator to help determine the value of reused and salvaged items. For the purposes of LEED documentation, project teams have the option to select the value to use when pursuing the MR Material Reuse credit. A salvaged material can have a purchase price value if the item is actually procured, but what about items currently in the owner's inventory? These existing items to be used for the project seeking certification were already purchased for another use and therefore were not purchased specifically for the project at hand. Project teams will then need to look to the replacement value for the items. The replacement value can be either the value if the product was purchased new for an equivalent item or it can be the price paid. The LEED reference guides indicate it is acceptable for project teams to use whichever value is higher when completing the calculations for the credit.

Once a month, the monitoring and reporting spreadsheet for this credit should be submitted with the other credits the team is pursuing to provide the team with a snapshot of progress. This is why it is important to set up the spreadsheets at the beginning of the project including the total material cost, as an incomplete form will not provide a status or percentage amount achieved.

Remember at the project's completion, if the calculations do not meet the minimum percentage threshold, salvaged materials can be then included in the construction waste calculations to help contribute toward earning those credits. Do not include any mechanical, electrical, or plumbing fixtures or any specialty items. Include only permanently installed items from CSI Divisions 03 through 10 and any reused foundations, site improvements, plantings, and paving items. LEED NC and CS projects reusing furniture may comply with this credit if the furniture is also included in calculations for MR credits 4 through 7 as well. With any of the rating systems, the qualifying furniture must have been purchased at least two years prior to the relocation.

Material Tracking: Documenting MR Credit 4: Recycled Content

The responsible party is encouraged to determine the materials that are most likely going to contribute to earning this credit as soon as possible. As each of those material submittals are received for review, the subcontractor should supply the documentation along with the rest of the product information. Specifically for this credit, the LEED coordinator will need to determine the preconsumer and postconsumer recycled content values and input the data into the monitoring and reporting spreadsheets. Remember from earlier, the only material with a default value is steel, as it is acceptable to assume a 25 percent postconsumer content if documentation cannot be obtained proving otherwise. The subcontractor will also need to supply the material cost, and that value will need to be conveyed into the spreadsheets as well. Some materials may be trickier than others, as they may contain multiple components. As previously stated, these materials will need to be evaluated based on weight as compared to the overall assembly. LEED CI projects must include furniture in the calculations, while NC and CS have the option to include it or not.

Once a month, the monitoring and reporting spreadsheet for this credit should be submitted, along with the other credits the team is pursuing to

SALVAGED MATERIAL BROKER'S PERSPECTIVE
Overcoming the Challenges of MR Credit 3: Materials Reuse

By Nathan Benjamin, LEED AP
Principal + Founder of PlanetReuse

Materials reuse (the purest form of recycling) is often passed over in even the most sustainable of projects. With only 6 to 8 percent of LEED-certified projects achieving materials reuse credits and 40 percent of all material going to landfills coming from the C&D industry, there is much to be done. MR Credits 3.1 and 3.2 are misperceived as challenging, more expensive, and difficult to understand and, as a result, very difficult to achieve. How do we change these misconceptions?

We can all incorporate more material reuse and divert materials from landfills by: (1) thinking about opportunities earlier in the process—adding a *reuse development phase* to the standard process; (2) thinking about a broad range of materials, not just wood; (3) understanding how the 5 percent/10 percent reuse credit amounts are really calculated; and (4) engaging a reuse consultant/broker to assist in the process.

PlanetReuse has found that the reuse development phase is the most important step among the four items listed. What is reuse development? It's a time during the project to evaluate reclaimed/reused opportunities. This step is best taken when decisions are not too far along for small changes and the LEED scorecard is still being developed. By engaging a broker/consultant at this phase, there is no time delay to the project, there are no additional costs, and it's a great way to look for cost savings while picking up a credit. Most people don't realize that, in general, to achieve the 5 percent reuse credit, for every $1 million in the overall project budget, you need only $13,500 of reused materials. These credits are very achievable.

Getting involved early and fully understanding the best ways to locate and coordinate reclaimed materials is key to achieving materials reuse credits. As a nationwide reclaimed construction material broker and consultant company, PlanetReuse becomes an invaluable team member that helps identify what people have and need and locates materials for projects. The PlanetReuse team builds on this information, coordinating with clients to get the right materials to commercial and residential projects when they need them, and provide confirmation of material origination for LEED MR credit documentation.

PlanetReuse has worked on many LEED-certified projects of all levels and Living Building Challenge Certified projects. Here are a couple of examples:

- For the Omega Center for Sustainable Living project in Rhinebeck, New York, PlanetReuse helped provide reclaimed doors, toilet partitions and accessories, dimensional lumber, plywood, and interior wood paneling (Figures 9.5 and 9.6). The design team commented in the process that they wished they had worked with PlanetReuse earlier in the process, as they could have located more reclaimed material options, helped on the schedule, and saved more money.

continued

Figure 9.5 The Omega Center for Sustainable Living in Rhinebeck, New York, incorporated salvaged materials, helping to earn LEED Gold certification. Image courtesy of PlanetReuse, LLC.

- The Greensburg School in Greensburg, Kansas, was completely destroyed by an F5 tornado. In rebuilding the LEED Platinum project, the design and owner team incorporated reuse opportunities whenever they could. PlanetReuse helped provide over 86,000 board-feet of wood siding, furring, Forest Stewardship Council (FSC) plywood, and interior wood cladding. The exterior siding was salvaged, blown-down cypress from Hurricane Katrina in Louisiana.

Not only does material reuse provide a great way to divert materials from landfills and save money on projects, it also provides a great educational outreach opportunity to allow those visiting the new facility to see the beautiful materials with a great reuse story to be told. Sustainability is all about changing our ways of doing things to better our planet. By changing the way we look at materials reuse, we can raise the number of projects achieving MR credits well beyond the current 6 to 8 percent rate.

Figure 9.6 The entryway of the Omega Center for Sustainable Living features the reclaimed wood paneling. Image courtesy of PlanetReuse, LLC.

provide the team with a snapshot of progress. At the end of construction, the data from the spreadsheet will be transferred to the LEED-Online credit submittal template proving compliance. As with all construction credits, it is advised to collect all documentation proving compliance, although only 20 percent of the documentation is required to be uploaded to LEED-Online.

Material Tracking: Documenting MR Credit 5: Regional Materials

As mentioned for the previous credit, the responsible party should have determine the materials that are most likely going to contribute to earning this credit to know which materials to monitor more closely during the submittal review process. This does not imply that other materials that could potentially contribute to earning the credit should be ignored, but instead to ensure that the "big ticket items" do comply.

As each of the submittals is received for review, the responsible party should review the subcontractor's documentation to ensure that both the extraction and manufacture locations are indicated, as well as the material cost for the product. The point of manufacture is the same as the location of final assembly. The LEED coordinator, or other responsible party, will then need to determine if both of those locations fall within the 500-mile radius from the project site. If the materials are in compliance with the credit, the locations and cost values will need to be entered into the monitoring and reporting spreadsheets. LEED CI projects must include furniture in the calculations, while NC and CS have the option to include it or not.

Remember, items that were locally salvaged and/or contain recycled content, rapidly renewable materials, or certified wood can also count toward this credit. For salvaged materials, the location from which the materials were salvaged functions as the extraction location, and the supplier's location where the items were purchased as the manufacturing location.

Just as with the previous credit, compliant products may be a part of an assembled product. When calculating compliance, the materials are based on *weight* as compared to the overall assembly.

Once a month, the monitoring and reporting spreadsheet for this credit should be submitted along with the other credits the team is pursuing to provide the team with a snapshot of progress. At the end of construction, the data from the spreadsheet will be transferred to the credit submittal template proving compliance. As mentioned previously, it is advised to collect all documentation proving compliance, although only 20 percent is required to be uploaded to LEED-Online.

Material Tracking: Documenting MR Credit 6: Rapidly Renewable Materials

Materials complying with this credit are typically determined during construction, as the minimum compliance threshold is lower than the previous two credits. The responsible party will need to collect the applicable product data proving that the credit requirements were adhered to. The material cost will need to be determined, as this credit is awarded based on purchasing and implementing a percentage of the total material cost, similar to most MR credits. LEED CI projects must include furniture in this credit's calculations, while NC and CS have the option to include the products or not. Just as with the two previous credits, compliant materials may be a part of an assembled product. When calculating compliance, the materials are based on weight as compared to the overall assembly.

As with MR Credits 3, 4, and 5, once a month the monitoring and reporting spreadsheet for this credit should be submitted along with the other construction side credits the team is pursuing to provide the team with a snapshot of progress. At the end of construction, the data from the spreadsheet will be transferred to the credit submittal template proving compliance. As mentioned previously, it is advised to collect all documentation proving compliance, although only 20 percent is required to be uploaded to LEED-Online.

Material Tracking: Documenting MR Credit 7: Certified Wood

This credit is a little different than the previously described MR credits in terms of material tracking. In order to achieve this credit, 50 percent of the total *new wood* purchased for the project must be FSC certified. Therefore, compliance is not based on the total material cost, but instead the total new wood material cost. NC and CS projects have the option to include temporary wood materials, but CI projects do not. NC and CS projects also have the option to include furniture in the calculations, but CI projects do not. Just as with the previously described MR credits, NC and CS projects that include furniture in one of the MR credits are required to add the value to the total material cost for each of the other MR credits as well.

This credit can be tricky for a number of reasons. It can be challenging to decipher the different types of FSC certifications for compliance. Typically, you will see three types: FSC Pure, FSC Mixed Credit, and FSC Mixed followed by a percentage. FSC Pure and FSC Mixed are both accepted at full value, while the latter FSC Mixed (NN percent) is valued at the percentage contained within the parentheses. For example, should documentation be submitted for a product with FSC Mixed (34 percent) and has a value of $28,000, the value contributing to the credit is $9,520. This credit also requires all wood products (including FSC-certified products) to be identified on a line-item basis along with the dollar value of each item. Coordination with each of the wood-supplying vendors is critical. Another challenge for compliance requires the responsible party to document the chain-of-custody (COC) number. For every invoice, the vendor's COC certificate number by an FSC-accredited certifier must be included.

This credit differs from the rest of the MR credits in terms of determining the contribution of assembly products. Whereas the previous credits based the components as a percentage of weight of the total assembly, FSC products can contribute based on weight, volume, or cost.

Once a month, the monitoring and reporting spreadsheet for this credit should be submitted along with the other credits the team is pursuing to provide the team with a snapshot of progress. At the end of construction, the data from the spreadsheet will be transferred to the credit submittal template proving compliance. Similar to the other MR credits, LEED-Online will require 20 percent of the documentation to be uploaded to prove compliance, but all backup documentation should be collected to be prepared for an audit.

Material Tracking: Documenting EQ Credit 4: Low-Emitting Materials

Just as with the other construction products and materials, when the contractor issues submittals for review, the VOC-related product information should be included to avoid any inappropriate purchases and delays at the end of the project. It is highly recommended to get all of the complying data in writing, as verbal confirmations are not accepted for the purposes of LEED compliance and documentation requirements. The VOC data needs to be compared to the coordinating reference standard (see Tables 9.1 and 9.2) to ensure that the maximum threshold has not been exceeded. If in compliance, the product data needs to be entered into the monitoring and reporting spreadsheets (see Appendix G). If the product data indicates that the VOC level is less than a certain value (i.e., < 50 g/L), and the maximum value is in compliance with the reference standard, list the maximum level in the coordinating

**Table 9.1 The VOC Maximum Thresholds for EQ Credit 4.1: Low-Emitting
Materials—Adhesives and Sealants Compliance**

Adhesives, sealants, and sealant primers must comply with the following limits for VOC content when calculated according to South Coast Air Quality Management District (SCAQMD) Rule #1168 effective July 1, 2005:

Architectural Application	VOC Threshold (g/L less water)
Carpet adhesives: Indoor	50 g/L
Carpet pad adhesives	50 g/L
Wood flooring adhesive	50 g/L
Rubber flooring adhesive	60 g/L
Subfloor adhesives	50 g/L
Ceramic tile adhesives	65 g/L
VCT and asphalt tile adhesives	50 g/L
Cove base adhesives	50 g/L
Drywall and panel adhesives	50 g/L
Multipurpose construction adhesives	70 g/L
Structural glazing adhesives	100 g/L
Specialty Applications	
PVC welding compounds	510 g/L
CPVC welding compounds	490 g/L
ABS welding compounds	325 g/L
Plastic cement welding compounds	250 g/L
Adhesive Primer for Plastic	550 g/L
Contact adhesives	80 g/L
Special purpose contact adhesives	250 g/L
Structural wood member adhesives	140 g/L
Sheet applied rubber lining operations	850 g/L
Top and trim adhesives	250 g/L
Substrate-Specific Applications	
Metal-to-metal adhesives	30 g/L
Adhesives for porous materials (except wood)	50 g/L
Plastic foam adhesives	50 g/L
Wood adhesives	30 g/L
Fiberglass adhesives	80 g/L
Architectural	250 g/L
Nonmembrane roof	300 g/L

Single-ply roof membrane	450 g/L
Other	420 g/L
Sealant Primers	
Architectural nonporous substrates	250 g/L
Architectural porous substrates	775 g/L
Other	750 g/L
Aerosol Adhesives per Green Seal Standard for Commercial Adhesives effective October 19, 2000 (GS-36)	
General-purpose mist sprays	65% VOCs by weight
General-purpose web sprays	55% VOCs by weight
Special-purpose aerosol adhesives	70% VOCs by weight

Table 9.2 The VOC Maximum Thresholds for EQ Credit 4.2: Low-Emitting Materials—Paints and Coatings Compliance

Paints must comply with the following limits for VOC content when calculated according to Green Seal Standard GS-11, 1st edition, Paints, as of May 20, 1993:	
Architectural Paints	**VOC Threshold (g/L less water)**
Flats	50 g/L
Nonflats	150 g/L
Anticorrosive and antirust paints applied to any interior ferrous metal substrates must comply with the following limits for VOC content when calculated according to Green Seal Standard GS-03, Anticorrosive Paints, 2nd edition, January 7, 1997:	
Architectural Paints	**VOC Threshold (g/L less water)**
Anticorrosive and antirust paints	250 g/L
Clear wood finishes, floor coatings, stains, sealers, and shellacs must comply with the following limits for VOC content when calculated according to South Coast Air Quality Management District (SCAQMD) Rule #1113, effective January 1, 2004:	
Architectural Coatings	**VOC Threshold (g/L less water)**
Clear wood varnishes	350 g/L
Clear wood lacquers	550 g/L
Floor coatings	100 g/L
Waterproofing sealers	250 g/L
Sanding sealers	275 g/L
All other sealers	200 g/L
Clear shellac	730 g/L
Pigmented shellac	550 g/L
Stains	250 g/L

spreadsheet. If the VOC content level surpasses the maximum allowable level, the submittal is rejected and a replacement product is needed (see VOC budget method for EQ 4.1 and 4.2 in the applicable reference guide). Remember, only products and materials used within the weather barrier and that are applied on-site need to comply, as products used outside or applied to products off-site do not need to be included in the tracking process. If the product is used as part of the barrier, it is best to include them in the submittal review process for the purposes of the LEED compliance.

Each month, the monitoring and reporting spreadsheets are included in the monthly reports to provide an update to the rest of the team, just as with the MR credits. It is best not to rely on the monthly reports should a product not comply with the coordinating credit. The submittal review process should be used to raise awareness of a noncompliant product.

At the end of construction, or when the last product is purchased, the product data is transferred to the applicable credit submittal template on LEED-Online to prove compliance for certification.

For EQ Credit 4.3, the materials and products need to be reviewed for certification compliance in addition to tracking the VOC content where applicable. For example, carpets need to be CRI Green Label Plus program certified, and the carpet adhesive VOC content needs to be documented. If the project is implementing both carpeting and hard surface flooring, 100 percent of the finished floor area must comply in order to earn the credit. EQ Credit 4.4, and for CI projects EQ Credit 4.5, documentation will also need to be gathered proving no urea-formaldehyde was used and Greenguard certification compliance. For Credit 4.4, be sure to also

monitor the adhesives used in the manufacturing process for laminated products, such as countertops, flooring, and doors. Also beware of "urea-formaldehyde free" advertising, as this may or may not address the binders that were used. Therefore, double-check the materials safety data sheets (MSDS) to ensure compliance. For Credit 4.5, project teams have the option to pursue either compliance Option 2 or 3 if Greenguard certification documentation is unavailable. As mentioned previously, SCS Indoor Advantage Gold will typically comply for Option 3. Whichever compliance option is chosen, verify the expiration date of the certification, as they expire each year, and log the manufacturer, product line, and dates of manufacture.

Once a month, the monitoring and reporting spreadsheet for this credit should be submitted along with the MR credits the team is pursuing to provide the team with a snapshot of compliance. Each of the credits within the EQ Credit 4 suite requires an "all-or-nothing" compliance strategy (unless using the VOC budget method), so it is important to monitor the products to be purchased and used on-site, but also to provide the team with a monthly progress report. At the end of construction, the data from the spreadsheet will be transferred to the credit submittal template proving compliance. Remember to collect all compliance-proving documentation and upload 20 percent of the documentation to LEED-Online.

The VOC Budget Method for EQ Credit 4.1 and 4.2

If an unapproved and/or noncompliant product is used within the weather barrier, it does not necessarily mean the team will not be able to pursue and earn the associated EQ low-emitting-materials credit (either EQ 4.1 or 4.2). In this case, the team will need

Table 9.3 Sample VOC Budget Method Calculation for EQ Credit 4.2

Product	Volume of Product Used	Maximum VOC Allowed	VOC Budget	Actual VOC Content of Product	VOC Used
Interior Primer	150 liters	50 g/L	7,500	91 g/L	4,550
Eggshell Paint	50 liters	150 g/L	7,500	0 g/L	0
Flat Paint	50 liters	50 g/L	2,500	97 g/L	48,50
Semigloss Paint	50 liters	150 g/L	7,500	0 g/L	0
Clear Wood Lacquer	38 liters	550 g/L	20,900	258/gL	9,804
TOTALS			45,900		19,204
					COMPLIANT

to pursue the VOC budget method. With this method, a comparison is conducted for the total VOCs used on site (in grams per liter) to a baseline total maximum allowable VOC levels to document an overall low-VOC performance. For each product used at the project site, the total volume amount of product used is multiplied by the maximum VOC limit and then again by the actual VOC content of the product. This results in a total allowable VOC content and total VOC content used. As long as the total used is less than the total allowed, the project is in compliance. This comparison is completed separately for applicable products per credit. Therefore, if a noncompliant paint product is used, sealants and adhesives are not included in the calculations, as they are part of a different credit. Table 9.3 provides a sample approach for EQ Credit 4.2: Low-Emitting Materials—Paints and Coatings.

Construction Waste Management

Each month, the LEED coordinator or responsible party will need to issue a monthly report including the progress for MR Credit 2: Construction Waste Management. Depending on the waste hauler and the collection strategy on-site, the coordinator will need to obtain a summary of or individual waste tickets for each container that leaves the site. Each container will need to be weighed and documented for the final destination of the materials collected. If the materials are collected in a commingled fashion and are sorted off-site, the sorting facility will need to provide a summary of the different materials collected within the container and where those materials are distributed to. If the materials are sorted on-site, the waste hauler will need to provide a ticket indicating how much the container weighs and where the container was brought to. The materials that leave a project site and are typically diverted from a landfill include wood, concrete, plastic, cardboard, dirt, asphalt, metals, and glass. The coordinator will also need to monitor the amount of waste that is sent to a landfill. Using the monitoring and reporting spreadsheets will help to track the progress on a monthly basis to include in the monthly report. This helps to ensure that the project stays on track to receive the intended amount of points for certification. At the end of construction, when the last container has left the site, the information is transferred to the credit submittal template on LEED-Online.

Construction Indoor Air Quality: Complying with SMACNA Requirements

During construction it is important to implement the Sheet Metal and Air Conditioning Contractors' National Association (SMACNA) guidelines, especially if the team is pursuing EQ Credit 3.1: Construction IAQ Management Plan—during Construction. As mentioned in the previous chapter, it is suggested to review the requirements of the credit with the entire construction team during an initial LEED training session. The construction IAQ management plan should be distributed to all of the subcontractors at this time, if this has not already been done. This plan will solidify the roles and responsibilities of the team, such as quality control. The plan should address the five SMACNA control measures to adhere to, as well as the protection of absorptive materials (Figure 9.7). To comply with EQ Credit

Figure 9.7 Elevating product storage protects against damage as suggested by SMACNA guidelines.

Figure 9.8 SMACNA-compliant practices include sealing off ductwork from dust and particulates.

3.1, the responsible party will need to complete the credit submittal template and upload the construction IAQ management plan and three IAQ reports containing pictures demonstrating compliance with the construction IAQ management plan. Following are the SMACNA control measures, with some tips for photo opportunities during construction:

- **Systems Protection.** Take pictures of the ductwork arriving and once installed but not yet in use where the plastic wrap is kept intact (Figure 9.8). Once the heating, ventilating, and air-conditioning (HVAC) system is operational, be sure to take pictures of the Minimum Efficiency Reporting Value (MERV) filters in place. Be sure to keep the mechanical room free and clear of any construction or waste materials.

- **Source Control.** Using low-emitting materials, sealing a surface to minimize odor, and keeping the containers of wet products closed and stored away are methods by which to comply with this SMACNA guideline.

- **Pathway Interruption.** Depressurizing the work area, pressurizing occupied spaces, segregating construction areas with barriers, relocating pollutant sources, or temporarily sealing the building are methods by which to adhere to this SMACNA control measure.

- **Housekeeping.** Photos of daily housekeeping activities such as using a high-efficiency particulate air (HEPA) vacuum and wet mopping to minimize dust are good examples showing compliance with this SMACNA guideline. Using a dust-collecting tools and equipment, such as drills and sanders, also would help to comply. Another example includes the removal of water accumulation and keeping the work area dry.

- **Scheduling.** An example of compliance could include the scheduling of construction activities for painting or floor sealing when absorptive materials, such as acoustical ceiling tiles, are not installed or stored on-site. This will help prevent the tiles from absorbing the emitted gases and prolonging the contamination. This control measure could also relate to work that occurs after substantial completion when a building may become occupied or for major renovation projects. Examples of compliance include creating a buffer zone to mitigate dust, noise, and odor, relocating occupants, continuous ventilation, staging work around occupancy hours, and maintaining negative pressurized work areas to prevent traveling odors.

It may also be helpful to create a weekly checklist to act as a reminder and for the contractor to complete. Table 9.4 provides an example of a checklist to refer to. The description of tasks should coordinate with the SMACNA control measure. For example, HVAC protection could include delivery of ductwork with plastic wrapping or the storage

Table 9.4 Sample Checklist

Date	SMACNA Guideline	Description of Task	Responsible Party	Photo?
	HVAC Protection			
	Source Control			
	Housekeeping			
	Pathway Interruption			
	Scheduling			

of the ductwork with plastic wrapping kept intact. If the HVAC system is to be operated during construction, ensure that the appropriate MERV filters are installed and replaced as needed and prior to occupancy. Housekeeping tasks could include wet sweeping, and source control tasks could include erecting barriers to contain construction areas or relocating pollutant sources.

It may also be helpful to post signs to relay the guidelines and practices to be followed during construction. The contractor is encouraged to assign the role of an IAQ manager to monitor compliance. Also, communication should already be under way concerning the compliance path for NC and CI teams pursuing EQ Credit 3.2: Construction IAQ Management Plan—before Occupancy. Remember, a flushout typically will extend the schedule, while air quality testing will typically add costs to the budget. A flushout may not be realistic given the time of year and climate conditions when the project will be completed, as it may be difficult to maintain the maximum relative humidity and minimum temperature levels. If pursuing air quality testing, be sure to monitor the schedule of the different trades to avoid overlapping of work where off-gassing could be prolonged and risk failing the tests. Also, require low-emitting cleaning products to keep contaminants levels in check, although a small-scale flush is typically completed prior to the testing to ensure compliance. Chapter 10 discusses

more details for EQ Credit 3.2 after construction is completed.

In summary, the responsible party should communicate with the contractor to ensure that photos are taken throughout construction (especially after ductwork is delivered) to document compliance and used to create three reports with at least six photos contained within, although there is not a specific number of photos required.

Monthly Reports

Monthly reports shall be issued to the owner or contractor (depending on roles, responsibilities, and contractual agreements) on a monthly basis. These monthly reports shall correlate with the LEED implementation plan discussed in the previous chapter and address MR Credits 3 through 7, MR Credit 2: Construction Waste Management, and each of the EQ low-emitting materials credits being pursued by the team. The IAQ report required for EQ Credit 3.1: Construction IAQ Management Plan—during Construction compliance shall be issued at least three times during construction in conjunction with the monthly progress reports.

A summary cover page is suggested to streamline progress updates. This cover page could also bring attention to outstanding and necessary information.

OWNER'S PERSPECTIVE
Pursuing LEED Certification

By Charley Ryan
Brooklyn Bowl

My partner, Peter Shapiro, and I came up with the idea for Brooklyn Bowl in 2000 when we hosted a company party at a bowling alley and thought we could create a superior place. We searched for the right location, on and off, for years. In 2006, we found what we wanted: the 1882 former Hecla Iron Works foundry in Williamsburg, Brooklyn. The space met our needs: massive wooden beams, high and irregular ceilings, brick walls, and 20,000 square feet of open space. Additionally, the zoning (mixed-use industrial) and the neighborhood were right.

Figure 9.9 The String bowling pin machines at the Brooklyn Bowl in New York use 75 percent less energy than typical machines. Photo courtesy of Adam Macchia.

continued

We retained the consulting services of GreenOrder, and to a lesser extent Buro Happold, to help us evaluate our chances for achieving LEED certification and find our way through the process. Their opinion was that it would be close; because the rules are more geared to influencing decisions made in new construction, many potential points did not apply to us and could not be scored. However, we made the fateful decision not only to build responsibly, but also to go for certification at the outset, and accordingly to register the project with Green Building Certification Institute (GBCI).

We minimized our water use wherever we could. In the bathrooms, we chose vandal-proof, flow-restricted lavatories that deliver only a half-gallon of water per minute. With wall-hung toilets, the best we could achieve was 1.28 gallons per flush, which undoubtedly will soon be improved in the marketplace. We wanted to use waterless urinals; this was disallowed for our old building by the City of New York, which may have been a blessing. We ended up with units that use one pint per flush, a huge savings compared to the standard. Due to these strategies, we were able to achieve a 43 percent reduction in water use.

In order to help us to optimize our performance, we installed energy-efficient pinspotters, reducing consumption there by 75 percent (Figure 9.9). Our HVAC plan features variable-frequency drive motors, CO_2 sensors, and four 10-foot ceiling fans by Big Ass Fans. Our system is smart and relatively small. We chose the most energy-efficient appliances throughout, and our stage lighting is almost exclusively light-emitting diode (LED). These fixtures reduce consumption by more than 90 percent compared to traditional incandescent lighting designs.

We concentrated on sustainable building material choices to help earn MR points, including installing rapidly renewable materials, like cork flooring in the green room and bowlers' lounge, and purchasing recycled and FSC-certified wood products (Figure 9.10). We were happy to be able to incorporate salvaged materials as well, to construct a performance stage covered in material 100 percent recycled from old truck tires, and to install glass dividers in the bar that are old, beautiful, and salvaged from the historic Brooklyn Navy Yard.

To comply with the intentions of the Indoor Environmental Quality category, we purchased low-emitting building materials such as adhesives, sealants, paints, and coatings. From Get Real Surfaces, we found soy-based concrete floor sealant and exterior waterproofing products that really work, with no environmental side effects.

The staff at GreenOrder, especially Pete Atkin and Caitlin Canty, divided up the project into teams within their office. Each team was charged with formulating a strategy to achieve compliance with each prerequisite and earn those credits. Sometimes this meant prodding, cajoling, or flat-out hectoring us. Their approach was welcomed and necessary, due to time restraints and the fact that we did not choose other consulting professionals carefully and specifically with our green aspirations in mind. We found out the hard way that they sometimes did not understand our mission, despite our attempts at communication, and even held the whole thing in contempt: "There's nothing green about this project," I heard from one "professional," and indeed that would have been true were the decision his to make. It is advisable to interview all prospective primary team members (including consultants, vendors, and

Figure 9.10 The design team of the Brooklyn Bowl in New York specified materials with recycled content, salvaged materials, FSC-certified wood products, and rapidly renewable materials throughout the facility, helping to earn the first LEED certification for a bowling alley! Photo courtesy of Adam Macchia

tradesmen) to gauge their LEED experience and interest in the issues. If you find there is real familiarity and experience beyond the buzzwords they almost all know, you will likely have an ally in this challenging endeavor—and you will need all the allies you can muster.

There was a major scramble at the end when we received our first review; about half of our points were approved, while the other credits were denied for various reasons. We had just a few weeks to respond to, answer, and clarify the questions that were technical in nature. Without GreenOrder's expertise and support, there is no question that we would not have succeeded as we did in our quest to become the world's first LEED-certified bowling alley!

We benefited from an avalanche of favorable publicity worldwide. We could not have predicted this, and our decision to build as we did was not based on any such expectation. Having said that, in hindsight the cost of our green aspirations, including the pursuit of LEED certification, was more than covered by the benefits of numerous interviews, newspaper and magazine articles, television coverage, and countless blogs.

The LEED process, although dense and bureaucratic, undoubtedly leads to more people making better decisions. We need more of that on planet Earth.

A submittal log is also a suggested inclusion to ensure no submittals have been overlooked or missed.

The LEED Documentation Notebook

The LEED coordinator may also be responsible for maintaining the LEED documentation notebook. This notebook remains on-site and is organized just as the LEED scorecard is: by categories and then prerequisites and credits. It includes the project-specific LEED scorecard and each of monthly reports summarizing the progress for each of the construction-side credits the team is pursuing. The LEED documentation notebook is the gathering place for all of the backup information to be delivered at the end of the project in case of an audit. For each prerequisite and credit applicable to the project, a copy of the completed LEED credit templates, applicable product data for material selection, final calculations, certifications for construction practices, procurement data, cumulative calculations, and other items as identified in the approved LEED implementation plan is required. The notebook typically will be reviewed at the pre-closeout meeting to verify completeness and then again at the closeout meeting.

10 Construction Completion

The construction phase can be the most exciting part of the project for some. It is the opportunity to see conceptual sketches come to life (Figure 10.1) and ideas to take a three-dimensional form (Figure 10.2). From a Leadership in Energy and Environmental Design (LEED®) perspective, the construction phase reveals the level of success, the true testament of effort. Although the project has achieved substantial completion and tasks are winding down, the work of the LEED Coordinator is not done yet! There are typically some outstanding tasks to be completed prior to submitting for a construction review with Green Building Certification Institute (GBCI). This chapter will detail those tasks, review the submission for certification review, and outline the tasks for postoccupancy.

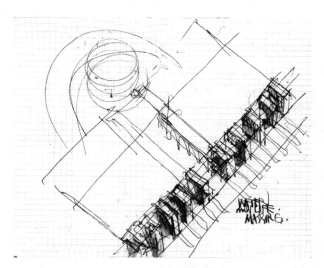

Figure 10.1 and 10.2 The Water + Life Museums in Hemet, California, from concept to reality. The project team, including Lehrer Architects, worked diligently to achieve the world's first LEED Platinum certified museum. Images courtesy of Benny Chan/fotoworks.

Tasks after Substantial Completion

The following details activities for LEED for New Construction and Major Renovations™ (NC) and LEED for Commercial Interiors™ (CI) project teams to address prior to the final certification submission to GBCI. These credits were not forgotten along the way, but are required to be addressed after the punch list is completed and the space is about to be occupied and not therefore available for LEED for Core and Shell™ (CS) project teams to pursue. CS project team members are encouraged to skip to the next section: Educating the Building Occupants.

EQ Credit 3.2: Construction Indoor Air Quality (IAQ) Management Plan, Before Occupancy

After all interior finishes are installed, the punch list is completed, all cleaning is finalized, the heating, ventilating, and air-conditioning (HVAC) system has been tested and balanced, and if the team is pursuing EQ Credit 3.2: Construction IAQ Management Plan—before Occupancy, either a flush-out will need to begin or air quality testing will need to take place. All Minimum Efficiency Reporting Value (MERV) filters should be changed out and replaced prior to pursuing either option. For NC projects, it is advised to have the furniture installation completed, although for CI projects it is required.

If pursuing Option 1: Flush-out, the team needs to determine if Path A or B is appropriate depending on the schedule availability and desired occupancy. Ensure that someone has been assigned the responsibility to document the flush-out dates, occupancy patterns, and delivery rates for outdoor air, and confirm that the relative humidity levels do not exceed 60 percent and the internal temperature does not drop below 60°F. This information will be necessary in order to write the narrative on the credit submittal template on LEED-Online.

If pursuing Option 2: Air Quality testing, as mentioned in the previous chapter, it is advised to ensure that only low-emitting cleaning products are used and perform a scaled-down version of a flush-out prior to testing. Typically, testing will take one day, but could require more time, depending on the size of the project. Verify that the testing is conducted within the breathing zone of the space (between three and six feet from the floor) and during normal occupied times. Be sure a team member is assigned the tasks of describing the testing process, including the dates, and recording the sample locations, including floor area, size, and ventilation used. This information will be included in the narrative documenting compliance, along with the test results. Remember, if the maximum contaminant levels are exceeded, retesting will be required after a flush-out is conducted in order to prove compliance, so be sure to document the locations from which the samples were taken.

EQ Credit 8.1: Daylight and Views—Daylight

For project teams that deferred Indoor Environmental Quality (EQ) Credit 8.1: Daylight and Views, Daylight from a Design Review and are pursuing Option 3, the daylight measurements need to be completed at this time. A hand-held light meter is used to record the daylight values based on a 10 × 10 grid. The responsible party will need to record the square footage of the regularly occupied areas that comply with the daylight requirements. Be sure to dedicate time to set up the grid and to measure the light values. Once completed, this documentation will need to be uploaded to LEED-Online proving compliance and the credit submittal template completed and signed.

Pre-Closeout Meeting

Although the LEED coordinator will need to visit the site periodically during construction, he or she may be required to attend two additional meetings after construction is completed. The first will be a pre-closeout meeting to review the LEED documentation notebook for completeness and identify any outstanding issues relating to final score and documentation requirements. The LEED documentation notebook was discussed in the previous chapter. The second is a closeout meeting to review the final LEED documentation notebook. At the closeout meeting, the project team will determine a final score for the project based on review of project performance and documentation. The LEED coordinator shall make an updated LEED documentation notebook available for this meeting. Note, if submitting for certification review, the final score is determined by GBCI.

Commissioning Activities

By the time construction is completed, the commissioning agent (CxA) must complete the systems manuals and deliver to the operations and maintenance (O&M) staff to complete Step 9 of the required commissioning (Cx) activities as part of Energy and Atmosphere (EA) Credit 3 (LEED CI EA Credit 2): Enhanced Commissioning. The O&M manuals need to include instructions for the operations and maintenance of the thermal comfort controls. The manual is also required to include the seasonal settings and changeovers and the limits of adjustments for manual controls. A maintenance and inspection checklist must also be included along with a schedule for the applicable building systems. Step 10 of the Cx activities is also required if the

team is pursuing the enhanced scope, but completing this step is not required in order to finalize the documentation for the purposes of LEED. This step requires the CxA to train the O&M staff and building occupants on a number of items in reference to the systems that were commissioned, such as the systems manuals, interactions with other systems and occupants, health and safety issues, and the different modes of operation. It is encouraged to schedule multiple training and orientation sessions as not to overwhelm the attendees by discussing multiple systems in one session.

Step 11 is required by the prerequisite requirements regardless if the credit is being pursued. This step addresses the summary Cx report. This report is intended to epitomize the entire Cx process of the project and includes the results of testing, all observations, and the agent's conclusions. Any deficiencies found and the resolution of those imperfections should be included in the notes. It should also address any issues to be verified at a later date due to seasonal limitations. The summary should discuss the alignment or misalignment with the owner's project requirements (OPR) and basis of design (BOD) as well. If the credit is also being pursued, the additional tasks should be included in the report, such as construction document and submittal review, the development of the systems manuals, and any training conducted.

The final task and Step 12 of the Cx process required for compliance with the Enhanced Commissioning credit, requires the CxA to visit the facility within 10 months after substantial completion for NC and CS projects and within 8 to 10 months for CI projects. The purpose of this visit is to confirm the systems are working correctly and the O&M staff is using and maintaining the equipment appropriately. Therefore, it is important to verify a contract exists requiring the CxA to revisit the project and there is a plan in place for corrective action. Note, the project does not have to wait until the site visit to submit for a final certification review with GBCI. Compliance of this final task is based on the honor system.

Educating the Building Occupants

Educating the building occupants is one part of the operational success of a LEED project. Focusing on the employees, it is critical the inhabitants will understand all of the sustainable features of the facility. The owner should be encouraged and excited to present all of the benefits of the new facility for the occupants to enjoy! Remember, the key is to not only operate and maintain the building after occupancy, but for it to perform the way it was designed. For example, if the dual flush toilets are not pointed out and occupants instructed on the proper use, the building might consume more water than necessary. If a project is pursuing the Innovation in Design (ID) credit for implementing a comprehensive signage program and/or tours for the community, this would be a perfect place to start with the building occupants.

An occupant educational program should address each key feature of the facility, starting with the Sustainable Sites (SS) category and finish with either the EQ or ID category. Each program will be specific to the project, but the following highlights some features and presents a few suggestions. The education should not stop after initial occupancy, as staff members that are hired after the initial training sessions should be informed of building capabilities and allowances as well.

Sustainable Sites

- **Public Transportation Access.** Provide schedules for the nearby bus routes and rail stations.

- **Bicycle Storage and Showers.** Point them out! Occupants may not realize that the adjacent gym will allow them to use the showers in the case the building in which they work does not have showers. Mention the environmental benefits and any incentives that may be available, such as maintenance reimbursements for bicycle tire changes and such.

- **Low-Emitting and Fuel-Efficient (LEFE) Vehicles.** Be sure to highlight the location of the reserved parking spaces or discount parking program available. Be sure to mention the advantages of the automobiles, especially if the company has purchased LEFE vehicles!

- **Carpool and Vanpool Reserved Parking.** Implement a ride-share board and encourage employees to take advantage of the program by offering incentives.

- **Greenfields and Open Space.** Be sure signage has been installed to designate the area to ensure it is preserved in the future.

Water Efficiency

- **Water Use Reduction.** Be sure to declare the percentage reduction goal and how it was calculated, as this strategy is key to achieving a noteworthy operational LEED building. Show the occupants the fixtures and explain how to use them properly. Implement a strategy to report any leaks or problems to have the issues addressed immediately.

Energy and Atmosphere

- **On-Site Renewable Energy.** Most everyone appreciates the beauty of renewable energy sources and the environmental benefits they offer. Be sure to present the amount of energy the system provides, such as a display monitor with daily production rates. It is one of the features to be visually appreciated by the common eye.

Materials and Resources

- **Storage and Collection of Recyclables.** This is another key feature of a successful LEED project, as the project was designed and constructed to support a recycling program and therefore should be used. The success of this strategy will not only be for the cleaning crew to be aware of the separate collection bins, but for the occupants to sort materials appropriately. Include an informative session to detail what waste goes in what bin and how the occupants can continue the efforts at home.

- **Construction Achievement Fun Facts.** Highlight the achievements during construction such as preserving the existing building, diverting a percentage of construction waste, or purchasing salvaged materials, materials with recycled content or manufactured locally, rapidly renewable materials, or certified wood products.

Indoor Environmental Quality

- **Environmental Tobacco Smoke (ETS) Control.** Be sure to review the smoking policy of the facility, including if and where smoking is allowed.

- **Controllability of Systems, Lighting and Thermal Comfort.** Be sure to review the lighting design and capabilities and encourage occupants to turn lights off when they leave. This effort should be coupled with turning off computers and other electronic equipment. The occupants should be informed of thermal comfort control locations and how to operate them.

- **Daylight and Views.** The occupants should be instructed on the shade and glare-control devices

and systems, as they might require manual operation. Some individuals might not be aware the controllability is available and then be disrupted during the workday.

Innovation in Design

- Be sure to present the occupants with any outstanding achievements not addressed under any of the main categories.

Training the Operations and Maintenance Staff

The previous section discussed one part of the operation success equation for a LEED project, while this section discusses the other: training of the O&M staff. These staff members will be directly responsible for monitoring the building performance and maintaining the equipment, spaces, and grounds and are therefore critical to the expected building performance achievements.

Just as with the education of the occupants, the training will need to be designed to address the specific systems and equipment installed for the project. As training will be quite elaborate, it is best to separate the training sessions not to overwhelm the staff members. The training strategy should address each key feature of the facility, starting with the SS category and finishing with either the EQ or ID category. The following highlights some of the critical components that may be included, but is not intended to be all-inclusive:

Sustainable Sites

- **Stormwater System.** The landscape manager should be presented with a maintenance plan, including a schedule to monitor performance and any guidelines for repairs and modifications. All plans and manuals should be provided as well. For projects with hopes of pursuing Existing Buildings: Operations and Maintenance (EBOM) certification in the future, a maintenance plan will help to contribute.

- **Alternative Transportation.** Just as with the other building occupants, the O&M staff should be advised on the options and incentives available. If refueling stations are provided on-site, be sure to the staff is aware of the safety and maintenance strategies associated with the feature or have a vendor under contract to maintain the stations.

- **Porous Paving.** Be sure to review the site activities that can impact the performance of the material, such as snow plowing.

- **Native and Adaptive Vegetation.** The O&M staff should be aware of the type of vegetation implemented on-site, as a meadow area could be destroyed by a lawn mower, while other species may need time to mature and grow in. If a temporary irrigation system is installed, it is important to clarify its intention and when it will be removed. Open areas to be used for natural infiltration should also be noted, as soil compaction from vehicle use can diminish the strategy.

- **Hardscape Areas and Roofing Materials.** Determine a schedule for regular cleaning activities to ensure the intended solar reflectance index (SRI) value is achieved. For hardscape areas, if an open-grid paving product was installed, be sure a schedule is developed for regular weeding. If a green roof was installed, be sure to review the maintenance requirements for the system.

- **Lighting Systems.** Be sure to review the lighting controls and determine a schedule for future inspections.

Water Efficiency

- **Fixtures and Systems.** Be sure to deliver the manuals for all systems and fixtures installed for the project. Each should be properly labeled, especially nonpotable water systems and pipes.

- **Waterless Fixtures.** Be sure to review the maintenance requirements for these fixtures and develop a schedule appropriate for the needs of the fixture.

- **Irrigation Systems.** Be sure to review the operation schedule for the system that is appropriate for the different seasons. The plans and system's details should also be provided to the landscape maintenance personnel for repairs and maintenance. The team should periodically verify the hardscape areas and/or building are/is not receiving water from the system. The landscape maintenance team should be encouraged to use mulch and compost where appropriate.

Energy and Atmosphere

- **Commissioning.** The CxA is traditionally responsible for the training of the O&M staff. The CxA will typically deliver a number of documents to the team to help ensure understanding and clarity. These documents commonly include the building operating plan, systems narrative, sequence of operations, preventative maintenance plan, and the commissioning report.

  - If the team is pursuing the Enhanced Commissioning credit, be sure to mention the follow-up meeting and schedule during the training sessions. This visit should be coupled with the EQ Thermal Comfort Verification credit if the owner is pursuing the survey effort. The survey should be conducted prior to the CxA's return to the site to implement any necessary corrective actions.

- **Efficiency Systems and Components.** The O&M staff should be provided with all of the plans, specifications, and manuals for operation, maintenance, and future renovations. The design team should share the results of the energy modeling exercise and the intended achievements for the project. Training sessions should focus on these anticipated achievements so that the staff can address noncompliance performance components. If a building management system was implemented, be sure to review how to use the software and all of the components it monitors. The staff should be encouraged to utilize the account setup for the project with the Environmental Protection Agency's ENERGY STAR Portfolio Manager to track the building's performance, which will assist in any future intentions to pursue EBOM certification.

- **Refrigerants.** If a phase-out plan is planned for a major renovation project, be sure to deliver the plan and address with staff members to ensure it is completed within five years. Equipment should be properly labeled with refrigerant usage. Remember, the goal is to minimize leakage during maintenance and removal.

- **On-Site Renewable Systems.** The O&M staff should be made aware of any maintenance contracts and/or requirements. Cleaning solar panels will ensure maximized production, so be sure to determine a cleaning schedule and assign responsibility to implement it. The system should be metered to track the intended production and use of the system installed.

- **Measurement and Verification (M&V).** Ensure that the staff is informed of the M&V plan to track usage and the corrective actions for discrepancies. Recalibration may be required for meters and submeters depending on the manufacturer and model, so be sure the requirements are noted in the maintenance schedule. The team should be encouraged to review the monthly reports to detect any irregularities.

Materials and Resources

- **Storage and Collection of Recyclables.** A recycling policy should be developed to address the collection and processing of waste to be recycled. Signage should be posted and replaced if damaged. Just as the occupants should be educated about which materials are to be discarded versus recycled, so should the O&M staff.

Indoor Environmental Quality

- **Air Delivery Monitoring.** Ensure that the building operator is aware of the minimum ventilation rates for each zone to ensure that they are maintained. The staff should all understand how to adjust the ventilation system and the CxA should review all the setpoints, control sequences, and recommended corrective actions. All exhaust systems should be periodically tested and maintained as detailed in the preventative maintenance plan that was developed specifically for the building. All CO_2 and airflow monitors shall be inspected and recalibrated as required.

- **Environmental Tobacco Smoke (ETS) Control.** Be sure to review the smoking policy of the facility including if and where smoking is allowed with all staff members and vendors.

- **Indoor Chemical and Pollutant Source Control.** The staff should be provided with the recommended practices for cleaning and maintaining the entryway systems. The Minimum Efficiency Reporting Value (MERV) filter replacement scheduled should be relayed to the team, as well as the proper location and disposal of hazardous chemicals.

- **Controllability of Systems.** Although the users are to be educated about the benefits of turning off the lights at the end of the work day, the O&M staff should also be aware of the controllability to help achieve intended energy performance and efficiency levels. The building operation plan should dictate the setpoints and schedules for automatic controls. All sensors should be addressed in the preventative maintenance plan for recalibration scheduling requirements. Where the building management system (BMS) can override and reset user settings, the staff should employ this capability at the end of the day and would therefore need to know how to do so.

- **Thermal Comfort.** Train the staff to understand the parameters of American Society of Heating, Refrigerating, and Air-Conditioning Engineers (ASHRAE) 55 standard and how to maintain compliance during operations.

- **Daylight and Views.** Be sure to review the goals of the daylight sensors and any other daylight control systems and how they are operated. The staff should be trained how to modify the system based on seasonal changes and determine an appropriate schedule to clean the interior and exterior shading devices to allow the intended amount of daylight to enter the space. This maintenance will also help to control dust and therefore, reflectivity issues.

LEED Online: Documentation Review

Similar to the documentation review after the construction documents (CDs) were issued, the LEED coordinator will need to work with the construction team in order to upload the documentation to LEED-Online to be reviewed. Most contracts will hold the final payments until certain items are received, such as manuals or the completion of the punch list; LEED documentation should not be any different. Just as with design team members, construction team members will move onto the next project and documentation will be forgotten and therefore, this contractual language could be critical.

Once all of the documentation is received and/or uploaded to LEED-Online, the LEED coordinator will be presented with the same task conducted during the design review: documentation review. This is the time all prerequisites and credits that might have been deferred from the design review, such as EQ Credit 5: Indoor Chemical and Pollutant Source Control, and EQ Credit 8.1: Daylight and Views—Daylight if pursuing Option 3, and all of the construction-side prerequisites and credits will be submitted for review with GBCI. Therefore, it is important to review all of the documentation to ensure clarity and consistency while proving compliance.

Similar to last time, the LEED coordinator is encouraged to confirm whether the streamlined path or full documentation path is appropriate and correct. Remember, the streamlined path requires the licensed professional to sign the licensed-professional exemption (LPE) form found at LEED-Online's LPE tab for applicable credits. If any tables or schedules were completed, the LEED coordinator shall ensure all the quantities and such are filled in correctly. Some prerequisites and credits require narratives; therefore, be sure to note if any are missing, and if not, read through them all to ensure accuracy and include reference to supporting documentation. Remember some of the questions from the design review to ask yourself: Are you overwhelmed with the information as you read through it? Is some supporting information difficult to read? Is the documentation uploaded upright, or does it need to be rotated? Are entry way system lengths noted? Are the building section, dimensioned as required? Are the calculations restated on the plans?

Sustainable Sites

SS Prerequisite 1: Construction Activity Pollution Prevention (for NC and CS projects). Although the LEED coordinator should have reviewed the erosion and sedimentation control (ESC) plan prior to the finalization of the Construction Documents phase, construction activities may require some revisions. Verify that the introduction includes the standard followed for compliance. There should be a list of all of the temporary and permanent control measures and a plan to implement those controls. During construction, frequent inspections are required to ensure the success of the control measures. The responsible party is required to submit dated photographs, an inspection log, or a written report of construction activities aligned with the prerequisite requirements.

SS Credit 5.1: Site Development, Protect or Restore Habitat. If a landscape architect is engaged on a project team with a previously developed site and is responsible for this credit, he or she can sign the LPE form and bypass listing all of the vegetation species implemented on site. The contractor will have to sign the submittal template indicating compliance during construction, *or* the responsible party can upload the site disturbance plan showing space limitations of construction activities.

SS Credit 7.1: Heat Island Effect—Nonroof. Verify that the site plan has been uploaded and is oriented correctly. The plan needs to clearly represent the compliance strategy including hardscape materials, square footage of hardscape areas, shading areas and hardscape locations, and the coordinating SRI value(s) for Option 1. If the team is pursuing Option 2, the drawings will need to show all of the parking available on-site and which stalls are located undercover. Regardless of the compliance path option selected, the submittal template needs to be correct and accurate. Be sure to make sure the responsible party has also uploaded the cut sheets for the hardscape materials with the SRI values listed.

Energy and Atmosphere

EA Prerequisite 1: Fundamental Commissioning, and EA Credit 3: Enhanced Commissioning (LEED CI EA Credit 2: Enhanced Commissioning). By this time the Cx report should be completed and all supporting documentation uploaded to LEED-Online. Verify that the OPR, BOD, and Cx plan are also uploaded and correctly updated. The LEED coordinator is also encouraged to review the submittal template for accuracy. As previously mentioned, Steps 1 through 9 need to be completed before submitting for certification review. As long as Steps 10 through 12 are confirmed to be completed, the prerequisite and credit can marked as complete and be submitted.

EA Credit 5 (LEED CI EA Credit 3): Measurement and Verification. Review the M&V plan to ensure the baseline energy use is defined, the postconstruction energy use is listed, the metering requirements, and the strategies for implementing the plan are all addressed, including responsibilities of the team members. The plan also should indicate how the data will be used and the details of corrective action if the results greatly differ from the baseline case. Ensure that the credit submittal template is completed (including reference to the supporting documentation) and signed and that the proper drawing(s), the narrative, and the M&V plan are uploaded to LEED-Online.

EA Credit 6: Green Power (LEED CI EA Credit 4: Green Power). The responsible party will need to complete the credit submittal template indicating how the energy consumption was estimated (Option

RECS PROVIDER PERSPECTIVE
EA Credit 6: Green Power—Some Common Misconceptions

By John Powers, LEED AP
Renewable Choice Energy

Figure 10.3 Cedar Creek Wind Farm in Colorado helps to produce clean, renewable energy. Photo courtesy of Brian Stanback, Renewable Choice Energy.

Having been U.S. Green Building Council (USGBC®) members since 2003 and provided green power to over 1,000 LEED projects, we have seen just about everything when it comes to the Green Power credit. Green power is one of the most cost-effective LEED credits and is the easiest to document (you just need a one-page purchase agreement and the letter template) but remains a bit misunderstood despite high adoption rates. It may be useful to address some of the most common misconceptions when it comes to purchasing green power for a LEED project:

- **"I am just 'buying' a LEED point."** This is the one we hear most often. It seems that most LEED guides do not tell you what you are actually getting when you purchase wind power (Figure 10.3). Buying renewable energy credits (RECs) helps new green power capacity to get built all over the United States, as it is a little cheaper to build a coal plant than a wind farm. RECs provide a financial incentive for developers to build clean technology, such as wind power, instead. Wind farm developers cite RECs as a core piece of the financing of any new wind farm—if nobody bought green power, much fewer wind farms and renewable facilities would come online. In fact, most of our customers are not even earning LEED points—they are buying green power because it is the right thing to do, as they want to reduce their carbon footprint or want to brand their business as more environmentally friendly. The USGBC recognizes the value of supporting clean energy, and they award you a LEED point for that. You are not just "buying a LEED point."

- **"Buying green power from a utility is fundamentally different from buying RECs."** The way that green power is tracked and traded in the United States is through RECs. Every time a wind farm or renewable facility produces one megawatt hour (MWh) of power and adds it to the national power grid, it "earns" one MWh renewable energy credit, so one-for-one. Since you cannot tell where the power actually goes once it gets on the national power grid, the owner of the REC gets to claim they are "green powered." This is the same for voluntary buyers, like LEED projects and compliance buyers. If your state has a mandate to purchase a certain percentage of green power by a certain year (10 percent by 2012 for instance), the way the utility can prove compliance is by owning RECs that correspond to 10 percent of their supplied power.

- **"I don't own my building so I can't buy green power" (more for LEED CI or EBOM).** There are simple ways to estimate your energy consumption whether you are submetered or not. The important thing is to do your best in estimating your usage and purchase enough green power to offset that usage. Whether that ends up being 99 percent or 101 percent of what you actually use is not as important.

---

1 or 2). Upload the contract to LEED-Online proving compliance.

Materials and Resources

MR Credit 1.1: Building Reuse—Maintain Existing Walls, Floors, and Roof (for LEED NC and CS projects). Confirm the calculations shown on the credit submittal form and the responsible party has uploaded the coordinating plans demonstrating the strategy for compliance. Be sure only one side of any reused interior structural walls, exterior walls, party walls, structural floors, and roof decks is counted. Verify that the appropriate plans and elevations have been uploaded and are noted correctly to indicate areas to be preserved.

MR Credit 1.2: Maintain 50 Percent Interior Non-structural Elements (for LEED NC and CI projects). Review the credit submittal template to verify it is completed correctly, including the narrative and calculations. Be sure only the square footage is included for reused finished ceilings and flooring areas. Walls calculations should be based on the finished area between the floor and the ceiling. Both sides of interior walls and door surface areas can be counted, whereas only one side of exterior walls is to be included in the calculations. Exterior windows and doors shall be subtracted, although exposed and finished surface areas of built-in casework shall be included. Verify the appropriate plans and elevations have been uploaded and are referenced on the credit submittal template. The plans should be noted correctly to indicate the areas that were preserved.

MR Credit 2: Construction Waste Management. Verify that the responsible party has completed the submittal template and the calculations are consistent in terms of the measurement for each of the waste types (i.e., volume or weight). Confirm the calculations do not include any land-clearing debris, hazardous materials, or excavated soil. Be sure the backup documentation, such as waste tickets and disposal locations and vendors, are noted for each type of material.

MR Credit 3: Materials Reuse. Verify that the responsible party has completed the template correctly and confirm the values and calculations. LEED-Online requires the responsible party to upload 20 percent of the supporting documentation, although the team is encouraged to maintain all of the documentation proving compliance.

MR Credit 4: Recycled Content. Ensure that the credit submittal template is accurately completed and documents the required information. Remember, preconsumer recycled content has half the value of postconsumer recycled content. Steel is the only material that can use a default 25 percent postconsumer recycled content value if the manufacturer or vendor is unable to provide a value to use (Figure 10.4). Also, take note of assembly material calculations to ensure that they were computed as a percentage of weight (and not cost). LEED-Online requires the responsible party to upload 20 percent of the supporting documentation to prove compliance, although the team is encouraged to maintain all of the documentation.

MR Credit 5: Regional Materials. Verify the credit submittal template is accurately completed and documents the required information. For materials salvaged from off-site, the salvage location or supplier's facility is used as the manufacturing location and the location in which the material was salvaged from as the extraction location. If the material was salvaged from on-site, the manufacturing and extraction location is the same as the site location. For materials with recycled content, the vendor location can be used as the extraction location if

the project team is finding it challenging to document the suppliers of the recycled content specific to their project. This is acceptable if the vendor that purchased the recycled materials can document that the materials were purchased from local vendors. Just as with the previous credit, LEED-Online requires the responsible party to upload 20 percent of the supporting documentation to prove compliance, although all documentation should be retained in case of an audit.

MR Credit 6: Rapidly Renewable Materials (for LEED NC and CI projects). Review the credit submittal template to ensure that it is completed correctly, including the calculations. LEED-Online requires the responsible party to upload 20 percent of the supporting documentation to prove compliance.

MR Credit 7: Certified Wood (Credit 6 for CS projects). Ensure that the submittal template includes a line-item approach for all new wood items purchased for the project and all of the chain-of-custody (COC) certification numbers for certified products. Verify that the correct value is assigned to the type of Forest Stewardship Council (FSC) certification. For example, if a wood product is FSC Mixed certified, the value must coordinate with the percentage value that is certified. If a new wood gym floor is FSC Mixed 65 percent, 65 percent of the value of the wood can be used toward credit compliance. If the gym floor is certified FSC Pure or FSC Mixed Credit, it is valued at 100 percent of the product cost. For the purposes of LEED, FSC Recycled and FSC Recycled Credit materials are not eligible to comply with this credit, but instead MR Credit 4: Recycled Content. Although LEED-Online requires the responsible party to upload 20 percent of the COC supporting documentation to prove compliance, the team is encouraged to maintain all of the COC documentation.

Figure 10.4 The Western Virginia Regional Jail in Salem, Virginia, constructed by Howard Shockey & Sons, Inc., was the first jail to earn LEED certification. The project's success was a result of diligent team coordination that started during design and continued through the construction process. The concrete used to construct the project, such as these cells, contributed to 12 percent of the overall recycled content contributing to earning MR Credit 4, while the steel contributed over 70 percent of the recycled content as compared to the total material cost for the project. Photo by Travis Hall, LEED AP of Howard Shockey & Sons, Inc.

Indoor Environmental Quality

EQ Credit 3.1: Construction IAQ Management Plan—during Construction. The responsible party will need to complete the credit submittal template, including confirmation of the operation of the HVAC system and listing the filter product information if the system was operated during construction. Verify that the construction IAQ management plan, filter cut-sheets (if applicable), and three IAQ reports have been uploaded, including pictures.

EQ Credit 3.2: Construction IAQ Management Plan—before Occupancy. Verify that the credit submittal template has been completed indicating the proper compliance path and includes a narrative. Review the narrative to confirm that the flush-out or testing details are included. Verify that both the construction IAQ management plan and, if pursuing Option 2, the air quality testing locations and results have been uploaded to LEED-Online.

EQ Credit 4: Low-Emitting Materials. Each of the credits within this suite requires individual credit submittal templates to be completed, signed, and submitted. The responsible party will need to transfer the information from the master monitoring and reporting spreadsheets to the coordinating LEED credit submittal template. Remember, some credits overlap with requirements, such as EQ Credit 4.1 and EQ Credit 4.3 for carpet adhesives. Therefore, the responsible team member will need to list the adhesive on both credit submittal forms to prove compliance for each credit being pursued. Be sure to verify that the certification is valid for CI teams pursuing EQ Credit 4.5 or NC and CS teams pursuing an innovation credit. LEED-Online will also require the responsible party to upload 20 percent of the supporting documentation to prove compliance, although the team is encouraged to maintain all of the documentation proving compliance in case the project is audited.

EQ Credit 7.1: Thermal Comfort, Design (LEED CS EQ Credit 7). Although this is listed as a design credit, due to the O&M manual documentation requirement, it is best submitted for a construction review. As suggested in Chapter 7, the mechanical engineer should have completed the credit submittal template, but the contractor will be the signatory. The narrative should be reviewed to ensure that the project space and use, climate zone, and an approach to the design of the systems to provide thermal comfort are all included. The ASHRAE 55 input factors will need to be entered on

the credit submittal form and then reviewed (if not done already). The calculation results based on the selected compliance path, the OPR and BOD documentation, and the O&M materials should all be uploaded to LEED-Online and referenced on the credit submittal template.

Innovation in Design and Regional Priority

The LEED coordinator should review each ID and Regional Priority (RP) credit prior to the submission to GBCI. Always review the credit submittal templates and ensure that they are signed. Verify that any required supporting documentation is also uploaded and clearly depicts the strategy and compliance. Remember, it is best to orient the documentation so that it is legible once opened and does not need to be rotated. All key information should be highlighted to draw the reviewer's attention to important concepts. Supporting documentation should be listed on the credit submittal template.

Submit for USGBC Construction Review

Similar to the submission activities for the design review, the construction review is conducted in the same fashion. The LEED coordinator will need to review all of the documentation as previously described. Additional certification review fees will also need to be addressed. The LEED coordinator should address the responsibility of these fees prior to the intended submission date to avoid any delays. After submitting for review, an email should be received indicating that the project has been submitted, and LEED-Online will indicate the project is under review. Just as with the design review, the review period typically will take 25 business days, but can depend on the demand for certification reviews at the time of submission. After the initial review is completed,

ARCHITECT'S PERSPECTIVE
Staying High Performance: Sustaining the Sustainability of Buildings

By Michael B. Lehrer, FAIA
Lehrer Architects LA

Figure 10.5 The solar panel system for the Water + Life Museums in Hemet, California, designed by Lehrer Architects with the consultation of Vector Delta Design Group Inc., generates 60 percent of the building's energy. Image courtesy of Benny Chan/fotoworks.

Creating a sustainable building is not only a matter of plans, materials, and codes. Of course, the right materials must be specified, the smart systems and designs chosen, and the appropriate actions—such as recycling excess materials during construction—should also be taken. But, unless the green and sustainable mandates are ultimately embraced by owners, there is no assurance that a building that is actually built green will be operated in a sustainable manner going forward.

Today, an architect is not only the designer, but must be an agent of change or, more aptly put, an emissary from the future. In the case of the recently constructed Water + Life Museums in Hemet, California, the clients did embrace green, and it can be confidently said that the buildings will be operated in a sustainable fashion for generations to come. Even so, going green is not the path of least resistance. It demands a time-consuming attention to detail and incredible persistence of cause.

continued

It was important that we not install a lot of sustainable systems that would be abandoned in following years, as building operational staff might change or might find the systems too vexing. Wherever possible, we designed or selected systems that would remain in use, due to ease of utility and maximum durability. Here are some of the energy-, water- and waste-saving materials, systems, and technologies that were employed:

- A rooftop and loggia solar panel system (Figure 10.5), which supplies 60 percent of the buildings' power needs is all the more remarkable given that the museums' desert location boasts one of hottest climes in North America. HVAC use can be very heavy and costly, especially on crowded summer days. The 50,000- square-foot solar system was overseen by Dr. Peter Gevorkian, author and recognized solar power expert and founder of the Vector Delta Design Group Inc. The 540-kilowatt solar-power system of 3,000 roof-mounted panels is strapped together to create large island platforms to withstand 120-mile-per-hour winds. The system is grounded and can withstand direct lightning strikes. It is nearly maintenance free; rooftop water nozzles were installed to allow for easy "hosing off" of panels to remove dust. "This system will function for a minimum of 30 years—probably beyond—and, after rebates, will pay for itself within seven years," says Gevorkian. "Moreover, it is a hedge against rising energy costs in the future. In a sense, it will be paying the museums back for decades." In addition to the utilitarian aspect of the solid solar panels, an artistic result emerged. The courtyard loggias are covered with panels made of silicon wafers set into translucent glass (Figure 10.6). They are a critical architectural feature, being about the sun's light—illuminating, dappling, and shading—as well as about the beauty of the capture of the sun's energy. The message is that architecture's work is to make necessity a virtue.

- Radiant heating and cooling water pipes were installed under the floors. This is a more logical place to concentrate temperature, as the museum has high ceilings that could wastefully capture the temperature when it is needed more toward the floor, where the people are. Embedded water pipes effectively alter ground-level temperatures with minimal energy consumption. This arrangement is largely controlled by a digital system and requires only routine and light maintenance.

- Special insulating glass was installed on 8,000 square feet of large, east-facing windows, deflecting heat from the morning sun, while letting sunlight in, with a very positive effect on ambience. To further reduce radiant heat gain, beautiful transparent thematic banners are hung in the windows, giving a pleasing reminder that "sustainable" can also be passive and low-tech. While the banners have a life span measured in years, the windows are permanent and require no management.

- The very shape of the buildings—with large solid bulwarks shielding recessed glass walls—helps reduce cooling costs. Recessed windows, of course, are a staple of traditional thick-walled Southwestern architecture, so in many ways, the museums fit into their surroundings. And, like the old buildings of the Southwest, the thick walls are maintenance free, adding another passive green feature.

- HVAC systems are monitored and controlled digitally, and all systems are monitored regularly off-site by online programs, eliminating the need for regular trips by motor vehicle. This is exemplary of green technology, which both reduces pollution and increases productivity.

- Interior systems have minimal effect on the daily workings of staff and visitors. Efficient, low-heat lighting is automatically dimmed when abundant natural light is evident. Low-flush toilets and waterless urinals require no more maintenance, and arguably less, than "regular" plumbing.

- Landscaping makes use of hardy desert plants, while rainwater is funneled into a designed creek bed that evokes the naturally found "braided streams" made up of sandstone and framed by boulders that resulted from the dam construction. Recycled water is used in a drip-irrigation system. This is another example of how green can result in less maintenance, not more. The typical garden of grass and exotic trees would require more water and fertilizer and be subject to botanical diseases that often afflict high-maintenance greenery. Green is not always green.

If merely erecting a museum to code is a monumental task, building to gain LEED certification is a documentation blizzard. Frank Gangi, construction manager, recalls trying to gain assurances from subcontractors that only recycled wood planks would be used in concrete formwork, and that excess materials from construction would be recycled. Indeed, more than 90 percent of the excess metal, wood, and other building materials were sold for scrap (a slight profit was made on that activity).

LEED certification entails another layer of action and record keeping. "It is certainly more difficult to build a LEED building, as the specs are different," says Gangi. "You run into special restrictions, such as limits on the off-gassing of materials and the use of certified wood. All these things have to be checked and then rechecked."

We can one day expect green buildings to become woven into the fabric of our society—just as seat belts, handicapped access, sunscreen, or recyclable bottles once seemed novel and now appear mundane.

The process of designing a sustainable building is not intuitive; it is a learned behavior, and experience will count for much going forward. The best architects (and owners) will not begrudge green, but will embrace the movement as a catalyst for change. Challenges beget opportunities for the agile architect and designer.

At the Water + Life Museums, we have shown that solar panels can be useful, economic, and beautiful, that naturally lit and enjoyable public spaces can be constructed while conserving energy and water consumption, and that the world need not be about zero-sum and trade-offs, but can engage in win-wins and add-ons.

Finally, to change the world, high-performance projects must stay high performing. Projects must answer the question: how do we sustain the sustainability of our projects?

Each sustainable project represents incremental change. Ultimately, to change the world, these changes must be broadly cultural and they must become second nature. Individuals come and go. Protocols must be designed that become embedded in the life of the building; they must be institutionalized. Training the first generation of building inhabitants is not enough because when they go, institutional memory will go with them. It takes time and commitment once the building is occupied to become a high-performing culture.

At Water + Life, we have an excellent model: comprehensive monitoring software and hardware tracks the operation and performance of all of the building systems. It is not only on-site, but it can be monitored by service companies and consultants, as well as owners and operators, in real time, anytime. With the system is place, the early and ongoing work to is engage the institution. We did it.

At Water + Life, it's working. With time and passion, it eventually becomes business as usual. That's the goal.

continued

Figure 10.6 The project team for the Water + Life Museums created a facility to endure with an approach cognizant of the operation and maintenance factors from the onset of the project. Image courtesy of Benny Chan/fotoworks.

a report summary will be available to download from LEED-Online summarizing the prerequisites and credits that were submitted for review and are expected to be awarded. Similar to the design review, the review team may also require clarification from the project team and is typically very clear on what additional information is required to be submitted by the means of a "Technical Advice" note provided for each prerequisite and credit. LEED-Online will revert back to the Construction Application phase if such information is required for clarification granting the team 25 business days to respond. At this time, the project team administrator should compile a checklist for each prerequisite and credit that requires clarification and assign each one to the responsible team member along with a deadline for completing the task. Once the clarification information is submitted, the GBCI review team should respond within 15 business days with final review comments. If the team received indication that a prerequisite or credit was denied and therefore will not be awarded, they have the opportunity to submit for a construction appeal for an additional fee. If the appeal is submitted, the project will move into the Construction Appeal phase. Project team members will have the opportunity to submit documentation to be reviewed and should receive review comments with 25 business days after the appeal fee has been paid for and processed. As previously recommended, it is best to avoid the appeal process and fees by submitting as much information as possible during the review process.

LEED after Occupancy? Or Occupancy after LEED?

As there are a few tasks to be completed, some others to be continued, and the owner may wish to seek EBOM certification, both questions could be applicable. After the building is occupied and training is completed, the efforts of the design and construction teams are in the hands of the staff, employees, and visitors. In terms of tasks to be completed, the owner may need to conduct a thermal comfort survey, the CxA may need to revisit the project within a year after occupancy, and the temporary irrigation system may need to be removed. Most of the strategies implemented should be continued, such as green power procurement and the use of low-emitting materials for repairs, touch-ups, and other future uses. If renovations are planned, the construction IAQ plan should be referenced to continue the efforts previously implemented. If renovations are intended, try to coordinate the effort while pursuing EBOM certification at least one year after occupancy. Many O&M efforts described previously could align with EBOM goals, such as conducting a waste stream audit or implementing a pest management plan could contribute toward earning EBOM certification in the future. Whether pursuing the next type of certification or not, always use the triple-bottom-line benefits and values to determine what is best for the project.

Appendix A: LEED Rating System Scorecards

Project Name
Date

LEED 2009 for New Construction and Major Renovation
Project Checklist

Yes ? No

Sustainable Sites — 26 Possible Points

Prereq 1	Construction Activity Pollution Prevention	Required
Credit 1	Site Selection	1
Credit 2	Development Density & Community Connectivity	5
Credit 3	Brownfield Redevelopment	1
Credit 4.1	Alternative Transportation, Public Transportation Access	6
Credit 4.2	Alternative Transportation, Bicycle Storage & Changing Rooms	1
Credit 4.3	Alternative Transportation, Low-Emitting & Fuel-Efficient Vehicles	3
Credit 4.4	Alternative Transportation, Parking Capacity	2
Credit 5.1	Site Development, Protection of Restore Habitat	1
Credit 5.2	Site Development, Maximize Open Space	1
Credit 6.1	Stormwater Design, Quantity Control	1
Credit 6.2	Stormwater Design, Quality Control	1
Credit 7.1	Heat Island Effect, Non-Roof	1
Credit 7.2	Heat Island Effect, Roof	1
Credit 8	Light Pollution Reduction	1

Water Efficiency — 10 Possible Points

Prereq 1	Water Use Reduction - 20% Reduction	Required
Credit 1	Water Efficient Landscaping	2 to 4
Credit 2	Innovative Wastewater Technologies	2
Credit 3	Water Use Reduction	2 to 4

Energy & Atmosphere — 35 Possible Points

Prereq 1	Fundamental Commissioning of Building Energy Systems	Required
Prereq 2	Minimum Energy Performance	Required
Prereq 3	Fundamental Refrigerant Management	Required
Credit 1	Optimize Energy Performance	1 to 19
Credit 2	On-Site Renewable Energy	1 to 7
Credit 3	Enhanced Commissioning	2
Credit 4	Enhanced Refrigerant Management	2
Credit 5	Measurement & Verification	3
Credit 6	Green Power	2

Materials & Resources — 14 Possible Points

Prereq 1	Storage & Collection of Recyclables	Required
Credit 1.1	Building Reuse, Maintain Existing Walls, Floors & Roof	1 to 3
Credit 1.2	Building Reuse, Maintain 50% of Interior Non-Structural Elements	1
Credit 2	Construction Waste Management	1 to 2
Credit 3	Materials Reuse	1 to 2

Yes ? No

Materials & Resources, Continued

Credit 4	Recyled Content	1 to 2
Credit 5	Regional Materials	1 to 2
Credit 6	Rapidly Renewable Materials	1
Credit 7	Certified Wood	1

Indoor Environmental Quality — 15 Possible Points

Prereq 1	Minimum Indoor Air Quality Performance	Required
Prereq 2	Environmental Tobacco Smoke (ETS) Control	Required
Credit 1	Outdoor Air Delivery Monitoring	1
Credit 2	Increased Ventilation	1
Credit 3.1	Construction IAQ Management Plan - During Construction	1
Credit 3.2	Construction IAQ Management Plan - Before Occupancy	1
Credit 4.1	Low-Emitting Materials, Adhesives & Sealants	1
Credit 4.2	Low-Emitting Materials, Paints & Coatings	1
Credit 4.3	Low-Emitting Materials, Flooring Systems	1
Credit 4.4	Low-Emitting Materials, Composite Wood & Agrifiber Products	1
Credit 5	Indoor Chemical & Pollutant Source Control	1
Credit 6.1	Controllability of Systems, Lighting	1
Credit 6.2	Controllability of Systems, Thermal Comfort	1
Credit 7.1	Thermal Comfort, Design	1
Credit 7.2	Thermal Comfort, Verification	1
Credit 8.1	Daylight & Views, Daylight	1
Credit 8.2	Daylight & Views, Views	1

Innovation and Design Process — 6 Possible Points

Credit 1.1	Innovation or Exemplary Performance	1
Credit 1.2	Innovation or Exemplary Performance	1
Credit 1.3	Innovation or Exemplary Performance	1
Credit 1.4	Innovation	1
Credit 1.5	Innovation	1
Credit 2	LEED® Accredited Professional	1

Regional Priority Credits — 4 Possible Points

Credit 1.1	Regional Priority: Specific Credit	1
Credit 1.2	Regional Priority: Specific Credit	1
Credit 1.3	Regional Priority: Specific Credit	1
Credit 1.4	Regional Priority: Specific Credit	1

Total — 110 Possible Points

Certified: 40 to 49 points, **Silver:** 50 to 59 points, **Gold:** 60 to 79 points, **Platinum:** 80 to 110 points

Source: www.usgbc.org/DisplayPage.aspx?CMSPageID=220

LEED 2009 for Core and Shell Development
Project Checklist

Project Name

Date

Sustainable Sites — 28 Possible Points

Yes	?	No			Points
			Prereq 1	Construction Activity Pollution Prevention	Required
			Credit 1	Site Selection	1
			Credit 2	Development Density & Community Connectivity	5
			Credit 3	Brownfield Redevelopment	1
			Credit 4.1	Alternative Transportation, Public Transportation Access	6
			Credit 4.2	Alternative Transportation, Bicycle Storage & Changing Rooms	2
			Credit 4.3	Alternative Transportation, Low-Emitting & Fuel-Efficient Vehicles	3
			Credit 4.4	Alternative Transportation, Parking Capacity	2
			Credit 5.1	Site Development, Protect or Restore Habitat	1
			Credit 5.2	Site Development, Maximize Open Space	1
			Credit 6.1	Stormwater Design, Quantity Control	1
			Credit 6.2	Stormwater Design, Quality Control	1
			Credit 7.1	Heat Island Effect, Non-Roof	1
			Credit 7.2	Heat Island Effect, Roof	1
			Credit 8	Light Pollution Reduction	1
			Credit 9	Tenant Design & Construction Guidelines	1

Water Efficiency — 10 Possible Points

Yes	?	No			Points
Y			Prereq 1	Water Use Reduction - 20% Reduction	Required
			Credit 1	Water Efficient Landscaping	2 to 4
			Credit 2	Innovative Wastewater Technologies	2
			Credit 3	Water Use Reduction	2 to 4

Energy & Atmosphere — 37 Possible Points

Yes	?	No			Points
Y			Prereq 1	Fundamental Commissioning of Building Energy Systems	Required
Y			Prereq 2	Minimum Energy Performance	Required
Y			Prereq 3	Fundamental Refrigerant Management	Required
			Credit 1	Optimize Energy Performance	3 to 21
			Credit 2	On-Site Renewable Energy	4
			Credit 3	Enhanced Commissioning	2
			Credit 4	Enhanced Refrigerant Management	2
			Credit 5.1	Measurement & Verification - Base Building	3
			Credit 5.2	Measurement & Verification - Tenant Metering	3
			Credit 6	Green Power	2

Materials & Resources — 13 Possible Points

Yes	?	No			Points
Y			Prereq 1	Storage & Collection of Recyclables	Required
			Credit 1	Building Reuse, Maintain Existing Walls, Floors & Roof	1 to 5

Materials & Resources, Continued

Yes	?	No			Points
			Credit 2	Construction Waste Management	1 to 2
			Credit 3	Materials Reuse	1
			Credit 4	Recycled Content	1 to 2
			Credit 5	Regional Materials	1 to 2
			Credit 6	Certified Wood	1

Indoor Environmental Quality — 12 Possible Points

Yes	?	No			Points
Y			Prereq 1	Minimum Indoor Air Quality Performance	Required
Y			Prereq 2	Environmental Tobacco Smoke (ETS) Control	Required
			Credit 1	Outdoor Air Delivery Monitoring	1
			Credit 2	Increased Ventilation	1
			Credit 3	Construction IAQ Management Plan - During Construction	1
			Credit 4.1	Low-Emitting Materials, Adhesives & Sealants	1
			Credit 4.2	Low-Emitting Materials, Paints & Coatings	1
			Credit 4.3	Low-Emitting Materials, Flooring Systems	1
			Credit 4.4	Low-Emitting Materials, Composite Wood & Agrifiber Products	1
			Credit 5	Indoor Chemical & Pollutant Source Control	1
			Credit 6	Controllability of Systems, Thermal Comfort	1
			Credit 7	Thermal Comfort, Design	1
			Credit 8.1	Daylight & Views, Daylight	1
			Credit 8.2	Daylight & Views, Views	1

Innovation and Design Process — 6 Possible Points

Yes	?	No			Points
			Credit 1.1	Innovation or Exemplary Performance	1
			Credit 1.2	Innovation or Exemplary Performance	1
			Credit 1.3	Innovation or Exemplary Performance	1
			Credit 1.4	Innovation	1
			Credit 1.5	Innovation	1
			Credit 2	LEED® Accredited Professional	1

Regional Priority Credits — 4 Possible Points

Yes	?	No			Points
			Credit 1.1	Regional Priority: Specific Credit	1
			Credit 1.2	Regional Priority: Specific Credit	1
			Credit 1.3	Regional Priority: Specific Credit	1
			Credit 1.4	Regional Priority: Specific Credit	1

Total — 110 Possible Points

Certified: 40 to 49 points, **Silver:** 50 to 59 points, **Gold:** 60 to 79 points, **Platinum:** 80 to 110 points

Project Name
Date

LEED 2009 for Commercial Interiors
Project Checklist

		Sustainable Sites	Possible Points: 21
Y	N	?	
		Credit 1	Site Selection	1 to 5
		Credit 2	Development Density and Community Connectivity	6
		Credit 3.1	Alternative Transportation—Public Transportation Access	6
		Credit 3.2	Alternative Transportation—Bicycle Storage and Changing Rooms	2
		Credit 3.3	Alternative Transportation—Parking Availability	2

		Water Efficiency	Possible Points: 11
Y		Prereq 1	Water Use Reduction—20% Reduction	
		Credit 1	Water Use Reduction	6 to 11

		Energy and Atmosphere	Possible Points: 37
Y		Prereq 1	Fundamental Commissioning of Building Energy Systems	
Y		Prereq 2	Minimum Energy Performance	
Y		Prereq 3	Fundamental Refrigerant Management	
		Credit 1.1	Optimize Energy Performance—Lighting Power	1 to 5
		Credit 1.2	Optimize Energy Performance—Lighting Controls	1 to 3
		Credit 1.3	Optimize Energy Performance—HVAC	5 to 10
		Credit 1.4	Optimize Energy Performance—Equipment and Appliances	1 to 4
		Credit 2	Enhanced Commissioning	5
		Credit 3	Measurement and Verification	2 to 5
		Credit 4	Green Power	5

		Materials and Resources	Possible Points: 14
Y		Prereq 1	Storage and Collection of Recyclables	
		Credit 1.1	Tenant Space—Long-Term Commitment	1
		Credit 1.2	Building Reuse	1 to 2
		Credit 2	Construction Waste Management	1 to 2
		Credit 3.1	Materials Reuse	1 to 2
		Credit 3.2	Materials Reuse—Furniture and Furnishings	1
		Credit 4	Recycled Content	1 to 2
		Credit 5	Regional Materials	1 to 2
		Credit 6	Rapidly Renewable Materials	1
		Credit 7	Certified Wood	1

		Indoor Environmental Quality	Possible Points: 17
Y	N	?	
Y		Prereq 1	Minimum IAQ Performance	
Y		Prereq 2	Environmental Tobacco Smoke (ETS) Control	
		Credit 1	Outdoor Air Delivery Monitoring	1
		Credit 2	Increased Ventilation	1
		Credit 3.1	Construction IAQ Management Plan—During Construction	1
		Credit 3.2	Construction IAQ Management Plan—Before Occupancy	1
		Credit 4.1	Low-Emitting Materials—Adhesives and Sealants	1
		Credit 4.2	Low-Emitting Materials—Paints and Coatings	1
		Credit 4.3	Low-Emitting Materials—Flooring Systems	1
		Credit 4.4	Low-Emitting Materials—Composite Wood and Agrifiber Products	1
		Credit 4.5	Low-Emitting Materials—Systems Furniture and Seating	1
		Credit 5	Indoor Chemical & Pollutant Source Control	1
		Credit 6.1	Controllability of Systems—Lighting	1
		Credit 6.2	Controllability of Systems—Thermal Comfort	1
		Credit 7.1	Thermal Comfort—Design	1
		Credit 7.2	Thermal Comfort—Verification	1
		Credit 8.1	Daylight and Views—Daylight	1 to 2
		Credit 8.2	Daylight and Views—Views for Seated Spaces	1

		Innovation and Design Process	Possible Points: 6
		Credit 1.1	Innovation in Design: Specific Title	1
		Credit 1.2	Innovation in Design: Specific Title	1
		Credit 1.3	Innovation in Design: Specific Title	1
		Credit 1.4	Innovation in Design: Specific Title	1
		Credit 1.5	Innovation in Design: Specific Title	1
		Credit 2	LEED Accredited Professional	1

		Regional Priority Credits	Possible Points: 4
		Credit 1.1	Regional Priority: Specific Credit	1
		Credit 1.2	Regional Priority: Specific Credit	1
		Credit 1.3	Regional Priority: Specific Credit	1
		Credit 1.4	Regional Priority: Specific Credit	1

		Total	Possible Points: 110

Certified 40 to 49 points   Silver 50 to 59 points   Gold 60 to 79 points   Platinum 80 to 110 points

Source: www.usgbc.org/DisplayPage.aspx?CMSPageID=145

Appendix B: Predesign Site Selection Checklist

LEED FOR COMMERCIAL INTERIORS

Path	Title	Base Building Questions	Building Compliant?	Status of Documentation
		SSc1 – Site Selection, Option 2 Checklist		
1	Brownfield Remediation	1. Is the site considered a brownfield according to a local, state, or federal agency? 2. Was asbestos remediation or other types of remediation ever conducted on site? 3. Was an ASTM E1903-97 Phase 2 Environmental Site Assessment ever conducted?		
2	Stormwater Design, Quantity Control	1. Does the maintenance staff refer to a stormwater management plan? 2. If not, is the building owner interested in developing and implementing one?		
3	Stormwater Design, Quality Control	1. Does the site treat stormwater runoff? How? 2. Are structural or nonstructural strategies used to improve runoff quality?		
4	Heat Island Effect, Nonroof	1. How many parking spaces are existing on site? Are any of the stalls covered or underground? 2. What is the materials used for hardscape areas? Are the SRI values compliant?		
5	Heat Island Effect, Roof	1. Does the building have a green roof? 2. What type of roofing materials are existing? What is the SRI of the material? Does the roof need to be replaced?		
6	Light Pollution Reduction	1. Are non-emergency luminaires shielded? 2. Does the building have an automatic control to shut them off? 3. Are there window shades installed?		
7	Water Efficient Landscaping, Reduce by 50%	1. Is there an irrigation system? If so, what kind of a system is it? 2. What kind of vegetation is implemented on site?		
8	Water Efficient Landscaping, No Potable Water Use or No Irrigation	3. Does the building harvest rainwater, or use grey water for irrigation? If not, is the owner interested in installing a cistern to collect rainwater? 4. Is there an existing landscape/irrigation plan on file?		
9	Innovative Wastewater Technologies	1. Does the building have the capacity to treat waste water on site? 2. What kind of plumbing fixtures does the building have? Are they efficient? 3. Does the building harvest rainwater or recycle grey water for sewage conveyance? 4. Is there the possibility that the building will upgrade its core plumbing fixtures, if they are not low-flow? 5. If building uses rainwater or graywater systems, is information available for those systems?		
10	Water Use Reduction, 30%	1. Does the building use water efficient plumbing fixtures? 2. Does it have automatic sensor, flow restrictors, metering controls? 3. If not, would it consider upgrading its existing fixtures to help converse water?		
11	On-Site Renewable Energy	1. Does the building have an on-site renewable energy system, such as photovoltaic panels that generates at least 5% of the building's energy needs? 2. If not, would the building owner consider installing a renewable energy system?		
12	Other Quantifiable Environmental Performance	1. Was the site design in compliance with the restrictions listed in LEED NC SSc1? 2. Does the building offer preferred parking for carpools or for low-emitting and fuel efficient vehicles and is compliant with LEED-NC SSc4.3? 3. Did the building protect or restore habitat on its site during development and is in compliance with LEED-NC SSc5.1? 4. Has the base building site design preserved open space according to LEED-NC SSc5.2? 5. Was the building designed to prevent mold or have provisions in place that are in accordance with the requirements of LEED for Schools EQc10? 6. Are there any other sustainable achievements not addressed that can be quantified?		

dms

LEED for New Construction Project Team Member Roles & Documentation Responsibilities

		Pre-Design	Schematic Design	Design Development	Construction Documents	DESIGN REVIEW	Construction	Substantial Completion	CONSTRUCTION REVIEW
Sustainable Sites									
SS	Prerequisite 1 — Construction Activity Pollution Prevention	CE	CE	CE	CE		GC	GC	CE
SS	Credit 1 — Site Selection	T	CE			O			
SS	Credit 2 — Development Density & Community Connectivity		O, A, CE			O			
SS	Credit 3 — Brownfield Redevelopment		O, CE, EC, GC			CE			
SS	Credit 4.1 — Alternative Transportation: Public Transportation Access	O	CE or LA			O			
SS	Credit 4.2 — Alternative Transportation: Bicycle Storage & Changing Rooms		O, LA, CE, A, MEP			A			
SS	Credit 4.3 — Alternative Transportation: Low-Emitting & Fuel-Efficient Vehicles		O, CE, MEP		CE	CE or A			
SS	Credit 4.4 — Alternative Transportation: Parking Capacity		O, CE		CE	CE or A			
SS	Credit 5.1 — Site Development: Protect or Restore Habitat		CE or LA				GC	GC	CE or LA
SS	Credit 5.2 — Site Development: Maximize Open Space		CE or LA			CE or LA			
SS	Credit 6.1 — Stormwater Design: Quantity Control		CE and LA			CE			
SS	Credit 6.2 — Stormwater Design: Quality Control		CE and LA			CE			
SS	Credit 7.1 — Heat Island Effect: Non-Roof		A, CE, LA				GC	GC	CE or LA
SS	Credit 7.2 — Heat Island Effect: Roof		O, A			A			
SS	Credit 8 — Light Pollution Reduction		CE, LD, A, MEP, O			LD			
Water Efficiency									
WE	Prerequisite 1 — Water Use Reduction: 20%	A, MEP		MEP		MEP			
WE	Credit 1 — Water Efficient Landscaping	CE, LA		LA		LA			
WE	Credit 2 — Innovative Wastewater Technologies	CE, A, MEP			MEP	MEP			
WE	Credit 3 — Water Use Reduction	A, MEP		MEP		MEP			
Energy & Atmosphere									
EA	Prerequisite 1 — Fundamental Commissioning of the Building Energy Systems	T	T	T	T			T	CxA
EA	Prerequisite 2 — Minimum Energy Performance		T		MEP	MEP			
EA	Prerequisite 3 — Fundamental Refrigerant Management	MEP	MEP	MEP	MEP	MEP			
EA	Credit 1 — Optimize Energy Performance		T		MEP	MEP			
EA	Credit 2 — On-Site Renewable Energy		O, MEP, A, CE		MEP	MEP			
EA	Credit 3 — Enhanced Commissioning	T	T	T	T			T	CxA
EA	Credit 4 — Enhanced Refrigerant Management	MEP	MEP	MEP	MEP	MEP			
EA	Credit 5 — Measurement & Verification		O, MEP, CxA				GC	CxA	
EA	Credit 6 — Green Power	O	O	O	O			O	
Material & Resources									
MR	Prerequisite 1 — Storage & Collection of Recyclables	A, O		A		O			
MR	Credit 1.1 — Building Reuse: Maintain Existing Walls, Floors, and Roof	A, S, O			A		GC	GC	A
MR	Credit 1.2 — Building Reuse: Maintain Interior Nonstructural Elements	A, O			A		GC	GC	A
MR	Credit 2 — Construction Waste Management	A, O		A			GC	GC	GC
MR	Credit 3 — Material Reuse	A, O			A		GC	GC	GC or A
MR	Credit 4 — Recycled Content	A	A	A	A		GC	GC	GC
MR	Credit 5 — Regional Materials	A	A	A	A		GC	GC	GC
MR	Credit 6 — Rapidly Renewable Materials	A	A	A	A		GC	GC	GC
MR	Credit 7 — Certified Wood	A	A	A	A		GC	GC	GC

Indoor Environmental Quality									
EQ	Prerequisite 1	Minimum IAQ Performance	MEP	MEP	MEP	MEP	MEP			
EQ	Prerequisite 2	Environmental Tobacco Smoke (ETS) Control	O, A, MEP, CE, LA				O			
EQ	Credit 1	Outdoor Air Delivery Monitoring	MEP	MEP	MEP	MEP	MEP			
EQ	Credit 2	Increased Ventilation	MEP	MEP	MEP	MEP	MEP			
EQ	Credit 3.1	Construction IAQ Management Plan: During Construction	MEP	MEP	MEP	MEP		GC	GC	GC
EQ	Credit 3.2	Construction IAQ Management Plan: Before Occupancy	MEP	MEP	MEP	MEP		GC	GC	GC
EQ	Credit 4.1	Low-Emitting Materials: Adhesives & Sealants	A	A	A	A		GC	GC	GC
EQ	Credit 4.2	Low-Emitting Materials: Paints & Coatings	A	A	A	A		GC	GC	GC
EQ	Credit 4.3	Low-Emitting Materials: Flooring Systems	A	A	A	A		GC	GC	GC
EQ	Credit 4.4	Low-Emitting Materials: Composite Wood & Agrifiber	A	A	A	A		GC	GC	GC
EQ	Credit 5	Indoor Chemical & Pollutant Source Control	A, MEP				A or MEP			
EQ	Credit 6.1	Controllability of Systems: Lighting	A, LD, MEP, O			LD	LD			
EQ	Credit 6.2	Controllability of Systems: Thermal Comfort	A, MEP			MEP	MEP			
EQ	Credit 7.1	Thermal Comfort: Design	MEP, A		MEP		MEP			
EQ	Credit 7.2	Thermal Comfort: Verification	O, CxA							
EQ	Credit 8.1	Daylighting & Views: Daylight 75% of Spaces	A, LD, MEP			LD	LD			
EQ	Credit 8.2	Daylighting & Views: Views for 90% of Spaces	A, LD			A	A			
Innovation & Design Process									
ID	Credit 1.1	Innovation in Design or Exemplary Performance	T	T	T	T	T	T	T	T
ID	Credit 1.2	Innovation in Design or Exemplary Performance	T	T	T	T	T	T	T	T
ID	Credit 1.3	Innovation in Design or Exemplary Performance	T	T	T	T	T	T	T	T
ID	Credit 1.4	Innovation in Design	T	T	T	T	T	T	T	T
ID	Credit 1.5	Innovation in Design	T	T	T	T	T	T	T	T
ID	Credit 2	LEED Accredited Professional	T	T	T	T		T	T	T
Regional Priority Credits									
RP	Credit 1.1	Regional Priority	T	T	T	T		T	T	T
RP	Credit 1.2	Regional Priority	T	T	T	T		T	T	T
RP	Credit 1.3	Regional Priority	T	T	T	T		T	T	T
RP	Credit 1.4	Regional Priority	T	T	T	T		T	T	T

dms LEED for Core & Shell Project Team Member Roles & Documentation Responsibilities	Pre-Design	Schematic Design	Design Development	Construction Documents	DESIGN REVIEW	Construction	Substantial Completion	CONSTRUCTION REVIEW
Sustainable Sites								
SS Prerequisite 1 — Construction Activity Pollution Prevention	CE	CE	CE	CE		GC	GC	CE
SS Credit 1 — Site Selection	T		CE		O			
SS Credit 2 — Development Density & Community Connectivity		O, A, CE			O			
SS Credit 3 — Brownfield Redevelopment		O, CE, EC, GC			CE			
SS Credit 4.1 — Alternative Transportation: Public Transportation Access	O		CE or LA		O			
SS Credit 4.2 — Alternative Transportation: Bicycle Storage & Changing Rooms		O, LA, CE, A, MEP			A			
SS Credit 4.3 — Alternative Transportation: Low-Emitting & Fuel- Efficient		O, CE, MEP		CE	CE			
SS Credit 4.4 — Alternative Transportation: Parking Capacity		O, CE		CE	CE			
SS Credit 5.1 — Site Development: Protect or Restore Habitat		CE or LA				GC	GC	CE or LA
SS Credit 5.2 — Site Development: Maximize Open Space		CE or LA		CE or LA				
SS Credit 6.1 — Stormwater Design: Quantity Control		CE and LA			CE			
SS Credit 6.2 — Stormwater Design: Quality Control		CE and LA			CE			
SS Credit 7.1 — Heat Island Effect: Non-Roof		CE and LA				GC	GC	CE or LA
SS Credit 7.2 — Heat Island Effect: Roof	A	A	A	A	A			
SS Credit 8 — Light Pollution Reduction		CE, LD, A, MEP, O			LD			
SS Credit 9 — Tenant Design & Construction Guidelines	T		O		O			
Water Efficiency								
WE Prerequisite 1 — Water Use Reduction: 20%		A, MEP		MEP	MEP			
WE Credit 1 — Water Efficient Landscaping		CE, LA		LA	LA			
WE Credit 2 — Innovative Wastewater Technologies		CE, A, MEP		MEP	MEP			
WE Credit 3 — Water Use Reduction		A, MEP		MEP	MEP			
Energy & Atmosphere								
EA Prerequisite 1 — Fundamental Commissioning of the Building Energy Systems	T	T	T	T			T	CxA
EA Prerequisite 2 — Minimum Energy Performance		T		MEP	MEP			
EA Prerequisite 3 — Fundamental Refrigerant Management	MEP	MEP	MEP	MEP	MEP			
EA Credit 1 — Optimize Energy Performance		T		MEP	MEP			
EA Credit 2 — On-Site Renewable Energy		O, MEP, A, CE		MEP	MEP			
EA Credit 3 — Enhanced Commissioning	T	T	T	T			T	CxA
EA Credit 4 — Enhanced Refrigerant Management	MEP	MEP	MEP	MEP	MEP			
EA Credit 5.1 — Measurement & Verification: Base Building		O, MEP, CxA			MEP			
EA Credit 5.2 — Measurement & Verification: Tenant Metering		O, MEP		MEP	MEP			
EA Credit 6 — Green Power	O	O	O	O			O	
Material & Resources								
MR Prerequisite 1 — Storage & Collection of Recyclables	A, O		A		O			
MR Credit 1 — Building Reuse: Maintain Existing Walls, Floors, and Roof		A, S, O		A		GC	GC	A
MR Credit 2 — Construction Waste Management	A, O		A			GC	GC	GC
MR Credit 3 — Material Reuse	A, O		A			GC	GC	GC or A
MR Credit 4 — Recycled Content	A	A	A	A		GC	GC	GC
MR Credit 5 — Regional Materials	A	A	A	A		GC	GC	GC
MR Credit 6 — Certified Wood	A	A	A	A		GC	GC	GC

Indoor Environmental Quality									
EQ	Prerequisite 1	Minimum IAQ Performance	MEP	MEP	MEP	MEP	MEP		
EQ	Prerequisite 2	Environmental Tobacco Smoke (ETS) Control	O, A, MEP, CE, LA				O		
EQ	Credit 1	Outdoor Air Delivery Monitoring	MEP	MEP	MEP	MEP	MEP		
EQ	Credit 2	Increased Ventilation	MEP	MEP	MEP	MEP	MEP		
EQ	Credit 3.1	Construction IAQ Management Plan: During Construction	MEP	MEP	MEP	MEP		GC	GC	GC
EQ	Credit 3.2	Construction IAQ Management Plan: Before Occupancy	MEP	MEP	MEP	MEP		GC	GC	GC
EQ	Credit 4.1	Low-Emitting Materials: Adhesives & Sealants	A	A	A	A		GC	GC	GC
EQ	Credit 4.2	Low-Emitting Materials: Paints & Coatings	A	A	A	A		GC	GC	GC
EQ	Credit 4.3	Low-Emitting Materials: Flooring Systems	A	A	A	A		GC	GC	GC
EQ	Credit 4.4	Low-Emitting Materials: Composite Wood & Agrifiber	A	A	A	A		GC	GC	GC
EQ	Credit 5	Indoor Chemical & Pollutant Source Control	A, MEP				A or MEP		
EQ	Credit 6	Controllability of Systems: Thermal Comfort	A, MEP			MEP	MEP		
EQ	Credit 7	Thermal Comfort: Design	MEP, A		MEP		MEP		
EQ	Credit 8.1	Daylighting & Views: Daylight 75% of Spaces	A, LD, MEP			LD	LD		
EQ	Credit 8.2	Daylighting & Views: Views for 90% of Spaces	A, LD			A	A		
Innovation & Design Process									
ID	Credit 1.1	Innovation in Design or Exemplary Performance	T	T	T	T	T	T	T	T
ID	Credit 1.2	Innovation in Design or Exemplary Performance	T	T	T	T	T	T	T	T
ID	Credit 1.3	Innovation in Design or Exemplary Performance	T	T	T	T	T	T	T	T
ID	Credit 1.4	Innovation in Design	T	T	T	T	T	T	T	T
ID	Credit 1.5	Innovation in Design	T	T	T	T	T	T	T	T
ID	Credit 2	LEED Accredited Professional	T	T	T	T		T	T	T
Regional Priority Credits									
RP	Credit 1.1	Regional Priority	T	T	T	T		T	T	T
RP	Credit 1.2	Regional Priority	T	T	T	T		T	T	T
RP	Credit 1.3	Regional Priority	T	T	T	T		T	T	T
RP	Credit 1.4	Regional Priority	T	T	T	T		T	T	T

dms

LEED for Commercial Interiors Project Team Member Roles & Documentation Responsibilities

			Pre-Design	Schematic Design	Design Development	Construction Documents	DESIGN REVIEW	Construction	Substantial Completion	CONSTRUCTION REVIEW
Sustainable Sites										
SS	Credit 1	Site Selection	T	CE			O			
	Path 1	Brownfield Redevelopment			O, CE, EC, GC		O or CE			
	Path 2	Stormwater Design: Quantity Control			O, CE and LA		O or CE			
	Path 3	Stormwater Design: Quality Control			CE and LA		O or CE			
	Path 4	Heat Island Effect: Non-Roof			CE and LA		O, CE, or LA			
	Path 5	Heat Island Effect: Roof	A	A	A	A	O or A			
	Path 6	Light Pollution Reduction			CE, LD, A, MEP, O		O or LD			
	Path 7	Water Efficient Landscaping, Reduced by 50%		CE, LA		LA	O or LA			
	Path 8	Water Efficient Landscaping, No Potable Use or No Irrigation		CE, LA		LA	O or LA			
	Path 9	Innovative Wastewater Technologies		CE, A, MEP		MEP	O or MEP			
	Path 10	Water Use Reduction: 30%		A, MEP		MEP	O or MEP			
	Path 11	On-Site Renewable Energy		O, MEP, A, CE		MEP	O or MEP			
	Path 12	Other Quantifiable Environmental Performance	T	T	T	T	T			
SS	Credit 2	Development Density & Community Connectivity			O, A, CE		O			
SS	Credit 3.1	Alternative Transportation: Public Transportation Access	O	CE or LA			O			
SS	Credit 3.2	Alternative Transportation: Bicycle Storage & Changing Rooms		O, LA, CE, A, MEP			A			
SS	Credit 3.3	Alternative Transportation: Parking Capacity	O, CE		CE		CE			
Water Efficiency										
WE	Prerequisite 1	Water Use Reduction: 20%		A, MEP		MEP	MEP			
WE	Credit 1	Water Use Reduction		A, MEP		MEP	MEP			
Energy & Atmosphere										
EA	Prerequisite 1	Fundamental Commissioning of the Building Energy Systems	T	T	T	T			T	CxA
EA	Prerequisite 2	Minimum Energy Performance			T	MEP	MEP			
EA	Prerequisite 3	Fundamental Refrigerant Management	MEP	MEP	MEP	MEP	MEP			
EA	Credit 1.1	Optimize Energy Performance: Lighting Power			T	LD	LD			
EA	Credit 1.2	Optimize Energy Performance: Lighting Controls			T	LD	LD			
EA	Credit 1.3	Optimize Energy Performance: HVAC			T	MEP	MEP			
EA	Credit 1.4	Optimize Energy Performance: Equipment and Appliances		O, A, MEP			MEP			
EA	Credit 2	Enhanced Commissioning	T	T	T	T			T	CxA
EA	Credit 3	Measurement & Verification		O, MEP, CxA			MEP			
EA	Credit 4	Green Power	O	O	O	O			O	
Material & Resources										
MR	Prerequisite 1	Storage & Collection of Recyclables	A, O		A		O			
MR	Credit 1.1	Tenant Space - Long-Term Commitment	O	O	O	O	O			
MR	Credit 1.2	Building Reuse		A, O		A		GC	GC	A
MR	Credit 2	Construction Waste Management	A, O		A			GC	GC	GC
MR	Credit 3	Material Reuse	A, O		A			GC	GC	GC or A
MR	Credit 3	Material Reuse: Furniture and Furnishings	A, O		A			GC	GC	O or A
MR	Credit 4	Recycled Content	A	A	A	A		GC	GC	GC
MR	Credit 5	Regional Materials	A	A	A	A		GC	GC	GC
MR	Credit 6	Rapidly Renewable Materials	A	A	A	A		GC	GC	GC
MR	Credit 7	Certified Wood	A	A	A	A		GC	GC	GC

Indoor Environmental Quality										
EQ	Prerequisite 1	Minimum IAQ Performance	MEP	MEP	MEP	MEP	MEP			
EQ	Prerequisite 2	Environmental Tobacco Smoke (ETS) Control	O, A, MEP, CE, LA				O			
EQ	Credit 1	Outdoor Air Delivery Monitoring	MEP	MEP	MEP	MEP	MEP			
EQ	Credit 2	Increased Ventilation	MEP	MEP	MEP	MEP	MEP			
EQ	Credit 3.1	Construction IAQ Management Plan: During Construction	MEP	MEP	MEP	MEP		GC	GC	GC
EQ	Credit 3.2	Construction IAQ Management Plan: Before Occupancy	MEP	MEP	MEP	MEP		GC	GC	GC
EQ	Credit 4.1	Low-Emitting Materials: Adhesives & Sealants	A	A	A	A		GC	GC	GC
EQ	Credit 4.2	Low-Emitting Materials: Paints & Coatings	A	A	A	A		GC	GC	GC
EQ	Credit 4.3	Low-Emitting Materials: Flooring Systems	A	A	A	A		GC	GC	GC
EQ	Credit 4.4	Low-Emitting Materials: Composite Wood & Agrifiber	A	A	A	A		GC	GC	GC
EQ	Credit 4.5	Low-Emitting Materials: Systems Furniture and Seating	A	A	A	A		GC	GC	GA, A, or O
EQ	Credit 5	Indoor Chemical & Pollutant Source Control	A, MEP				A or MEP			
EQ	Credit 6.1	Controllability of Systems: Lighting	A, LD, MEP, O			LD	LD			
EQ	Credit 6.2	Controllability of Systems: Thermal Comfort	A, MEP			MEP	MEP			
EQ	Credit 7.1	Thermal Comfort: Design	MEP, A			MEP	MEP			
EQ	Credit 7.2	Thermal Comfort: Verification	O, CxA							
EQ	Credit 8.1	Daylighting & Views: Daylight 75% of Spaces	A, LD, MEP			LD	LD			
EQ	Credit 8.2	Daylighting & Views: Views for 90% of Spaces	A, LD			A	A			
Innovation & Design Process										
ID	Credit 1.1	Innovation in Design or Exemplary Performance	T	T	T	T	T	T	T	T
ID	Credit 1.2	Innovation in Design or Exemplary Performance	T	T	T	T	T	T	T	T
ID	Credit 1.3	Innovation in Design or Exemplary Performance	T	T	T	T	T	T	T	T
ID	Credit 1.4	Innovation in Design	T	T	T	T	T	T	T	T
ID	Credit 1.5	Innovation in Design	T	T	T	T	T	T	T	T
ID	Credit 2	LEED Accredited Professional	T	T	T	T		T	T	T
Regional Priority Credits										
RP	Credit 1.1	Regional Priority	T	T	T	T		T	T	T
RP	Credit 1.2	Regional Priority	T	T	T	T		T	T	T
RP	Credit 1.3	Regional Priority	T	T	T	T		T	T	T
RP	Credit 1.4	Regional Priority	T	T	T	T		T	T	T

O = Owner, A = Architect, MEP = Engineer, CE = Civil Engineer, LA = Landscape Architect, S= Structural
LD = Lighting Designer, EC = Environmental Consultant, CxA = Commissioning Agent, GC = Contractor, T = Team

Appendix D: Design versus Construction Prerequisites and Checklists

LEED for New Construction
Certification Review Submittal

			Certification Submittal
Sustainable Sites			
SS	Prerequisite 1	Construction Activity Pollution Prevention	Construction
SS	Credit 1	Site Selection	Design
SS	Credit 2	Development Density & Community Connectivity	Design
SS	Credit 3	Brownfield Redevelopment	Design
SS	Credit 4.1	Alternative Transportation: Public Transportation Access	Design
SS	Credit 4.2	Alternative Transportation: Bicycle Storage & Changing Rooms	Design
SS	Credit 4.3	Alternative Transportation: Low-Emitting & Fuel-Efficient Vehicles	Design
SS	Credit 4.4	Alternative Transportation: Parking Capacity	Design
SS	Credit 5.1	Site Development: Protect or Restore Habitat	Construction
SS	Credit 5.2	Site Development: Maximize Open Space	Design
SS	Credit 6.1	Stormwater Design: Quantity Control	Design
SS	Credit 6.2	Stormwater Design: Quality Control	Design
SS	Credit 7.1	Heat Island Effect: Non-Roof	Construction
SS	Credit 7.2	Heat Island Effect: Roof	Design
SS	Credit 8	Light Pollution Reduction	Design
Water Efficiency			
WE	Prerequisite 1	Water Use Reduction: 20%	Design
WE	Credit 1	Water Efficient Landscaping	Design
WE	Credit 2	Innovative Wastewater Technologies	Design
WE	Credit 3	Water Use Reduction	Design

Energy & Atmosphere			
EA	Prerequisite 1	Fundamental Commissioning of the Building Energy Systems	Construction
EA	Prerequisite 2	Minimum Energy Performance	Design
EA	Prerequisite 3	Fundamental Refrigerant Management	Design
EA	Credit 1	Optimize Energy Performance	Design
EA	Credit 2	On-Site Renewable Energy	Design
EA	Credit 3	Enhanced Commissioning	Construction
EA	Credit 4	Enhanced Refrigerant Management	Design
EA	Credit 5	Measurement & Verification	Design
EA	Credit 6	Green Power	Construction
Material & Resources			
MR	Prerequisite 1	Storage & Collection of Recyclables	Design
MR	Credit 1.1	Building Reuse: Maintain Existing Walls, Floors, and Roof	Construction
MR	Credit 1.2	Building Reuse: Maintain Interior Nonstructural Elements	Construction
MR	Credit 2	Construction Waste Management	Construction
MR	Credit 3	Material Reuse	Construction
MR	Credit 4	Recycled Content	Construction
MR	Credit 5	Regional Materials	Construction
MR	Credit 6	Rapidly Renewable Materials	Construction
MR	Credit 7	Certified Wood	Construction
Indoor Environmental Quality			
EQ	Prerequisite 1	Minimum IAQ Performance	Design
EQ	Prerequisite 2	Environmental Tobacco Smoke (ETS) Control	Design
EQ	Credit 1	Outdoor Air Delivery Monitoring	Design
EQ	Credit 2	Increased Ventilation	Design
EQ	Credit 3.1	Construction IAQ Management Plan: During Construction	Construction
EQ	Credit 3.2	Construction IAQ Management Plan: Before Occupancy	Construction
EQ	Credit 4.1	Low-Emitting Materials: Adhesives & Sealants	Construction
EQ	Credit 4.2	Low-Emitting Materials: Paints & Coatings	Construction
EQ	Credit 4.3	Low-Emitting Materials: Flooring Systems	Construction
EQ	Credit 4.4	Low-Emitting Materials: Composite Wood & Agrifiber	Construction
EQ	Credit 5	Indoor Chemical & Pollutant Source Control	Design
EQ	Credit 6.1	Controllability of Systems: Lighting	Design
EQ	Credit 6.2	Controllability of Systems: Thermal Comfort	Design
EQ	Credit 7.1	Thermal Comfort: Design	Design
EQ	Credit 7.2	Thermal Comfort: Verification	Design
EQ	Credit 8.1	Daylighting & Views: Daylight 75% of Spaces	Design
EQ	Credit 8.2	Daylighting & Views: Views for 90% of Spaces	Design

Innovation & Design Process			
ID	Credit 1.1	Innovation in Design or Exemplary Performance	**Design or Construction**
ID	Credit 1.2	Innovation in Design or Exemplary Performance	**Design or Construction**
ID	Credit 1.3	Innovation in Design or Exemplary Performance	**Design or Construction**
ID	Credit 1.4	Innovation in Design	**Design or Construction**
ID	Credit 1.5	Innovation in Design	**Design or Construction**
ID	Credit 2	LEED Accredited Professional	Construction
Regional Priority Credits			
RP	Credit 1.1	Regional Priority	Construction
RP	Credit 1.2	Regional Priority	Construction
RP	Credit 1.3	Regional Priority	Construction
RP	Credit 1.4	Regional Priority	Construction

LEED for New Construction
Design Review Checklist

Sustainable Sites

- ☐ Credit 1: Site Selection
- ☐ Credit 2: Development Density & Community Connectivity
- ☐ Credit 3: Brownfield Redevelopment

  Credit 4: Alternative Transportation
  - ☐ Public Transportation Access
  - ☐ Bicycle Storage & Changing Rooms
  - ☐ Low-Emitting & Fuel-Efficient Vehicles
  - ☐ Parking Capacity
- ☐ Credit 5.2: Site Development, Protection or Restore Habitat

  Credit 6: Stormwater Design
  - ☐ Quantity Control
  - ☐ Quality Control
- ☐ Credit 7.2: Heat Island Effect, Roof
- ☐ Credit 8: Light Pollution Reduction

Water Efficiency

- ☐ Prerequisite 1: Water Use Reduction
- ☐ Credit 1: Water Efficient Landscaping
- ☐ Credit 2: Innovative Wastewater Technologies
- ☐ Credit 3: Water Use Reduction

Energy & Atmosphere

- ☐ Prerequisite 2: Minimum Energy Performance
- ☐ Prerequisite 3: Fundamental Refrigerant Management

- ☐ Credit 1: Optimize Energy Performance
- ☐ Credit 2: On -Site Renewable Energy
- ☐ Credit 4: Enhanced Refrigerant Management

Materials & Resources

- ☐ Prerequisite 1: Storage & Collection of Recyclables

Indoor Environmental Quality

- ☐ Prerequisite 1: Minimum IAQ Performance
- ☐ Prerequisite 2: ETS Control
- ☐ Credit 1: Outdoor Air Delivery Monitoring
- ☐ Credit 2: Increased Ventilation
- ☐ Credit 5: Indoor Chemical & Pollutant Source Control

  Credit 6: Controllability of Systems
  - ☐ Lighting
  - ☐ Thermal Comfort

  Credit 7: Thermal Comfort
  - ☐ Design
  - ☐ Verification

  Credit 8: Daylight & Views
  - ☐ Daylighting
  - ☐ Views

Innovation & Design Process

- ☐ Credit 1: Innovation or Exemplary

LEED for New Construction
Construction Review Checklist

Sustainable Sites

☐ Prerequisite 1: Construction Activity Pollution Prevention

☐ Credit 5.1: Site Development, Maximize Open Space

☐ Credit 7.1: Heat Island Effect, Non-Roof

Energy & Atmosphere

☐ Prerequisite 1: Fundamental Commissioning of Building Energy Systems

☐ Credit 3: Enhanced Commissioning

☐ Credit 5: Measurement & Verification

☐ Credit 6: Green Power

Materials & Resources

Credit 1: Building Reuse

☐ Maintain Existing Walls, Floors & Roof

☐ Maintain 50% of Interior Non-Structural Elements

☐ Credit 2: Construction Waste Management

☐ Credit 3: Materials Reuse

☐ Credit 4: Recycled Content

☐ Credit 5: Regional Materials

☐ Credit 6: Rapidly Renewable Materials

☐ Credit 7: Certified Wood

Indoor Environmental Quality

Credit 3: Construction IAQ Management Plan

☐ During Construction
☐ Before Occupancy

Credit 4: Low-Emitting Materials

☐ Adhesives and Sealants
☐ Paints and Coatings
☐ Flooring Systems
☐ Composite Wood and Agrifber Products

Innovation & Design Process

☐ Credit 1: Innovation or Exemplary

☐ Credit 2: LEED Accredited Professional

**LEED for Core and Shell
Certification Review Submittal**

			Certification Submittal
Sustainable Sites			
SS	Prerequisite 1	Construction Activity Pollution Prevention	Construction
SS	Credit 1	Site Selection	Design
SS	Credit 2	Development Density & Community Connectivity	Design
SS	Credit 3	Brownfield Redevelopment	Design
SS	Credit 4.1	Alternative Transportation: Public Transportation Access	Design
SS	Credit 4.2	Alternative Transportation: Bicycle Storage & Changing Rooms	Design
SS	Credit 4.3	Alternative Transportation: Low-Emitting & Fuel-Efficient Vehicles	Design
SS	Credit 4.4	Alternative Transportation: Parking Capacity	Design
SS	Credit 5.1	Site Development: Protect or Restore Habitat	Construction
SS	Credit 5.2	Site Development: Maximize Open Space	Design
SS	Credit 6.1	Stormwater Design: Quantity Control	Design
SS	Credit 6.2	Stormwater Design: Quality Control	Design
SS	Credit 7.1	Heat Island Effect: Non-Roof	Construction
SS	Credit 7.2	Heat Island Effect: Roof	Design
SS	Credit 8	Light Pollution Reduction	Design
SS	Credit 9	Tenant Design and Construction Guidelines	Construction
Water Efficiency			
WE	Prerequisite 1	Water Use Reduction: 20%	Design
WE	Credit 1	Water Efficient Landscaping	Design
WE	Credit 2	Innovative Wastewater Technologies	Design
WE	Credit 3	Water Use Reduction	Design
Energy & Atmosphere			
EA	Prerequisite 1	Fundamental Commissioning of the Building Energy Systems	Construction
EA	Prerequisite 2	Minimum Energy Performance	Design
EA	Prerequisite 3	Fundamental Refrigerant Management	Design
EA	Credit 1	Optimize Energy Performance	Design
EA	Credit 2	On-Site Renewable Energy	Design
EA	Credit 3	Enhanced Commissioning	Construction
EA	Credit 4	Enhanced Refrigerant Management	Design
EA	Credit 5.1	Measurement & Verification: Base Building	Design
EA	Credit 5.2	Measurement & Verification: Tenant Metering	
EA	Credit 6	Green Power	Construction
Material & Resources			
MR	Prerequisite 1	Storage & Collection of Recyclables	Design
MR	Credit 1.1	Building Reuse: Maintain Existing Walls, Floors, and Roof	Construction
MR	Credit 1.2	Building Reuse: Maintain Interior Nonstructural Elements	Construction
MR	Credit 2	Construction Waste Management	Construction
MR	Credit 3	Material Reuse	Construction
MR	Credit 4	Recycled Content	Construction

MR	Credit 5	Regional Materials	Construction
MR	Credit 6	Certified Wood	Construction
Indoor Environmental Quality			
EQ	Prerequisite 1	Minimum IAQ Performance	Design
EQ	Prerequisite 2	Environmental Tobacco Smoke (ETS) Control	Design
EQ	Credit 1	Outdoor Air Delivery Monitoring	Design
EQ	Credit 2	Increased Ventilation	Design
EQ	Credit 3.1	Construction IAQ Management Plan: During Construction	Construction
EQ	Credit 4.1	Low-Emitting Materials: Adhesives & Sealants	Construction
EQ	Credit 4.2	Low-Emitting Materials: Paints & Coatings	Construction
EQ	Credit 4.3	Low-Emitting Materials: Flooring Systems	Construction
EQ	Credit 4.4	Low-Emitting Materials: Composite Wood & Agrifiber	Construction
EQ	Credit 5	Indoor Chemical & Pollutant Source Control	Design
EQ	Credit 6	Controllability of Systems: Thermal Comfort	Design
EQ	Credit 7	Thermal Comfort: Design	Design
EQ	Credit 8.1	Daylighting & Views: Daylight 75% of Spaces	Design
EQ	Credit 8.2	Daylighting & Views: Views for 90% of Spaces	Design
Innovation & Design Process			
ID	Credit 1.1	Innovation in Design or Exemplary Performance	Design or Construction
ID	Credit 1.2	Innovation in Design or Exemplary Performance	Design or Construction
ID	Credit 1.3	Innovation in Design or Exemplary Performance	Design or Construction
ID	Credit 1.4	Innovation in Design	Design or Construction
ID	Credit 1.5	Innovation in Design	Design or Construction
ID	Credit 2	LEED Accredited Professional	Construction
Regional Priority Credits			
RP	Credit 1.1	Regional Priority	Construction
RP	Credit 1.2	Regional Priority	Construction
RP	Credit 1.3	Regional Priority	Construction
RP	Credit 1.4	Regional Priority	Construction

LEED for Core & Shell
Design Review Checklist

Sustainable Sites

- ☐ Credit 1: Site Selection
- ☐ Credit 2: Development Density & Community Connectivity
- ☐ Credit 3: Brownfield Redevelopment

  Credit 4: Alternative Transportation
  - ☐ Public Transportation Access
  - ☐ Bicycle Storage & Changing Rooms
  - ☐ Low-Emitting & Fuel-Efficient Vehicles
  - ☐ Parking Capacity
- ☐ Credit 5.2: Site Development, Protection or Restore Habitat

  Credit 6: Stormwater Design
  - ☐ Quantity Control
  - ☐ Quality Control
- ☐ Credit 7.2: Heat Island Effect, Roof
- ☐ Credit 8: Light Pollution Reduction
- ☐ Credit 9: Tenant Design & Construction Guidelines

Water Efficiency

- ☐ Prerequisite 1: Water Use Reduction
- ☐ Credit 1: Water Efficient Landscaping
- ☐ Credit 2: Innovative Wastewater Technologies
- ☐ Credit 3: Water Use Reduction

Energy & Atmosphere

- ☐ Prerequisite 2: Minimum Energy Performance
- ☐ Prerequisite 3: Fundamental Refrigerant Management

Energy & Atmosphere, con't

- ☐ Credit 1: Optimize Energy Performance
- ☐ Credit 2: On-Site Renewable Energy
- ☐ Credit 4: Enhanced Refrigerant Management

  Credit 5: Measurement & Verification
  - ☐ Base Building
  - ☐ Tenant Metering

Materials & Resources

- ☐ Prerequisite 1: Storage & Collection of Recyclables

Indoor Environmental Quality

- ☐ Prerequisite 1: Minimum IAQ Performance
- ☐ Prerequisite 2: ETS Control
- ☐ Credit 1: Outdoor Air Delivery Monitoring
- ☐ Credit 2: Increased Ventilation
  - ☐ Credit 5: Indoor Chemical & Pollutant Source Control
  - ☐ Credit 6: Controllability of Systems, Thermal Comfort
- ☐ Credit 7: Thermal Comfort, Design

  Credit 8: Daylight & Views
  - ☐ Daylighting
  - ☐ Views

Innovation & Design Process

- ☐ Credit 1: Innovation or Exemplary

LEED for Core & Shell
Construction Review Checklist

Sustainable Sites

- ☐ Prerequisite 1: Construction Activity Pollution Prevention

- ☐ Credit 5.1: Site Development, Maximize Open Space
- ☐ Credit 7.1: Heat Island Effect, Non-Roof

Energy & Atmosphere

- ☐ Prerequisite 1: Fundamental Commissionin of Building Energy Systems
- ☐ Credit 3: Enhanced Commissioning
- ☐ Credit 6: Green Power

Materials & Resources

- ☐ Credit 1: Building Reuse, Maintain Existing Walls, Floors & Roof
- ☐ Credit 2: Construction Waste Management
- ☐ Credit 3: Materials Reuse
- ☐ Credit 4: Recycled Content
- ☐ Credit 5: Regional Materials
- ☐ Credit 6: Certified Wood

Indoor Environmental Quality

Credit 3: Construction IAQ Management Plan

- ☐ During Construction
- ☐ Before Occupancy

Credit 4: Low-Emitting Materials

- ☐ Adhesives and Sealants
- ☐ Paints and Coatings
- ☐ Flooring Systems
- ☐ Composite Wood and Agrifber Products

Innovation & Design Process

- ☐ Credit 1: Innovation or Exemplary
- ☐ Credit 2: LEED Accredited Professional

**LEED for Commerical Interiors
Certification Review Submittal**

Sustainable Sites			Certification Submittal
SS	Credit 1	Site Selection	**Design**
	Path 1	Brownfield Redevelopment	**Design**
	Path 2	Stormwater Design: Quantity Control	**Design**
	Path 3	Stormwater Design: Quality Control	**Design**
	Path 4	Heat Island Effect: Non-Roof	**Design**
	Path 5	Heat Island Effect: Roof	**Design**
	Path 6	Light Pollution Reduction	**Design**
	Path 7	Water Efficient Landscaping, Reduced by 50%	**Design**
	Path 8	Water Efficient Landscaping, No Potable Use or No Irrigation	**Design**
	Path 9	Innovative Wastewater Technologies	**Design**
	Path 10	Water Use Reduction: 30%	**Design**
	Path 11	On-Site Renewable Energy	**Design**
	Path 12	Other Quantifiable Environmental Performance	**Design**
SS	Credit 2	Development Density & Community Connectivity	**Design**
SS	Credit 3.1	Alternative Transportation: Public Transportation Access	**Design**
SS	Credit 3.2	Alternative Transportation: Bicycle Storage & Changing Rooms	**Design**
SS	Credit 3.3	Alternative Transportation: Parking Capacity	**Design**
Water Efficiency			
WE	Prerequisite 1	Water Use Reduction: 20%	**Design**
WE	Credit 1	Water Use Reduction	**Design**

Energy & Atmosphere

EA	Prerequisite 1	Fundamental Commissioning of the Building Energy Systems	Construction
EA	Prerequisite 2	Minimum Energy Performance	Design
EA	Prerequisite 3	Fundamental Refrigerant Management	Design
EA	Credit 1.1	Optimize Energy Performance: Lighting Power	Design
EA	Credit 1.2	Optimize Energy Performance: Lighting Controls	Design
EA	Credit 1.3	Optimize Energy Performance: HVAC	Construction
EA	Credit 1.4	Optimize Energy Performance: Equipment and Appliances	Design
EA	Credit 2	Enhanced Commissioning	Design
EA	Credit 3	Measurement & Verification	Design
EA	Credit 4	Green Power	Construction

Material & Resources

MR	Prerequisite 1	Storage & Collection of Recyclables	Design
MR	Credit 1.1	Tenant Space - Long-Term Commitment	Construction
MR	Credit 1.2	Building Reuse	Construction
MR	Credit 2	Construction Waste Management	Construction
MR	Credit 3	Material Reuse	Construction
MR	Credit 3	Material Reuse: Furniture and Furnishings	Construction
MR	Credit 4	Recycled Content	Construction
MR	Credit 5	Regional Materials	Construction
MR	Credit 6	Rapidly Renewable Materials	Construction
MR	Credit 7	Certified Wood	Construction

Indoor Environmental Quality

EQ	Prerequisite 1	Minimum IAQ Performance	Design
EQ	Prerequisite 2	Environmental Tobacco Smoke (ETS) Control	Design
EQ	Credit 1	Outdoor Air Delivery Monitoring	Design
EQ	Credit 2	Increased Ventilation	Design
EQ	Credit 3.1	Construction IAQ Management Plan: During Construction	Construction
EQ	Credit 3.2	Construction IAQ Management Plan: Before Occupancy	Construction
EQ	Credit 4.1	Low-Emitting Materials: Adhesives & Sealants	Construction
EQ	Credit 4.2	Low-Emitting Materials: Paints & Coatings	Construction
EQ	Credit 4.3	Low-Emitting Materials: Flooring Systems	Construction
EQ	Credit 4.4	Low-Emitting Materials: Composite Wood & Agrifiber	Construction
EQ	Credit 4.5	Low-Emitting Materials: Systems Furniture and Seating	Construction
EQ	Credit 5	Indoor Chemical & Pollutant Source Control	Design
EQ	Credit 6.1	Controllability of Systems: Lighting	Design
EQ	Credit 6.2	Controllability of Systems: Thermal Comfort	Design
EQ	Credit 7.1	Thermal Comfort: Design	Design
EQ	Credit 7.2	Thermal Comfort: Verification	Design
EQ	Credit 8.1	Daylighting & Views: Daylight 75% of Spaces	Design
EQ	Credit 8.2	Daylighting & Views: Views for 90% of Spaces	Design

Innovation & Design Process			
ID	Credit 1.1	Innovation in Design or Exemplary Performance	Design or Construction
ID	Credit 1.2	Innovation in Design or Exemplary Performance	Design or Construction
ID	Credit 1.3	Innovation in Design or Exemplary Performance	Design or Construction
ID	Credit 1.4	Innovation in Design	Design or Construction
ID	Credit 1.5	Innovation in Design	Design or Construction
ID	Credit 2	LEED Accredited Professional	Construction
Regional Priority Credits			
RP	Credit 1.1	Regional Priority	Construction
RP	Credit 1.2	Regional Priority	Construction
RP	Credit 1.3	Regional Priority	Construction
RP	Credit 1.4	Regional Priority	Construction

LEED for Commercial Interiors
Design Review Checklist

Sustainable Sites

☐ Credit 1: Site Selection

☐ Credit 2: Development Density & Community Connectivity

Credit 3: Alternative Transportation

☐ Public Transportation Access
☐ Bicycle Storage & Changing Rooms
☐ Parking Availability

Water Efficiency

☐ Prerequisite 1: Water Use Reduction

☐ Credit 1: Water Use Reduction

Energy & Atmosphere

☐ Prerequisite 2: Minimum Energy Performance

☐ Prerequisite 3: Fundamental Refrigerant Management

☐ Credit 1: Optimize Energy Performance

o Lighting Power
o Lighting Controls
o HVAC
o Equipment and Appliances

☐ Credit 3: Measurement & Verification

Materials & Resources

☐ Prerequisite 1: Storage & Collection of Recyclables

☐ Credit 1.1: Tenant Space – Long-term Commitment

Indoor Environmental Quality

☐ Prerequisite 1: Minimum IAQ Performance

☐ Prerequisite 2: ETS Control

☐ Credit 1: Outdoor Air Delivery Monitoring

☐ Credit 2: Increased Ventilation

☐ Credit 5: Indoor Chemical & Pollutant Source Control

Credit 6: Controllability of Systems

☐ Lighting
☐ Thermal Comfort

Credit 7: Thermal Comfort

☐ Design
☐ Verification

Credit 8: Daylight & Views

☐ Daylighting
☐ Views

Innovation & Design Process

☐ Credit 1: Innovation or Exemplary

LEED for Commercial Interiors
Construction Review Checklist

Energy & Atmosphere

☐ Prerequisite 1: Fundamental Commissioning of Building Energy Systems

☐ Credit 2: Enhanced Commissioning

☐ Credit 4: Green Power

Materials & Resources

☐ Credit 1.2: Building Reuse

☐ Credit 2: Construction Waste Management

☐ Credit 3.1: Materials Reuse

☐ Credit 3.2: Materials Reuse, Furniture & Furnishings

☐ Credit 4: Recycled Content

☐ Credit 5: Regional Materials

☐ Credit 6: Rapidly Renewable Materials

☐ Credit 7: Certified Wood

Indoor Environmental Quality

Credit 3: Construction IAQ Management Plan
☐ During Construction
☐ Before Occupancy

Credit 4: Low-Emitting Materials
☐ Adhesives and Sealants
☐ Paints and Coatings
☐ Flooring Systems
☐ Composite Wood and Agrifber Products
☐ Systems Furniture and Seating

Innovation & Design Process

☐ Credit 1: Innovation or Exemplary

☐ Credit 2: LEED Accredited Professional

Appendix E: Owner's Project Requirements Template and Basis of Design Sample

700 Mattison Avenue
Asbury Park, NJ 07712
P: 732-988-8850
F: 732-988-9596
www.eneractivesolutions.com

Client Name

Project Title

(Street Address, City, State)

Owner's Project Requirements

I. General Requirements

A. The [Project Name] will be designed in accordance with all state adopted codes, complete with any local amendments. For the project location in [City], [State], this includes, but is not limited to, the 2006 set of International Codes (Building, Mechanical, and Fuel Gas), the 2005 National Electric Code, and the 2006 National Standard Plumbing code. The adopted state energy code and anticipated LEED requirements discussed in the remainder of this document further reference the energy standard of ASHRAE 90.1-2004.

II. Owner and User Requirements

A. The [Project Name] encompasses approximately [XXX,XXX] square feet of floor area for use office space with user amenities including a conference rooms, kitchenette pantry, and staff lounge.

III. Environmental and Sustainability Goals

A.   At a minimum, the project shall meet the requirements of, and be fully certified as, a LEED [LEED Category] project at the "[Platinum, Gold, Silver, Certified]" level. A "[Platinum, Gold, Silver]" certification level has been identified as a target "reach" benchmark.

B.   The *most current* LEED point checklist put forward shall be referred to for representation of the intended areas targeted for point accrual at any point in the design/construction process. In accordance with the most recent LEED checklist distributed *to date*, the subsequent requirements include, but are not limited to, the following:

   a.   Building shall be within ½ mile of a commuter rail line, or ¼ mile of two or more bus lines. *(LEED-CI SSc1-3.1)*

   b.   Bicycle storage and convenient shower/changing facilities shall be provided for a minimum of 5% of tenant occupants. *(LEED-CI SSc3.2)*

   c.   Based on tenant occupancy requirements, building shall use 30% less water than the water use baseline calculated for tenant space after meeting Energy Policy Act of 1992 fixture performance requirements. *(LEED-CI WEc1.2)*

   d.   No CFC refrigerants shall be used in any system. *(LEED-CI EApr3)*

   e.   Daylight responsive controls shall be installed within 15 feet of windows and skylights in all regularly occupied spaces to adjust lighting levels accordingly. (LEED-CI EAc1.2)

   f.   HVAC system component performance shall be demonstrated to comply with the standard level detailed in ASHRAE 90.1 2004. *(LEED-CI EApr2)*

   g.   Tenant space shall increase levels of energy conservation beyond the pre-requisite standard by utilizing appropriate zon*ing and controls* in the following manner: *every solar ex*posure must have a separate zone control, interior spaces must be separately zoned, and private offices and specialty occ*upancies (confe*rence rooms, kitchens, etc.) must have active controls capable of sensing space use and modulating the HVAC system in response to space demand. *(LEED-CI EAc1.3 opt A)*

   h.   90% (as a percentage of rated power) of all possible ENERGY STAR appliances shall be ENERGY STAR rated. *(LEED-CI EAc1.4)*

   i.   *Contract Docu*ments shall incorporate the commissioning process as an integral part of the building fit-out. Furthermore, a commissioning plan shall be developed for reviewing system requirements with the building O&M staff and finalizing the resolution of any outstanding commissioning related issues within eight to ten months after final acceptance. *(LEED-CI EAc2 and LEED-CI EApr1)*

j. An area serving the entire building will be set aside for the collection / separation / storage of recyclable material. *(LEED-CI MRpr1)*

k. A construction waste management plan shall be developed to quantify at least 75% of construction, demolition, and packaging debris is diverted from the landfill. *(LEED-CI MRc2.1 & 2.2)*

l. Materials, including furnishings, shall be 20% recycled content (post-consumer + ½ pre-consumer). *(LEED-CI MRc4.1 & 4.2)*

m. A minimum of 20% of all construction and furnishing material shall be manufactured within a 500 mile radius of the project site. *(LEED-CI MRc5.1)*

n. A minimum of 10% of all construction and furnishing material shall be extracted, harvested, recovered, or manufactured within a 500 mile radius of the project site. *(LEED-CI MRc5.2)*

o. 5% of the total dollar value of construction material and furnishings shall be made from plants that are typically harvested within a 10-year or shorter cycle. *(LEED-CI MRc6)*

p. 50% of all wood based products and materials shall be certified in accordance with the Forest Stewardship Council's Principles and Criteria. *(LEED MRc7)*

q. Indoor air quality plan shall incorporate, at a minimum, ASHRAE Standard 62 unless adopted codes set a higher requirement. *(LEED-CI EQpr1)*

r. Tobacco smoke control shall be incorporated into the design. *(LEED-CI EQpr2)*

s. An indoor air quality management plan shall be put into place for the construction phase. *(LEED-CI EQc3.1)*

t. An indoor air quality management plan shall be put into place for the pre-occupancy phase. *(LEED-CI EQc3.2)*

u. Adhesives and Sealants, Paintings and Coatings, Carpet, Composite Wood and Adhesives, and Furniture and Seating shall comply with low emissivity requirements. *(LEED-CI EQc4)*

v. Lighting control shall be provided for at least 90% of building occupants and all multi-occupant shared spaces. *(LEED-CI EQc6.1)*

w. Tenant space shall comply with ASHRAE Standard 55-2004, Thermal Environmental conditions for Human Occupancy, and a method to monitor conditions shall be implemented to ensure system performance to the desired criteria. *(LEED-CI EQc7.1 & 7.2)*

x. An educational program effort shall be undertaken and documented for a possible Design and Innovation Credit. *(LEED-CI IDc1.1)*

y. A green housekeeping effort shall be attempted for a possible Design and Innovation Credit. *(LEED-CI IDc1.2)*

z. A re-usable mugs/dishes program shall be attempted for a possible Design and Innovation Credit. *(LEED-CI IDc1.3)*

aa. Additional measures shall be taken to increase water efficiency above the threshold identified in LEED credit WEc1.2. *(LEED-CI IDc1.4)*

IV. Energy Efficiency Goals

A. Energy performance shall be illustrated so that the overall lighting power and HVAC system energy performance meets the ASHRAE 90.1-2004 baseline.

    a. All trades shall coordinate their design accordingly.

V. Special Indoor Environmental Requirements

A. Luncheonette and copy areas shall have adequate ventilation and exhaust to accommodate any associated equipment.

B. Server Rooms and Data Centers shall have independent units to maintain the required air quality requirements for the installed equipment.

VI. Equipment and Systems Expectations

A. All fit-out systems shall show consideration for an acceptable level of initial capital investment, while meeting the adopted building codes and LEED requirements, as well as conforming to other project requirements set forth in this document.

VII. Building Occupant and O&M Personnel Expectations

A. Occupants shall have independent lighting and HVAC control within their zones, and shall be adjustable to suit changing needs.

B. Lighting control for all common areas shall have the capability of being programmable in a time-of-day-schedule, with temporary override buttons controlling multiple zones.

C. Equipment training should be included in the project specifications and be complemented with an overall Operations & Maintenance manual complete with all necessary information including, but not limited to, equipment model numbers, valve schedules, maintenance schedules and instructions, replacement part lists.

D. As built drawings should be provided at projects completion.

Client Name

Project Title

(Street Address, City, State)

Building Energy Systems
Basis of Design

I. HVAC System

B. *Narrative Description of System*

    a. Cooling and heating of the building spaces is accomplished by a combination of Base Building systems and supplemental systems provided by the tenant. A roof-top air-cooled air conditioning penthouse system with variable speed fan motors is existing. The penthouse unit provides cooling and heating air to the tenant space by means of a vertical duct riser in the building shaft. New and re-used variable air volume (VAV) boxes and fan-powered variable air volume (FPB) boxes are used to serve individual tenant zones. FPB's are provided with electric re-heat coils.

    b. An air-cooled split-system type supplemental unit is provided by the tenant for cooling needs at the MDF room. The unit provides dedicated cooling to the MDF room and shall operate during occupied hours and after hours.

    c. Existing electric baseboard heaters shall be re-used at the Reception area for additional heating.

C. *Reasons for System Selection*

    a. The supplemental systems selected for tenant use at the MDF room was selected because the space requires cooling on a 24 hour basis.

D. *Load Calculations*

    a. Load calculation method/software: Calculation software utilized is Trane Trace 700.

    b. Summer outdoor design conditions: 91 °F drybulb, 73 °F wetbulb.

    c. Winter outdoor design conditions: 14 °F drybulb.

    d. Indoor design conditions: 75 °F cooling; 70 °F heating.

    e. Internal heat gain assumptions:

Space	Lighting Load	Plug Load	Occupant Load	Infiltration Load	Other:
Typical office spaces	1.10 W/ft²	1.0 W/ft²	1 person per 150 ft² (average)	0 btu/h	15 cfm ventilation air per person
Typical conference and team room spaces	1.30 W/ft²	0.25 W/ft²	1 person per 25 ft² (average)	0 btu/h	15 cfm ventilation air per person
MDF Room	160 W	9200 W	0 btu/h	0 btu/h	

     f.   Calculated cooling loads and system size:

System/Air Handler ID	Calculated Peak Cooling Load	Selected System Cooling Capacity
AC-1-1	32,000 Btu/hr	33,000 Btu/hr

    E.   *Sequence of Operations*

       a.   Sequence of Operations can be found on design drawings M-201 and M-202.

II. Indoor Lighting System

    A.   *Narrative Description of System*

       a.   Light Fixtures with description, lamp and ballast types:
          1. F1:   Recessed 6" aperature downlight
                    (32w TTT lamp)

          2. F1A: Recessed 6" aperature downlight – dimming
                    (32w TTT lamp with dimming ballast)

          3. F2:   Recessed 6" aperature wall washer
                    (26w TTT lamp)

          4. F2A: Recessed 6" aperature wall washer – dimming
                    (26w TTT lamp with dimming ballast)

          5. F3:   Recessed linear
                    (54w T5 lamp)

6. F4: Recessed 3" aperature downlight
   (37w MR16 lamp)

7. F4A: Recessed 3" aperature downlight – dimming
   (37w MR16 lamp with dimming ballast)

8. F6: Recessed 2x2 indirect
   (10w BIAX lamp)

9. F6A: Recessed 2x2 indirect with daylight harvesting
   (10w BIAX lamp)

10. F7: Recessed 2x2 parabolic
    (31w T8 lamp)

11. F8: Linear direct/ indirect 4ft pendant
    (54w T5HO lamp)

12. F8A: Linear direct/ indirect 8ft pendant
    (54w T5HO lamp)

13. F8B: Linear direct/ indirect 4ft pendant with daylight harvesting
    (54w T5HO lamp)

14. F8C: Linear direct/ indirect 8ft pendant with daylight harvesting
    (54w T5HO lamp)

15. F9: Linear direct/ indirect pendant
    (50w MR16 and 40w G13/T8 lamps)

16. F10: Large decorative pendant
    (40w D45/ E14 lamp)

17. F11: Small decorative pendant
    (13w CFL 4 pin lamp)

18. F12:   Undercabinet task lights
(20w T5 lamp)

19. F13:   Cove lights
(28w T5 lamp)

b. The design of the lighting control system includes the following measures:

1. Areas within 15 feet of the perimeter windows, including enclosed perimeter offices, open work stations, and conference rooms and team rooms, incorporates the use of a "daylight harvesting" lighting control which dims the lighting in areas indicated with respect to the amount of available outside lighting, to reduce the amount of energy used.
2. Open tenant areas, including workstations and corridors, are controlled by a centralized lighting control system, set to operate during building occupied hours. System includes over-ride switches in several open area zones.
3. The large conference room includes a dimming system with multiple dimmer and switch controls.
4. Other enclosed spaces, not at the perimeter, include local light switch controls.

B. *Reasons for System Selection*

a. Reasons that the selected lighting system is a better choice than alternatives include:

1. The specified 2x2 indirect light fixtures (F6 and F6A) for the private offices, copy center and team rooms provide improved lighting distribution than the conventional parabolic fixture therefore requiring less fixtures.
2. The specified linear pendants (F8, F8A, F8B and F8C) for the open office is an ideal fixture since it provide a wider range of distribution for both direct and indirect lighting therefore reducing the number of fixtures. This fixture also has the added benefit of having the daylight harvesting sensors built-in as a standard.
3. The specified wide spread downlights (F1 and F1A) used at the main circulation isles provide the required lighting with a wider spread since the lamping is vertical. The downlights also highlight the main isles of egress in the open office areas.
4. The F9 pendant fixtures (with the direct and indirect features) allow for more control of the lighting environment as the needs arise; therefore reducing the total power consumption.

C. *Lighting Design Criteria*

Space Type	Illumination Design Target (footcandles)	Source of Target (e.g. IES Standard, Owner Requirement)	Other Lighting Design Criteria: *[e.g. CRI, CCT]*
Open office	35-45 FC	Owner requirement	3500K lamps
Private office	35-45 FC	Owner requirement	3500K lamps
Conference Rooms	35-45 FC	Owner requirement	3500K lamps
Pantry	35-45 FC	Owner requirement	3500K lamps

D. *Lighting Power Design Targets*

Space Type	ASHRAE 90.1-2004 Lighting Power Allowance (watts/ft^2)	Lighting Power Design Target (watts/ft^2)
Open office	1.1 W/SF	>15% below allowable
Private office	1.1 W/SF	>15% below allowable
Conference Rooms	1.3 W/SF	>15% below allowable
Pantry	1.2 W/SF	>15% below allowable

III. Water Heating System

A. *Narrative Description of System*

    a. Water heating system for the potable domestic water for tenant use includes a point of use electric water heater at the Pantry area. This heater is sized at 2500 W.

B. *Reasons for System Selection*

    a. The water heating system design was selected to improve system efficiency and cost. An individual heating system at the local point of use allows for flexibility in the system operating hours and demand load. In addition, it would not require the wasted energy inherent in energizing a centralized system for times when a small heating demand is required. A cost savings is included in the heating system design by limiting the length of piping for circulating domestic water. A centralized system would require long runs of horizontal piping to serve all points of use.

C. *Water Heating Load Calculations*

    a. Load calculations for the water heating system are based on hot water demand tables (based on gallons per hour at each fixture type), as listed in ASHRAE design guidelines, in 2007 Applications handbook Chapter 49.

Appendix F: Sample Construction IAQ Management Plan

[This document should be project specific. All text in italics is intended to be guidance for customizing the plan specific to the project. Refer to the SMACNA guidelines for more information on specific strategies]

Project Information

General Contractor: Name
Address
. Phone

Contact Person: Name

Project:
Address:

Project Type:

Plan Goals *(Modify as required to address project specific goals)*

Achieving LEED certification requires a team effort in the areas of site selection and development, water reduction, energy efficiency, material and product selection, and indoor environmental quality. The strategies to address these components are addressed during design and implemented during construction. A Construction Indoor Air Quality (IAQ) Management Plan is designed to present best practices for managing IAQ during and after construction and prior to occupancy per the Control Measures of the Sheet Metal and Air Conditioning Nation Contractors Association (SMACNA) IAQ Guidelines for Occupied Buildings under Construction, 2007, Chapter 3. The goal of the plan is to reduce or eliminate contamination and pollution of materials by dust, debris or odor, and to reduce the potential of long-term pollution of interior environments by construction materials. Additionally, the plan aspires to reduce the negative implications from environmental conditions, such as heat, cold, humidity, and moisture.

Plan Summary *(Modify as required to address project specific goals)*

The Construction IAQ Management Plan describes strategies and procedures for the General Contractor and each of the Subcontractors to follow, such as handling and storing materials, protecting work in place, managing potential contaminants through source control, housekeeping, and scheduling of materials during construction. The plan also explains the tasks required by LEED for inspection during construction, project closeout, system start-up, and building flush-out or air quality testing.

Intent

To decrease indoor air quality problems resulting from the construction *or renovation* process in order to help support the Comfort and the well-being of construction workers and building occupants.

Requirements

Develop and implement an Indoor Air Quality (IAQ) Management Plan for the construction and pre-occupancy phases of the building, as follows:

1. During construction, meet or exceed the recommended Control Measures of the SMACNA IAQ Guidelines for Occupied Buildings Under Construction, 2007, Chapter 3.

2. Protect stored on-site or installed absorptive materials from moisture damage.

3. During construction, if permanently installed air handlers are operated, provide filtration media with a Minimum Efficiency Reporting Value (MERV) 8 at each return air grille, as determined by ASHRAE 52.2-1999. Replace all filtration media as necessary during construction and prior to occupancy.

4. Prohibit smoking on the project site. *[Not required but a suggestion]*

Communication

[Describe the project specific approach to communicating the IAQ goals for the project. Each of the subcontractors should receive a copy of the plan, as well as any tracking forms they will need to complete for the submittal process. Will the goals and progress be discussed at the weekly meetings? What kind of training will be provided? Will there be signage to reinforce the strategies?]

Strategy

[Describe IAQ scope of work as it pertains to the project: will air handlers be used, quality control measures, and any tools to be used to help support goals]

SMACNA Guidelines

SMACNA IAQ Guidelines include protection of HVAC systems, source control, pathway interruption, house-keeping, and scheduling.

PROTECTION

[Project specific strategies should be outlined including the operation of air handlers during construction and MERV filter requirements. Although it is best if the system is not used during construction. The strategies should specifically address the elimination or reduction of dirt, debris, and dust and assign responsibilities for quality control. The strategies should address daily activities, as well as weekly or monthly tasks to be completed. The following sections are suggested but not required. For each strategy listed, describe the project specific approach, as appropriate.]

HVAC Systems

- HVAC Return Side Protection:
- HVAC Central Filtration:
- HVAC Supply Side Protection:
- Duct Cleaning:

Building Shell:

- Mechanical Rooms:
- Insulation:
- Drywall:

- **Finish Materials:**

Source Control

[Project specific strategies should address low-emitting materials or the measures to reduce the emission of VOCs within the weatherproofing system. The strategies should address daily activities, as well as weekly or monthly tasks to be completed. The following sections are suggested but not required. For each strategy listed, describe the project specific approach, as appropriate.]

Product Substitutions:

Modifying Construction Equipment and Operation:

Changing Work Practices:

Local Exhaust:

Cover or Seal:

Pathway Interruption

[Project specific strategies should address the measures to reduce the contamination of occupied or clean areas. The strategies should address daily activities, as well as weekly or monthly tasks to be completed. The following sections are suggested but not required. For each strategy listed, describe the project specific approach, as appropriate.]

Depressurization Of The Work Area:

Pressurize Finished Or Occupied Space:

Erect Barriers to Contain Construction:

Relocate Pollutant Sources:

Temporarily Seal the Building:

Housekeeping

[Project specific strategies should address cleaning activities to reduce the contamination of occupied or clean areas, as well as HVAC equipment. This includes the removal of water after rainfall inside the building and the final cleaning prior to occupancy. The strategies should address daily activities, as well as weekly or monthly tasks to be completed. The following sections are suggested but not required. For each strategy listed, describe the project specific approach, as appropriate.]

Dust Control:

Spill Control:

Cleaning Materials:

HVAC Equipment Cleaning:

Scheduling

[Project specific strategies should address methods to reduce the contamination of absorptive materials, damage of materials, and disruption of occupied areas. The following sections are suggested but not required. For each strategy listed, describe the project specific approach, as appropriate.]

Sequence of Work:

Scheduling of Materials:

Building Flush-out and/or Air Quality Testing:

Documentation

[Describe the project specific approach to documenting compliance with the IAQ plan, such as photographs, inspections, and meetings. Assign the responsibility of the task and how often the task should be completed.]

LEED Submittals:

LEED Requirements:

Provide photographs that demonstrate consistent adherence to the construction IAQ management plan and LEED credit requirements. With each photograph, identify the SMACNA approach adhered to.

Sample MR Credit 2 Tracking Form

GENERAL CONTRACTOR

NAME OF PROJECT
City, State

DESIGN MANAGEMENT SERVICES

					Waste Type						
Pickup Date	Residual	Paper	Wood	Metal	Plastic	Glass	Gypsum	Asphalt	Comingled		Total
TOTAL	0.00	0.00	0.00	0.00	0.00	0.00	0.00	0.00	0.00		0.00

TOTAL WASTE	$0.00
TOTAL WASTE DIVERTED	0.00
% OF WASTE DIVERTED	**0%**

For LEED NC, CS, and CI Projects

50% Diverted	1 point
75% Diverted	1 point
ID Credit 1: Exemplary Performance 95%	1 Point

3 Points Possible (Teams are encouraged to verify if RP Credit is available)

Sample MR Credit 4 Tracking Form

GENERAL CONTRACTOR

NAME OF PROJECT
City, State

DESIGN MANAGEMENT SERVICES

Materials and Resources - Credit 4: Recycled Content

				Total Project Value	$3,000,000.00					
				Default Value (if applicable)	45%			(not to be used for CI projects)		
				Total Material Cost (Default or Actual)	$1,350,000.00					

SUBMITTAL NUMBER	SECTION NUMBER	SECTION NAME	MANUFACTURER	MATERIAL OR PRODUCT	Product Value	% Preconsumer	% Postconsumer	Contributing Product Value	Source of Documentation
4	054000	Cold-Formed Metal Framing	XYZ Manufacturer	Metal Studs	$10,000.00	37%	17%	$3,550.00	Manufacturer Letter
25	095113	Acoustical Ceiling Tiles	ABC Manufacturer	123 Acoustical Ceiling Tiles	$32,000.00	23%	1%	$4,000.00	Manufacturer Letter
				Product Value Subtotal	$42,000.00			$7,550.00	

TOTAL VALUE OF RECYCLED CONTENT	$7,550.00
TOTAL % OF RECYCLED CONTENT	**0.56%**

For LEED NC, CS, and CI Projects

10% Recycled Content	1 point
20% Recycled Content	1 point
ID Credit 1: Exemplary Performance 30%	1 Point

3 Points Possible (Teams are encouraged to verify if RP Credit is available)

Sample MR Credit 5 Tracking Form

GENERAL CONTRACTOR

NAME OF PROJECT
City, State

DESIGN MANAGEMENT SERVICES

Materials and Resources - Credit 5: Regional Materials

				Total Project Value	$3,000,000.00			
				Default Value (if applicable)	45%			
				Total Material Cost (Default or Actual)	$1,350,000.00			

SUBMITTAL NUMBER	SECTION NUMBER	SECTION NAME	MANUFACTURER	MATERIAL OR PRODUCT	Product Value	Extraction Distance from Project Site	Manufacturing Distance from Project Site	Source of Documentation
4	054000	Cold-Formed Metal Framing	XYZ Manufacturer	Metal Studs	$10,000.00	26 mi	57 mi	Manufacturer Letter
25	095113	Acoustical Ceiling Tiles	ABC Manufacturer	123 Acoustical Ceiling Tiles	$32,000.00	341 mi	235 mi	Manufacturer Letter
				Product Value Subtotal	$42,000.00			
				TOTAL VALUE OF REGIONAL MATERIALS	$42,000.00			
				TOTAL % OF REGIONAL MATERIALS	3.11%			

For LEED NC and CS Projects		For LEED CI Projects	
10% Manufactured & Extracted Regionally	1 point	10% Manufactured Regionally	1 point
20% Manufactured & Extracted Regionally	1 point	20% Manufactured & Extracted Regionally	1 point
ID Credit 1: Exemplary Performance 30%	1 Point	ID Credit 1: Exemplary Performance 30%	1 Point
	3 Points Possible		3 Points Possible

(Teams are encouraged to verify if RP Credit is available)

Sample MR Credit 6 Tracking Form

GENERAL CONTRACTOR

NAME OF PROJECT
City, State

DESIGN MANAGEMENT SERVICES

Materials and Resources - Credit 6: Rapidly Renewable Materials

		Total Project Value	$3,000,000.00
		Default Value (if applicable)	45%
		Total Material Cost (Default or Actual)	$1,350,000.00

SUBMITTAL NUMBER	SECTION NUMBER	SECTION NAME	MANUFACTURER	MATERIAL OR PRODUCT	Product Value	Percentage Compliant	Contributing Product Value	Source of Documentation
5	096229	Cork Flooring	XYZ Manufacturer	Cork Flooring	$10,000.00	100%	$10,000.00	Vendor Letter
42	064214	Wood Paneling	ABC Manufacturer	Wheatboard Panels	$7,000.00	75%	$5,250.00	Website Letter

				Product Value Subtotal	$17,000.00		$15,250.00	
				TOTAL VALUE OF RAPIDLY RENEWABLE MATERIALS	$15,250.00			
				TOTAL % OF RAPIDLY RENEWABLE MATERIALS	1.13%			

For LEED NC and CS Projects		For LEED CI Projects	
2.5% Rapidly Renewable	1 point	5% Rapidly Renewable	1 point
ID Credit 1: Exemplary Performance 5%	1 Point	ID Credit 1: Exemplary Performance 10%	1 Point
	2 Points Possible		2 Points Possible

Sample MR Credit 7 Tracking Form

GENERAL CONTRACTOR

NAME OF PROJECT
City, State

DESIGN MANAGEMENT SERVICES

Materials and Resources - Credit 7: Certified Wood

SUBMITTAL NUMBER	SECTION NUMBER	SECTION NAME	MANUFACTURER	MATERIAL OR PRODUCT	Product Value	Percentage Compliant by Weight	Potential Contributing Product Value	Percentage Certified	Contributing Product Value	COC Certificate Number
12	096400	Wood Flooring	XYZ Manufacturer	Wood Flooring	$40,000.00	90%	$36,000.00	100%	$36,000.00	Vendor Letter
31	061623	Subflooring	ABC Manufacturer	Subfloor	$7,000.00	100%	$7,000.00	0%	$0.00	Website Letter
58	082100	Wood Doors	XYZ Manufacturer	Doors and frames	$55,000.00	75%	$41,250.00	75%	$30,937.50	
18	061101	Wood Framing	ABC Manufacturer	Blocking	$3,567.00	100%	$3,567.00	100%	$3,567.00	

| | | | | Product Value Subtotal | $105,567.00 | | $87,817.00 | | $70,504.50 | |

TOTAL VALUE OF WOOD PRODUCTS $105,567.00
TOTAL VALUE OF CERTIFIED WOOD PRODUCTS $70,504.50
% OF CERTIFIED WOOD PRODUCTS **66.79%**

For LEED NC and CI Projects
50% FSC Certified 1 point
ID Credit 1: Exemplary Performance 95% 1 Point
2 Points Possible

Sample EQ Credit 4 Tracking Form

GENERAL CONTRACTOR

NAME OF PROJECT
City, State

dms

Indoor Environmental Quality - Credit 4: Low Emitting Material													
SUBMITTAL NUMBER	SECTION NUMBER	SECTION NAME	EQ LEED CREDIT	CONTRACTOR	MANUFACTURER	MATERIAL OR PRODUCT	EQ4.1 ADHESIVES AND SEALANTS- VOC LEVEL	EQ4.2 PAINTS AND COATINGS - VOC LEVEL	VOC LIMITS	EQ4.3 FLOORING CERTIFICATION	EQ4.4 NO UREA FORMALDEHYDE	EQ4.5 SYSTEMS FURNITURE & SEATING (FOR CI ONLY)	COMMENTS
3	99100	Painting	EQ4.2	ABC Subcontractor	XYZ Manufacturer	123 Paint - Interior Primer	n/a	0 g/L	50 g/L	n/a	n/a	n/a	

Sample Submittal Form

GENERAL CONTRACTOR

PROJECT NAME
City, State

dms

DESIGN MANAGEMENT SERVICES

Submittal log

SUBMITTAL #	Subcontractor	Product	Product Value	Salvaged	Recycled Content	Regional	Rapidly Renewable	FSC	Adhesives & Sealants	Paints & Coatings	Flooring	No Urea	Notes		Additional Submittal dates	
					MR4	MR5	MR6	MR7	EQ4.1	EQ4.2	EQ4.3	EQ4.4				

Endnotes

Chapter 1

1. USGBC, *LEED Reference Guide for Green Interior Design and Construction* (Belmont, CA: Professional Publications, 2009), xiv.
2. USGBC website, www.usgbc.org/DisplayPage.aspx?CMSPageID=295.
3. USGBC, p. xiv.
4. Ibid.
5. Ibid.
6. Ibid., p. 1.
7. USGBC website, www.usgbc.org/DisplayPage.aspx?CMSPageID=1989.
8. Ibid.
9. NIBS Whole Building Design Guide website, www.wbdg.org/project/buildingcomm.php.
10. USGBC website, www.usgbc.org/DisplayPage.aspx?CMSPageID=1989.
11. USGBC, p. xii.
12. USGBC website, www.usgbc.org/ShowFile.aspx?DocumentID=6715.
13. USGBC website, www.usgbc.org/ShowFile.aspx?DocumentID=6473.
14. GBCI website, www.gbci.org/Certification/Resources/cirs.aspx.
15. Ibid.
16. Ibid.
17. GBCI website, www.gbci.org/Libraries/Certification_Resources/Policy_Manual.sflb.ashx.
18. Ibid.

Chapter 2

1. 7 Group and Bill Reed, *The Integrative Design to Green Building* (Hoboken, NJ: John Wiley and Sons, 2009), 15.

Chapter 3

1. Whole Building Design Guide website, www.wbdg.org/project/buildingcomm.php.

Chapter 4

1. USGBC website, www.usgbc.org/DisplayPage.aspx?CMSPageID=1779.

Chapter 5

1. USGBC, *LEED Reference Guide for Green Building Design and Construction* (Belmont, CA: Professional Publications, 2009), xxiii.

Chapter 6

1. USGBC, *LEED Reference Guide for Green Building Design and Construction* (Belmont, CA: Professional Publications, 2009), 170.
2. USGBC (2009). *LEED Reference Guide for Green Interior Design and Construction*, p. 103.
3. USGBC (2009). *LEED Reference Guide for Green Building Design and Construction*, p. 179
4. Ibid., p.181.
5. Ibid., p.196.
6. Ibid., p.197.
7. Ibid., p. 247.
8. Ibid., p. 264.
9. USGBC (2009). *LEED Reference Guide for Green Interior Design and Construction*, p. 155.
10. Ibid., p. 162.
11. USGBC, *LEED Reference Guide for Green Building Design and Construction*, (2009), p. 247.
12. Ibid., p. 291.
13. Ibid., p. 322.
14. USGBC (2009). *LEED Reference Guide for Green Interior Design and Construction*, pgs. 189–190.
15. USGBC, *LEED Reference Guide for Green Building Design and Construction*, (2009), p. 393.
16. USGBC (2009). *LEED Reference Guide for Green Interior Design and Construction*, p. 284.
17. Ibid., p. 281.
18. Ibid., p. 300.

Chapter 8

1. USGBC, *LEED Reference Guide for Green Building Design and Construction* (Belmont, CA: Professional Publications, 2009), 226.
2. Ibid., p. 227.

Chapter 9

1. USGBC, *LEED Reference Guide for Green Building Design and Construction* (Belmont, CA: Professional Publications, 2009), 624.

Index

The abbreviation fig. following a page number indicates an illustration or a photograph; a letter t after a page number denotes a table.

WILEY BOOKS ON Sustainable Design

 ## Environmental Benefits Statement

This book is printed with soy-based inks on presses with VOC levels that are lower than the standard for the printing industry. The paper, Rolland Enviro 100, is manufactured by Cascades Fine Papers Group and is made from 100 percent post-consumer, de-inked fiber, without chlorine. According to the manufacturer, the use of every ton of Rolland Enviro100 Book paper, switched from virgin paper, helps the environment in the following ways:

Mature trees	Waterborne waste not created	Water flow saved	Atmospheric emissions eliminated	Soiled Wastes reduced	Natural gas saved by using biogas
17	6.9 lbs.	10,196 gals.	2,098 lbs.	1,081 lbs.	2,478 cubic feet